THE ESSENTIAL RAYMOND DURGNAT

edited by
HENRY K. MILLER

A BFI book published by Palgrave Macmillan

First published in 2014 by
PALGRAVE MACMILLAN

on behalf of the

BRITISH FILM INSTITUTE
21 Stephen Street, London W1T 1LN
www.bfi.org.uk

There's more to discover about film and television through the BFI.
Our world-renowned archive, cinemas, festivals, films, publications and learning resources are here to inspire you.

Palgrave Macmillan in the UK is an imprint of Macmillan Publishers Limited, registered in England, company number 785998, of Houndmills, Basingstoke, Hampshire RG21 6XS. Palgrave Macmillan in the US is a division of St Martin's Press LLC, 175 Fifth Avenue, New York, NY 10010. Palgrave Macmillan is the global academic imprint of the above companies and has companies and representatives throughout the world. Palgrave® and Macmillan® are registered trademarks in the United States, the United Kingdom, Europe and other countries.

Cover images: (front) © couch; (back) *Tonite Let's All Make Love in London* (Peter Whitehead, 1967), Lorrimer Films
Designed and set by couch
Printed in China

This book is printed on paper suitable for recycling and made from fully managed and sustained forest sources. Logging, pulping and manufacturing processes are expected to conform to the environmental regulations of the country of origin.

British Library Cataloguing-in-Publication Data
A catalogue record for this book is available from the British Library
A catalog record for this book is available from the Library of Congress

ISBN 978–1–84457–451–3 (pb)
ISBN 978–1–84457–452–0 (hb)

CONTENTS

PREFACE/V
INTRODUCTION: THE DIVIDED SELF/1

PART 1: AUTEUR WARS
INTRODUCTION/7
1.1 'Standing Up for Jesus'/13
1.2 'Who Really Makes the Movies?'/25
1.3 'Cat and Mouse Games'/31
1.4 'Michael Powell'/34
Annotations/41

PART 2: JET-PROPELLED PHOTOGRAPHS
INTRODUCTION/46
2.1 'Flyweight Flicks'/49
2.2 *'Wholly Communion'*/50
2.3 'Underground Film Festival
    Programme Notes'/52
2.4 'Asides on Godard'/52
2.5 'Ker-Plow!'/58
2.6 'Dwoskin's Dream-Films'/59
2.7 'London Film-Makers' Co-operative
    Catalogue Entries'/60
2.8 *'Tonite Let's All Make Love in
    London'*/61
2.9 *'One Plus One'*/63
2.10 'Cutting With a Keen Edge'/67
Annotations/69

PART 3: IMAGES OF THE MIND
INTRODUCTION/73
3.1 'Fake, Fiddle and the Photographic
    Arts'/77
3.2 'Images of the Mind I: Throwaway
    Movies'/91
3.3 'Images of the Mind II: Ebb and
    Flow'/99
3.4 'Images of the Mind III: The
    Impossible Takes a Little Longer'/105
3.5 'Images of the Mind IV: Style and
    the Old Wave'/109
Annotations/112

PART 4: BRITAIN THROUGH THE
    LOOKING GLASS
INTRODUCTION/115
4.1 'Brain Drains: Drifters, Avant-Gardes
    & Kitchen Sinks'/117
4.2 'TV's Young Turks'/123
4.3 'The Great British
    Phantasmagoria'/129
4.4 *'Sexual Alienation in the Cinema'*/139
Annotations/143

PART 5: CALIFORNIA SPLIT
INTRODUCTION/145
5.1 'Montage Rides Again!'/152
5.2 'Pacific Film Archive Programme
Notes'/156
5.3 'From Signs to Meanings'/160
5.4 'Popeye Pops Up'/172
Annotations/187

PART 6: LOOKING BACK
INTRODUCTION/191
6.1 *'About John Ford'*/193
6.2 'A Skeleton Key to Stephen
Dwoskin'/197
6.3 'Cooped in a Co-op?'/201
6.4 'Jean-Luc Godard: His Crucifixion and
Resurrection'/204
6.5 'Resnais & Co.: Back to the Avant-
Garde'/210
6.6 'Aiming at the Archers'/215
6.7 'The Prewar Bs: Rewards and
Fairies'/227
6.8 'Remembering Michael Powell'/230
Annotations/233

APPENDIX I: PACIFIC FILM ARCHIVE
PROGRAMMES/237
APPENDIX II: TOP TENS/240
INDEX/242

PREFACE

It is tempting to believe that film culture has changed as much in the twelve years since Raymond Durgnat's death as in the half-century during which he was a published critic. His byline belongs to an almost vanished world of print magazines. Durgnat wrote for *Film*, *Films*, *Film Comment*, *Film Quarterly*, *Film Dope*, *American Film* and, especially, *Films and Filming*. Sometimes he was found in *Art and Artists* and *Books and Bookmen* too. He contributed to *Cinim*, *Cinema*, *Cineaste*. For a time he co-edited *Motion* and was given space in *Movie*. In two discrete periods he appeared in *Sight and Sound* and the *Monthly Film Bulletin*. In the late 1960s he was a presence in *IT* and *Oz*; and, in the same years, in the *Burlington Magazine* and the *British Journal of Aesthetics*. He also wrote for *Positif* and *Midi-Minuit Fantastique*.

Yet what he wrote anticipated our digital age. 'Ten years from now,' he wrote in 1968, 'movies may be as throwaway as pen and paper.' Ten years later he foretold 'the end of cinema's magnificence. With pocket TV sets, people will be able to watch movies as they sit on a bus or train, stopping and starting when it's convenient.' 'For the first time in history,' he wrote in 1982, 'the cultures of all times are simultaneously available. It's less like enjoying a vantage point than drowning in information.' He predicted that 'Word and image processors *plus* video cameras *plus* computer mail and networking *plus* videotapes will let everybody cook up his own moving image-text combos.' Well before the possibilities of digital image manipulation had begun to be realised, Durgnat championed films which went beyond 'the limitations of photographic realism'.

Far from being trapped in time, he has come into his own. Though this book pays tribute to the very diverse band of publications in which its contents first appeared by simulating their various house styles, it is meant for the present.

Over the years of its gestation I have incurred many debts to colleagues, friends and family. I want to thank in particular Patricia Aske; Rebecca Barden; Charles Barr; Justin Bengry; Judy Bloch; Donald Brett; Liz Bruchet; Ian Christie; Michel Ciment; Richard Combs; Sophia Contento; Kieron Corless; Paul Cronin; David Curtis; Manolis Daloukas; Gareth Evans; Will Fowler; David Gale; Nancy Goldman; Jean-Pierre Gorin; Brian Hunter; Ian Johnson; Stella Keen; Lucinda Knight; Brighid Lowe; Tom Luddy; Hannah Mowat; James Naremore; Neil Parkinson; Frank Pike; Al Rees; James Riley; Jayne Ringrose; Jonathan Rosenbaum; Yvonne Salmon; Melanie Selfe; A. C. H. Smith; Rob Vasey; Edwin N. Vidler; Rob White; Peter Whitehead; Emma Wilson; Leila Wimmer; Mandy Wise; and the staffs of the BFI Library and Cambridge University Library.

Henry K. Miller, Cambridge, 2014

The editor and publisher also wish to thank Kevin Gough-Yates for permission to reproduce work by Raymond Durgnat.

Evening Standard, 29 November 1949

INTRODUCTION: THE DIVIDED SELF

'As a schoolboy', Raymond Durgnat recalled in 1965, 'I often played truant to go to the pictures, and now that I'm a lecturer in "Studies Complementary to the History of Art" I'm an even firmer believer in the "truancy" theory of art.'[1] Movies like 'that bad-taste thunderclap' *Duel in the Sun* (1946) 'strengthened my schoolboy revolt – not revolt exactly, but respectful dissent – from edifying influence'.[2] He compared himself with the protagonist of *The Guinea Pig* (1948), a tobacconist's son 'scholarshipped up' from 'Walthamstow, E17, a terrible low district', where Durgnat was educated 'at an excellent grammar school founded in 1527'.[3] The influence of the Sir George Monoux was edifying indeed, and 'literary to the point of being blind. My grammar school teachers insisted that I drop even its sloppy-go-lucky art class for "Eng. Lit." and extra Latin.'[4]

> In 1950 I went to see [André Cayatte's] *Les Amants de Vérone*, eleven times in seven days. First to study [Jacques] Prévert's crackling yet poetic dialogue, and then to try and remember exactly how it worked as a visual succession. I came away baffled, frustrated, with nothing to show but some visually illiterate sketches and a few sentences which I dared show nobody, so hopelessly trivial were they in terms of literary content.

> But those images had hit me with their rhythm. They asserted the richness of a third dimension which in film criticism then was in its deepest point of eclipse: film as a graphic art.

Grammar School Eng. Lit., meanwhile, meant F. R. Leavis, the Great Tradition and attempted inoculation 'against the multitudinous counter-influences – films, newspapers, advertising – indeed, the whole world outside the class-room'.[5] Durgnat, a Baudelaire-reading jazz trumpeter who spent his weekends exploring Soho and the docks when not at the pictures, may have relished these counter-influences, but he was also a star pupil and editor of more than one school magazine. Nor were his teachers unresponsive: one sent an example of his work to Richard Winnington, film critic of the *News Chronicle*, and Winnington wrote back with encouragement. In December 1950 he won a place to study English Literature at Pembroke College, Cambridge, and a variety of scholarships to take him there.

At Pembroke's suggestion Durgnat took a year out, during which time he published his first articles in the British Film Institute's *Monthly Film Bulletin* and *Sight and Sound*, recently taken over by a group of critics from the Oxford film magazine *Sequence*, led by editor Gavin Lambert. University was further delayed by National Service, to which Durgnat intended to conscientiously object until dissuaded at the last moment by Pembroke's senior tutor. During his two years in the Royal Army Education Corps, some of it spent in Hong Kong, as reflected in his second *Sight and Sound* piece 'Oriental Notebook', he wrote a book on film which his future publisher Faber and Faber was not alone in rejecting.

Finally in the autumn of 1954, at the age of twenty-two, he went up to Cambridge, where his supervisors included the Leavisite D. H. Lawrence specialist Harry Coombes.

Durgnat took refuge in the cinema but wrote little, an anomaly perhaps explained by the title and tenor of his single *Granta* contribution, 'A Critique of Critics', published in June 1955. Castigating his fellow student reviewers for, among others failings, their 'adulation of Hitchcock', he concluded that 'perhaps not until professors and pedants get their hooks into the Tenth Muse will she command the attention she deserves'.[6]

His final year coincided with a national watershed at once political and cultural. 'Suez served to rally the first of a series of youthful "waves",' wrote Durgnat from the vantage of 1968, 'whose selfless indignation was doubtless sharpened by the denial of equalities and opportunities in a stagnant society. The first wave were the "Angry young men", and the brief boom in the New Left.'[7]

A quintessential Angry Young Man himself, Durgnat identified with – or projected himself on to – Jimmy Porter, the class-warrior antihero of *Look Back in Anger*. John Osborne's play, which opened at the Royal Court Theatre in May 1956, was twice televised that autumn, and twice came to Cambridge the following year, 'reached and revealed a new audience whose existence had been unsuspected, not only by the film industry, but by almost all the cultural "establishments"', Durgnat wrote a decade later.[8] 'The audience has the satisfaction, the liberation, of hearing its own smouldering discontents fierily expressed.'[9] Durgnat's Porter 'was unlucky enough to win a scholarship, intellectualise his gift of the gab, feel the full pressure of grammar-school earnestness'.

The play sent ripples through British film culture. Its director Tony Richardson was part of the *Sequence–Sight and Sound* circle, some of whose members had become film-makers. In February 1956 they had launched 'Free Cinema' with a National Film Theatre programme comprising Richardson and Karel Reisz's *Momma Don't Allow*, Lorenza Mazzetti's *Together* and Lindsay Anderson's *O Dreamland*. In the Autumn 1956 *Sight and Sound*, by then edited by Penelope Houston, Anderson (no grammar-schoolboy he) issued what became a famous manifesto for politically committed criticism, 'Stand Up! Stand Up!', illustrated by a photograph of Richardson's stage production and endorsing Porter's nostalgic lament, eleven dispiriting years after the 'glorious' Labour victory of 1945, for the lack of 'good, brave causes'.

Suez, which both shattered Britain's remaining imperial pretensions and made it seem as though the imperialist 'old gang', in Porter-speak, were still in charge, provided a cause of a kind, and the New Left emerged in its wake. In the spring of 1957 'Stand Up! Stand Up!' was reprinted in the first issue of *Universities and Left Review* (*ULR*) alongside essays by E. P. Thompson and Stuart Hall. It was at this moment, and with special significance for the New Left, that Richard Hoggart's *The Uses of Literacy* appeared, described by Durgnat as 'perhaps the most influential attempt made in Britain to cope with the challenge of the mass media'.[10] Many of its readers recognised themselves in Hoggart's 'Scholarship Boy', as discussed in the second *ULR*, uprooted beneficiaries of the 1944 Education Act which had brought the grammar schools into the state system.

Durgnat was a scholarship boy, but as the son of Swiss immigrants, thrown around the country as a wartime evacuee, he may have known Hoggart's 'sense of no longer really belonging' before he took his eleven-plus exam.[11] Whereas for Hoggart the contradiction between homework and the 'magazines which are never mentioned at school' was a source of shame and insecurity, for Durgnat it became a reason for defiance.[12] Hoggart thought that his anxious but committed few had 'special value' in an increasingly affluent society that was in 'danger of reducing the larger part of the population to a condition of obediently receptive passivity, their eyes glued to television sets, pin-ups, and cinema screens'.[13] Durgnat discerned in such passages the continuation of 'the Matthew Arnold–F. R. Leavis tradition' in post-war clothing.[14]

A branch of this tradition was being challenged in 1956 by another intellectual coterie with which Durgnat was more closely aligned. In August the Independent Group of artists and critics, based at the Institute of Contemporary Arts, came to public attention as part of an exhibition, 'This Is Tomorrow', at the Whitechapel Gallery. Fascinated by the imagery of American consumerism, and by its violent undercurrents, Independent Group artists like Eduardo Paolozzi and Richard Hamilton were especially interested in science-fiction movies. The group's room at the Whitechapel was dominated by the presence of Robby the Robot from the recently released *Forbidden Planet*. Its spokesman Lawrence Alloway recalled that 'our feeling was never that we were slumming, or getting away from it all, or not being serious'.[15]

Durgnat was predisposed to embrace Alloway's proposition that 'unique oil paintings and highly personal poems as well as mass-distributed films and group-aimed magazines can be placed within a continuum rather than frozen in layers in a pyramid', as against the Arnoldian–Leavisian approach taken by Alloway's immediate quarry, 'T. S. Eliot and his American followers'.[16] As Durgnat wrote in 1964,

> Those intellectuals of my generation who interested themselves in jazz, in the cinema, in science-fiction, in American comics, did not 'capitulate' to the 'pressures' of the mass media; on the contrary. We deliberately chose them – or rather intuitively responded to them – both as artistic pleasures unsullied by the assumptions of our schoolmasters, and for their 'subversive', vulgar view of human nature [...] we felt fonder of the screaming teen-age girls who worshipped Elvis than of those who deprecated and bewailed this mass hysteria.[17]

At the height of the Suez emergency in November 1956, Durgnat and his friends were in a 'delirium of interpretation' over another film cherished by the pop artists, *Invasion of the Body Snatchers*, which opened in Cambridge on the day British troops landed in Egypt, and was discussed 'at mesmerised length [...] Harry Fainlight saw it as an anti-Zen-Buddhism film – for the pod state of no desire, no attachment is all but nirvana.'[18]

The year 1956 was also a watershed personally. In October Pembroke arranged for Durgnat to begin a course of psychotherapy at the Tavistock Clinic in London. He was treated by a young psychiatrist who had joined the clinic, and begun to train at the Institute of Psychoanalysis, only that month: R. D. Laing, then nearing completion of the book that would make him famous, *The Divided Self*. Laing, who had been working with schizophrenic patients in Glasgow and

Varsity, 27 October 1956

characterised the Tavistock as 'an organization that dealt with normal people', nonetheless took his patients seriously and 'addressed myself to the best of my sensibility and intelligence to what they were on about'.[19] Most Tavistock treatment was done in groups, but Durgnat was seen individually by Laing every week for more than two years, and in some capacity thereafter.

On graduating in the summer of 1957 Durgnat began what he called his 'Cloister-and-the-Hearth alternation between the film industry and the groves of academe'.[20] With the strong support of his supervisors he was offered a state studentship for postgraduate research on 'Aspects of French influence on Eng. Lit. in C19'. He was also offered a three-month position as a trainee writer at the Associated British Picture Corporation at Elstree. He chose the latter and, despite being kept on, regretted it. ABPC was largely committed to churning out routine, quota-filling fare, and was by the late 1950s, when television was cutting into the regular family audience and cinemas were closing in scores, 'too nervous to actually make any movies'.[21] In 1958 Warner Bros, which had a commanding stake in the company, began to turn the studios over to small-screen production. Thus Durgnat attempted to win a second studentship two years after turning down the first.

His proposed theme this time was a study of 'Literary Style and Techniques in relation to Psychology and Psychoanalysis', which would 'do for prose what Rudolph Arnheim did for art in "Art and Visual Perception"'; though he also mentioned an alternative, stemming from his day job, 'a study of box-office factors in commercial films; why some stories please the public enormously and others closely resembling them fall very flat'.[22] This was impossible at Cambridge, and Durgnat's application, which was eventually made to King's College London, was poorly focused. His supervisors were more cautious than before, and Pembroke sought reassurance from Laing about Durgnat's mental state. Laing replied that 'he is "erratic", but his personality has become much less turbulent in the last three years'.[23]

> I have not read anything that he has written, but from his speaking there is no doubt that he has quite an exceptional psychological understanding. He is genuinely gifted in this respect, and as with so many people who have such a gift, he has been wild and unstable in his life.

It is known that Laing discussed cultural questions in his sessions, including the Angry Young Men.[24] One of Durgnat's referees recorded that he had been 'moving towards the psychoanalytic discussion of literature' after he began treatment, and that his college essays were 'supported by a reading of the major psychological texts'.[25] Laing's remarks on Durgnat's 'psychological understanding' suggest an arrangement as much educative as therapeutic. 'I was in no way committed to the idea that they had come to see me for *psychotherapy*,' he once claimed. 'They had come to see me for a consultation as to what I could contribute to their life positively, which might not be a recommendation to get into therapy, it might be anything, absolutely anything.'[26] In any case Durgnat's application failed, and by the end of 1959 he contemplated going into teaching.

Fate intervened. Writing in the Winter 1959–60 *Sight and Sound*, Sir William Coldstream, Slade Professor of Fine Art, announced the appointment of a lecturer in film by University College London, and invited applications for two postgraduate studentships, to be housed at the Slade. The scheme was to be funded by industry bodies including ABPC, with assistance from the BFI. UCL's appointee was Thorold Dickinson, director of *Gaslight* (1940) and a central figure in international film culture since the 1930s.

Thorold Dickinson at the Slade (Courtesy the Slade Archive)

The studentships for 'research in some aspect of the Film' were formally advertised at the end of March. Durgnat was among the seven to be interviewed by a UCL–BFI panel in July. Dickinson was in New York, finishing his time as head of Film Services at the UN, but his two favoured candidates, Durgnat and Don Levy, came through.

The Slade itself being unprepared, teaching began at Dickinson's Chelsea home in the autumn of 1960. Durgnat's application promised versions of three of his future books – *Films and Feelings*, *A Mirror for England* and *Jean Renoir* – on top of his 'study of box-office factors'.[27] 'The idea', he recounted some decades later, 'was to give movie analysis some roots in industry and market pressure, public taste in particular, and it sounds easy, but the big problem was how to square it with all the prejudices built into high culture finessing.'[28] Or, as he put it closer to the time: 'Why do people find spiritual satisfaction in movies which according to film appreciators shouldn't work at all, but do?'[29] The hour of the professors had arrived. Durgnat was at last a student of 'film as a graphic art' – but still vitally a truant.

Notes
1. Durgnat, 'Film Goes to the Movies', *Film*, Winter 1964–5, p. 23.
2. Durgnat, 'Martin Scorsese: Between God and the Goodfellas', *Sight and Sound*, June 1995, p. 22.
3. Durgnat, 'Vote for Britain!' (2), *Films and Feelings*, May 1964, p. 12.
4. Durgnat, 'Towards Practical Criticism', *AFI Education Newsletter*, March–April 1981, p. 10.

5. F. R. Leavis and Denys Thompson, *Culture and Environment: The Training of Critical Awareness* (London: Chatto and Windus, 1933), p. 1.
6. Durgnat, 'A Critique of Critics', *Granta*, 4 June 1955, pp. 35–6.
7. Durgnat, 'Fading Freedoms/Latent Fascisms & Hippie High Hopes: A Paranoid Guide' (2), *Oz*, no. 12, c. May 1968, n.p. The second wave was the satire boom; the third was the underground.
8. Durgnat, 'Loved One' (1), *Films and Filming*, February 1966, p. 20.
9. Ibid., p. 21.
10. Durgnat, 'The Mass Media: A Highbrow Illiteracy?', *Views*, no. 4, Spring 1964, p. 55.
11. Richard Hoggart, *The Uses of Literacy* (London: Chatto and Windus, 1957), p. 239.
12. Ibid., p. 242.
13. Ibid., p. 258.
14. Durgnat, 'The Mass Media', p. 55. Durgnat's conception of this tradition may have derived from another classic of the early New Left, Raymond Williams's *Culture and Society*, published in 1958.
15. Lawrence Alloway, '"Pop Art" Since 1949', *Listener*, 27 December 1962, p. 1085.
16. Lawrence Alloway, 'The Long Front of Culture', *Cambridge Opinion*, no. 17, c. December 1959, p. 25.
17. Durgnat, 'The Mass Media', p. 51. Elvis entered the British chart for the first time in May 1956.
18. Durgnat, rev. *Invasion of the Body Snatchers*, in *Films and Filming*, February 1969, p. 50.
19. Bob Mullan, *Mad to be Normal: Conversations With R. D. Laing* (London: Free Association Books, 1995), p. 148; p. 171.
20. Robert Murphy (ed.), *The British Cinema Book* (London: British Film Institute, 1997), p. xi.
21. Durgnat, 'Culture Always is a Fog', *Rouge*, no. 8, 2006, n.p.
22. Pembroke College Archive: Letter from Raymond Durgnat to William Anthony ('Tony') Camps, Senior Tutor, Pembroke College, 21 January 1959.
23. Pembroke College Archive: Letter from R. D. Laing to Tony Camps, 2 April 1959.
24. Allan Beveridge, *Portrait of the Psychiatrist as a Young Man: The Early Writing and Work of R. D. Laing, 1927–1960* (Oxford: Oxford University Press, 2011), p. 283.
25. Pembroke College Archive: Reference by J. B. Broadbent, Assistant Tutor, King's College, Cambridge, 11 February 1959.
26. Mullan, *Mad to be Normal*, pp. 321–2.
27. UCL Records Office, AR 13 3(b).
28. Jeffrey Richards, *Thorold Dickinson: The Man and His Films* (London: Croom Helm, 1986), p. 179.
29. Durgnat, 'Film Goes to the Movies', p. 26.

The Essential Raymond Durgnat

PART 1
AUTEUR WARS

INTRODUCTION

Just as Durgnat joined the Slade in the autumn of 1960, the season of the *Lady Chatterley* trial and the general release of *Psycho*, there began a revolution in transatlantic film culture. Earlier that year the student critics of *Oxford Opinion*, partly inspired by what they had seen of *Cahiers du Cinéma*, had mounted an assault on 'the standards and prejudices of this country's cinematic establishment'.[1] By this they meant principally the BFI, in particular 'the attitude', typified by 'Stand Up! Stand Up!', 'which exalts right-mindedness above form, style, and technique', and *Sight and Sound*'s consequent low valuation of such *Cahiers* favourites as Samuel Fuller. In response, Penelope Houston, posing the question 'Samuel Fuller or John Ford?', accused the young men of misusing art as 'something for kicks' and violence as a 'stimulant',[2] while Richard Roud charted *Cahiers*'s decline into 'crypto-fascist' nuttiness.[3]

Simultaneously, in the film society magazine *Film*, *Oxford Opinion*'s Ian Cameron reiterated his critique for a larger audience. BFI criticism, he wrote, 'could have been written entirely from the plot synopsis [...] To judge a film on anything other than its style is to set up the critic's own views on matters outside the cinema against those of its maker. This is gross impertinence.'[4] The argument, which began even as the *Cahiers* critics' first films were appearing in London, spread into the Sunday papers and weeklies, and on to the radio. In December, the month Truffaut's *Shoot the Pianist* opened in the West End, Lawrence Alloway gave his qualified support to the Oxford critics on the Third Programme. Meanwhile John Osborne, with the French example in mind, lamented that such rows were 'substitutes for creativity' in Britain.[5]

The argument was also carried on abroad, in San Francisco's *Film Quarterly* and in the *New York Film Bulletin*, one of whose critics, Andrew Sarris, had recently made his debut for the *Village Voice* with a paean to *Psycho* and 'the wild young men of *Cahiers*'.[6] Cameron and his colleagues gained allies at home including Robin Wood, whose critical debut had been a piece about *Psycho* for *Cahiers* itself. They were also able to gain the material backing of Nicholas Luard, trust-funded business partner of Peter Cook in the Establishment Club, which opened in October 1961, and publisher from the following spring of the fledgling *Private Eye*. Published by Luard, edited and beautifully designed by Cameron, the pilot issue of *Movie*, with contributions from Sarris and Claude Chabrol as well as the British auteurists, was dated June 1962.

Durgnat wasn't in it. Nor had he written for *Sight and Sound* since 'Oriental Notebook' in 1954. Since April 1960 he had been a regular reviewer for a publication less exalted than either of these, *Films and Filming*. Part of the 'Seven Arts' group of similar titles – *Plays and Players*, *Dance and Dancers*, etc. – founded by the eccentric publisher Philip

Dosse, *Films and Filming* had a higher circulation – about 25,000 – than any other 'serious' film magazine, though its seriousness was not everywhere recognised. Perhaps not unrelatedly, 'it was the only mainstream, pre-decriminalisation, mass-circulation publication in Britain to remain successful while actively courting a queer market segment', most noticeably in the small ads.[7] Its editors Peter Baker and Robin Bean, who seem to have taken a broadly non-interventionist stance towards their writers' work, were endlessly generous with space, considerably less so with pay.

With his first feature article, 'A Look at Old and New Waves', Durgnat conveyed his mixed feelings about the official *nouvelle vague* by recalling the early 1950s, when a '"new wave" of the Occupation (Clouzot, Clément, Cayatte, Autant-Lara) suddenly belted out a batch of furious, brutally energetic protest films'.[8] In the month *Sight and Sound* took on *Cahiers* and *Oxford Opinion*, he published an appreciation of Claude Autant-Lara,[9] a director Truffaut had attacked in his essay 'A Certain Tendency in French Cinema' for 'his nonconformism, his "advanced" ideas and his fierce anti-clericalism'[10] – qualities Durgnat valued – and belittled *Cahiers*'s 'notorious adulation' of Hollywood craftsmen as 'a case of artists enthusing over talents convenient for their own development'.[11] Yet he praised *Shoot the Pianist* and called Truffaut 'the Cinema's key stylist'.[12]

Shortly before the first *Movie* appeared, Durgnat made his debut in another little magazine, *Motion*, which had been founded in 1961 by Ian Johnson, a student at the LSE. Lacking Luard's means, *Motion* used 'an old and sometimes battered typeface', Johnson recalls, but it had set a high standard with its first two issues and had a print-run of 5,000 against *Movie*'s 9,000, no mean achievement.[13] It served as British distributor for the *New York Film Bulletin*, and (in theory) vice versa. To its third issue Durgnat contributed 'The Apotheosis of Va-Va-Voom', an analysis of Robert Aldrich's *Kiss Me Deadly* (1955) – loved in Paris, all but ignored in London, and therefore ripe for auteurist revaluation. Instead he wrote of the commercial cinema as 'a "group art"', 'designed to appeal to, and to embody the beliefs, values, hopes and fears of a group, of a culture, rather than those of the artist himself'.[14]

The first *Movie*, conversely, included a 'talent histogram' that ranked directors from 'Great' to 'Talented' and downwards. Much of its second issue was given over to the 'Brilliant' Otto Preminger, much of its fifth to the 'Great' Howard Hawks. *Movie* did not last long as an almost-monthly – Nicholas Luard Associates went bankrupt in June 1963, soon after which the magazine went into hibernation – but its eleven issues during 1962–3 were a decisive factor in the auteurist turn in critical opinion. The Hawks issue, dated December 1962, coincided with a Hawks retrospective at the National Film Theatre, first mounted at New York's Museum of Modern Art by *Movie* and *NYFB* contributor Peter Bogdanovich. In the spring of 1963 came the first version of Sarris's *The American Cinema*, with its more enduring categories ('Less than Meets the Eye', 'Lightly Likeable', etc.), in a special issue of New York's *Film Culture*.

Durgnat was unimpressed. A year later he wrote that 'it became apparent with each succeeding issue of *Movie* that they worshipped their talent histogram with the same unswerving devotion that *Sight and Sound* lavished on their chosen few. However vicious some of the surface conflicts have been, criticism has stayed very much the same in terms of fundamentals.'[15] Some of these fundamentals would be called into question in the fourth *Motion*. The *Motion* 'Companion to Violence and Sadism in the Cinema', which Durgnat assembled with Johnson at Durgnat's family home in Chingford, was published simultaneously with Durgnat's first book, the 'Motion Monograph' *Nouvelle Vague*, in

The Newcomers (1964): 'a life of books and films and hats'

February 1963. The *Movie* critics, sharing at least some of Houston's assumptions, had taken umbrage at her 'something for kicks' line. The *Motion* 'Companion' reappropriated it.

Wasn't art, in a manner of speaking, for kicks? To deny the possibility was to cut away art's roots in ritual. Durgnat had defended screen violence in his maiden *Sight and Sound* article, which began: 'Because violence is a leading characteristic of the postwar world, it is reflected in a good deal of contemporary art'.[16] 'An essential part of films like *Psycho* and *Peeping Tom*', he had argued in his first *Films and Filming* series, 'Erotism in Cinema', in 1961, 'is that the whole pattern of guilt, terror, suspicion, pity, hope-against-hope and so on, is brought into play. [...] One would completely misunderstand the way *Psycho* orchestrates the audience's feelings if one tried to make a distinction between the "sexual" elements and the others.'[17] (Here, presumably, were the 'Freudian components' of Durgnat's Slade thesis at which Thorold Dickinson 'bristled'.)[18]

The argument was put with more force and sarcasm in *Motion*'s opening pages, after a series of citations that juxtaposed Houston's remarks with gobbets from Freud and Artaud. Taking its cover image from Mario Bava's banned *Black Sunday* (aka *The Mask of the Demon*, 1960), the 'Companion' was an A–Z – not a histogram, nor a pantheon – of the disreputable, with entries on science-fiction, monster movies and 'Dentures, Death by'. Johnson provided a seminal piece on *Peeping Tom*, almost universally reviled on its release in 1960 and a shared passion of the two editors, while Durgnat's contributions included a note on the recently released *Dr. No*. Dated for the month before the release of the Beatles' first LP and the outbreak of the Profumo scandal, it was, according to Johnson, 'our best-selling issue, especially in Soho'.[19]

On 30 April, Durgnat promoted the 'Companion' with an 'evening on Violence in the Cinema' at the ICA, titled 'The Art of Scaring You to Death'. Later, the magazine made a cameo appearance in John Boorman's *The Newcomers*, a television documentary about a young couple living in Bristol, broadcast in the spring of 1964 on the newly launched BBC 2. The 'Companion' is shown in a montage sequence introducing the series's subjects, Alison and Anthony Smith, in the first episode. According to Anthony, seen reading it, the magazine was in fact 'specially planted' by Boorman 'to flesh out the cinéaste image of us that he wanted. *The Newcomers* was billed as a documentary but the BBC later allowed that it would be more accurately described as "television's first novel".'[20] The voiceover accompanying the sequence defines a generation – that of *Motion*'s contributors and readers, perhaps – as much as a couple:

> the first Welfare State people, succoured on free school milk and weaned on social security. They're both successes of the system. They passed eleven-plus, won scholarships to university, received grants, allowances, and bursaries. [...] Godless, uninhibited, people without ties [...] living the all-night talking life, a life of books and films and hats and time-consuming games: a long quest for the good life.

Motion's next, and last, issue, given the title 'Puritans Anonymous', would shape the subsequent course of Durgnat's career. Its centrepiece, 'Standing Up For Jesus', is an extended Jimmy Porter rant against Arnold, Leavis, Hoggart, grammar schools, Eng. Lit., the New Left, Free Cinema and, above all, *Sight and Sound*, subsumed together under the general heading of 'puritanism'. It is also, as this list suggests, an agonised reckoning with Durgnat's own background.

Decades later, writing about René Clément's 'ancienne vague' *Gervaise* (1956), Durgnat observed that, despite its fame, Truffaut's 'strange, challenging diatribe' 'A Certain Tendency', whose targets included *Gervaise*'s screenwriters, 'was not reprinted in his book *The Films in My Life*'.[21] Of his own diatribe, which likewise 'involves some central questions', he told interviewers that 'I'd let it be reprinted, but given footnotes and frameworks around it.'[22] 'Puritans Anonymous' was the last *Motion* for the usual reasons, 'shortage of both money and time', rather than any backlash, but it did lead to Durgnat's exclusion from the most powerful institution in British film culture, the BFI – and not only Durgnat's.[23] In 1977 Dickinson wrote to his former student that Houston had 'barred you and the Slade – and me for that matter – from Sight & Sound'.[24]

Durgnat's formal studies at the Slade had ended in mid-1961, but his connection with Dickinson's department, whose activities included screening series and seminars, continued through the decade. In early 1965, Dickinson told an interviewer that Durgnat 'is turning out what is in fact a thesis of his work here. He was here from '60 to '61 and in '65 all these masses of notes had been boiled down to this statement about cinema which is running as a serial and it's very interesting reading.'[25] It is probable that 'Erotism in Cinema' derived from the same source, but the first instalment of what was billed as 'a series of articles on style in film-making', based on the Slade thesis, had appeared in the December 1964 *Films and Filming*.[26] Readers were advised that it was 'designed to raise your temper to bursting point'.

The penultimate part, 'Who Really Makes the Movies?', takes on the auteur theory. Expanding on 'The Apotheosis of Va-Va-Voom', it reveals Durgnat's affinities with the similarly sceptical Alloway, who had written in *Movie* that 'To consider movies primarily as unique products of single controlling individuals to the same extent that poems and paintings can be so considered has vitiated a great deal of ambitious film criticism.'[27] Gently chiding his hosts, Alloway had gone on to recommend that the critic discover 'to what extent themes and concepts present in them can be found in movies by other, and for this purpose, less distinguished, directors'.[28] Durgnat's essay, consciously or coincidentally, takes up what Alloway called 'the necessity for considering movies in groups not necessarily dependent upon directors'.[29]

It helped that Durgnat did not consider many of the auteurists' chosen few very distinguished. Hitchcock, the only director other than Hawks whom *Movie* rated 'Great', was a partial exception. In the October 1960 *Films and Filming* Durgnat had written that '*Shadow of a Doubt* was the last Hitchcock film which was not a good joke (or tedious, like *I Confess* and *The Wrong Man*)', which was more or less the *Sequence–Sight and Sound* position; but this is likely to have been before he saw *Psycho*, which very quickly became a touchstone film, and forty years later the subject of his last book.[30] 'Cat and Mouse Games', the concluding part of his final *Films and Filming* series 'The Strange Case of Alfred Hitchcock', published in 1970, did not appear in the book of that title four years later, perhaps because of its concentrated ambivalence.

The last *Motion* had promised a future issue on 'the British cinema and the British character'; six months later, in the spring of 1964, Durgnat began a series on the same theme for *Films and Filming*.[31] The avowed purpose of 'Vote for Britain!', published on the eve of the General Election that ended thirteen years of Conservative rule, was 'to trace some of the less obvious ways in which British films reflect ideological controversy'.[32] More specifically, it set out to explore through popular British cinema the question why, despite the post-war Labour government, the Welfare State and the end of Empire, 'old ways, old institutions, miraculously held good; every year we heard of a balance-of-payments crisis and every year we were a little more affluent; in 1945 the working-classes had half a mind to "soak the rich," by 1953 "they" were "ours" again'.[33]

The approach owed something to Siegfried Kracauer's 1947 classic *From Caligari to Hitler*, the difference being that most of Durgnat's examples were run-of-the-mill, barely remembered. Method and matter could hardly have been less fashionable. The *Movie* critic V. F. Perkins had condemned Kracauer's book in the *Oxford Opinion* on the grounds that 'it neglects the aesthetics of the cinema in favour of politics and sociology'.[34] And *Movie*'s first issue began with an editorial statement on 'The British Cinema' which contained the Truffautian declaration that 'the British cinema is as dead as before. Perhaps it was never alive'.[35] 'Vote for Britain!' did indeed neglect the aesthetics of the cinema; but one of its subjects, rated merely 'Competent or ambitious' in *Movie*'s histogram, was considered by Durgnat to be a true auteur: Michael Powell.

Despite Durgnat's harsh words about auteurism, there were ties between *Motion* and *Movie*. Wood had contributed a close reading of Joseph Losey's *The Criminal* (1960) to the 'Companion' – Losey being the one 'British' director whom *Movie* rated as 'Brilliant' – and Charles Barr and Gavin Millar, who formed the second cohort at the Slade in 1961–2, had written for both magazines. Thus *Movie*, which had come back for what turned out to be three issues in 1965, published 'Michael Powell' in the autumn number, over the pseudonym O. O. Green. As Perkins has recalled, it was allowed in 'because it was going against the critical consensus and anything that was intelligently argued, well written and went against the critical consensus was grist to our mill'.[36]

That consensus was formidably dense. By writing about Powell and Pressburger, Durgnat was by no means bringing forgotten figures into the auteurist light: their films were kept in circulation in commercial cinemas long after release. *A Matter of Life and Death* (1946) was revived in Cambridge on three separate occasions in 1956–7, while *The Life and Death of Colonel Blimp* (1943) and *The Red Shoes* (1948) were both shown there at least once in the same year. But within elite film culture antipathy to the Archers was a common denominator uniting otherwise opposed or historically distinct critical schools.

Movie's hostility to British cinema and the press outcry over *Peeping Tom* only bolstered what was already an orthodoxy. Lindsay Anderson had anathematised the Archers in *Sequence*; and those nameless critics to whom Durgnat credits Powell's reputation as a 'technician's director' are likely to have included Richard Winnington, who called the *Red Shoes* ballet 'an essay in complicated camera trickery for its own sake'.[37] As Durgnat wrote in 1967, 'from the mid-'30s until the mid-'50s, film criticism in English was dominated by writers who were strongly influenced by, or actively engaged in, the British documentary tradition'.[38] This domination was in turn only the national aspect of 'the dogmatic realism which ravaged film criticism from Grierson until Bazin', and indeed Kracauer.[39]

Durgnat's description of Powell as 'an upholder, through its lean years, of the Méliès tradition' is an allusion to Kracauer's *Theory of Film: The Redemption of Physical Reality*, published in 1960, in which Kracauer argued that 'film is essentially an extension of photography and therefore shares with this medium a marked affinity with the visible world around us'.[40] Kracauer thus regarded Méliès, whose 'main contribution to the cinema lay in substituting staged illusion for unstaged reality' as aesthetically illegitimate.[41] Dismissing *The Tales of Hoffmann* (1951) as 'cinema estranged from itself', he wrote that Powell and Pressburger 'retrogress from all that is fresh in Lumière to Méliès's theatrical *féeries'*.[42] Meanwhile André Bazin, in his 1958 essay 'The Evolution of Film Language', wrote of the eclipse of 'plastic expressionism' in the sound era.[43]

The third part of 'Vote for Britain!' was a savage attack on the Grierson school, and in his thesis, as we shall see in more detail, Durgnat sought to debunk the theoretical underpinnings of Kracauer and Bazin in order to reclaim film as a graphic art. In the second part, published in the same year as the Powell piece, he wrote that 'while the old-fashioned film criticism is still permeated with the assumption that the cinema is at its "best" when it records "real life", the cinema in fact accommodates fantasies and fairytales of every kind and style', naming Powell's *The Thief of Bagdad* (1940), the first film he could remember seeing, as an example.[44] Realism, Durgnat quoted G. W. Pabst as saying, 'is a means, not end'; a means to 'showing, surely, something deeper than the surface of life', something 'invisible to the camera-eye'.

Nonetheless, the strength of the consensus, and the hold it exerted over Durgnat, is suggested by his relative hesitancy, especially over the *Red Shoes* ballet, which he would in later and more confident years describe as '*the* peak of cinema'.[45]

The consensus against the Archers was, moreover, political as well as aesthetic, again dividing Durgnat's sympathies. As he observed in the first part of 'Vote for Britain!', *A Matter of Life and Death* 'makes perennial Conservative criticisms of the Welfare State', and 'the imagery is always High Tory [...] – another form of romanticism, which English audiences very much enjoy even when they only half-believe it'.[46] Powell and Pressburger had, as Durgnat made clear many years later, 'ready access to government circles'; *The Battle of the River Plate* (1956), for example, had its Royal Command Performance just as the Suez emergency began.[47] *The Queen's Guards* (1961), in which Suez was symbolically avenged, went 'too far for public taste in asserting the gentlemanly tradition', too far also for Durgnat.[48]

In another mood, however, just as Jimmy Porter secretly admired his Blimpish father-in-law Colonel Redfern, so Durgnat was perversely attracted by Powell's pre-Suez, pre-1945, even pre-1914 outlook, which had little in common with modern conservatism. ('You're hurt because everything is changed,' Alison Porter tells her father in Osborne's play. 'Jimmy is hurt because everything is the same.') 'One of the things to be trumpeted in the favour of the Establishment, God bless its heraldic little socks,' Durgnat wrote in his 'Companion' entry on *Dr. No*, 'is that it maintains a healthy anarchic vigour, a proper admiration for guts, grit and attack as virtues in themselves, against the heavy moralizing drizzle that has mildewed English "committed" criticism from the foundations up,' words which may help explain his belief that Powell was 'the only director' equipped to film Bond as Ian Fleming had imagined him.[49]

The relationship which Durgnat proposes in his last sentence between Powell and various directors of the *nouvelle vague*, though more mysterious at first glance, is perhaps more significant still. Viewed through this international lens, Powell is seen to have presaged what Durgnat described in his thesis as the push of the 'pendulum of style slowly back from the "realistic" to the "expressionistic"', a process which was in full swing when he published it, and which he found more exciting by far than the exhumation of the Hollywood past.[50]

1.1 STANDING UP FOR JESUS

The root cause of the critical condition of English film criticism is the old triple threat. Matthew Arnold outflanked the philistines by selling culture to the agnostic puritans as something next to cleanliness but more deeply interfused that rolls through all things. Since then a high moral purpose has become the homegrown equivalent of the deep symbolical meaning beloved of our Teutonic cousins; and D. H. Lawrence joins the Puritans' Committee of 100, along with John Calvin, John Knox, William Prynne and other founder-members of the Lady Chatterley fan-club. The second stab-in-the-back comes from the literature courses at university where 18-year-olds are required to turn out weekly essays in each of which they solemnly "evaluate" Wordsworth, Milton, Webster, etc., and often from the vantage point of, society hopes, total virginity where sex, violence, death and even barrack-room camaraderie are concerned, discuss whether the "texture" of Fielding, Hardy or Baudelaire "reproduces the authentic density of lived experience". Not surprisingly the victims, who also have exams to worry about, study the critics and skim the texts, which are apt to be confusing. Nor are the disciplines of criticism furthered by the more dogmatic Leav(is)ites who by confusing democratic with demotic imagine that all culture is for all and that you don't need background knowledge to understand Shakespeare, Dante or "Finnegans Wake". All it needs is the grandiose claim to be "objective" in one's aesthetic responses for a total collapse of criticism into a collection of schools which not only can't communicate, but can't even disagree without jeering.

The last twist of the knife is that as the Anglo-Saxon culture puritan braces himself against the temptation to relax in the opium-dens of light entertainment, he treats all entertainers and artists as putative drug-peddlers whose work has to be carefully scrutinised before it may be allowed to communicate. In fact, the more earnest a critic is, the more incapable he tends to become of seeing a moral or a meaning unless it's so crashingly simple that any artist above the level of hack would have thrown it away before he began. Hence English arty criticism noodles endlessly round foredoomed attempts to equate "good" style with "true" (i.e., good) attitudes to life and bad with bad. And, my word, there's plenty of bad – what that Satan gets up to! he's got that entertainment industry sewn up tight! Who but Screwtape could have inspired the virtuous Anglo-Saxon working man to prefer entertainment to high seriousness, and pushpin to poetry.

The Absent Minded Professor
Deplorable as this preference may be, it's hardly as deplorable as the gulf which these cultural assumptions themselves created between the lowbrow public and the university-educated art world and artists. It's hardly as deplorable as the assumption that no man of good taste would prefer the joie-de-vivre implicit in B.B.'s b and bs to hearkening unto the Messianic wailing and moaning of T-for-Tiresias S. Eliot, O. M. And it's hardly as deplorable as the solemn charlatanry of the Hoggartites, who purport to survey the mass media and whine for censorship without a good word for Jerry Lewis, Bugs Bunny, "Mad", "Galaxy", Humph, Thelonious Monk, Bootsie and Snudge, singers like Eartha Kitt, Edith Piaf, Cleo Laine, songs like "September in the Rain" or "Tell Laura I Love Her", etc., and, to put it mildly, etc.

In a word the present generation of British left-wing intellectuals have never so much as dreamed of founding their cultural attitudes on left-wing attitudes, but have fallen hook, line and sinker for the petit bourgeois notions picked up in the sixth forms of grammar schools whose main purpose is still to segregate the white collar workers of tomorrow from those rough, swearing working-classes; notions fatally reinforced by thoughtless theories of "objectivity" popular at university, where adolescence inevitably seeks something which will combine the certainties of both science and religion while necessitating no discipline of one's own whims and prejudices.

.... And Sons of Flubber

To this tradition the reigning house at Dean St. is heir. That the best of intentions, and a sincere belief that their personal responses were the absolute cat's whiskers, go with it we do not deny, indeed, we are anxious to stress, nor are these attitudes peculiar to "Sight and Sound". Only in the writing of Peter John Dyer did they become so marked as to be unpleasant. Apparently incapable of using critical techniques so as to clarify, deepen, explore a film's meaning, he seemed, and seems, totally unaware that an artist is something more than an examinee being given a credit, a passmark or a whigging. When in one notorious article he applied the terms "exhibitionism", "obsessions", "consulting-room horrors", "sexual fatality" to films by Bergman, Chabrol, Truffaut, Bolognini and Visconti, it became apparent that his main concern was to punish an artist for portraying (or having any sympathy for) the sort of weakness which (a) he, P.J.D., felt he was himself far above, and (b) which wasn't freely confessed in Surbitonian chit-chat. Had he said "These films upset me" or "I don't like these films" or "We don't wish to know that" or even "My experience of experience of rape, murder, sexual perversity and consulting-room horrors is so wide that I know these films don't show what really goes on" we could have respected him, but his own delicate prudery consorts strangely with the trenchancy of his vocabulary. Anyway, as Peter John Dyer said of Ingmar Bergman, "As Ernest Bevin said of George Lansbury, "He's been a martyr carting his own faggots around quite long enough. It's time someone obliged with a match."" When a match was applied, in the pages of "Film", Mr. Dyer went up with a whoosh.

The Same Old New Staggerers

But there is more than one strand of cultural tradition involved in the evolution of the Dean St. clique. Ever since the oft-lamented departure of Gavin Lambert, "Sight and Sound" has been a sort of pushmi-pullyou, with the editorial office straining to a sort of middle-of-the-road Lib-Lab culture, and the Red Flaggers tugging it towards notions of commitment in the narrowest and most puerile sense. Between 1955 and 1960 the paper had talked itself into misinterpreting and dismissing English and American films with something of the self-defeating bigotry which had characterized "L'Ecran Francais" in its Stalinist days. There were exceptions, of course: musicals – which can be enjoyed without having to sort out one's ideas (even here it was following a politique des auteurs laid down in the Gavin Lambert days – it missed "Give A Girl A Break" because it was directed by Donen who according to its theories was only Gene Kelly's sidekick). Anything by John Ford, even "Mogambo" with its difficult-to-obtain shots of gorillas was – well; one can't say that "The Wings of Eagles" is NOT a glorification of American militarism but then, there is something so healthy about all those open-air Westerns, isn't there? There's no connection, of course, between the individualism, the expansionism, the violence of the old-fashioned, pre-"Broken Arrow" Western and brinkmanship? no connection, in the American mind, between the bugles-and-flag ethos of the U.S. Cavalry and the U.S. Marines? or to come down to more recent times, no significance in the fact that John Ford lent his old Commie-baiting pal John Wayne a hand in cutting "The Alamo", where the Mexicans are undoubtedly the Communists and maybe the massacre is nuclear war? I'm not saying John Ford is a Fascist, I'm not saying he never made "The Grapes of Wrath" (21 years ago), I'm saying he's an American patriot and hardly anti-militarist. So why were S & S so upset over the spate of war films during the '50s? if John Ford can make "They Were Expendable", can't we all? To be "against" war films as such is fatuous unless you are also against (a) fighting Nazism and (b) fighting back in Korea. But the general public has never wanted war films which attributed some courage and dignity to the sacrifices which they made.

The first article I ever cut out for my scrapbook, in 1938, at the tender age of 5, was "Will the Bomber Always Get Through?" By the age of 8 I was sleeping through the Blitz, at the age of 12 the German atrocity stories were in full flood and Vansittart was saying "Geld the lot", at about 13ish I was being V-I'd and V-2'd, at the sophisticated age of 14 I saw the Belsen shots in "The True Glory" (shown free and compulsory in schools), and the news of the first atomic bomb gave this avid s-f fan an eerie frisson. At 20 I was bayoneting straw men and enjoying the refined moral influence of the barrack-room (which was hardly coarser than that of at least 3 of the schools I'd been to). So exactly how is the X certificate coarsening my sensibilities?

The truth is that there is no logic at all, either aesthetic or Socialist, in the "Sight and Sound" horror at war films. It's sheer Lansburyism, the pacifistic reflexes of middle-class "refinement", like its perpetual obeisance to censorship. What masquerades as vaguely leftish goodness is really middle-class fear of the brutal and licentious proletariat. Only today there is a still more specific subsection – working-class youth.

The examples of committed criticism vouchsafed us in S & S (and for that matter "Definition") were depressing in the extreme. Lindsay Anderson sang a revivalist hymn, "Stand up, stand up for Jesus, Ye soldiers of the cross, Lift high his royal banner, It may not suffer loss," and sang it in close harmony with the Sons of the U.S. Cavalry.

One only wishes he hadn't also aspired to be the Sankey and Moody of film criticism, and it's not surprising that he got his ideological wires crossed in every one of his Free Cinema films which has any ideological significance. When at a rally of the Joint Council for Education Through Art a friend of mine rose and suggested that on the evidence of "O Dreamland" Mr. Anderson hated and despised the workers there was a good solid round of applause from the hall – in which I didn't join, but which I understood. As for "Every Day Except Christmas", Captain Anderson paints so glowing a picture of the jolly, hardworking British squaddie, always grumbling and rough with his tongue, but loyal at heart, so loyal that as he drives his lorry down the rolling English road he switches on the radio to listen to the Epilogue and God Save the King (or did we have a Queen already?), then, without a doubt, the Conservative government, the capitalist system and Fords of Dagenham, whose contented employees are currently bleeding them to death, have done the proletariat proud. All it needed was the Blessing of the Trucks by Father Karl Malden. Lindsay Anderson has produced at least one classic, "Thursday's Children", his Aldermaston film is deeply moving and we have a high opinion of "This Sporting Life". If the New Left hadn't been so sanctimonious about Free Cinema already we'd write an article in its praise. But while on the subject of Free Cinema, let's face it, "Nice Time" with its distaste for all those nasty X-certificate films was about as left-wing as a pep talk by Lord Hailsham. Even when Free Cinema got down to direct propaganda it could do so only by discreetly twisting social realities. "We Are the Dear Little Lambeth Boys" might have been subtitled "I Was A Teen-Age Little Lord Fauntleroy". At least it has like "Momma Don't Allow" the elementary merit of spoofing the toffs, but even Norman Wisdom films do that, and in any case MDA, while a fair enough picture of the "Fishmonger's Arms", isn't typical of the wider jazz movement, which was pushed just as hard by grammar school boys, as by working-class youth, who, on the whole, preferred and still prefer those trashy pops (and don't come the old Acker with us, mate). I quite admit that it was a tour de force to get those earthy workers' faces on the screen, more like themselves than they ever had been in those Grierson Instructionals, and that Free Cinema prepared Messrs. Reisz, Richardson et al. for the big break which they seized with both hands and of which they made splendid use. I still don't want to see those Free Cinema films unless I have to, and it's not because they're badly made but because I can see how neatly the directors have squared them with middle-class prejudices.

By and large, committed critics show very little interest in how accurately the films they criticize reflect society. They refer films to their own broad slogans, not to the realities which the films purport to reveal. Lindsay Anderson goes haring away after so idiosyncratic an interpretation of "On the Waterfront" that the next issue of S & S abounded in counter-interpretations (well, three, anyway); and one suspects that Mr. Anderson under the guise of attacking the last reel is really attacking the last reel but one in which Terry alias Elia turns stoolie and squeals to a certain Congressional Committee. His main criticism of the film is that if it had been truly Socialist it would have shown the dockers banding together to right their wrongs. But one of the disturbing features of the New York waterfront racket was the extent to which the men connived or were cowed into conniving with the union's attempt to keep the racketeers in power; in fact (after the film was finished) despite the efforts of an uncorrupt union, **and** of the government, **and** of the press, the men voted the corrupt officials back into power, where they remain. The points of detail which outraged Mr. Anderson were quite correct: there was not just **one** Mr. Big but many of them (the shipping companies), a Catholic priest did take a conspicuous part in exposing the racketeers. I suspect, though I don't know, that why Terry had to turn to the government was that if his fellow-workers had turned out to be noble savages and righted their wrongs for themselves, the film might have been seen by American audiences as yet another proof that there's never any need for government interference in industry. Terry has to face Friendly afterwards to prove to the dockers that he still is, and acted as, one of them; his sacrifice will, it is hoped, inspire them to become conscious of themselves as a class, to the solidarity which they haven't got. The film is not a study in Fascist leadership, but in martyrology – just like "Earth". Johnny is the audience-identification figure: "this is what **you** must do, you must stand up for Jesus". Why is the great gate so forbidding at the end? Because Kazan wants to remind us that the bosses are no more the dockers' friends than Johnny Friendly is, that work isn't always such fun as it is in "Every Day Except Christmas".

Undoubtedly there's a romantic streak in the film; I maintain there is a romantic streak in Mr. Anderson, but that wouldn't justify my calling him Fascist, disgustingly cynical, or even, really, deviationist. It would incidentally have been nice if someone on S & S had noticed that "Wild River" has an open justification of "Socialistic" planning.

Why do we bring up so old a criticism? Because examples of "social" criticism by "committed" critics have been so few and far between, and because this particular article established the New Left's tradition of denouncing films, not by reference to their actual social accuracies or inaccuracies, but by their relation to a set of dogmatic slogans about what left-wing orthodoxy was. To be sure, S & S ran an effort vaguely focusing on, yes, of course, what else is there, The Youth of Today, with its alarming Method acting, its evil motorcycling and rock 'n' roll, which Nannie Don't Allow.[*]

* To this Sunday School atmosphere, Robert Vas, now departed, brought a welcome touch of reality.

Jimmy Porter at the pictures: *Look Back in Anger* (1959)

If In Doubt Sloganise

Even more depressing, though, is one's suspicion that even when our "committed" critics do have a direct acquaintance with social reality they sloganise everything into a caricature of itself. "Definition" ran a long article asking itself whether Flaherty wasn't a bit of a romantic really (no prizes offered for the correct answer) and characteristically it didn't do so by comparing (say) "Nanook of the North" with how Eskimos live, or "Moana" with how South Sea tribes live, but by comparison with theories elastic (i.e. vague) enough to cover all these forms of social organisation. Even more typical, alas, was an article on "Look Back In Anger", where Stuart Hall argued that "the film is **not** about the sex-and-love life of the James T. Porters, and the occasions when Jimmy threatens to bash Alison over the head far outweigh and outnumber the tight clinches"; and implied that the publicity still which implied that was a typical film industry lie. But the simplest spectator knows enough about Strindberg-type love-hate to resolve this ludicrous dichotomy between bashing and clinching – or they wouldn't be able to make head nor tail of David O's "Duel in the Sun". "The sexual and human relationship between Jimmy and Alison is a metaphor for the social relationship between Jimmy and the world." By "world " Mr. Hall presumably means the upper-middle-class ethos, which must of course have weighed pretty heavily on Jimmy down in the market-place sweet-stall. But if we rule out the love-story, what are the social significances of Helena and Cliff? what class significance can Mr. Hall find for such little details as the fact that Jimmy is more contented with Helena than with Alison but loves Alison more than Helena? Of course the film is about class and of course Mr. Hall is justified in reacting when critics try to dismiss a play or film because they don't like its protagonists (a fault from which left-wing criticism is hardly immune). But Mr. Hall seems to grudge the film its non-political meanings. The still which said "Look Back In Anger" was a love story was absolutely right. One reason why "Look Back In Anger" was the best English film since goodness knows when (and maybe still is, though we don't claim to have seen every English film made since goodness knows when – we mean this like other critics decide on the Ten Best Films Of All Time), is because it frankly admits that Porter is his own co-executioner (with society) and that one of the obstacles to his finding a cause to fight for is the closed-shop insularity of the English working-classes. It is because the film has all sorts of themes, political, social, emotional, that it is so splendid and true.

Not that it hasn't a snide defeatist streak — Alison's miscarriage brings it within the atmos-phere of gynaecological moralising accepted by Schlesinger and quietly left ambiguous by Reisz — while like Celia Johnson and Alan Bates our old friend Mr. Porter sees the moral light on a railway station, which is nothing to do with nationalisation (Enter Dr. Beeching, pursued by a diesel). It's a thousand pities that since "The Entertainer" Osborne himself has capitulated to the left-wing moralists and produced a thin and sour strip-cartoon ("Paul Slickey") and a thin and solemn one ("Luther"), as if bidding for the title of the neuras-thenics' Al Capp (The second play does have the merit of a timid return to ethical com-plexity; it goes without saying that we like "Under Plain Cover" better than the B feature). But the reader can see why we have looped our way from criticism criticism into film crit-icism. The "chastening" of all our working-class heroes by the desire for affluence (Heather Sears, Shirley Anne Field), by the equation of working-class wisdom with funda-mentalist moralising ("Right's right and wrong's wrong and all this tones-of-grey nonsense is self-indulgence" as the Peggy Mount surrogate booms in "A Kind of Loving"), and by a private stoicism and loyalty (Jimmy Porter) — all this is the artists' *honest* acknowledge-ment of the bankruptcy of Socialist-puritan fundamentalism in our period when the work-ing-class is being (relatively) emancipated. The New Left's sudden recrudescence of hymn-singing, its desperate attempts to reduce Osborne's play to the pious simplicities of a Wayside Pulpit are just what they seem; a regressive revivalism.

For the same reason committed critics relish the flags and bugles of a Ford picture while shuddering at the truly contemporary bitterness of "Run of the Arrow". It is the com-mitted critics who are unable to grasp that Ray's films are worth noticing carefully not only because of their plastic language but because of their concern with man in society ("Rebel Without A Cause", "The Savage Innocents"). Just because of their intellectual fundamen-talism they are constantly attacking, despising, ignoring film-makers who in some ways at least are on their own side (e.g. 'On the Waterfront', 'Kiss Me Deadly', 'La Loi', 'On the Beach', 'En Cas de Malheur', 'Notte Brava', all Losey's British films until 'The Criminal').

The only way one can tackle the issue of commitment, or even clarify the disagreements, is by starting from the ground up, e.g. what is culture for anyway? has it a moral duty to be propaganda, or is it highbrow beer-and-skittles, or is it anti-propaganda in the name of that refractory thing, human nature, or what, or all four together or at different times, and if so, when is it which? Maybe Socialists should make a point of seeing films which view the world through Tory eyes? maybe their opponents have some useful things to teach them? Why shouldn't Socialists be interested in, and sympathetic to, Tory or Fascist or Buddhist or Eskimo artworks for the same reasons that we hope Catholics are interested in Protestant films or modern democrats in Elizabethan drama or the Tories in what we think? Why shouldn't Socialists say to one another or to the world at large, "Do go and see "Triumph of the Will" again and again and again, you've never seen such a persuasive account of Fascist idealism, now at last we can really feel Fascism from the inside?" Ergo, "Triumph of the Will" is a great film — whether your interest in it is one of "Quicquid agunt homines", of "There, but for the grace of God, go I" or of psychological espionage or self-enlightenment. There is our attitude, we may be wrong, but instead of discussing issues S & S promptly took refuge in a smokescreen of insults ("cultural gauleiters") and Bloomsbury woolliness. "The governing characteristic of English critical writing seems to be its empiricism, its innate dis-trust of theory and reluctance to draw dividing lines." But the governing characteristic of Dean St. critical writing is that it never sees the necessity of theorising because it hasn't yet grasped that attitudes other than its own merit the courtesy of consideration.

The Case of the Bloodstained Bathtub

Faced with the challenge of new ideas, Nannie's instinctive reaction is to shut the door quick. "Nicholas Ray or Satyajit Ray? Samuel Fuller or John Ford?" she asks. Answer: why not both? You might as well say "Soup or sweet" or "Laurel or Hardy" or "Sight **or** Sound" (as critics did in the thirties) or "painting *or* literature". S & S's inability to think is bound up with its inability to adjust. Because its thoughtless responses are its guide, a *different* response is felt to somehow undermine its authority. It can't conceive that another critic might like Fuller for some reasons and Ford for other reasons. Miss Houston scathingly cites an "Oxford Opinion" remark: "In "Party Girl" there is a shot of a girl lying with her hands dangling in a bath full of water which is red from the blood of her slashed wrists. Even by Ray standards it is outstandingly beautiful." Oh how morbid. But if you turn to the next article in the same issue of S & S what do you find? Richard Roud is attacking Fereydoun Hoveyda's criticism of "Party Girl" and writes: "Every remarkable shot is mentioned. (Though not, curiously enough, the one I consider the most beautiful ... The camera frames the wall at eye level and then slowly descends to the girl, whom we see bent over the tub, her hair and arms streaming down into the blood-filled bath.)" One would have thought that Miss Houston would have discussed the issue with her collaborator. "I know that unlike those horrible Teddy Boys from the dreaming spires of the Oxford liberal magazine you are not hungry for kicks at any price, so would you explain to me where the sublimity of this shot lies for you?"

But no. Her colleague's opinions are a closed book to her, and when they are expressed by the "wrong" side they are, it is discreetly implied, ludicrous and disreputable. (Mr. Roud, trying to outsmart Hoveyda, falls into another naivety: he raises his discreet eyebrows because Hoveyda doesn't rhapsodise over his own favourite bloodbath.) The trouble with the S & S non-theory is that it is an assortment of prejudices and habits which thinks it is the broadest possible, the biggest and best, range of tastes. Actually, its scope, minimal in the first place, is, not increased, but diminished by the play of the contradictions beneath the mask of tolerant eclecticism. The "form or content" debate exemplifies the process. Penelope Houston, reasonably, insists that the cinema is about human relationships NOT spatial relationships. One gathers that she would also subscribe to Mr. Roud's contention that content is "like" literature and ideas, while form is "like" painting. One more effort and S & S would have hauled itself out of the form-or-content quagmire altogether. Form is "like" painting; but painting has a "content", and this content is carried in the form (shapes, colours, etc.) so that in a painting the "spatial relationships" may well "be" the human relationships. Similarly, in literature, literary meanings often depend on the *form* of the phrases (rhythm alliteration, etc.), so that, there too, form = idea. The form of a phrase is itself a phrase inflecting the phrase. Ideational and formal content interinfluence each other and *both are content*. Form is part of the content and "content" is only part of the "content". Abstract painting and music are both "pure form", the ideational content may be absolutely nil. According to the Houston–Roud non-theory, they have no content at all and are presumably insignificant, as being only about spatial and harmonic relationships.

The only formulation which begins to make sense is to say that the "spatial relationships" in Ray, Lang, Antonioni, Mizoguchi et al. are the human relationships in metaphor; and that spatial metaphors are no more recondite and baffling than saying, with W. C. Fields, "He has apple cheeks, cauliflower ears and mutton-chop whiskers." But for Mr. Roud the camera-movements in "L'Avventura" are just "patterns in the carpet". In an article called "Novel Novel Fable Fable" he turns his back decisively on the only possible solution to the "form or content" debate (a solution which admittedly solves nothing but at least has the merit of opening a new avenue of questions); and discovers that not all stories are novels. One of these days literary critics will stumble on "The Canterbury Tales", "The Decameron", "Le Morte d'Arthur", "The Rime of the Ancient Mariner", and, as for that strange work "Gulliver's Travels", it can safely be said that its author, Dean Swift, may yet turn out to be the Samuel Beckett of the New Wave. In fact, of course, a look in 90% of films films for what Mr. Roud looks for in novels novels is as silly as looking for impressionism in Henry Moore or for Rembrandt character in "Tom Jones".

Take away the simplistic distinction between "form" and "content" and the whole 'Sight and Sound' aesthetic collapses. Even Mr. Roud's attempt at compromise in "The French Line" is left with its literary ideas on the one hand, and its patterns in the carpet on the other, and never the twain shall meet. A film critic without something of a painter's eye is like an opera critic who's tone deaf. But like so many people who can only visualise things in terms of words and ideas, Mr. Roud can't steer clear of a solipsistic and jeering verbal tone (= style = content), which amounts to a caricature of the "line" which he purports to be (a) describing and (b) criticising. For example, after noting that French critics are generally kinder to many American films than English, he proceeds, "It may be difficult for English people to think of Detroit as El Dorado, but it is undeniable that American life in all its forms exercises a very strong hold over present-day young French intellectuals." Leaving aside for a moment the hold it exercises over present-day young English intellectuals (and the function of "trendhounds" as the Kremlinologists of democracy), our main point is Mr. Roud's snide gibes: he caricatures the French *interest* in America as a gullible Utopianism ("El Dorado…") and mysteriously sums up "American life in all its forms" as "Detroit" (why not "New Orleans" or the "West Coast"?). He seems incapable of seeing things in a direct, neutral way: "French intellectuals are interested in America because in American films they recognise predicaments akin to their own and respond with sympathy and insight to the attempted solution." Hence, French Marxists ("Positif") are as interested in American films as the critics of "Cahiers". Mr. Roud's way of putting things is as ludicrous as insinuating that Lindsay Anderson thinks capitalism is Heaven on earth because he enjoys films about the U.S. Cavalry. His own spotty grasp of social realities is revealed by his attempt to attribute the French interest in America to a 20th-century reaction against Cartesianism, which he equates with restraint, rationalism and moderation. Not a word about the French Revolution, the Paris Commune and other little "Cartesian" tiffs. For Mr. Roud history *is* philosophy. And this one-for-one relationship between culture (i.e. taste) and politics turns up again when Mr. Roud concludes that Michel Mourlet is crypto-Fascist (and slightly nutty) on the grounds that Mourlet (a) thinks Charlton Heston has a splendidly male screen personality and (b) admires Lang, Losey (who is a left-winger), Preminger, Walsh, Cottafavi and Don Weis. Mourlet writes: "Charlton Heston by his existence alone gives a more accurate definition of the cinema than films like "Hiroshima Mon Amour" or "Citizen Kane"" and Mr. Roud thinks this is very peculiar. But Mourlet is right and Mr. Roud is the eccentric. Since about 1910 the aesthetic of the commercial cinema has been based on the star, on *personality* and, far from being an invention of the Mammon Studios this developed first in Italy and independently in India and Japan. By what process of thought Mr. Roud equates male strength with Fascism I hate to think — I should have thought such an equation was just what "Triumph of the Will" wanted its audience to make, and if something about Charlton Heston is quasi-Fascist, the Western is quasi-Fascist. But Mr. Roud can't say about Mourlet's opinion, simply, "I don't agree, I think it's mistaken", he has to accuse Mourlet of having a swastika embossed in his soul. Cripes. My all-time favourite film star is Lillian Gish in Griffith's early films, presumably this makes me an honorary member of the Ku Klux Klan.

Sense and Sensuality

All this politicization of taste got so ludicrous that, of course, we have been witnessing over the last two years, the fighting retreat of S & S from the bloody crossroads of semi-commitment, to land plump in the slender arms of "Lola". After giving "Cahiers" a few gratuitous kicks (for all the wrong reasons), S & S sets about imitating it. First, the heavyweight intellectual quotes (Aristotle, Thomas Mann, Balzac). Then, the blobs-and-stars on the back of the MFB. The Catholic streak of "Cahiers" is a bit much, and its addiction to woolly Hegelian dialectics are, as they say in the trade, inimitable, fortunately – I thought we were in for it when we were treated to a comparison between Bergman and oxymoron. But anyway, S & S, after preening itself on its lack of cut-and-dried theories, duly came up with a cut-and-dried theorist, Eric Rhode, who saw films as paradigms of Augustinianism, humanism, existentialism and Rhodeism. At least he brought his basic principles out into the open and in his coldly spherical way ("Art is a cold sphere" as Fats Waller said to Dizzy Gillespie) he said some interesting things. But his tone of superiority, his way of alighting upon films from some private moral stratosphere, and a hypochondriac obsession with psychological "normality" accorded ill with the sympathy needed to respond to works of art, and which with the simple-minded muddle-headedness of his philosophical notions, augured more than a touch of Dyerism. At times he wrote like film criticism's answer to Colin Wilson. His notion of "Centrality" seems to equate humanism with some sort of classicism; he seem to think it entails or favours the well-constructed plot; he believes that the plot which contrasts "the stable world" with "some disruptive force" and then shows the world returning to "its natural harmony" was and in some ways still is particularly useful or true; and seems vaguely to connect that sort of plot with "humanism" whereas the other sort of plot is linked to existentialism (which, for good measure, is demonstrably psychotic).

Yet the notion of the world not having an inner core or "essence" isn't peculiar to existentialism at all, it's also built into the assumptions of English pragmatism and scepticism – you wouldn't call Hume or Russell or Ayer "existentialists", at least not without remarking that you are playing musical chairs with conventional terminology. It's equally quaint to imply a comparison between something called Naturalism (which doesn't mean, as you'd think, realism, but determinism) and "riotous fantasy" of the mind (All those Surrealistic dancing-girls). But what do all these huge notions mean when you get down to cases? I call myself a humanist critic and indeed a scientific humanist critic and I tend to translate existentialism back into pragmatism (i.e. paradox into compromise), an English tendency, but I don't and never did believe that the plot which contrasts "the stable world" with "some disruptive force" and shows the world returning to "its natural harmony" was more useful or true than any other, in fact I'd say it's a conventional wish-fulfilment. Now I come to think of it, I have always presumed that "the stable order", far from being "harmonious" was naturally an unstable equilibrium of any number of diverse forces, hit on by chance, and of no metaphysical permanence, i.e. I believe that it is in the nature of Nature not to be bothered about what man wants, and that often the happy end to one's life's story comes in the middle, or at the beginning, or not at all. So I suppose I am a stoic scientific humanist critic, except that I'm a hedonist in the vulgar and materialistic (i.e. Bertrand Russell) sense, and as at the drop of a hat I'll set about having a bash at psycho-analysing a film and feeling I'm doing something vaguely interesting, and as I regularly vote Labour and my immediate target would be to see Britain run on Swedish lines politically, you'd have to say I'm a Socialist Freudian Epicurean stoic scientific humanist critic. So much for philosophical pigeonholes; you need at least 57 holes to hold one pigeon, and I haven't even begun to tell you what a loveable character I have.

Of course "A Bout de Souffle" is full of "discontinuities" if you're looking for "continuities" resembling the assumptions of the eighteenth-century neo-platonist parish-pump. Yet the action and plot of Godard's film makes perfect sense; so far as theme, relationships, motivations and narrative determinism are concerned the film is absolutely conventional, as straightforward as "Quai des Brumes".

Philosophically, Mr. Rhode's standpoint is that of arriere-garde neo-platonism onto which psycho-analytical terminology has been grafted. The attempt is frequent these days, and the graft won't last. While it lasts, the effect is of super-Augustinianism: the inquisitor can psycho-analyse his victim and condemn him for his "repressions". A cerebrality like Manicheanism appears again in Mr. Rhode's solo effort on eroticism, which "proved" by a couple of twists of phrase that *only* death gives sensuality its meaning. This profound sentence makes just as much sense back to front ("only sensuality gives death its meaning") but you might just as well say "only death gives language its meaning" or "only death gives pickled onions their meaning". What he seems to be trying to say is, "Don't believe all this superficial rubbish about breasts and bodies, that's all very unhealthy, we're all thoughtful skeletons really." It's an eerie article on the erotic that mentions neither passionate love nor reproduction, which in the human species is sexual – the death instinct's little joke, presumably. He mentions four films as being sensual (and says he's only seen one or two more): "Ossessione" (yes, I had a crick in my neck too, when I came out), "Casque d'Or", "Que Viva Mexico", "Le Dejeuner Sur l'Herbe", and writes, "Only in Eisenstein's case is it fairly certain that he was not primarily motivated by nostalgia." But if Marie Seton's biography is anything to go by then Eisenstein was the most likely to have been motivated by nostalgia – I don't suppose it's necessary to dwell on the homosexual elements in Eisenstein's and Visconti's films? Mr. Rhode's non-reaction before the scene of Nadia Gray on the fur in "La Dolce Vita" is peculiar – I saw the film twice and both times the audience "felt" the fur – it's Mr. Rhode who doesn't, because in the cinema, as feelies haven't been invented yet, sensuousness is in the mind of the beholder, just as in literature it's in the mind of the reader. But how can you react sensuously to a film when all the time you're worried about whether it's healthy or what philosophical football team the director plays for or whether the jump-cuts are psychotic or not?

Mr. Rhode's interest in personal hygiene even leads him to say, about Visconti, "There is something wrong somewhere when a nobleman makes a film entirely about Sicilian fishermen; and the fault doesn't lie only with social conditions and the desire to expose social wrongs. I feel that Visconti (though perhaps to a lesser degree than his contemporaries) is trying in his work to escape from the complex issues, from the uses of intelligence." There's no possible defence, of course, against a suggestion so vague that it might as well apply to Lindsay Anderson, Tony Richardson, Karel Reisz, or anybody who comes from one class or country but habitually makes films about people from another. If Eric Rhode doesn't diagnose directors as sick because they don't put their own problems on the screen, Peter John Dyer will diagnose them as sick because they do.

In "The Listener" Mr. Rhode's view of human nature has gradually become less hypochondriac and mellower: his "Sight and Sound" period illustrates puritanism's last stand; it becomes agnostic and philosophical and talks about "maturity" when it means "salvation". Mr. Rhode's articles were interesting and his departure leaves S and S without a thinker, sinking slowly back to safely non-philosophical, non-committed earth, in short, to Bloomsburyite waffling about aesthetics-qua-aesthetics of which there is a delirious specimen in an article with a sensitively twee bit of anti-syntax en tete, "How Art Is True?" (How true is art, how is art true, is? true; how; art! – aw, shucks).*

And then who, as they say in the grunt-and-groan racket, will unmask Arkadin the Mystery Man of Semi-committed criticism? "Movie" thinks it's John Russell Taylor, but we don't mind who it is. Anyway impregnable behind his anonymity, he remarks, "surely it is an unhealthy sign when those who are ostensibly criticising a film devote so much of their space instead to criticising other critics". Touche, Monsieur Pussycat, and et tu, brute, come to that, you've just had a delicate go at John Coleman, Isabel Quigley, Dilys Powell and several others. We haven't a clue as to why you do it, but we do it because:–

(1) too many of the critics criticised here make the bland, and, alas, so often *unconscious* assumption that the relationship of critic to film-maker is that of examiner to examinee. Fellini is such a bungling idiot that he can't even stage a strip-tease excitingly, Brooks, Aldrich, Losey, Fuller, Minnelli, never try to do anything that a critic can't sum up off the cuff, the critic may have moral ideas *about* a film but there are rarely moral ideas *in* a film, Visconti and Bergman are just walking about waving their sores in the air, etc. This assumption of superiority leads inevitably to a critical negligence whereby these critics restrict their responses to the run of films to a level of sophistication *below* that of the *average* film director, to the level of the *least* intelligent spectator. Superior in *depreciation*, they are far and away *inferior* in appreciation to Mr. and Mrs. Bloggs.

(2) We must head off the inevitable smear that this is an attack on film criticism. The Dean St. clique still thinks it is film criticism generally, despite accumulating evidence to the contrary. So accumulating that even S & S has finally blossomed out in highbrow quotations (just like "Cahiers"), has contrived to discover Hawks and Losey (just like "Cahiers"), Frank Tashlin (in time for "Bachelor Flat", that is, ten years after the first really glorious Tashlin film, "Susan Slept Here"), has asked "Why don't we take horror films seriously?" (the answer is, we always have), and then, aghast at its own daring covered up quickly with "but not seriously seriously" (as you were), has given a Fuller film two stars. But if anyone *else* does it, they're hungry for kicks …

(3) It's very odd how the whole commitment debate went through without reference to "Positif". One would have thought that on strategical grounds alone "committed" critics (or their half-hearted champions) would have been glad to direct attention to the work of their French comrades-in-arms. But of course, sneering at "Cahiers" (even while you emulate its "confusionism") is much easier than seeking to understand one's allies. Above all, one is never in danger of not feeling superior, is one? "Positif" calls itself "la revue du cinema la plus aggressive": being openly rude, it manages to be less offensive than S & S. Sometimes, we feel, it is too quick on the trigger. Its sometimes very sharp divisions between "left" and "right" attitudes can-

* The post-Dyer M.F.B. veers to the more genial but pays for it by inconsistency. Worse, the anonymity of many reviews makes it impossible to make allowances for critics' idiosyncrasies.

not really be applied in Britain, although "Positif" may well still dislike our feeling that there are right-wing critics whose opinions interest us more, and to whom in many ways we feel nearer, than those on the left. We don't think of film criticism as a form of political activity, but are committed in the sense that we have opinions, and see no reason for not bringing them to bear on films. We cite "Positif" because it is (a) committed and (b) its cultural equipment enables it to grapple with contemporary films of all kinds. Opening past issues at random we find incisive and enthusiastic reviews of: "The Girl Can't Help It", "Odds Against Tomorrow", "La Dolce Vita", "Time Without Pity", "El Cochechito", "Rocco and his Brothers", "Peeping Tom", "Look Back In Anger", "Le Bel Age", "Strangers When We Meet", "The Bells Are Ringing", "The Virgin Spring". If S & S do after all still want to be committed they might with advantage take lessons from "Positif" (and from "La Methode", "Premier Plan", "Contre-Champ") and forgo their opportunistic derivations from "Cahiers".

(4) It's high time our highbrows dropped their supercilious (S & S) or paranoid (Hoggart) attitude to the mass media and mitigated their lofty disinterest in what the general public wants and why.

(5) We believe there is a necessity for critical disagreements, counter-interpretations, cross-purposes, debates. We are not quibbling with S & S because they didn't enthuse over the films we liked. Nor have we merely culled a Golden Treasury of Howlers – which no critic can altogether avoid. We are saying that just as "Definition" killed committed criticism, so "Sight and Sound" with its unique prestige has over the last ten years done more to keep English film criticism naive than no criticism at all would have done.

If it now wants to take notice of any of these criticisms, it's very welcome. No-one will be more pleased than we will.

—

The cover of the Spring '63 is obviously neo-"Movie", suggesting another fashionable shift of emphasis: if you can't sneer 'em out of court, imitate 'em. As always, the "outside" contributions are the most interesting: Geoffrey Nowell-Smith not only grasps some of the basic issues in the "S & S"–"Movie" needle-match (nth round) but actually contrives to treat "Movie" with courtesy. Arkadin, the Doctor Death of film criticism, gets submission grips on a couple of obvious deadbeats, but his try at reconciling his rationalist principles with out-Cahiering "Cahiers" in uprooting adorable turnips is feeble because he still hasn't grasped the rules of the game and still can't decide whether or not to take himself seriously. A survey of "Blockbusters" tries to be toughly practical about the trade, but can't make it because neither of the authors has a clue as to what or why or how the public "sees" films. For example: of "Spartacus": "the audience warmed to the well-staged gladiatorial contests and left the moralising to look after itself". Not at my local Odeon they didn't; they responded to all the moral climaxes and cheered two of them. The British public isn't as stupid as "Nice Time"-besotted "intellectuals" seem to imagine.

SOURCE: *MOTION*, NO. 6, AUTUMN 1963, 25–8, 38–42

1.2 WHO REALLY MAKES THE MOVIES?

Questions of style inevitably bring us to the debates over the so-called *auteur* theory currently sprawling through the flock of new American film magazines. Our concern is not to discuss the arguments in all their aspects but to concentrate on those which concern the issue of style and personal vision.

The first point is that an *auteur* theory as such is central to the old 'British school' of film criticism, running from Rotha and Grierson through the British Film Institute of the '30s and '40s to *Sequence* and *Sight and Sound*. Their *auteurs* have been men like Eisenstein, Pudovkin, Flaherty, Huston, Ford, Cocteau and so on. Interest waxes and wanes, but by and large they are named and considered with respect. Other directors have had periods as *auteurs* – Lang, Hitchcock and Vidor through the '20s and '30s, Capra in the '30s, Minnelli in the '40s – but almost all their later films are 'out'. So are such 'post-war' directors as Fuller, Preminger, Kazan and Ray. These critics attached great importance to a director's having an individual vision or style, so they felt quite at home with people like Ingmar Bergman and Antonioni (once they had been discovered on the continent), Ophuls, Wajda, Truffaut, Godard and so on. The 'documentary' tradition also induced them to attach a certain importance to 'social consciousness', of the rather obvious liberal type typified by *I Was A Fugitive From A Chain-Gang* (LeRoy), *Fury* and *You Only Live Once* (Lang). *Scarface*, *The Front Page* and *Sergeant York* (Hawks) – though they positively disliked the more tormented post-war films like *On the Waterfront* (Kazan), *The Big Heat* (Lang), *Run of the Arrow* (Fuller) and *The Young Savages* (Frankenheimer). Probably the last Hawks film to have widely enthusiastic reviews in these circles was *Red River* (1948).

The young critics never questioned the importance of a director's possessing an individual vision or style, and Andrew Sarris, the one coherent Anglo-Saxon exponent of *auteur* theory, extended it to cover 50 or 60 Hollywood directors, including such 'forgotten men' as Allan Dwan. In general, the main dispute was over post-war Hollywood directors (this, according to one rumour, was only because many of the younger critics had hardly seen any pre-war films). They took their cue quite slavishly from the second generation of critics of *Cahiers du Cinéma*, the '55–'63 flotilla of 'Hitchcocko-Hawksiens', who included such directors-to-be as Truffaut, Godard and Chabrol. In England the *Cahiers* line was usually simplified down to baby-talk about details of style (though Robin Wood matched the cultural depth of the French critics). They deliberately and somewhat perversely ignored the 'social consciousness' of all films including their own favourites (Nicholas Ray's). This importation of the *Cahiers* line, simplified as it was, shook *Sight and Sound* into finding a neo-platonic equivalent of *Cahiers*' philosophising over points of style, a change which rendered it largely turgid as well as muddleheaded. There can be no doubt, however, that the efforts to substitute one set of idols for the traditional culture-figures had the wholly excellent result of extending critical interest to many directors hitherto dismissed as beneath serious consideration.

It's still worth remarking that, substantial as was the debt of so many young English critics to *Cahiers du Cinéma*, the French magazine was doing no more than follow in the footsteps of two magazines edited by Jean-George Auriol, *Du Cinéma* between the wars, and *La Revue du Cinéma* which before 1950 was devoting major reviews to such 'non-U' films as Dassin's *Brute Force*, Charles Vidor's *Gilda*, William Dieterle's *Love Letters*, and all Hitchcock's American films. There's nothing new in French intellectuals' adoption of American films. Most French critics have been exploring Hollywood as widely as *Cahiers*

The Apotheosis of Va-Va-Voom: *Kiss Me Deadly* (1955)

since the end of the war, and even earlier. The veteran Henri Agel, a Roman Catholic whose books are published by a Dominican publishing house, has never seen anything paradoxical in taking seriously such films as *Duel in the Sun* and Hawks's *Monkey Business*.

The importance attached to a 'personal vision' by the older critics has provoked the 'rebels' to rise to the bait and feel very concerned to show that Howard Hawks, say, has a personal vision and style, presumably altogether different from, say, Otto Preminger's. But the importance of this can be questioned, from the most traditional of all approaches to art.

The concise OED gives us a second sense of the word 'style'. Style is also the 'collective characteristics of the writing or diction or artistic expression or way of presenting things or decorative methods proper to a person or school or period or subject, manner exhibiting these characteristics'. In other words, a director's vision or style may be of great interest and sincerity even when it is shared by a great many directors – just as in architecture one speaks of collective styles – Norman, Early English, decorated perpendicular, Tudor, Queen Anne, and so on. Similarly, in literature there are 'groups' of artists who have many opinions and mannerisms in common – the 'Metaphysicals', the 'neo-classicists', and so on. The purpose of art is not to express individuals, particularly, but feelings, attitudes and values of any kind, and a film may be of considerable cultural significance even if it is quite anonymous – just as medieval religious paintings, stained glass windows, certain poems (*Beowulf*) or buildings (the Taj Mahal) reveal little or nothing about the individual man who painted, wrote or designed them. Most folk art is anonymous, by definition, but nonetheless poignant and significant. A cathedral may be altered by one generation after another (with no one mind 'in control'!) but still be of artistic importance. In fact the notion of culture is arrived at by taking as significant those elements which artists have in common. *Kiss Me Deadly* isn't important because it 'reveals' Aldrich. Aldrich is important because *Kiss Me Deadly* (and one or two of his other best films) reveals America – and us all.

The fact that a director has an 'individual' style doesn't make his films interesting (unless you collect film styles like some people collect quaintly-shaped inkpots). Enid Blyton, Marie Corelli and Amanda McKittrick Ros all have 'individual' visions and styles, and are undoubtedly *auteurs*, but this doesn't make them great creative artists.

A peculiarity of the *auteur* theory is that all the auteurs seem to be directors. But many important creative personalities are producers – one thinks of Mark Hellinger, and of David O Selznick, who virtually directed some of his films 'through' his directors, reputedly bombarding them with 50-page telegrams telling them exactly how a given scene ought to be played. Selznick is an *auteur* – *Portrait of Jennie* is 1 per cent Dieterle, 99 per cent Selznick. Several screenwriters are *auteurs* – Philip Yordan in Hollywood, Bryan Forbes in Britain, Carl Mayer in Germany, Jacques Prévert in France. As Renoir remarked: '… anyone that says that *Les Enfants du Paradis* is Carné's film is crazy. It's Jacques Prévert's. Prévert was the dominant personality. Not that Carné is not a good director – but I think he was born to be a good director of great writers.' Renoir continues: 'Sometimes it can even be the actor who dominates – take the Mary Pickford films, for example.' The mere fact that the public follows stars proves that a star is an *auteur*. So are 'undirectable' actors like George Arliss and Charles Laughton, certain personalities (Louise Brooks, Robert Mitchum), and, particularly, comedians like Jerry Lewis and Laurel and Hardy.

It isn't unknown for excellent parts of an *auteur*'s film to be directed by someone else (the chariot race of Wyler's *Ben-Hur* and the landrace of Anthony Mann's *Cimarron* were both directed by Andrew Marton, the exteriors of Corman's *The Terror* by Monte Hellman). *Gone With the Wind* has a consistent visual style through all its changes of director because it was masterminded by Selznick and storyboarded by William Cameron Menzies. Nominally an art director, Menzies created the visuals of many British and American films; his own directorial efforts suffer from a poor story sense and slightly stilted acting, but he is certainly an *auteur*, and many directors have enjoyed the praise for effects which were actually Menzies's.

Many films bear the marks of several auteurs. *Le Crime de Monsieur Lange* is 100 per cent Prévert, and 100 per cent Renoir – total 200 per cent. *Duel in the Sun* is 80 per cent Selznick and 80 per cent Vidor – total 160 per cent. But a good film is always a subtle balance of creative energies and ascendancies, especially in Hollywood where until recently the *auteur* was at bay against the production line system imposed by such men as Louis B Mayer and Harry Cohn.

Some brilliant films have been made by directors who, for one reason or another, have not emerged as consistent *auteurs*. One thinks of Joseph H Lewis's *Gun Crazy*, E E Reinert's *Quai de Grenelle*, Norman Panama and Melvin Frank's *Li'l Abner*. And who is the auteur of such weird and brilliant one-shots as *The 5,000 Fingers of Dr T* (director, Roy Rowland), *Gilda* (director, Charles Vidor), *This Island Earth* (director, Joseph M Newman)? The full list of credits offers no clue. As Renoir said, 'A good film is a miracle', that is, a series of happy accidents … Inevitably, a mediocre or bad film by a 'great' director will be of more interest to connoisseurs than a mediocre or even a good film by a mediocre director. Renoir's *Le Déjeuner Sur L'Herbe* might have been the work of two men, containing as it does one sequence of sheer genius (the disturbed picnic) in a context whose dithering incompetence results (one hopes) from a wrong theory pushed to the limit. Any artist's inspiration results from a conflict, that is, a precarious balance of attitudes and emotions, and there's nothing illogical in, for example, my own feeling that King Vidor's *North-West Passage* and *H M Pulham Esq* are as nauseating as such films as *Hallelujah* and *Ruby Gentry* are superb. However charmed we may be by *The Enchanted Island* it's no use pretending that *The Most*

Dangerous Man Alive, by the same producer-director (Benedict Bogeaus-Allan Dwan) is anything but a stinkeroo. Conversely, Benedek's strange decline casts no reflection on his achievement in *The Wild One*. Often, film auteurs, like novelists and poets, die before their death – like Tay Garnett, Stanley Donen, Edward Dmytryk, Robert Siodmak.

A special form of *auteur* is the *anti-auteur* – the man who delights in adopting different themes and styles for each of his films – for example, Fred Zinnemann in America, René Clément in France and Alberto Lattuada in Italy. Ford has had two distinct styles – his 'open-air' style (*Stagecoach*) and his 'expressionistic' style (*The Informer*, *The Long Voyage Home*). It's a pity he's never explored the region where these two tones and views of life meet and conflict.

Another kind of creative personality may come to dominate the cinema's history, not simply because of his own films, but because of his creative fertility – the German scenarist Carl Mayer, the Italian writer Cesare Zavattini, were both one-man mass movements. So to some extent was Gregg Toland – whose deep-focus expressionism was used extensively in Ford's *The Long Voyage Home*, *before* Welles took it up for *Citizen Kane*.

Although many of Hollywood's directors are *auteurs* it is quite possible to speak of an overall Hollywood 'style' – in that, whether the narrative is fast (La Cava's *Stage Door* possibly holding some sort of world record) or slow (Henry King's *Snows of Kilimanjaro*), there is a certain tautness, a spareness of intention, a lack of distraction from the principal story points. There are none of the asides one finds in, say, Renoir or Becker and which European directors generally are more inclined to entertain. Hollywood would never have invented such 'European' ideas as the *temps-mort*, or the stylistic pot-pourri of Truffaut. American films seem to be enclosed by their subjects, and the dramatic tensions are calculated with a Protestant rigour. European directors often deliberately relax the story so as to dwell on the sprawl and irrelevance of 'off-moments' (which after all constitute 80 per cent of life).

Similarly there is a Hollywood tradition that it's cissy to pan where a cut would do – the latter being faster, smoother, tauter. The preference for camera-movements over cuts is primarily a European tradition (Murnau, Renoir, Ophuls) which Hitchcock's *Rope* reduced to a boring 'exercise de style'. In general it seems true to say that Hollywood directors show less variety of theme and approach than European ones. This is because Europe is culturally more diversified than America, dedicated as the latter is to the moulding of immigrants into one cultural pattern. However, I should say that such directors as Hitchcock (sometimes), King Vidor or Samuel Fuller show a 'European' extent of individuality, whereas, say, Hawks and Preminger don't.

Of course, one can group individualists, in America as in Europe, into 'schools'. After Preston Sturges 'died', his vein of sick humour was asserted by Billy Wilder, from whose failing grasp the torch was snatched up by Stanley Kubrick. In fact one can group and re-group Hollywood directors in all sorts of ways, depending on which points of style one finds interesting. There are 'soft' directors (Frank Borzage, Allan Dwan in *The Enchanted Island*) and 'bleak' directors (Hawks, Jack Arnold, Boetticher), 'muscular' directors (King Vidor, Fuller, Walsh, Richard Fleischer, Anthony Mann) and 'tightlipped' directors (Lang, Mann, Hawks). There are 'women's' directors (Cukor, Minnelli), 'theatrical' directors (Cukor, Wyler), 'actor's' directors (Cukor, La Cava), 'novelist' directors (Mankiewicz, Brooks). There are TV directors, whose visuals are often ragged (like Delbert Mann's, and Frankenheimer's, except when he carbon-copies Hitchcock) but who have a powerful acting sense. There are 'plush' directors (George Sidney, Douglas Sirk, Quine, Edwards). There are the 'tearaways' (Don Siegel, Phil Karlson).

There are directors whose forte is what we have called 'mise-en-scene' – Nicholas Ray, Boetticher, Minnelli, Jack Webb. Douglas Sirk approaches a plush weepie like *Imitation of Life* with a dry calculation which introduces a sense of lonely alienation not unlike Antonioni's (this doesn't make him worthy of a 'cult', but is interesting to notice, for the commercial cinema, by curious processes of its own, is often ahead of 'art' films). There are essentially 'middle-class' directors (Wyler, Zinnemann, both with a pessimistic under-current). There are 'fake liberals' (George Stevens), 'flabby liberals' (Wyler) and the younger, tougher, more courageous men (Wise, Brooks, Daves in his Westerns). There are even more bitter, virulent men (Aldrich, Losey). There are 'right-wing' directors (Leo McCarey, John Wayne, Ray Milland). There are deeply ambivalent figures like Ford, Fuller and King Vidor. There are the 'intellectuals' – Huston (who joins Losey, Buñuel and Jacques Becker in the group of great moralists), Arthur Penn, Elia Kazan.

But none of these directors can be contained within such a classification. Cukor's *Heller in Pink Tights* reveals his affinities with Vincente Minnelli. Wyler's *Ben-Hur* resembles Fleischer's *Barabbas* in its use of symbolism, its 'staging', its sense of physique. Raoul Walsh, lyricist par excellence of male exuberance, endows parts of *The Lawless Breed* with a soft, feminine delicacy (or is this the contribution of an art director?). One can almost describe *Moonrise* (Borzage), *The Night of the Hunter* (Laughton) and *The Enchanted Island* (Dwan) as Hollywood's tattered rearguard of Griffith-spirited films. Yet, with *Wild River* Kazan returns to a romantic lyricism not far in spirit from Borzage and Dwan. And curious affinities link otherwise completely different films and directors. The use of depth and space by Budd Boetticher (a genuine *auteur*) in *Ride Lonesome* is very reminiscent of Roman Polanski's in *The Knife in the Water* (which could easily be transposed into terms of a Boetticher Western). *The 41st* is Russia's answer to *Duel in the Sun* (and vastly inferior), in climax (shotguns), style and love-hate theme. Kazan is the most European of American directors – *Rocco* is Visconti changing his style after *On the Waterfront*, while the immigrant story of *The Anatolian Smile* is Kazan following the 'immigrant' story of *Rocco*.

The paradox is not that the various groups of *auteur* theorists accept the films that they do but that they reject so many films which would seem to be on their wavelength. Ray's *Rebel Without A Cause*, Fuller's *Run of the Arrow*, Vidor's *Ruby Gentry*, Lang's *The Big Heat*, Aldrich's *Attack*, Kramer's *On the Beach*, arouse the ire, contempt, or, at best, indifference of the older critics who, however, lavish praise on the canny escapism of John Ford. Conversely the younger critics, prizing themselves on their sense of style, seem to make nothing of George Sidney's *Pal Joey* or his very beautiful *Jeanne Eagels*, or even of Corman's horror rhapsodies, while applauding every time such limited stylists as Hawks and Preminger manage to move the camera from A to B. Those whom they admire as moralists are all sophisticated entertainers who carefully tailor their message so as not to offend their audience (Hitchcock, Preminger) and they praise for his maturity a director (Hawks) whose films, charming as they are, rarely move outside a range of agreeable cliché which almost any other American director can handle, and at some time or other has.

One can understand why French intellectuals take them seriously. Their very simplicity can have a tonic, and very real, value, as a corrective to the debilitating worship of culture and sensitivity for its own sake. But it's as well to remember that Hawks moves on the easiest, simplest, wavelength of his (mass) audience's responses – even to his 'deadpan' way with emotion, which is an American cliché. Hemingway shares it, but his work has a quality of pain, of waste, which Hawks complacently ignores.

Preminger is another minor figure with an inflated reputation among the *auteur* critics. He is at his best in the 'modest' films made when he was 'trapped' within the system – *Fallen Angel, Laura, Angel Face, The Man With The Golden Arm* and *Anatomy of a Murder* – all have a real feeling for the enigmatic quality of human relationships, and an authentic atmosphere of sordid anguish. But the ambiguity *in* these small-scale subjects gets into his treatment *of* the later, 'bigger' themes, which consequently become as boring as they are non-committal. If he makes *Saint Joan* there's Shaw's play for the agnostics, Greene's screenplay for the Catholics, Jean Seberg for the 'teen-agers of the Middle West, Richard Widmark for the 'industrial halls', and Anton Walbrook, Felix Aylmer and John Gielgud for the 'carriage trade'. (Nobody minds this sort of calculation – but with Preminger it always shows.) *Exodus* does for Israel what *Giant* does for Texas (nothing) while on the most controversial issues of all *Advise and Consent* and *The Cardinal* contrive to say nothing of interest at all; they don't even manage to annoy anybody, except Cardinal Spellman. Only *Anatomy of a Murder* can even stand comparison with such attacks on American complacency as Richard Brooks's *Deadline* and *Elmer Gantry*, Wilder's *Stalag 17*, and Wyler's *Carrie* and *Detective Story*. And Preminger's best films aren't specifically Preminger – they're part of the '40s wave of 'tightlipped misogyny' (*Gilda, The Outlaw, Leave Her to Heaven, The Lady From Shanghai*). Even his masterpiece, *Laura*, is one of a deluge of '40s films about portraits and missing women (*Rebecca, Phantom Lady, Pandora and the Flying Dutchman, Portrait of Jennie, One Touch of Venus*). As for Preminger's *Lady Windermere's Fan*, it is possibly the worst film ever produced in Hollywood. That Preminger's films all show the mark of a definite artistic personality is beyond question; whether that personality is an interesting one is another question altogether. My own feeling is that, in this second, all-important, sense, Preminger isn't an *auteur* at all.

Given the Hollywood system, it's evident that a director's name can be no guarantee of quality. For example, Lang's *The Big Heat* is a key film from any point of view; the attempt to repeat its success in *Human Desire* is a flop from any point of view; while *Blue Gardenia* is hardly recognisable as a Lang film. Similarly, Ray's *Party Girl* is as inept as his *Rebel Without A Cause* and *The Savage Innocents* are invaluable. Donen's and Kelly's musicals are classics (when will MGM revive *Give a Girl a Break*?) yet his comedies are insipid. All Hitchcock's films for Paramount and Universal are interesting or first-rate, but all his films for Selznick and (bar one, *Strangers On a Train*) Warners are below par.

Every critic will of course have a greater temperamental affinity with some auteurs than with others. But perhaps the best way of 'valuing' Hollywood – and Europe for that matter – is not by selecting certain auteurs as 'in' and others as 'out', but by picking those individual films which most subtly, vividly and fully crystallise the ranges of feeling asserted by the whole body of films together with those which go out into undiscovered country, and those which pick on themes otherwise ignored as too hot to handle (Hollywood was half-killed by its fear of controversy). By choosing the best films of (for example) Aldrich, Arnold, Boetticher, Brooks, Cassavetes, Daves, De Mille, Donen, Dwan, Ford, Fuller, Hawks, Hitchcock, Huston, Kazan, Mankiewicz, Mann, Minnelli, Ray, Sidney, Sirk, Tashlin, Ulmer, Wilder, Wise, Wyler, Zinnemann, *et al.*, one's canon of films has much greater variety. It also saves one from having to see the dreary or pusillanimous films which all these directors have perpetrated from time to time. No doubt each reader will have his own suggestions for Hollywood's twenty best post-war films …?

But in any case one shouldn't despise the thought and style of so many fascinating films which probably won't make the Top Twenty (or even Hundred). One thinks of Ulmer's

The Essential Raymond Durgnat

atmospheric *The Man from Planet X*, Gregg Tallas's *Siren of Atlantis*, Minnelli's 'communi-cations' comedy *The Bells Are Ringing*, Joseph H Lewis's *The Big Combo*, Dwan's *The Enchanted Island*, and many others. And however one approaches these films it is absurd to try and consider the visual style in isolation from the quality of the ideas and attitudes which go with it, or to dismiss the immense dramatic power of, say, Delbert Mann's *The Middle of the Night*, just because its visuals aren't elegant. Nor is the mass audience a bunch of innocent 16-year-olds standing in any great need of instruction in whatever prim-itive moral points Preminger and Hawks manage to put across to them.

SOURCE: *FILMS AND FILMING*, APRIL 1965, 44–8

1.3 CAT AND MOUSE GAMES

THE STRANGE CASE of Alfred Hitchcock poses many interesting critical issues. On the one hand, Truffaut, whose criticism of 'le cinema de papa', when it was French, was so destruc-tive, sits at the feet of his London-Hollywood guru with a respect which would be touch-ing if it weren't so inappropriate. The big Secker and Warburg tome is fascinating when the indulgent, sometimes testy, master and wilful acolyte discuss, as distinguished practi-tioners, the gnostic lore of technical execution and audience manipulation. They talk on equal terms, and Truffaut's nostalgias nicely dovetail with Hitchcock's wise assurance. At the same time, the text intermittently possesses the involuntary comedy of a dialogue between the deaf. Truffaut, moving in his little world of Platonic love and preconceptions, misses so many leads and clues and corrections in Hitchcock's answers; while Hitchcock disdains Truffaut's moral metaphysics except insofar as they correspond to the everyday, popular, intuitive morality which Hitchcock understands so clearly. Truffaut misses, too, Hitchcock's evident respect for 'pure cinema', that is, for the very ideas against which Bazin and *Cahiers* led the original charge. It's ironical, too, that Truffaut after so savagely dismissing the 'well-constructed script' should, not just mince matters, but not even raise them, with a director whose scripts are unsurpassably classic in construction. Truffaut, as an interviewer, is a mouse, whereas the ideal interviewer is, if not a ferret, at least a retriever. The text remains two fascinating monologues.

We are used by now to the way young men adore in their grandfathers even more extreme versions of what they fight in their fathers, and young European intellectuals revere in their American grandfathers every nuance of a morality which they would rightly dismiss if proposed by a French director.

The position would be complicated enough were it merely a matter of extreme views col-liding – dismissal versus adulation, 'mere entertainer' versus 'prophet' – and of a possible, intermediate, position. But preferences for different periods and aspects within periods are involved; one man's nostalgia is another's unreality, what one man respects as a challenge another despises as 'nasty', and so on and so forth. What one respects as the preoccupa-tions of an *auteur*, bore another as monotonous repetition; what one ascribes to Hitchcock seem to another a property, either of the genre or of the period to which a particular film belongs. And indeed to tackle the spiritual phenomenon of Hollywood one needs not only an *auteur* theory and a *genre* theory but a *period* theory, a theory to cover the endeavour by artist-entertainers to express, not themselves, but their audience, a theory of formulae (whereby, for instance, *Repulsion* is a permutation of *Psycho*), and a theory of the symbiotic relationship between art and entertainment. Not the least merit of Robin Wood's Hitchcock book is that he says, simply: Hitchcock's films deserve to be taken seriously.

Hitchcock's long work, consistent/repetitive in some ways, diverse in others, challenges, also, the monolithic tendencies that recent controversies have brought to *auteur* theory. It's often assumed that to defend, say, *Vertigo*, one must also defend *Stage Fright*, or that to attack the cliché facilities of *Foreign Correspondent* is to put the skids under *North-By-North-West*, that Hitchcock was never very inspired between 1921 and 1939 but always very inspired between 1939 and 1969, that an *auteur* who isn't always brilliant is never brilliant, that an *auteur* who isn't always an *auteur* is never an *auteur*. All these assumptions, without which few of the arguments about *auteur* theory make sense, are revealed as nonsensical the moment one applies them to the other arts. No-one would dream of arguing that because *The Pilgrim's Progress* is a masterpiece, every text and tract and allegory that John Bunyan wrote is of other than very highly specialized interest. Criticism has always allowed that a man might have *his* masterpiece, that, for any one of a million reasons, and combination of reasons he might, once or twice, rise above himself, and produce a classic in which much that he otherwise expresses moderately well, or boringly, here finds an eloquent form and finesse. No artistic paradox, no critical innovation, is involved, in our ultra-traditional view that Hitchcock is just such an artist, and that the question is not whether to be pro-Hitchcock or anti-Hitchcock or pro-English Hitchcock and anti-American Hitchcock or, as the general tendency of this essay runs, anti-Balcon Hitchcock, pro-Maxwell Hitchcock, pro-Montagu/Balcon Hitchcock, anti-Selznick Hitchcock, anti-Warner Brothers Hitchcock, and pro-post-*Rear Window* Hitchcock, but to discriminate between superficially and theoretically similar films, and see which convincingly pose complex and valuable insights in terms of human experience. Critics being individuals, we'll never absolutely agree, but our discussion will be more sophisticated, subtle and demanding as we restore to films, and to scenes within films, their individuality and specificity, as we look for nuances in experience rather than patterns of symbols in isolation.

Hitchcock's films are all the more intriguing for his curious combination of versatility, limitation and self-restriction. In his early romances, something tentatively bitter and sombre evokes Julien Duvivier – albeit a nonconformist Duvivier, that is to say, bound by moral claims to a cynical but stern prudence, whereas the Frenchman's cultural background allows amorality and its sensitive, yet ruthless, cynicism. (It's interesting to relate Truffaut's pessimism with Duvivier's; and for *Les 400 Coups* read *Poil de Carotte*). Hitchcock's gifts as a vignettist set one wondering whether he mightn't have become the screen equivalent of a Simenon or a Graham Greene – two writers whose work he has, rather surprisingly perhaps, shown no inclination to tackle. One wonders whether, behind the 'master of suspense', there isn't a broader, more dramatic, director, who can't quite find himself within the moral ambit proposed by *Downhill* and *The Manxman*, and who loiters on the periphery, as with the gigolo-hero of *Young and Innocent*, or the patriotic prostitution theme of *Notorious*.

Hitchcock may indeed be one of those interwar English directors, like Anthony Asquith and Thorold Dickinson, both of whom made, in passing, super-Hitchcockian films (*A Cottage On Dartmoor* and *Orders To Kill*; *Gaslight* and *Secret People*) and whose spiritual range couldn't be unfolded within the climate of their country and period. The films of Asquith and Dickinson show an acquaintance with high culture of which Hitchcock's show none – an absence which, perhaps, facilitated his responsiveness to commercial formulae and to the American style. Artistically, though, the culture within which Hitchcock worked levelled with John Buchan rather than Simenon and French populism, with Daphne du Maurier rather than Dostoievski. It's obviously not a matter of reading, but of the spiritual flexibility and reach of the culture within which he works. Hitchcock, locked within non-conformism, plays cat and mouse with it, accepting, denying, denying his denial, querying his acceptance, counterpointing severity with cynicism, indulgence with paranoia, playing a cat and mouse game with challenge and prudence, fear and complacency, optimism and pessimism. Mostly it's fixed. His best films are those in which the cat doesn't just play with the mouse, but catches and eats it.

In much the same way, Hitchcock's technical flexibility and virtuosity has a smack of the avant-garde about it. In the '20s, Asquith can out-Hitchcock Hitchcock, before Hitchcock, in one sequence of *A Cottage On Dartmoor*, switch to matching Pabst in the Gallipoli landing sequence of *Tell England*; the '30s see his experimental impulse dry, and die; the lyrical impulse jets forth one last time in *The Young Lovers*. Thorold Dickinson, who is the true lion of English style, the English Visconti, before Visconti, can assert, but cannot continue to impose, his immense potentialities within a cinema whose spiritual and stylistic mediocrity suits the national character: defensive, safe, and sorry. Hitchcock's styles span what one might call the Lindgren-era conceptions of the late '20s and '30s (quick cutting, 'pure' cinema), to the revival, collaterally with Ophuls, of the Murnau style, and through to the para-TV interviews of *Psycho*. His reasons, often, are practical ones; yet their result is aesthetic also. Hitchcock's flexibility, like Renoir's, reminds just how durable and resourceful the cinema's conventional, classical mainstream is, how smoothly its qualities may be blended with changes which every avant-garde hard-sells as a 'new language' but which always turns out to be a new idiom – useful indeed, but not so revolutionary that its eventual justification isn't a new compromise. Truffaut, interviewing Hitchcock, is renouncing his own criticism – which probably explains why it's as bad, though in a defensive, rather than an aggressive way, a new compromise. His readiness for technical innovation and variation is counterpointed by another flexibility; an affable-cynical readiness to draw in his horns, in response to a commercial failure, and, in anticipation thereof, to go so far and no further; without, however, remaining content with a few stock favourites, as Hawks has done. Hitchcock has retained a certain initiative. He complains that *Secret Agent* broke a basic rule, of featuring a negative hero; but he still makes *The Wrong Man*, with its even more negative hero; and just how positive are the successive heroes of *Psycho*? He says he thought *Psycho* would not be a great box-office success, just as he says he planned it as a fun picture, and perhaps the two statements aren't contradictory. Perhaps he did in fact aim it at the guignol-horror public, rather than the larger family public, and in so doing gave himself more rope than usual, to hang his moral restraint and unleash the full dynamism of the macabre. Of all his films it comes nearest to that food-to-waste subject which he dreamily described to Truffaut, but done in human terms. A dissolve links the eye with the plughole: 'Norman has pulled the chain'. One may prefer those films which come nearest that pitiless derision (*Sabotage*, *Vertigo*, *Psycho*, maybe, in their way, *Murder*, *Rope* and *The Birds*), or find an equivalent, a religious sense of the absurd, in seediness, like *The Man Who Knew Too Much*. Hitchcock would then be a Céline who has not lost his moral finesse …

But Hitchcock's gifts are too diverse for any one criterion to apply. Hitchcock the anti-Surrealist exists only in interaction with Hitchcock the dramatist, that dissatisfying, promising, fascinating figure who serves Eden Phillpotts, Galsworthy, O'Casey, Hall Caine, well enough, very well, indeed, for their time, yet subtly betrays *Under Capricorn*, *I Confess* and *The Wrong Man*. When Chabrol and Rohmer indicate their preference for the Maxwell-

B.I.P. period rather than the Montagu/Balcon period, they are, in effect, preferring Hitchcock the dramatist to Hitchcock the concocter of picaresque comedy-thrills. Whatever one's reserves, the preference points towards a central crux of Hitchcock's work; a certain dryness, an apparent need for a framework other than the natural movement of the human heart, a framework provided by literary material, or by the thriller framework, with its concealments, subterfuges and enigmas. As a dramatist, Hitchcock is a vignettist. Yet his cameos may derive strength and breadth from a variety of factors – the local colour of *Blackmail*, the discreetly reinforced expressionism of *Murder*, the sudden flare-ups of his religious absurdity, certain concatenations of circumstances, notably the growing socio-psychological realism of American films through the '60s. Perhaps Hitchcock's best will endure as among those minor but favourite classics about which critics can never agree if their best effects are due to a mixture of contrivance and luck, or to the wind blowing where it listeth…

SOURCE: *FILMS AND FILMING*, NOVEMBER 1970, 35–7

1.4 MICHAEL POWELL

For some time now Michael Powell has been fashionably dismissed by critics as a "technician's director", a virtuoso of the special effect, with a joltingly uneven story-sense, for whom, indeed, a narrative was only an invisible thread permitting the startling juxtaposition of visual beads. To observers of the simplistic distinction between "style" and "content", he seemed a stylist and a rhetorician, camouflaging an absence of idea by a weakness for the grandiose, out-of-context effect.

There is indeed a sense in which he can be described as Britain's answer to Abel Gance (and it won't be very long before he, too, has his N.F.T. season). Both directors have a weakness for patriotic sentiment (Powell's more veiled than Gance's), both have a weakness for optical shocks. (Gance's "the camera becomes a snowball" could be paraphrased by "the camera becomes an eyeball", when the pink-and-mauve eyelid-lining closes over the screen in *A Matter of Life and Death*). And both seek to ornament *melodrama* by visual style rather than by re-thinking the *drama*.

The myth of Powell as a "mindless eye" was challenged when Raymond Durgnat established what he labelled the "High Tory" moral of *A Matter of Life and Death*. The film then ceases to be an assemblage of technical effects and of metaphysical tags: whatever its weaknesses (which themselves indicate the spirit of its time and class) it has a consistent theme and "body", and its various episodes and ingredients appear as spokes radiating from a central hub. An inability to think in terms of "content" must be attributed, not to Powell, but to his critics, who didn't see that the film was as political as *The Life and Death of Colonel Blimp*. It's ironic that the fiercest attack on the film (as decadent, sadistic, Fascist, and what-have-you) came, not from left-wing critics, who didn't even see that it was an anti-Socialist film, but from E. W. and M. M. Robson whose ideological position was very near Powell's own.

But though "High Tory" morals and atmospheres are clearly discernible in other Powell films such as *I Know Where I'm Going*, and *The Queen's Guards*, our concern here is not with any similarities between Michael and Enoch. Indeed, the heroine of *I Know Where I'm Going* renounces the materialistic marriage offered her by the tycoon, to embrace values more traditional, more rural, more spiritual, and more mysterious. The director's 'typical hero' is a 'country gentleman'; he takes a romantic view of the military life; and, as Richard Winnington remarked at the time of its release, a basic idea of *A Canterbury Tale* was "to endow an accidental wartime excursion to Canterbury with the hushed, bated magic of the Pilgrim's Way, to link in mystic suggestion the past and the present ...."

"In mystic suggestion ...." It would be a pity if the political interpretation, however correct, of Powell's films obscured another source of his inspiration, a source whose mixture of strengths and weaknesses is the subject of this article – an article making no claim to be the exhaustive survey which his work deserves.

For, if Michael Powell is an "eccentric technician", it is in the sense of that proverbially English phenomenon, an eccentric Colonel. When stiff-upper-lip Colonels retire from such matter-of-fact activities as strategy and gunnery, they proverbially embrace strange, soggy systems of mystical belief. This type of hard-edged soft-centred mysticism is not exclusively English and commoner than one might think: Doris Lessing described her father's in "In Pursuit of the English"; the Amberson family patriarch is another specimen; and so is General de Gaulle. Similarly, when the brilliant technician Powell leaves off, there begins a man who dabbles in mysticisms and romantic emotions of every kind: not only the "Kiplingism" of his English officers and countryside, but in his fables for the Celtic fringe (*The Edge of the World*, *I Know Where I'm Going*, *Gone to Earth*), in pagan spiritual forces repelling Christian nuns from Himalayan peaks in *Black Narcissus*, in the fate-time warp of *A Matter of Life and Death*, in the hothouse world of opera-ballet (*The Red Shoes*, *Tales of Hoffmann*, *Oh, Rosalinda!*, *Honeymoon*), in the hallucinated soul (*The Small Back Room*, *Peeping Tom*).

Indeed, his adaptation of Nigel Balchin's novel illustrates his penchant for opening up the romantic veins of his "sober" subjects, by blossoming into an (ill-advised) expressionist sequence as David Farrar, in grip of the D.T.s, sees himself trying to scramble the sheer smooth sides of a Kong-sized whisky bottle. The most powerful passage in *The Battle of the River Plate* is the camera's chilling inspection of the battleship's grey, silent mass, a vast, complex killing-city, a technological Moby Dick, conspicuously invested with a Satanic nobility. And its naval battles catch, visually, the gaudy fervours of the battle paintings in regimental messes. Powell's interest in technological devices enables him to transpose into contemporary terms this underlying romanticism. The veteran officer of *The Queen's Guards* hauls his crippled frame about the room on a complex rig-cum-cradle. Peeping Tom's movie-camera has two very optional extras: the front leg of the tripod conceals a blade with which he bayonets sufficiently beautiful subjects, and, as he photographs their dying agonies, a distorting mirror replacing the reflector enables them to share the show, and re-infect them with their own fear, squared. *Cinéma-vérité* cuts to the quick .... Here Powell's sense of apparatus attains a convulsive poetry.

Somehow, Powell seems born into the wrong period. Had he, and the cinema, and Technicolor, been born during any of the periods celebrated in Mario Praz's "The Romantic Agony", he might have been working with the cultural grain instead of against it. Admittedly his "romantic-expressionist" films chime in with a post-war English nostalgia for period exoticism. The multi-millionaire (Eric Portman) of Terence Young's *Corridor of Mirrors* openly felt he was born in the wrong century and built Renaissance Venice in his grounds to prove it. Thorold Dickinson's *The Queen of Spades*, Michael Relph and Basil Dearden's *Saraband for Dead Lovers*, Lean's Dickenses, Korda's *An Ideal Husband* and Olivier's Shakespeare, all register this middlebrow escapism from '40s austerity. But

Powell's craving is more audacious, more interesting, more constant, more uncertain, as he turns this way and that, restlessly seeking out different genres, styles, symbols.*

Its (Tory) political overtones apart, I Know Where I'm Going asserts the antagonism of the orderly, money-based world of the heroine (Wendy Hiller) to the irrational but wise worldliness of Celtic myth. Paganism overwhelms Christianity – the heroine tries to say her usual prayers, but the real occult force is making a wish while counting the roofbeams of the eerie cottage. The bluestocking heroine's Shavian brashness about money is queered by wayward Celtic winds-and-waves. She is worked upon by a group of Celtic females (Pamela Brown, Sybil Thorndike) whose "wisdom" is disturbing rather than reassuring. They have the glances of eagles – indeed, the hero (Roger Livesey) has an eagle's nose and an elderly "Major" is training a golden eagle which bears the young man's name. Altogether the film neatly, nicely dovetails the "magic" world with that of ration books and faulty telephone-cabins, maintaining a nice ambiguity – the curious British blend of knowledge that the romantic-occult isn't true, with a wish to believe that somehow it might be. Only at one point is the Celtic myth debased to the domesticated whimsy of middle-class romanticism. The young laird finally braves a family curse forbidding him from entering his ancestors' keep – and finds the curse was actually a challenge, ambiguously concealing from all but the first to defy it a liberation from its reputation. A legend about lovers chained together to drown "parallels" a modern story about lovers being "chained" together in marriage. Maybe Powell intends to stress that country gentry Toryism mustn't be too traditional, must continue tradition by defying it, and be more like brain surgeons than Blimps: all three characters, incidentally, are played by Roger Livesey. One might suspect that Powell is merely exploiting the myths to provide a little "local colour". But, if he disbelieves the specific myths, his fondness for myth reveals a serious belief in the wayward natural forces which myths maintain against our too-tidy reason. He has never quite managed to bring their full power into his films. There are constantly hints, jabs of it: a close-up of the eagle tearing a rabbit's ear off; nature, for Powell, is not just an inspirational calendar, but also a Nietzschean whirl of blood and death. The heroine bribes a foolish young boatman to defy the storm; but the hero sails the boat through the treacherous whirlpool, overcoming those forces with a protective manliness, which, like those of the Hebridean islanders who dwell on The Edge of the World, is itself a force of wild nature. Even the defensive comic relief about Tory-Celtic "eccentricity" has a sharpness of its own – as the women kiss their kin on the mouth, as the peppery old eagle-tamer dodders about with a featherduster and a hairnet, looking mildly like Oliver Hardy in drag, and calling the hero "potty" for considering marriage.

Less dated than Brief Encounter, I Know Where I'm Going isn't dissimilar in theme and tone. Its story enables Powell to integrate his somewhat centrifugal qualities in a way which doesn't recur until Peeping Tom.

In each film of Powell's, this romantic urge sports a different livery – co-existing with the everyday and with an only mildly pusillanimous humour (the Heavenly Messenger is always heralded by the smell of fried onions). Its recurrent forms are political Toryism

* Emeric Pressburger, a Hungarian scriptwriter, shared joint producer-writer-director credit with Michael Powell on all his films from "The Life and Death of Colonel Blimp" until "Ill Met By Moonlight". Their relative share and influence is impossible to determine, since Powell's solo efforts before and after are not markedly different from the tandems. Possibly Pressburger abetted Powell's interest in less obviously commercial subjects. His solo efforts since the break-up were "Twice Upon A Time" (1953), a pedestrian "moppet-saves-marriage" story, and "Miracle in Soho" (1957), a sickening local-colour piece, directed by Julian Amyes.

Powell and Pressburger also produced a film, directed by Derek Twist, "The End of the River" (1947), in which Sabu, a native who has come up the Amazon to discover civilisation, beats a homicide rap by pleading "fate".

("Country Gentry Freedom Works"), professional soldiering (especially our gallant Prussian foes*), and ballet-opera – suggesting that it is these forms that seem to Powell to survive the hardheaded tests which he does in fact apply. His central problem as an artist has been his tendency to fall between the two stools of romanticism and realism, to "escape from" (or schematise) the latter, yet only "play with" the former. The two aspects of his vision remain flawed and, as it were, unconvinced – leading to a third besetting vice, a summary way with human emotion. Romantic in potentiality is his daring way with technical effects – a huge Technicolor close-up of an eyelid closing, seen from within, or the camera panning to and fro with a ping-pong ball until Time stops and players and balls stand transfixed. Yet, all too often, the technical fireworks are frittered on merely decorative details: in *The Elusive Pimpernel* abstract patterns appear, but only to give us visual equivalents of a sneeze. And yet Powell never deigns to give such patterns a deeper pretext and add "abstract expressionism" to his repertoire of artistic effects.

His weaknesses are displayed in his four ventures into opera-ballet. *The Red Shoes* revived the Rouben Mamoulian tradition. Banal in its view of ballet-life, schematic in its romantic view of art as that blend of the sublime and the diabolical which Bergman propounded with vastly greater sophistication and force in *Summer Interlude* and *The Face*, *The Red Shoes* has suffered the fate usually endured by works of art which, otherwise uninspired, show a new stylistic flexibility (in colour palette); instantly overpraised, they appear infuriatingly pretentious for years afterward before finding their own level – an honourable one. It survives for some lyrically coloured scenes and for a climactic ballet which, despite some ugh touches perpetrated by Powell's notoriously erratic taste, blends, by and large, an effective simplicity à la Kelly–Donen with an expressionism which was Powell's and Heckroth's own – drifting pieces of sad, sickly cellophane suggesting gaiety's futility, some sharp colour discords.

It's to Powell's credit that, seemingly bored with this simplicity, he banked everything on an all-stops-out expressionistic clutter for *Tales of Hoffmann*. This gallimaufry of Gothicisms, this pantechnicon of palettical paroxysms, this meddle-muddle of media, this olla podrida of oddsbodikins, this massive accumulation of mighty midcult Wurlitzerisms, follows Offenbach's operetta faithfully and fills in filmically by ballet, decor and by-play, seeking, moreover, an operatic visual style with a total disdain of plausibility. The artists have turned their back on current "interpretative" fashions and sought to recapture the full-blown romantic surge.

To object to the overloading, to the clutter *per se*, is like objecting to the "thickness" of Keats, of Poe. It cocktails up many of nineteenth century romanticism's idioms: the Greek, the Gothic, Balzacian courtesans, doppelgangers, the devil, sexual oddities (Pamela Brown in drag), and, over and over, art as diabolical. It's not courage this film lacks; it's taste, in the sense of economy of means; it's ugly, in an inexpressive way, ugly even when the theme requires beauty. One need only compare the awkward way in which humans and puppets are symbolically mingled in a quadrille with the similar mixture in the nightclub scene in Marcel L'Herbier's *La Nuit Fantastique*, a film made by an academic who, however, had grown up within a climate infected by Surrealism, by the sombre, toughly Marxist poetry of Prévert–Carné, by Delluc, by Vigo. Powell–Heckroth have as inspirational heritage and trampoline the visual culture of Ye Olde Junke Shoppe.

---

* In "The Spy in Black" (gallant U-Boat Captain Conrad Veidt), "49th Parallel" (the resourceful U-Boat crew), "The Life and Death of Colonel Blimp" (Blimp's Prussian "oppo", Anton Walbrook), "The Battle of the River Plate" and "Ill Met By Moonlight".

Unreservedly successful are those sequences whose embellishments are photographic rather than architectural – Moira Shearer in dragonfly tights, photographed through a smudged green filter; or a split screen showing four elevations of Moira Shearer in white with a black-cloaked porteur who emerges into a black background. Though frequently overblown to the point of gruesomeness, the film is incessantly breathtaking, an effect which survives repeated viewings; perhaps, after all, it's a bad taste classic, and the predominant word there is "classic"; in his autobiography Joseph von Sternberg pays a generous tribute to the haunting quality of its visuals.

The next film in the series, *Oh, Rosalinda!* is a four-power "Fledermaus", a weird and, to my mind, rather wet blend of opéra-bouffe and topical satire, with The Bat topically metamorphosed into a sort of Harry Lime of love. Powell lovingly adds absurdities of his own to the operatic convention – a duet sung over the telephone is interspersed with short snatches of dance. Made relatively cheaply (the sets are painted rather than built) it oddly misuses its high-voltage battery of talents – Michael Redgrave has more dancing to do than Ludmilla Tcherina. As for *Honeymoon*, which floated into only a few cinemas here, despite its inclusion of La Tcherina's stunning "total-theatre"-type-ballet, "Les Amants de Teruel", criticism cannot speak fairly of a film so hacked by its distributors. Since then Powell has abandoned the field of filmed opera-ballet.

Black Narcissus, *The Elusive Pimpernel* and *Gone to Earth* represent Powell's Lyceum streak. The first contrasts the Anglican nuns (Mother Superiored by Deborah Kerr) in their lofty Tibetan convent whose spiritual serenity is rudely disrupted by the Himalayan heights, by local superstitions, by the silent and immoveable "holy man" whose superhuman asceticism shames them, by the cynical Oriental wisdom of the local ruler (Esmond Knight), by the earthy physicality of David Farrar, who rides on a donkey with his hairy, sexy legs dangling, and typifies *l'homme moyen sensuel*, by homesickness, by jewel-in-nosed dancing girl Jean Simmons, symbolising Oriental sensuality, and by Kathleen Byron as the sex-maddened sister who, trying to murder the Mother Superior, only falls to her death in her sinful scarlet dress from the very bell which dared challenge the sullen, deep tone of the Tibetan mountain-horns. Alas not even Jack Cardiff's glittering colour photography of Jean Simmons's tawny-and-green eyes can redeem Rumer Godden's story from its fatal defect (shared by *The Greengage Summer*), a clumsy chopping to-and-fro between a basically "naice" idea of English life, a tourist's idea of the exotic, and screaming-and-strangling melodrama.

Similarly, *The Elusive Pimpernel* is sapped by the naivety of the Baroness Orczy elements, which P and P accept but endeavour to camouflage by their pictorial virtuosity – quite "hand-held" in its effect is a dazzling game of Blind Man's Buff where the aristocratic ladies blindfold George III with a black scarf from under one corner of which he and we can see a whirling circle of sumptuously creamy bosoms. Attempts are made to liven up that stock and static scene where a lady alone at her dressing table receives and reads an important note – here, she finds it on the floor and stretches herself out at full length in order to read it. Powell has certainly escaped the visual stuffiness of Korda's *Lady Hamilton*. But why take Orczyism on its own terms in the period of Burt Lancaster, Kirk Douglas and Robert Mitchum?

As a result of Korda's hook-up with Selznick, P and P find themselves struggling with sultry passion in *Gone to Earth* (or *The Wild Heart* in the U.S.A. and on B.B.C. T.V.), with Jennifer Jones as Shropshire's answer to Pearl Chavez. *Duel in the Sun* is a bad taste masterpiece which is also a good taste masterpiece, for its vulgarity is that of its conviction. Throughout the British film, the American star seems *yearning* for someone to make a passionate film round her, to whirl her into it. From King Vidor's film she remembers, pos-tures, gestures. But Powell, stilted or shy, like so many compatriots of his generation, in the presence of erotic intensity, fears embarrassment and ridicule, cuts away to "local colour" (harpists, landscapes) and *faux-naif* cliché (the bad squire's black boot stamps on the girl's rosy posy). Powell's respect for unfashionable genres is in itself admirable but so often he accepts what is worst rather than what is best in them. A schematic colour sym-bolism proves thin compensation for dramatic hollowness; the red of the huntsman con-trasts with the black of the churchgoing middlegroups, both groups being concerned, in their different ways, to hunt down the fey fox heroine. The result is neither Selznick nor Mary Webb – for romanticism is passion creating its own universe, or it is nothing.

The recent deluge of Technicolor horror might have offered Powell a congenial climate for his lyrical propensities, and it's characteristic of his ever-astonishing mixture of gifts that his near-miss to a masterpiece, *Peeping Tom* is a very different kettle of fishiness. The storyline is excessive enough to carry any amount of dramatic weakness, and still be breath-taking; in a sense, it needs a "cool" style, for the Peeping Tom cameraman (Carl Boehm) is secretive, passionless, lonely. As appropriate to a study in repressions and inhi-bitions, the film is built on symbols and references, which have been admirably schema-tised by Ian Johnson. The eye-mirror-camera motif recalls the brain surgeon with his *camera obscura* in *A Matter of Life and Death* (another "cutting *voyeur*"), and reminds us that P & P's trademark as "The Archers" was a close-up of an arrow smacking into a bulls-*eye*. Little need to dwell on the erectility of the bayonet-tripod, while Mark Lewis's job as a *focus-puller* underlines the *voyeur's* association of seeing with sexual protuberance. The old woman who "sees through" the quiet young man to his real nastiness is blind. (Indeed, she's related to the Celtic women with their "second sight"; for Anna Massey, playing her daughter, looks like Pamela Brown in *I Know Where I'm Going*.) Mark has his tripod, the old woman has her stick. He has his mirrors, she has her wisdom. The Oedipal situation is lovingly elaborated. Mark paraphrases on his "models" the experiments his father, a world-famous psychologist, inflicted on him – experiments on the effect of fear – throwing a lizard (cold-eyed phallic "snake") onto his bed, shining a bright light in his eyes, showing him his own films. Mark has kept his father's films of the experiments; also shots taken by his father of his stepmother, a bosomy young thing whom he married six weeks after Mark's mother's death and who looks like the nude models whom Mark earns pocket-money by photographing (notably Pamela Green, here garnished with a disfigured lip). The film abounds in films-within-films (opening with Mark's new film of a murder, and taking in its stride both the film on which Mark is working at the studio and Mark's father's films of the young Mark). The film's plethora of in-jokes out-Cahiers *Cahiers*. Mark's father is played by Michael Powell; the director of the feature film is played by Esmond Knight, who is blind; the hero is called Mark Lewis, presumably after the scriptwriter, who is Leo Marks; the Esmond Knight character is called Arthur Baden, Baden-*Powell* being the man who looks after little boys and trained their characters. Mark gets involved mainly with red-headed women – most Powell heroines are redheads too – Mark describes himself as a correspondent from *The Observer* and his father tells him to "Look at the sea" – "Look at the see" being what his victims do in the *mirror* which replaces the *reflector*. The black-and-white flashbacks to "clinical" child-torture relate to the coloured present in a way rem-iniscent of Resnais's *Nuit et Brouillard*. This film is built on refusing to allow the audience to hate the torturer, on a cold hysteria of frustrated indignation, stoked up by such a sac-rilegious idea as casting Moira Shearer as a bitch, fit fodder for a sensitive sex murderer.

'You don't get that in *Sight and Sound*': *Peeping Tom* (1960)

In the last split-second, Mark, in a dying hallucination, is reconciled with his long-dead father. Here art reveals, again, its diabolic root, and reconciliation with the diabolic is an underlying *leitmotif* in Powell – in the close association between the gallant Prussian soldier and the Nazi cause, in the cruel paganism of *I Know Where I'm Going*. The hero, there, subdues nature, or rather survives it, because he has nature's intensity. Indeed, Powell has a fondness for leading men with a certain sharp, hard intensity about them – Roger Livesey, Marius Goring, Anton Walbrook, and, in a different modality, David Farrar, just as his women are often half-witches. Yet, ironically, the one film in which he needed to explore emotional intensity in depth – *Peeping Tom* – depends on what is, in effect, the deadpan pleasantness of Carl Boehm, and the dimension therefore lacking is more vividly asserted in *Repulsion*, by the confluence of Catherine Deneuve's nervous tension and Roman Polanski's eye for the eerie. In this game of hide-and-seek between the inhibited and the diabolical, the patriotic and the exotic, the traditional and the technological, the Tory and the pagan, Powell's work finds much of its fascination and its disquiet.

His two most satisfying films are, perhaps, *Peeping Tom* and the child's Arabian Nights fantasy *The Thief of Bagdad* (1940), for which he shares directorial credit with Ludwig Berger (German specialist in trick-and-costume films) and Tim Whelan (an efficient Hollywood craftsman). This too carries many distinctly Powellian notations – almost its first shot is of a painted eye on a boat's prow, surging up into close-up, its story (by Miles Malleson) includes the theft of the all-seeing eye (*Peeping Tom*!) from a Tibetan temple (*Black Narcissus*!); the giant genie from the bottle (beautifully incarnated by Rex Ingram, who played God the Father in *Green Pastures*) prefigures the gigantic bottle in *The Small Back Room*; its tricks with fate-and-time parallel *A Matter of Life and Death*. If it never quite transcends the sphere of children's film to become an adult's fantasy too, it remains one of the classic screen fantasies, worthy of Roy Rowland's *The 5,000 Fingers of Dr. T* and of Joseph Von Baky's *The Incredible Adventures of Baron Munchausen*; its scope and audacity, its morning freshness, reduce Cottafavi's *Hercules Conquers Atlantis* to small

The Essential Raymond Durgnat

beer. It's characteristic of the Powell paradox that his two best films should be an epic for grown-up children and a very queasy study of a tormented childhood.

Whence this contrast, this centrifugality? The comparison with King Vidor is pertinent. Vidor, intellectually, perhaps, less sophisticated, or at least less cautious, than Powell, has retained just that Wagnerian authenticity of emotional excess which gives his films that genuine mysticism, their quality of that strange thing, a Nietzschean pantheism. But Powell lived in a class and a country which suspects, undermines, is embarrassed by, emotion; his diversity of qualities rarely find their holding context. Between himself and Hoffmann he interposes the opera-ballet convention; whereas the (American) Corman–Crosby team, in their horror films, blend Poe, Wilde, Freud and colour expressionism into a coherent universe. It would not be altogether unreasonable to see Powell's indirectness as the Pirandellism of scepticism, to see Powell's ballet films as preludes to an *8½* which he hadn't the egotism to make. One would dearly like to see him tackle those science-fiction subjects which have a built-in excess – C. L. Moore's "Shambleau", Richard Matheson's "I Am Legend", Damon Knight's "The Analogue Men". And he is the only director who could bring to the screen *Fleming's* James Bond.

He remains an upholder, through its lean years, of the Méliès tradition. His films shed not a little light on English thought and the English soul, in its restraints, its pusillanimity, its nostalgia for a German expressionism, its coy amorality. At their least convincing, they hold one's attention and give pleasure by their very unexpectedness, in theme as in decoration, and, in this sense, they relate to certain films of Quine, Godard, Varda, Demy, Cottafavi and others.

SOURCE: *MOVIE*, NO. 14, AUTUMN 1965, 17–20

ANNOTATIONS

STANDING UP FOR JESUS

[p. 13] The **Committee of 100** was an offshoot of the Campaign for Nuclear Disarmament. | **"Galaxy"** *Science Fiction* magazine, publisher of Isaac Asimov, Ray Bradbury, Robert Heinlein, *et al.* | **Humph**rey Lyttelton, responsible for the first British top-twenty jazz hit, 'Bad Penny Blues', in July 1956. | **Bootsie and Snudge**, a television sitcom set in a gentleman's club. | [p. 14] The **reigning house at Dean St**, i.e. the Soho headquarters of the BFI. | Dyer's **notorious article** was 'London Festival', *Sight and Sound*, Winter 1960–1. | Ian Cameron had in fact already demonstrated Dyer's plagiarism **in the pages of "Film"** for September–October 1960; Ian Jarvie followed up in the March–April 1961 issue. | Delmer Daves's **"Broken Arrow"** (1950) was noted for its sympathetic portrayal of American Indians. | The Sir George Monoux was indeed **V-2'd**, though without serious casualties. | [p. 15] **"Definition"**, founded in 1960, was a short-lived little magazine associated with the New Left. | The **Joint Council for Education Through Art** conference 'Artist, Critic and Teacher', staged at the National Film Theatre, was covered by Paddy Whannel in the Summer 1958 *Universities and Left Review*. | Anderson's **"Every Day Except Christmas"**, which debuted in the third Free Cinema programme in May 1957, was sponsored by **Fords of Dagenham**. | Anderson's **Aldermaston film** *March to Aldermaston* (1959), was collectively made and credited to the Film and Television Committee for Nuclear Disarmament. | Alain Tanner and Claude Goretta's **"Nice**

Time" (1957) had appeared in the same programme as *Every Day Except Christmas*. | **Lord Hailsham** was a Conservative politician prominent in the party's crises during 1963, including the Profumo affair. | **"We Are the Dear Little Lambeth Boys"**, i.e., Karel Reisz's *We Are the Lambeth Boys*, included in the final Free Cinema programme in March 1959, and reviewed by Richard Hoggart in the Summer 1959 *Sight and Sound*. | The **Fishmonger's Arms** was a trad jazz venue in Wood Green, not far from Durgnat's family home. | [p. 16] Anderson's **interpretation of "On the Waterfront"**, which explains the earlier reference to **Father Karl Malden**, appeared in the January–March 1955 *Sight and Sound*. | **"Earth"** (1930), Dovzhenko's poetic tribute to collectivisation, a film society standard. | Durgnat reviewed Kazan's **"Wild River"** on release in the August 1960 *Films and Filming*. | Anderson addressed **The Youth of Today** in the Summer 1957 *Sight and Sound*. | In his 1957 essay 'Get Out and Push!' Anderson had used **Nannie**, or 'Nanny', to characterise smothering, censorious British establishment culture. | [p. 17] **Stuart Hall** discussed *Look Back in Anger* in the first issue of *Definition*, dated February 1960, under the title 'Jimmy Porter and the Two-and-Nines'. | [p. 18] Durgnat has in mind the **gynaecological moralising** of John **Schlesinger**'s *A Kind of Loving* (1962) and **Reisz**'s *Saturday Night and Sunday Morning* (1960). **Alan Bates** starred in the former. | The infamous **Beeching** report, which led to the destruction of much of Britain's railway network, was published in March 1963. | **Al Capp**, the cartoonist behind *Li'l Abner*, a favourite of Durgnat's. | Osborne's **"Under Plain Cover"** debuted together with *The Blood of the Bambergs* in a programme titled 'Plays for England' at the Royal Court in July 1962. | **Heather Sears** in *Room at the Top* (1958); **Shirley Anne Field** in *Saturday Night and Sunday Morning*. | **Peggy Mount** played a domineering mother-in-law in *Sailor Beware* (1956). | With his comparison of Ford with Fuller's **"Run of the Arrow"**, Durgnat begins his response to Penelope Houston's 'The Critical Question', from which he takes the expression **"cultural gauleiters"**. | [p. 19] **Fereydoun Hoveyda's criticism of "Party Girl"** appeared in *Cahiers du Cinéma*; Richard Roud criticised Hoveyda in turn in 'The French Line'. Both his and Houston's articles appeared in the Autumn 1960 *Sight and Sound*. | Penelope Houston used the Henry Jamesian 'The Figure in the Carpet' as title for her article on Hitchcock in the Autumn 1963 *Sight and Sound*, hence, possibly, **"patterns in the carpet"**. | Roud's **"Novel Novel Fable Fable"** was in the Spring 1962 issue. | [p. 20] **Michel Mourlet**, leader of the MacMahonist tendency – the MacMahon being a Parisian cinema that often showed films by **Lang, Losey**, *et al.* – and editor of its house journal *Présence du Cinéma*. Mourlet's homage to Charlton Heston, as quoted by Roud, appeared in *Cahiers*. | [p. 21] According to his *Motion* special on the *Nouvelle Vague*, Durgnat's **all-time favourite star** had been Clara Bow (or Jerry Lewis) quite recently. | The **heavyweight intellectual quotes** are from Eric Rhode's 'Why Neo-Realism Failed', in the Winter 1960 *Sight and Sound*. | **Bergman and oxymoron** were discussed by Eleanor McCann in 'The Rhetoric of *Wild Strawberries*', in the same issue. | **"Art is a Cold Sphere"** is really Rhode, citing Mann. | The undergraduate Durgnat had written a damning piece about the 'pipsqueak prophet' **Colin Wilson**, author of the Angry Young Man bestseller *The Outsider*, in the 1 December 1956 issue of the Cambridge newspaper *Varsity*. | [p. 22] **Rhode's solo effort on eroticism**, 'Sensuality in the Cinema', in the Spring 1961 *Sight and Sound*. | [p. 23] Tom Milne's **"How Art Is True?"** was in the Autumn 1962 number. | **Arkadin** was *Sight and Sound*'s anonymous gossip columnist; the **criticising other critics** line is from the Autumn 1962 instalment; **seriously seriously** is from Summer 1962. | [p. 24] **The cover of the Spring '63** issue, which had a new design, included a still from Jacques Demy's *La Baie des Anges* (1963). | **Geoffrey Nowell-Smith** had written for *Oxford Opinion*.

WHO REALLY MAKES THE MOVIES?

[p. 25] **Andrew Sarris** discussed **50 or 60 Hollywood directors** in the Spring 1963 'American Directors' issue of *Film Culture*, the basis for his 1968 book *The American Cinema*. | **Jean George Auriol** founded *Du Cinéma* in 1928; it became *La Revue du Cinéma* in 1929 and folded three years later. In 1946 Auriol began another magazine with the same name; it too folded after three years. Two of its contributors, André Bazin and Jacques Doniol-Valcroze, went on to found *Cahiers du Cinéma*. | [p. 27] **As Renoir remarked** in the *Guardian*, 9 November 1961.

CAT AND MOUSE GAMES

[p. 31] Truffaut's **big Secker and Warburg tome** *Hitchcock* was published in Britain in 1968. | [p. 32] **Robin Wood's Hitchcock book** *Hitchcock's Films* was published in 1965. | Michael **Balcon** was Hitchcock's first producer, at Gainsborough, in the mid-1920s. | John **Maxwell** was studio chief at British International Pictures, where Hitchcock made *Blackmail* (1929). | Ivor **Montagu** worked with Hitchcock at Gainsborough, notably on *The Lodger* (1926), and then in the mid-1930s at Gaumont-British, where Balcon was head of production. | [p. 33] Ernest **Lindgren**, curator of the BFI's National Film Library from its foundation in 1935 almost until his death in 1973, was an influential exponent of Soviet montage theory. | Hitchcock's **food-to-waste subject**, which he first discussed making as early as 1928, would have covered a day in the life of a city. | **Chabrol and Rohmer**'s *Hitchcock* was published in 1957.

MICHAEL POWELL

[p. 34] Abel Gance's **N.F.T. season** took place in July–August 1965; Powell's first came in December 1970–January 1971. | **E. W. and M. M. Robson** attacked Powell in their pamphlet *The Shame and Disgrace of Colonel Blimp*, published in 1944. | As of 1965, **Enoch** Powell was known for his maverick free-market views, but had yet to make the 'rivers of blood' speech that would define him in the popular imagination. As this paragraph suggests, he was a Tory at once High and, in his materialism, Low. | [p. 35] Durgnat, quoting Alex Comfort, described **Mario Praz's "The Romantic Agony"**, first published in 1930, as a catalogue 'of the morbid pre-occupations of the Romantics – sadism, diabolism, the character of woman as Medusa and bitch, the exaltation of suffering and corruption' ('Cupid v. the Legions of Decency', *Films and Filming*, December 1961, p. 17). It was a major source for his writings on Hitchcock. | [p. 36] In March 1964, just as his 'Vote for Britain!' series began to appear, Durgnat saw *Brief Encounter* (1945) laughed off the screen at the Baker Street Classic. In *A Mirror for England* (London: Faber and Faber, 1970), he explained the change in audience sensibility thus: 'Jimmy Porter came along' (p. 180). | [p. 38] The **Lyceum** gave its name to a kind of full-blooded Victorian melodrama, still being staged at the theatre on the eve of the Second World War. | **Pearl Chavez** is the name of Jennifer Jones's character in *Duel in the Sun*. | [p. 41] Durgnat hymned the Roger **Corman**–Floyd **Crosby team** in similar terms in the concluding paragraphs of the *Films and Filming* version of his thesis. They more than once collaborated with **Richard Matheson**. | For Durgnat, **Pirandellism** meant self-reflexivity, detachment and alienation, as opposed to emotional participation and identification. | He disapproved of the Pirandellism of Richard **Quine**'s *Paris When it Sizzles* (1964), but was warmer towards *Strangers When We Meet* (1960) and *How to Murder Your Wife* (1965).

Notes

1. V. F. Perkins, "'Fifty Famous Films 1915–45'", *Oxford Opinion*, no. 38, 30 April 1960, pp. 36–7.
2. Penelope Houston, 'The Critical Question', *Sight and Sound*, Autumn 1960, p. 163.
3. Richard Roud, 'The French Line', *Sight and Sound*, Autumn 1960, p. 171.
4. Ian Cameron, 'All Together Now', *Film*, September–October 1960, p. 13.
5. John Osborne, 'Schoolmen of the Left', *Observer*, 30 October 1960, p. 17.
6. Andrew Sarris, 'Movie Journal', *Village Voice*, 11 August 1960, p. 8.
7. Justin Bengry, '*Films and Filming*: The Making of a Queer Marketplace in Pre-Decriminalization Britain', in Brian Lewis (ed.), *British Queer History: New Approaches and Perspectives* (Manchester: Manchester University Press, 2013), p. 244.
8. Durgnat, 'A Look at Old and New Waves', *Films and Filming*, July 1960, p. 28.
9. Durgnat, 'The Rebel With Kid Gloves', *Films and Filming*, October 1960, p. 11; p. 38.
10. François Truffaut, 'A Certain Tendency in French Cinema', in Peter Graham (ed.), *The French New Wave: Critical Landmarks* (London: BFI/Palgrave Macmillan, 2009), p. 44. Originally published as 'Une Certaine Tendance du Cinéma Français' in the January 1954 *Cahiers du Cinéma*.
11. Durgnat, 'On the Crest of the "Wave"', *Films and Filming*, October 1960, p. 40.
12. Durgnat, rev. *Shoot the Pianist*, in *Films and Filming*, February 1961, pp. 29–30.
13. Email to editor, 31 January 2013.
14. Durgnat, 'An Art Form', *Motion*, no. 3, Spring 1962, p. 3.
15. Durgnat and Peter Armitage, 'Ten Years That Shook An Art', *Film*, Summer 1964, p. 33.
16. Durgnat, 'Ways of Melodrama', *Sight and Sound*, August–September 1951, p. 34.
17. Durgnat, 'The Dark Gods', *Films and Filming*, October 1961, p. 16.
18. Jeffrey Richards, *Thorold Dickinson: The Man and His Films* (London: Croon Helm, 1986), p. 179.
19. Email to editor, 31 January 2013.
20. Email to editor, 24 October 2013.
21. Durgnat, entry on *Gervaise*, in Frank N. Magill (ed.), *Magill's Survey of Cinema: Foreign Language Films* (Englewood Cliffs: Salem Press, 1985), p. 1222.
22. Durgnat, 'Culture Always is a Fog', *Rouge*, no. 8, 2006, n.p.
23. Email to editor, 31 January 2013.
24. BFI Special Collections: Thorold Dickinson, Box 47, Folder 2: Letter from Thorold Dickinson to Raymond Durgnat, 5 February 1977.
25. Slade Film Department Archive, Box 7: Letter from *Times Educational Supplement* to Thorold Dickinson, 5 February 1965.
26. Durgnat, 'This Damned Eternal Triangle', *Films and Filming*, December 1964, p. 14.
27. Lawrence Alloway, 'Lawrence Alloway on the Iconography of the Movies', *Movie*, no. 7, March 1963, p. 4.
28. Ibid.
29. Ibid., p. 5.
30. Durgnat, 'On the Crest of the "Wave"', p. 40.
31. *Motion*, no. 6, Autumn 1963, p. 62.
32. Durgnat, 'Vote for Britain!' (1), *Films and Filming*, April 1964, p. 9.
33. Ibid., p. 10.
34. Perkins, "'Fifty Famous Films'", p. 37.

35. 'The British Cinema', *Movie*, no. 1, June 1962, p. 3. Credited to 'V. F. Perkins on behalf of the editorial board', but with significant input from Robin Wood.
36. Quoted in Leila Wimmer, *Cross-Channel Perspectives: The French Reception of British Cinema* (Oxford: Peter Lang, 2009), p. 282.
37. *News Chronicle*, 26 July 1948, p. 2.
38. Durgnat, *Franju* (London: Studio Vista, 1967), p. 9.
39. Durgnat, 'Brain Drains: Drifters, Avant-Gardes & Kitchen Sinks', on p. 122 of this volume.
40. Siegfried Kracauer, *Theory of Film: The Redemption of Physical Reality* (New York: Oxford University Press, 1960), p. ix.
41. Ibid., p. 32.
42. Ibid., p. 155. Kracauer revered and had written a book about Offenbach, the composer of both *The Tales of Hoffmann* (1881) and *Le Voyage dans la Lune* (1875), the '*opéra-féerie*' on whose imagery Méliès had drawn for his 1902 fiilm of the same name.
43. André Bazin, 'The Evolution of Film Language', in Peter Graham (ed.), *The New Wave* (London: Secker and Warburg in association with the British Film Institute, 1968), p. 38. Originally published as 'L'Évolution du Langage Cinématographique' in the first volume of Bazin's *Qu'est-ce que le Cinéma?* in 1958.
44. Durgnat, 'Truth is Stranger than Fiction', *Films and Filming*, January 1965, p. 44.
45. See Appendix II.
46. Durgnat, 'Vote for Britain!' (1), p. 12.
47. Durgnat, 'The Powell and Pressburger Mystery', *Cineaste*, December 1997, p. 17.
48. Durgnat, 'Vote for Britain!' (1), p. 13.
49. Durgnat, 'Doctor No', *Motion*, no. 4, February 1963, p. 16. Durgnat seems not to have known that Powell had directed three episodes of the television series *Espionage* (1963–4), one of them written by *Peeping Tom* screenwriter Leo Marks, a former cryptographer who had, like Ian Fleming, worked in intelligence during World War II. Powell went on to produce Marks's partly autobiographical *Sebastian* (1967).
50. Durgnat, 'Expressing Life in Celluloid', *Films and Filming*, May 1965, p. 45.

PART 2
JET-PROPELLED PHOTOGRAPHS

INTRODUCTION

Word of the New York underground reached *Films and Filming* in early 1964. The March issue's editorial column contained an account of the legal difficulties encountered by Jack Smith's *Flaming Creatures* (1963) which Durgnat had received from his university friend Harry Fainlight. 'Perhaps the film's most important achievement', wrote Fainlight from the Lower East Side, 'is in the converting of the materials of pornography (however partially) into art. [...] After the Action Painters and the Beats, the film underground will provide the next big wave.'[1] The column went on to give the address of Smith's distributor, the New York Film-Makers' Co-operative, and to relay news from Kenneth Anger of his new film *Scorpio Rising* (1963), 'a fantasy about the young men in leather who ride fast motor-cycles'.[2]

Both films were shown at the ICA in June 1964, during a season organised by the NYFMC, but it was not until the following year that underground movies found a regular home in London. Early in 1965 the suburban schoolteacher, sound poet and small-press publisher Bob Cobbing joined the staff of Better Books on Charing Cross Road, bringing with him his circle of artists and writers, and also his avant-garde film society Cinema 61, renamed Cinema 65. Durgnat, who had recently started lecturing at St Martin's School of Art, directly opposite Better Books, signed up. 'The first programme that really registered with me was [...] *Scorpio Rising*', he recalled; 'it really got under the American umbrella pretty quickly, and one of the things we were always trying to do was to see if there was anything specifically English by way of avant-garde'.[3]

Durgnat soon helped bring to attention one director as just that: Jeff Keen, whose films had bewildered audiences on the amateur circuit but found a much more receptive scene at Better Books. 'I think it's all to do with the exasperations of being young, gifted and British, and having nothing better to do in that stagnant land than gnaw one's friends to death', Durgnat told an American audience in 1977, describing Keen's early films as 'brisk pick-ups on pop art themes' and 'the best and fastest footnotes to *Look Back in Anger*' – in other words, right under Durgnat's personal umbrella.[4]

On 19 May 1965 Allen Ginsberg, whose poem 'The Change' Cobbing had earlier published as a pamphlet, gave a reading at Better Books to an audience that mixed the local little magazine crowd with the entourages of Ginsberg and Andy Warhol. Lawrence Ferlinghetti and Gregory Corso were also in Europe; Bob Dylan had played the Albert Hall ten days earlier – Ginsberg had appeared in the famous 'Subterranean Homesick Blues' film clip – and thus Ginsberg's companion Barbara Rubin booked the same venue for 11 June to host what was finally named the International Poetry Incarnation. Ginsberg encouraged the British poets, above all his friend Fainlight, to take part; and in parallel the task of filming the event, which had originally been assigned to Rubin, an NYFMC insider, fell instead to a recent Slade graduate, Peter Whitehead.

The result, *Wholly Communion*, opened at the Academy Cinema on Oxford Street in May 1966, billed with *Fists in the Pocket*, the debut feature of another Slade film-maker, Marco Bellocchio. The success of the original reading was such that, according to Cobbing's associate Jeff Nuttall, 'the Underground was suddenly there on the surface, in open ground with a following of thousands', and its instigators and attendees felt encouraged to go further.[5] In late 1965 Durgnat's poem 'A Voice from Limbo' was included alongside contributions from Ginsberg and Ferlinghetti in *Long Hair*, one of a handful of publications to come out of the Incarnation, edited by sometime Better Books manager Barry Miles and John 'Hoppy' Hopkins. A short time later Durgnat and Miles became involved in an attempt to open a branch of the New York Film-Makers' Co-op in London.

In the spring of 1966, NYFMC founder Jonas Mekas wrote an open letter to 'World Film-Makers' announcing that Rubin would soon travel to London 'to organize a huge Benefit show (at the Albert Hall) for the London Center', which would act as a European distribution hub and 'permanent showcase to our work (as well as the budding British & Continental undergrounds)'.[6] From the very start, however, relations among the British, among the Americans, and between the two groups, were sketchy. Neither the Albert Hall show nor Rubin materialised; in her place came Harvey Matusow, a divisive character on both sides of the Atlantic. The London Film-Makers' Co-operative would never have close ties with its nominal parent body, functioning instead as a more ambitious version of Cinema 65. As well as Durgnat, Cobbing, Keen and Whitehead were all involved in its confused gestation.

The LFMC's launch coincided with that of *IT*, Britain's first underground paper, in October 1966. The occasion was marked by a week-long 'Spontaneous Festival of Underground Movies' at the Jeanetta Cochrane Theatre, then controlled by *IT* co-founder Jim Haynes. The programme included Antony Balch and William Burroughs's *Towers Open Fire* (1963); films by Anger, Hilary Harris, Willard Maas, Marie Menken and Stan Brakhage; and a selection of shorts from the Slade–Better Books axis. As well as Whitehead there was Don Levy; as well as Keen there was John Latham, a veteran of various Better Books happenings and, like Durgnat, a lecturer (at least notionally) at St Martin's. Also in the programme was a new name, Stephen Dwoskin, a New Yorker who had been part of the conjoined Co-op and Factory scenes before moving to London.

Cobbing had long planned to publish a film magazine, for which Durgnat had suggested dozens upon dozens of possible titles, none of which Cobbing used. The first issue of *Cinim* appeared at about the time of the Jeanetta Cochrane season, and included some of Durgnat's 'Asides on Godard'. These had been written in the spring of 1966, when there were three new Godard films playing in London's art cinemas: *Une Femme Mariée* (1964) at the Berkeley; *Alphaville* (1965) at the Academy, billed with Chris Marker's *La Jetée* (1962); and *Pierrot le Fou* (1965) at the Cameo-Poly. 'I must say I'd be delighted if you saw fit to use them all (in any order or interwoven with anything),' Durgnat had told Cobbing, 'but do of course cut if you prefer.'[7] The full or fuller set appeared in a 1967 *Movie* collection edited by Ian Cameron.

At the start of 1967 a reluctant Durgnat was recruited to replace Matusow as LFMC chairman. The main difference between the Co-op and Cinema 65 was the institution of open screenings at Better Books, the value of which Durgnat, at least in retrospect, rather doubted. 'The ratio of shit to tolerability was about nine to one,' he recalled, 'because it was a great era of euphoric narcissism.'[8] There were however moments of co-operation under his chairmanship, as when Cobbing and fellow sound poet Annea Lockwood collaborated on the soundtrack for Keen's *Marvo Movie* (1967). There were also moments of exhilaration. 'Magic was created', Durgnat recalled of the underground nightclub UFO, where LFMC films were shown, 'when *Scorpio Rising*, with its shots of leathered motor-cyclists tinkering with their machines, was projected on to the Soft Machine pop group, live, with their guitars and feedback sounds.'[9]

Durgnat's appreciation of Dwoskin appeared in the second *Cinim*, which Dwoskin himself designed, in the summer of 1967. By then Cobbing's tenure at Better Books was under threat from new, more puritanical management. Almost the last programme there, on 4 August, included the underground film which had inspired Dwoskin in New York, and drawn Durgnat's attention in London: *Flaming Creatures*. Over the months that followed the Co-op, after moving to Haynes's newly opened Arts Lab, was gradually taken over by a younger set of film-makers who prevailed, according to Durgnat, 'because they were more dedicated, and had more time, and were more narrow-minded'.[10] At the end of September, having overseen the writing of the LFMC's first catalogue, Durgnat mounted at the ICA what was effectively his last stand, advertised as follows:

The London Film-Makers' Co-operative will present 'An Underground Trip', an evening of underground movies on tuesday, september 26.

'A movie is underground if –
– it has been produced on a shoestring basis, and for love, not for money;
– it has happily resigned itself to being banished from cinemas, TV, and all mass media; and if
– it has that indefinable aura of knowing itself to be in spiritual, social, artistic and/or technical bad taste.

In the affluent USA home movies are commoner than diaries. The era of cinema as technology is closing, that of movie diaries, poems, graffiti, is at hand. In less affluent Britain the mental breakthroughs needed are slower to come. The LFMC hopes to be midwife.'[11]

Two of the Slade film-makers Durgnat had championed in the LFMC debuted their first features shortly afterwards: Levy with *Herostratus*, which included footage from *Wholly Communion*, and that film's director with *Tonite Let's All Make Love in London*. (The title came from a poem Ginsberg wrote for Fainlight a few days before he read it at the Albert Hall.) As he began shooting in mid-1966, Whitehead described it as an attempt to chart the 'revolution in England' that had taken place over the preceding decade.[12] He planned to 'go back to John Osborne with *Look Back in Anger* when it all started – and trace through the theatre, cinema, books and pop painting and POP, the gradual growth towards a Mass Media motivated conscious culture'.[13] The film's first movement, 'Loss of the British Empire', cuts between Trooping the Colour – shot, unlike *The Queen's Guards*, without permission – and a hippy in *Sergeant Pepper*-style uniform.

Durgnat was a regular contributor to *IT*, and to the other principal underground paper *Oz*, but usually as a dissenting voice. Britain's never-ending balance-of-payments crisis led in November 1967 to devaluation and in March 1968 to an austerity budget, signalling the end of the post-war boom and prompting Durgnat to wonder whether 'all those flower people will be reduced to beatniks and Bohemians (remember them? all cords and beer)'.[14] At the same time he looked forward with scepticism towards the prospect of the underground going on the rates, writing that Labour arts minister Jennie Lee's visit to the Arts Lab may herald the kiss of death'.[15] His review of Godard's *One Plus One* (1968), filmed in London, contains his reflections on the counter-culture after he had kicked his 'underground habits'.[16]

Durgnat had by then parted ways with the LFMC, which had been 'infected' by the 'aesthetic extremism, etiolation of content, and mystic negligence of intelligent intervention' typical of New York minimalism.[17] Latham, Levy and Whitehead more or less abandoned film-making around the end of the decade, while Keen and Dwoskin had little to do with the new regime. Durgnat emerged convinced of the 'continuum between commercial production and underground production', and that the underground was only the precursor to a much wider diffusion of film-making technology.[18] 'What the guitar is to the '60s,' he wrote at the end of 1967, 'the ciné-camera will be to the '70s.'[19]

2.1 FLYWEIGHT FLICKS

Why take notes when you could take pictures? An 8mm camera is the ballpoint of the visual world. Soon (and the sooner the better) people will use camera-pens as casually as they jot memos today. Film-makers will make "rough-drafts" of their films as rapidly as painters dash off preliminary sketches. And the narrow gauge can take finished works of art.

First of the 8mm poets to operate in Britain is Brighton-based painter Jeff Keen, who may prove to have pioneered a new "Brighton school". At last Britain has its own avant-garde. Keen has been using 8mm since 1961. His films use "pop"-art imagery and the casual spectator may at a first glance see in them all the themes that are fashionable among young painters: "pixilated" American comics are intercut with motor-cyclists, Gagarin-rockets, monsters, jazz sessions, "Pull My Daisy"-type goofing of glossy advertisements, and references to as extensive a range of writers as Mickey Spillane, Antonin Artaud and Piero Heliczer. But these motifs are galvanised by a new kind of movie sense. To take one example from a welter of innovations: The cameraman rides pillion on a motorbike which twists round and round another. The camera-eye follows the rider of the other machine, while tilting and tracking up and down from his head to his gauntlets and boots. The intricate weave of movements and counter-movements has a giddy excitement that recalls action-painting and justifies Keen's own manifesto: "Cinema here needs the kind of jolt the great American exhibition gave to painting about four years ago …" Not that Keen rejects the past: Eisenstein, Cocteau, Buñuel and Kirsanoff are among his points of reference.

I've written unkind things about avant-garde preciosity and solemnity in the past. But behind Keen's visual dynamism, his gags and flip good humour, lies a spiritual resilience, a sense of direction, that lifts them altogether clear of the "easy-fashionable" bracket. As Keen puts it: "When words fail – use your teeth!" He cuts, not with scissors, but with a scalpel – a jet-propelled one! The purely visual rhythms even of his *silent* films have the spectator tapping his feet as if to music. Depending as they do on wit and movement rather than on photographic texture, they prove that mini-cinema can pack a good strong middleweight punch.

For me, Keen's *Like The Time Is Now* (10 mins), *Wail* (8 mins), *Instant Cinema* (2 mins) stack up alongside little gems like McLaren's *Boogie-Doodle* and Len Lye's *Colour Box*. Let's hope some enlightened distributor of short films soon makes them available, on 8 or 16mm.

SOURCE: *FILMS AND FILMING*, FEBRUARY 1965, 61

2.2 *WHOLLY COMMUNION*

Ever since the schoolmarm spirit succeeded in misrepresenting the rebellious passions of the romantic poets as inoffensive 'uplift', poets have been caught between, on the one hand, appealing to a public educated enough to appreciate their complexities, but withdrawn in a kind of blind distaste from everyday realities and vulgarities, and, on the other hand, touching the more numerous public which was healthily less snobbish but lacked that cultural background without which most modern, or, for that matter, ancient, poetry is to all intents and purposes so incomprehensible as to be an enigma. The new wave of 'beatnik' poets and their contemporaries, however eccentric and way-out, at least represent a coming-together of the poetry medium and some popular attitudes. It's no accident that through such figures as Donovan, Bob Dylan and Joan Baez, this kind of poetry is beginning to link up with 'pop' music; and some highly profitable cultural collisions and mixings seem imminent.

A first and highly encouraging eruption occurred when a poets' co-operative hired the Royal Albert Hall on June 11 last year, and, against all expectations, all but filled the huge auditorium. Indeed, they would probably have filled it completely had the management not deliberately turned away latecomers, under the pretence, which it must have known to be false, that no seats remained. One suspects that their real objection was to a poet's use of that four-letter word because of the harm which the word would do to their moral characters. But the Establishment's hostility is a backhanded compliment, and the event is for poetry what the success of *Look Back in Anger* was for the modern English theatre.

A great deal of the night's excitement is caught in Peter Whitehead's film (a twin to the paperback of the same name); it is all the more astonishing for being made by a one-, repeat, one-man unit. Some roughnesses of reporting, concentrated mainly in the first half of the film, help to recapture the actual atmosphere of the occasion, which was as improvised as a jam-session; and the film is not just a newsreel so much as a piece of cinéma-vérité, as it penetrates, through the 'event', to feelings and hopes, as in the spirited exchanges between the chairman (Alexander Trocchi), a heckling spectator, and the poet Harry Fainlight, anguishedly persevering in reading his brilliant and nightmarish anti-epic of LSD visions, *The Spider*.

One regrets that one's attention is ruinously distracted from Gregory Corso's reading by the camera's trying to look past, or through, two bobbing heads in the foreground; one develops a certain sporting interest in the pas-de-trois between heads and camera but personally I could have done without this sequence. On the other hand, there is a long, astonishing sequence where Allen Ginsberg's reading is accompanied by the strange, writhing, haunting movements, something between hand-jive and *Swan Lake*, performed by an anonymous, lovely girl in the audience, movements which, more eloquently than any

Harry Fainlight remonstrates with Allen Ginsberg's finger in *Wholly Communion* (1965)

ballet, because of their very naturalness, are terrifying in their quiet revelation of anguish, beautiful in their abstruse, serene generosity, and poignantly eerie in their combination of the two moods. In an atmosphere encouraging of wild effects, the camera is admirably restrained; there are no unnecessary zoom-shots (except one or two where the photographer was having to guess what would happen next), the use of 'frozen-frame' is discriminatingly linked to the poetic text, the moments of black screen are very successful, and the fade-out line both witty and touching.

The revelation of the evening was, perhaps, the extent to which many modern poems which, though likely on the page to seem rhymeless, formless, senseless and pointless, reveal an unexpected power in performance – as when Adrian Mitchell, with all the scathing bitterness of an Alan Sillitoe hero, rips off his *Stunted Sonnet*, or when the Austrian poet Ernst Jandl delivers his 'sound poems' of abstract syllables – a genre which, on paper, looks thin and twee, but which, as here, forcefully and rhythmically declaimed, goaded the audience into roars of excited approval, just like the chantings of Dizzy Gillespie's drummer, Chano Pozo. Some of the poets are poor performers (and often the snippet shown isn't fair to the poem); but if the film is interesting, rather than ideal, for those who want only 'pure poetry', it's an admirable demonstration of 'performed poetry'. Other readers include Michael Horovitz, Lawrence Ferlinghetti and Christopher Logue, while the proceedings are dominated by the amiably bearish, bushy-bearded Ginsberg and the lean, lunar serenity of Alexander Trocchi. Almost every poem, poet and performance spurs reflections, alas, rather beyond the scope of a film review, which must restrict itself to indicating the fascinations of a film which pulverizes previous British essays at filming poetry (notably the B.F.I.'s cretinous *Poet and Painter* series) and records the first big eruption of the too-long-quiescent poetic volcano.

SOURCE: *FILMS AND FILMING*, JUNE 1966, 53–4

2.3 UNDERGROUND FILM FESTIVAL PROGRAMME NOTES

Wholly Communion
The greatest show on earth. Under the big top of London's famed Albert Hall a menagerie of LSD-maddened poets strike fire from iron curtains and stiff upper lips. Ferlinghetti, Fainlight, Horovitz, Adrian Mitchell, Allen Ginsberg, Yevtushenko and all. Filmed and edited by Peter Whitehead, the 1-man movie crew, straight back from his Irish safari with the Rolling Stones (**Charley is My Darling**) on their concert tour. Peter Whitehead's Lorrimer Films also published the book of the film, and the translated script of **Alphaville**.

Books
The film that became a happening. Abstract animation of partially destroyed books, screened on to the human form clothed in books. Truly three-dimensional. John Latham graced the recent DIAS symposium with the burning of his skoob towers. He has a destroyed-book, painted relief in the Tate gallery.

Wail and Like the Time is Now
Jeff Keen makes films on shoestrings and then blows them up to 8mm. They race through the projector at 24 f.p.s. and it feels like 240 f.p.s. His middle name is Speedy Gonzalez. His midget movies are the Mighty Mouse of the film world. His speed of light technique whips comicstrips, news images, doldrums and exhaust pipes into a St. Vitus's dance of death. But don't turn to your neighbour as the credits come up or you'll miss the whole movie. Jeff Keen also paints (joint exhibition with Jeff Nuttall) and edits **The Amazing Ray-Day** and **Zipp-Zapp** from Future City Press, 14 St. Michael's Place, Brighton.

Time Is
Not just an underground movie, but a clandestine one. Made for an educational film unit to explain the theory of relativity to college students and schoolkids, the racing style makes time turn turtle and come up draped in the seaweed of Surrealism. Full fathom five the theories lie, and have suffered a sea-change, Into something rich and strange … Levy didn't let his producers see the movie until it was too late, and they couldn't do much about it. All they could do was cut out some of the 'violence', and distribute a bowdlerised version under some such title as **A Question of Time**.

Don Levy directed **Ten Thousand Talents**, a vicious exposé of Oxbridge pretension (and masturbation) awarded at Knokke-le-Zoute and widely shown round Bleecker St. Putting the last snips to **Herostratus**, two and a half spectrum-coloured hours on the adman's London now.

SOURCE: *IT*, 31 OCTOBER–13 NOVEMBER 1966, 9

2.4 ASIDES ON GODARD

I. God, Godard, Godot.
Godard is of Swiss Calvinist stock. His art is a basically Protestant one. Grey, ascetic images reduce the world to a concept of itself. He photographs Karina like Dreyer photographs

Falconetti, but reduces her to just a face, mysterious, melancholy, ethereal even in gaiety, where Dreyer's images are sculptural, anguished. There's flesh in Dreyer, despite the resonances, resemblances between flesh and stone, which, asceticism apart, carry the implication that people are real and strong like stone, like rocks of ages. But in Godard everything is a grey, jerky flow. Godard's is an art of the plastic age, of fluent, pliable, putty characters.

Godard's words-on-images suggest an agnostic, nay nihilistic Bresson, and indeed the Catholic critic Henri Agel accused Bresson of Jansenism, which is a heresy with many Calvinistic connections. Godard's is a Calvinistic mind astray in a Godless, soulless world, a world of accidents which because they lack essence, lack even a felt existence …

II. Godard and the Death of E. M. Forster

Godard films which seem to me ludicrously bad fascinate several people whose opinions I respect, and I explain their infatuation as follows (which infuriates them). His evocations of an emotionally and morally lost world would appeal to my acquaintances' disillusionment, their pain, as nice, idealistic, upper-middle-class liberals, finding themselves in today's cool, fluid, cynical world. His despair catches their own melancholy. His best films are those where feelings of pain and loss are most plausible: *A Bout de Souffle*, *Le Petit Soldat* and one or two passages in *Pierrot le Fou*, notably the beautiful ending. The feelings are plausible because the characters have positive, focused desires, the frustration of which we observe.

There are of course other reasons for responding to Godard's duller films. One may be a connoisseur of remarkable idioms and styles. One may be sceptical to the point of nihilism, suffering from a moral and emotional impotence behind which lies just the breath of remorse that appears in Godard's films. Godard is, in a sense, the ghost of Losey, the Losey of moral anti-matter. Losey is a violent puritan, Godard a broken one. In Losey there's a certain fascination with moral nihilism. One can imagine *Le Petit Soldat* filmed by Losey. But Godard's *King and Country* would reduce Hamp's pain to a wry shrug.

Or one may admire Godard's bad films because of their sense of the world as unreal – a schizophrenic art for a schizophrenic epoch. But for myself, I'm bored with art that's merely symptomatic: it goes straight into the Light Entertainment category, when, at least, it entertains. I prefer analysis, diagnosis, prognosis and, if only by implication, intimations of a new synthesis.

And Godard's lesser films say nothing that hasn't been said better by, say, Malle's *Le Feu Follet*, Welles's *The Trial*, Antonioni's *L'Avventura*, Bergman's *The Silence*, Losey's *The Damned*; not to mention 'commercial' films like *The Mistress*, *The Doll*, or *The World Ten Times Over* (which, as a study of prostitution, nihilism and non-communication, makes *Vivre sa Vie* look like moron glacé).

III. Hear Me Talkin' to Ya …

But it may be said that Godard's films are not about their dramatic subjects, which are only pretexts. *Vivre sa Vie* is not about prostitution, but about communication. To which one may reply that:

1. there's no reason why a film shouldn't be about two things at the same time: say, the experience of prostitution, linking with difficulties of communication, and that:
2. Godard's stylistic sensitivity and originality is at its sharpest when it gears in with his subject-matter.

One thinks of his most painful film, *Le Petit Soldat*. It is almost a Bressonian soliloquy over a silent film (yet a very modern silent film), as Coutard's fingertip-held camera hosepipes along rooftops or flicks from one face to the next. Certain photograms have an almost orthochromatic anguish; natural sounds are eerily excluded (again, like Bresson, dematerializing the world); the streetscapes are as evocative as those of Kirsanoff's *Ménilmontant*.

Throughout the film alternates a quality of semi-abstraction and of beautifully textured moments, notably the virtual *pas-de-deux* between photographer and model, though that too is a pun, and is spiritualized by the music of Haydn – a nice reference: advertising art has a graceful formality. Godard has a fine ear for such original affinities. There's a car journey as winding and endless as *Vertigo*. The back of Karina's head becomes a mask. The reiteration of '*A quoi tu penses?*' relates the photographic session and the torture session. Michel Subor's cut-price Brando is a just-about-adequate mouthpiece for Godard's paradoxes, including a remark which furnishes the key to Godard's moral vision: 'Perhaps it is with remorse that liberty begins.' Otherwise, Godard is the worst director of actors since Sternberg and Bresson; and how can he not be, when he does not believe in feelings?

But Godard's *pointillisme* of ideas lacks a backbone (aesthetic and moral – the two are one) in *Vivre sa Vie* and *Une Femme Mariée*. The pimp suddenly goes off into the vocabulary of an RTF documentary about prostitution (and a doctor rambles off into impersonal vaguenesses about contraception). Sex is shown by day, in a white sunlit hotel room, with cars passing, so becomes as cold as a white towel. Brice Parain discourses on the necessity of detachment and philosophy (which is pouring water on a drowning pussycat). The two studies in woman, prostitute and wife, are studies in philosophical perfidy, in knowing and lying. Even the views of Paris that appear and just fade out, in the 'album' style that was quite orthodox in silent films, here have an eerily cold, elegiac meaning, by contrast with current syntax, where we expect an establishing shot to lead into some emotionalising action. One thinks of the photographs of Eugène Atget. Hence, too, the private jokes: Karina as the tart is going to be, or has been 'in films' with, she says, Eddie Constantine, a flash-forward to *Alphaville*.

The play of gestures in Godard yields a code about doubt. In *A Bout de Souffle*, Belmondo dying rubs his thumb over his lips, a gesture which Seberg catches from him at the end. Lemmy does it too. In *Charlotte et son Jules,* Belmondo, startled, wipes his expression off his face like one of the three Stooges, after Charlotte, too, whimsically wipes an expression on and off and on and off.

Godard works engagingly on the spectator's awareness that his film is a film, e.g. the narrator-hero speaks the credits (*Histoire d'Eau*), the hero addresses the audience (*Pierrot le Fou*); the effect is at once insolent and elegiac, intimate and forlorn.

Vivre sa Vie is an ironical title; that's the one thing the heroine doesn't do. Instead, she is reduced to an unfeeling object. First, her heart leaves her mind, then her perceptions quit her body, then she lets herself be sold, and then she's shot; total separation. Like *Une Femme Mariée* it's about talk-about-being only being beating-about-the-bush and not being the being itself. In the later film the child has his simple rules; the humanist intellectual stresses that man must understand before he affirms (Godard neither understands nor affirms). The wife lies, the husband assents in her lies by his complacency, and lies too; the doctor's 'authoritative', impersonal vocabulary outrages the dignity of the individual to whom he speaks.

Similarly, *Alphaville* isn't science-fiction at all. It isn't even what one could call 'conceptualist art', as when Raymond Roussel, Boris Vian, J. G. Ballard or for that matter Alain Resnais in *L'Année Dernière à Marienbad* allow to exist 'impossible worlds' whose right to existence is a purely verbal, conceptual one: theological worlds. But in *Alphaville*, the technological references are simply a network of metaphors. If Godard talks about 'galactic space' and shows us a car driving down a road it's because seeing a road as 'galactic space' is a characteristic schizophrenic experience and Godard is talking about schizophrenia. Schizophrenic too are the neg-pos reversals as Lemmy flees. The schizophrenia is not only that of Overkill, but of well-adjustment in our bourgeois-technological world. *Mon Oncle*'s house was an oasis in it; Lemmy fights his way out of it.

IV. Godard As Philosopy's Con-man

Godard's films like Losey's go in twos – two on flirtation (*Tous les Garçons s'appellent Patrick*, *Histoire de l'Eau* – where the flood background becomes, by virtue of inserts of newsreel aerial views, as extensive and ominous as the spread of *Alphaville*), two on cool, flip Belmondo being quit by his woman (*Charlotte et Son Jules*, *A Bout de Souffle*), two on war and murder (*Le Petit Soldat*, *Les Carabiniers*), two on women (*Vivre Sa Vie*, *Une Femme Mariée*), two on passion (*Le Mépris*, *Pierrot le Fou*), two on madness vs. logic (*Alphaville*, *Pierrot le Fou*).

Yet, precisely because he withdraws from reality, they're all the same film; the whole of *Alphaville* is merely a tautology of the overtones in *A Bout de Souffle*. Missing in *Vivre sa Vie*, lyrical as it is, are the humanity and the nuances that appear in so much conversation by non-artists. To take another girl who lived her life, one thinks of Christine Keeler: 'Ward said it was all right provided I never developed the mentality of a prostitute.' There's a better story about split personality in that remark than Godard's berserk exploitation of the notion of unreality. Especially when linked with: 'My life revolved around him from morning to night. We were like brother and sister.'

A Bout de Souffle and *Le Petit Soldat* are perhaps Godard's best films because, jump-cuts apart, they are completely traditional in their conception, construction and dialogue. Indeed, they are models of their kind. The traditional qualities provide a holding context for divergences from tradition, the deliberate dips into unreality. After the second film, Godard's nihilism and sense of unreality leave the picture for the paint, and begin to sabotage his style. (It's curious how many film cynics do this. Allégret and Clouzot turned commercial; in this art-film-era, Godard turns 'anti-commercial' …)

Godard's obtrusive anti-commercial appeal is facilitated by his in-jokes (we all like to feel we're In), by his very verbal, literary approach, and by what may seem to be an avant-garde style. Yet all his experiments with narrative amount to a compromise between the narrative and the essay: a characteristic novelist's technique, from Fielding's digressions, many of which were art about art, to Aldous Huxley's, and in this Chris Marker's and Agnès Varda's movies have gone far beyond Godard's: being more demanding, they are less popular. Godard's 'impressionism', in his literary approach to real life (which he takes care not to approach too closely), in his sense of unreality, he reminds one of the first cinematic *avant-garde*, of Delluc's *Fièvre* and L'Herbier's *Eldorado*, which were also weary mood-pieces. Delluc used what he fondly hoped was a Symbolist approach; L'Herbier used appliqué optical tricks, which rarely worked except as *ideas*, because they were the work of a literary man who thought in terms of visual ideas rather than of visual experiences. In contrast, Godard exploits with commendable aplomb the mish-mash of word and image, of seen word, the stream of word-over-glimpse, which are characteristic perceptual modes of the 'sixties and are a major reason for his fascination. But Godard's films have the same ethereal ring, the same preciosity.

As a philosopher, however, Godard is Colin Wilson with a sense of humour. *Alphaville* has amusing ideas (the cinema with tip-up seats; the execution like a happening; Lemmy using an old safety-razor, like the G-Man; the loving parodies of Spillane, e.g. 'I shoot first because life's too short to ask questions').

The best in Godard is in his verbal gags, often extremely sad. One might well compile a little book of his reflections: 'The Wisdom of Jean-Luc Godard', and I would rather read the script of *Alphaville* and imagine the film, than see Godard's clumsy transcription. But the major ideas are old hat and square (Who's afraid of the big bad Computer) as well as plagiarisms (word-revision and novel-writing machines from *1984*, computers and seedy Akim Tamiroff from *The Trial*). And most of the visual effects are crummy by comparison with, say, Dick Lester.

Many of his best scenes are filmed anecdotes (like the man with the tune in *Pierrot le Fou*). Often, hopes and ideals are fossilised into paintings or books – notably the big comic-strip tome featured so ostentatiously in *Pierrot le Fou*. Its heroes, a band of engagingly craven rascals called *Les Pieds Nickelés*, lived out this hero's nostalgia for innocence and action, a nostalgia which he, in fact, lives out, only to end in an emptiness as utter as if he had stayed at home. Godard's eye for visual symbolism is a penetrating one: the sticks of explosive which Pierrot drapes over his shoulders at the end resemble waxen Icarus wings. Nor is the symbolism over-simplistic: if Pierrot paints his face blue before dying, is it blue for the sky, blue for the blues, blue like Picasso's blue or blue in neo-Dada meaninglessness? It's for all these things …

Smart as his philosophical gags are, they coexist with a curious philosophical archaism. *Alphaville* introduces us to *conscience* as an innate entity, to the *inherent* comprehensibility of words, to an *amor vincit omnia* sentimentality, that hark back, if not to Thomism, at least to Platonism, an approach to man and to cultural values that one would have thought Freud had finished with once and for all.

There are those who cling to traditional notions of rationalism and objectivity. There are those who can accept neither traditional notions nor depth-psychology, and engage in existentialist tussles with 'the absurd' or '*le néant*', especially if they're from the Catholic (*Cahiers du Cinéma*) or the Anglican (*Sight and Sound*) bourgeoisie. Or they may return to religion, or wish they could (Malcolm Muggeridge is just Cardinal Heenan out of drag). Or they may feel driven to reject all -isms, and to feel that the only integrity is in incessant doubt, non-affirmation, subversion. Or they may accept notions of the unconscious, and so still believe in causes, structures, emotions, and in 'subversion' by lucidity rather than doubt. There is no unconscious in Godard. He is a systematic doubter, not so much of outside reality, which appears in his work as neutral, but of the mind, because there is nothing in his mind between the conscious purpose and nothingness. Again, his approach is extremely archaic: the last gasp of Cartesianism. From 'I think, therefore I am' to 'I'm not sure what I think, therefore I don't exist'.

V. Godard and the Paras

The under-the-sheets love-scene in *A Bout de Souffle* could be the least erotic bed-scene ever filmed. Godard's *Le Mépris* is about sexual-emotional diffidence, Moravia's *noia*. The emotional listlessness and the grey, flimsy non-sensuousness of his films suggest that

Anna Karina's lovers have all taken being flip to the point of impotence, and sit there watching her obsessively. From the cool to the frigid. Karina is not Godard's anima and ex-wife, but his posthumous life, his nirvana, his ghost (castrated, sensitive, passive, alive). He watches her try to live (that is to say, be tortured, prostituted and shot by personifications of his confused indifference).

Alphaville is the emotional emptiness, the whirring-and-clicking of Godard's mind, against which Lemmy-Bogey-the-man-Belmondo-wishes-he-were protests. But he protests by the hysteric reflex of an unthinking brutality ('life's too short to ask questions'), recalling Spillane's Mike Hammer, and, of course, the nihilist acquiescence of *Le Petit Soldat*. What a contrast with Franju's *Judex*, where the violence is only a pretext for the magic of tenderness! *Alphaville* is just another version of *Our Man Flint*. In both cases our brutal hero sets out against the scientists who with their computers and their artificial paradise turn women into pleasure-units.

Aldrich said so much about it all in *Kiss Me Deadly* – his *tour-de-force* of 'dehumanised style'.

In France, Godard is commonly called Fascist; in England he has become the darling of the sensitive plants of *Sight and Sound*. Without calling all nihilists Fascists, perhaps we should take more seriously the nastiness in Godard's films.

Le Petit Soldat is morally as gripping as it's depressing, like *Psycho*. Our hero veers from bragging about his blandness over the men he's killed to proving how sensitive he is ('eyes Velazquez-grey or Renoir-grey?'). Concentration camp commandants were great at loving classical music, and the OAS fought for the sake of Western culture. Godard's hero is half-redeemed by being so weak, so green, so wistful. He's a bad Nazi rather than a good one; a putty-Nazi.

Not that Godard is a 'para'; his diffidence cuts both ways. But the comparison with Antonioni, whose characters share the anguish, the doubt, the non-feeling, of Godard's, isn't irrelevant. Godard's shrug off grief, turn flip and empty; Antonioni's don't lose their moral compass-points, hold on to their humanity. Not that Godard lacks lucidity about this. '*Aprés tout, je suis con ...*' says Belmondo in *A Bout de Souffle*. And Godard's attitude is one of complicity rather than of contempt. Complicity with the morally contemptible is one of the major artistic modes of our time, from the *acte gratuit* in Gide to Camus's *L'Etranger*, and innumerable commercial films, e.g. René Clément's *Plein Soleil*. Thus Antonioni's films have their overtones of archaism: his characters are worthy, and they care about not caring. His films have a brooding, Bergman-like intensity. Godard's characters' recognition of their own '*connerie*' may be a plus feature, but it isn't necessarily a redeeming one. At the time of the OAS crisis, Antonioni's characters would do what they could, while Godard's characters would do nothing, and rapidly be sodomised by the Paras mushrooming in the grey skies.

Godard wears dark glasses to hide from the world the fact that he's in a permanent state of ocular masturbation, rubbing himself off against anything and everything on which his eye alights. The flicking glance of his camera is the constant dribble of premature ejaculation. It is an unseeing stare. Godard keeps babbling on about the world being absurd because he can't keep an intellectual hard on long enough to probe for any responsive warmth.

SOURCE: *THE FILMS OF JEAN-LUC GODARD* (LONDON: STUDIO VISTA, 1967), 147–53

Better Books' paperback department, Better Bookz (Photograph by Simos Tsapnidis, © Manolis Daloukas)

2.5 KER-PLOW!

Is it a flaming creature? Is it a blonde cobra? No, it's the Underground Movies movement!

There was the documentary movement in the '30s, the Free Cinema boys in the '50s. Each had their crowded hour of glorious life and before they faded rejuvenated the jaded arteries of cinema.

Now every hip, beat or Liverpool poet carries a cine-camera in his mental baggage. So here come the Underground movies – the Dadamentary movement, the Freak-Out Cinema boys, the hip-flip-trip mini-gauge brigade.

The London Film-Makers' Co-operative exists to help, and arrange showings, lectures, etc., for the makers of hip, beat, experimental, way-out, or just plain-but-interesting, movies on any gauge.

Acting Chairman is critic Raymond Durgnat, well-known old sweat of *films and filming* columns.

Anyone interested in travelling by Underground, and how to find it, please contact him c/o *films and filming*, or write to LFMC, Better Books, Charing Cross Road, W.C.2.

SOURCE: *FILMS AND FILMING*, JULY 1967, 38

2.6 DWOSKIN'S DREAM-FILMS

I've seen <u>Alone</u> three times. After the first time, I was left with a vague impression that it was one long take of a lonely girl in bed, halfheartedly trying not to masturbate, and then despite herself, indulging.

After the second view, I thought of Warhol, and of Stroheim − of a Warhol who had disciplined his showmanship enough to "bat it and run"; that is to say of a Warhol whose De-Mille-nnial weakness for the supercolossal had been replaced by the terse toughness of a Howard Hawks; and of a Stroheim who had freed himself of his Griffithian ethic.

At the third view, I began to count the cuts (33) as if to assure myself that they were there. I nearly began counting the one softly repeated chord engineered by Ron Geesin as a tocsin for the images; and I grew infatuated with the shadows on Zelda's face − chunky shadows of pullulating grain.

The Swedish short <u>Enligt Lag</u> showed a convict masturbating, and then cut to an expressionistic image of a lonely figure scrambling out of a gravel-pit. This grain is that gravel. That metaphor becomes this form. Not until the third view did the grain emerge from shadow, because this is a well-made film with the old-fashioned virtues which are newer than new.

It tells a story; and telling a story is the only way of not repeating oneself. Because the story is told only in three or four gestures, and could happen tonight or any night, it is also as timeless as that lone, de-musicalised note.

The note resembles a ghost's pulse-beat. The drifting it depicts is also a fight. (There is pain in the emptiness.) And the despair it reveals is beyond self-pity; the honesty in it, beyond pity. For some, the film is a photograph of total despair. For me it is the only matter-of-fact film about eroticism ever made.

The film is fiercely anti-subjective. Everything is vaporised, except this rendezvous of a physiology with its own loneliness. The girl's fantasies are painfully absent, yet lucidly so − no flaming creatures in shadow gardens, no door marked gents opening on to burning christmas trees in the empty grate, no strip cartoons stuck to a patch of bare brick beyond her bed. Or maybe this girl is so far gone that her finger is only her finger and no dreams live. The primitivism of the act is matched by the camera, invariably full-face to her bedstead, and by the editing, pitted by shadows that now block out her eyes, now mass under her cheekbones, now caress the long, lean legs whose posture evokes the compositions of Pabst (another master of erotic energy wasted in squalor). Perhaps squalor is the wrong word − there is an eerie solemnity to the nothingness, like the rite of a priestess.

<u>Chinese Checkers</u>, by contrast, is a fiesta. A lesbian fiesta certainly, but at least it's a bicycle made for two. But can we really speak of <u>homo</u>sexuality when the partners are <u>hetero</u>-geneous as the softly-insisting Oriental girl and the strong-jawed brightly confused friend-antagonist of the game? Once again, a Pabstian link occurs; one thinks of the chess-game ascendancy between Queen and her victim in <u>L'Atlantide</u>. Here, the girls drift, as in a dream, from a game to a form of communication that communicates nothing, but <u>Chinese Checkers</u> is not so much avant-garde as stone-age in its deeply pre-Bazin cinema: low angles, contre-jour (whites of the eyes glimmering in grisaille), first-person, reverse angles; etc.

After the first viewing, I had the impression that the camera looks up at the Chinese girl from or below board-level, while looking more evenly at her white victim; almost as if Dwoskin had amused himself by this ultra-classic use of camera-angles; but that he had done this so non-committally that they take on a new sense entirely, a dreamlike dislocation of levels.

At a second view, I began to doubt if the camera-angles had any such one-for-one significance, and wondered if I had not happened only to remember the angles as and when they fitted the glances. That first-person reverse angling is authentic too, and never mechanical. Each shot makes us one of the girls <u>absorbing</u> the other, by a kind of cannibal osmosis. Perhaps this is why the film disturbs and enriches us more than the orthodox encounter would do. With a childlike candour the camera looks in at two perverse young mothers, and a highly sexual film establishes an erotic archetype.

It is <u>never</u> a peeping tom film; the point of it being that we are drawn into it; we <u>become</u> both girls, each as mysterious as the other, each a mass of psychic being, pure feminine energy.

I would hazard that this film is a direct rendering of a dream. And to dream in celluloid so impeccably is a tour-de-force of fidelity. One thinks less of Robbe-Grillet than of Maya Deren.

<u>Sleep</u> and <u>Solo</u> are lighter hearted. In particular, <u>Solo</u> touches at times on the sprightly whimsy of the world of Ken Russell. <u>Sleep</u> might be termed a jocular mock-up of Kuri's <u>Chair</u>. A pair of soles (those of a sleeping girl?) move restlessly about under the lower edge of a sheet. (Again the unvarying <u>Alone</u> angle.) The image is underscored by Ron Geesin's lively music until what we accept as the "dormant" state reveals an opaque life as unremitting as that of day. Why film feet rather than a sleeping face? Perhaps because feet have a faint air of the blackly comic about them, whereas watching a face would make us feel too powerful or too tender. Ron Geesin's piano occasionally mickey-mousing the feet's jabs and twitches makes them resemble malformed hands, or the stunted fingers of some thalidomide pianist. What are toes after all, if not near-fingers that have suffered centuries of cramp, like Chinese footbinding? They are also very sprightly things, those feet, the toes sprouting and wiggling with daffodil joy.

At a first view, I was disappointed to find <u>Solo</u> evoking the Temperance Seven/Biographic/Mukkinese Battle Horn vein of Edwardian spoof-nostalgia. (A youth polishes a huge horn among audio-visual incunabula.) I prefer Dwoskin in his bleaker, weirder dream key. But at a second view, the film spoke in new accents. The black sun of Dwoskin's melancholy began showing a rim round the shape of the film's whimsy. And this takes a darker turn when the hero's audio-visual museum of a room is infested suddenly with nude fantasms, while a comedian from the days of Edison-Bell chortles out a whiskery song about being happy every day.

SOURCE: *CINIM*, NO. 2, SUMMER 1967, 7–8

2.7 LONDON FILM-MAKERS' CO-OPERATIVE CATALOGUE ENTRIES

JEFF KEEN
MARVO MOVIE
Movie wizard initiates shatterbrain experiment Eeeow! – the fastest movie film alive – at 24 or 16 fps even the mind trembles – splice up sequence 2 – flix unlimited, and inside yr very head the images explode – last years models new houses and such terrific death

scenes while the time and space operator attacks the brain via the optic nerve – will the operation succeed – will the white saint reach in time the staircase now alive with blood – only time will tell says the movie master – meanwhile deep inside the space museum...

Hire fee: £3 0 0, 5 mins, colour, sound

JOHN LATHAM
TALK
An abstract movie by the notorious bibliophobe and Skoob erector. Blobs and dots tumble and tremble about in patterns which at once please the eye and baffle the mind. Some see it as a visualization of party chit chat. For others it is a formal exercise in kinetic art. Whatever one thinks, and even if one doesn't, this is a welcome new move in the too rare Fischinger tradition.

Hire fee: £1 5 0, colour, silent, 7 mins

SPEAK
is his second attack on the cinema. Not since Len Lye's films in the thirties has England produced such a brilliant example of animated abstraction. "Speak" is animated in time rather than space. It is an exploration in the possibilities of a circle which speaks in colour with blinding volume. "Speak" burns its way directly into the brain. It is one of the few films about which it can truly be said "it will live in your mind."

Hire fee: £2 15 0, colour, 11 mins

SOURCE: LONDON FILM-MAKERS' CO-OPERATIVE CATALOGUE, 1967

2.8 *TONITE LET'S ALL MAKE LOVE IN LONDON*

Marx denounced religion as the opium of the people. But more and more it's less the pulpit than the mass media that stupefy us with myths which we don't really believe but which colour our thinking and dim our sense of our own reality. In every myth there's a grain of truth – the bigger the better; exaggeration is always more plausible than invention. If the old myths stressed eternity, austerity, duty, pain and gloom, the new ones stress ephemerality, indulgence, liberty, pleasure and optimism.

Swinging London, by now, is such a myth – a welcome, disturbing minority way of life falsified into a city's brand-image by journalists, advertisers and everyone's daydreams. The economic trampoline beneath it is probably that for the first time working-class adolescents had money and freedom; the upper classes had no empire to be sent out to; the middle classes had lost their dynamism and their self-confidence. But such shifts have left most people, and institutions, untouched, so far. As Michael Caine tells his interviewer here, a capital city whose pubs shut at eleven is about as swinging as Highgate Cemetery, and, as David Hockney observes, London is to New York as Bradford is to London.

Near the beginning of Peter Whitehead's reportage his characteristically nimble camera roams over magazine covers and headlines – as if to stress that 'Swinging London' is as much an image as a reality. (A friend of mine always calls it 'Swingling London', to suggest 'swindling'.) The camera catches Donyale Luna off guard, and, as she nervously laughs, 'looking like a rag' (but a fascinating rag) in the Portobello Road – the myth comes to earth, and there's still no contact. At a light show a girl dances with her own shadow; beatnik buskers avert their faces. Lee Marvin, in his *Dirty Dozen* outfit, represents the typical, amiable American tourist, obliging with a few vapid remarks about mini-skirts. The inevitable *Playboy* smoothie is, sickeningly, there (it's surely the Playboy Club that David Hockney describes as 'a sort of rhythm-and-blues Angus Steak House, where the seats are so small it's like a children's tea-party').

The camera watches, as smooth, as critical, as a cat, waiting for the people to give themselves away, to come alive. The criticism is carried out on a moral plane also. Eric Burdon records 'When I Was Young', whose words are cut in with stockshots of the 1939–45 air war, and the gruelling purpose dominating the older generation's youth. A dollygirl, on a Big Wheel, talks about her freedom, and the camera zooms back to show her, high, alone and perilous, in her lofty cage, while the soundtrack twice repeats the last two words of her last sentence: 'You can do whatever you like and no-one cares'. David Hockney emerges from behind his 'Zoom' spectacles to discuss the way we live now with a blend of Bradford accents, Oxford high-table mannerisms, and flip thoughts, which in itself is a splendid commentary on our new social mobility. Some of the other interviewees are less enlightening (Andrew Oldham, Mick Jagger, Julie Christie) not because their thought isn't sensible, but because the easy English use of words is rooted in social and moral outlooks which no longer apply. Thus Alan Aldridge, shown painting flower and butterfly patterns on a girl's nude body, is asked if he doesn't think it's 'psychic masturbation', and can respond only with a sceptical shrug. The best accounts of themselves are given by the artists. David Hockney is almost the star of the film – apart, of course, from the camera – and Edna O'Brien is quite interesting – though not more so than the anonymous Cockney dollygirl who, having no image to bother about, just declares she doesn't believe in love, and draws all the common sense conclusions as to how a girl ought to behave.

One might have expected the freer, more varied canvas of a whole generation to have provided a 'bigger' film than the poetry reading of *Wholly Communion*. This hasn't happened, for, in a sense, the secret of that film was the stringently limiting conditions under which it was made, forcing Whitehead to a Houdini inventiveness of style. The camera's probing for focuses, its swinging zips and zooms, the glaring lights, the relentless drilling into a face or dwelling on a space, not only provided fascinating cinematic arabesques but gave an astonishing sense of immediacy. The Albert Hall offered a highly articulate, visual and dramatic spectacle on which the camera could dwell; the reality behind Swinging London is more complex and evasive. Its stars are less articulate and less likely to drop the mask which is their stock-in-trade. The camera seems to have been placed just where the mask might reveal the face; but they don't, quite; Julie Christie's only too formidable powers of self-deprecation are held on a tight leash, despite her melting 'You will be kind, won't you?' Nor are we taken into places where a 'peeping tom' camera might catch other naked truths. The film falls somewhere between cinéma-vérité and TV reportage – it's a tantalising, rather than a satisfying, entity. Understandably, perhaps, it omits the twilight and shadowy areas of the swinging. Personally, I can't help wishing Whitehead had printed the introductory credits over that extraordinary film of his which was part of *Oh!* at the Jeanetta Cochrane Theatre – when he simply took his colour camera down the underground and filmed all the real-life people, looking so strangely cowed and tired, as if all the responsiveness had been drained from them, into the neon-signs. And it might have fitted the 'hall of mirrors' effect of the electric media to have filmed himself filming, and preparing his interviewees for, the actual interviews, or lightly skating over the shadows ...

The film remains a rich and rewarding experience, both in terms of the phenomenon which it evokes, and in cinematic terms. The intercutting between Eric Burdon and the war-in-the-air images says, in a fascinatingly different style (not unlike Jeff Keen's) what Antonioni more portentously hints at through David Hemmings's purchase of a Spitfire airscrew in *Blow-Up*. Whitehead's gift of ironic counterpoints of word and image inspires the eerie sequence of flustered bouncers hurling Mick Jagger's female fans back across the footlights into the stalls, to the music of 'Lady Jane'. The idea of 'tromboning' the zoom-lens to and fro in time to the strains of the national anthem is another example of Whitehead's brilliant improvisations; his approach to editing is (whether in the camera or at the machine) much as George Martin and the Beatles use the sound produced by their instruments, playing it backwards, recutting it, using fuzz and reverberations as part of the sound, switching speed and pitch. The device of cutting all but a few frames from a sequence, and then printing them as 'stills' to give a 'stop-go' effect, is no mere gimmick, but absolutely right for suggesting the alienation, the unreality, the edgy beauty, the instability, of our bright, ephemeral, syncopated world. The cutting between the Pink Floyd sound and some bright hot colour patterns becomes abstract cinema in its own right – abstract cinema which has learned from light-shows how to have a thick, sensuous impact on its audience. One might talk about a 'Wagnerian' type of visual music, as distinct from the shriller, flimsier experiments of McLaren and others. The film bristles with fascinations of every kind and a comparison with Godard isn't at all uncalled for. Whitehead's film language, more nervous, less literary, is the next stage on.

SOURCE: *FILMS AND FILMING*, FEBRUARY 1968, 23–4

2.9 *ONE PLUS ONE*

Jean-Luc Godard meets Swinging London; the conjunction was too auspicious not to be ominous. Not that it was impossible to imagine the two surrogate-realities dovetailing. On both sides the equivocations are apparent. Godard's realism evokes the medieval scholastic doctrine of Realism (which corresponds to what we would call idealism) as opposed to nominalism (corresponding to our realism). His eye, alighting on reality, *abstracts*, however 'realistic' the idioms he employs. The visually concrete world separates out into symbolic-iconic-tactile-auditory aspects (or 'accidents'). Where a conventional, 'nominalist' director seeks to recreate, in a coherent whole, all he can sense of the diverse aspects of reality, from its surface to its meaning (meaning being the moral-dramatic values which constitute their 'holding centre', that is, their humanist, non-alienated 'essence'), Godard lets the accidents float off one another (why shouldn't a face be blue? ...), and concentrates, obsessively, on the deep absence of any meaning.

His London is a Nowhere Land – and fleet references to that Yellow Submarine (of nostalgia for togetherness) prompts the comparison with the Beatles' Nowhere Man, a lonely, bookish, madly, sadly, creative polymath. *Cinéma-vérité* of a Stones rehearsal (always the same song) is interspersed with 1) a sprinkling of shots of youngsters scrawling graffiti on walls, posters and cars, and 2) several longer episodes. Black Panthers sit around and read and talk in a car scrapyard, then shoot two white women in white shifts. A TV team interviews Anne Wiazemsky in a cool green forest and feeds her complex Marcuse-like propositions to which she replies 'No' or 'Yes'. Two somewhat sceptical coloured girl reporters interview a determined but somewhat bemused Black Panther. Maoist slogans and Hitler salutes are exchanged in a bookshop (not necessarily, as some critics have supposed, a dirty Soho one), run by a hippie reading aloud from, *inter alia*, *Mein Kampf*. Finally a film is being shot on a beach. Coloured guerrillas on the run try to help a white girl escape, then lay her on a huge camera boom which lifts her corpse, in some art-as-Elijah's-chariot apotheosis, up towards the sun. The image freezes (despite a continuing slow track-in) and – courtesy of the producers – is printed in a sequence of granular rainbow colours. With such perplexing juxtapositions goes the cut-up technique. Over various images (and faded-out dialogues) a voice reads from various, possibly apocryphal, texts. Predominant among them is a porno-political spy thriller whose characters, like *Alphaville*'s, have realistic-Surrealist names and aliases. A certain Marilyn gets involved with Trotskyites, a Governor of the B.B.C. lands his Starfighter in Biafra. The ideological *volte-faces* characteristic of our post-cold-war era (and of its unprecedentedly long historical awareness) suggests such pirouettes as: 'You're my kind of girl, Pepita', said Pope Paul, as he lay down in the grass, 'But I'm not going to rape you.' The clash of behavioural conventions is a happy one.

Godard's ideological evolution requires some comment. *Alphaville* seemed to affirm a nostalgia for good old-fashioned individualistic violence, as against the dehumanising machines. Since the events of May 1968, Godard has increasingly committed himself to a radical-anarchist left, to the Third World, to his variant of 'International Situationism'. *Le Petit Soldat* has signed on, after all, with Che; and Godard observes his redemption, with more hopefulness, but with a nagging scepticism …

His evolution from a nihilistic acquiescence, which could hardly have brought itself to object to Fascism, to these revolutionary affirmations, and indeed actions, parallels a general shift, from the apoliticism of the New Wave's peak years, as de Gaulle triumphed over an aggressive extreme right, to the radical activism of the Provos, Cohn-Bendit, Marcuse, *Black Dwarf*, *et al*. But just as the students were infinitely less menacing than the Generals' plot, so the tensions between radical revolutionism and a despairing withdrawal from society are weaker. They are weaker because revolution is less real a possibility than acquiescence in what the radicals would describe as the ongoing Liberal Fascism. *One Plus One* is about revolution *as* paralysis.

Godard's Black Panther guerrillas, real in the Congo, real in the USA, are purely hypothetical in London 1969. Their rootless pathos is the effect desired. The Marcusian interview is set in a forest recalling a menthol-fresh commercial (Godard's wife appears as a kind of visual-dramatic surrogate for Mick Jagger's Marianne Faithfull, whom Godard used in *Made in USA*. The director's wife for the star's, the French girl in the English film, the English girl in the American film …). *One Plus One* is an audio-visual meditation on the remoteness of radical action, on the curious ethereality, betrayed by vehemence, in radical thought. Are some Maoists *also* Fascists, an efflorescence of Western decadence? Who is really who and how many sides is he on?

In the gloss and polish of a recording studio, Mick Jagger sings: 'Please let me introduce myself, I'm a man of wealth and taste; I was here when Jesus Christ had his moment of doubt and pain; I made damn sure that Pilate washed his hands and sealed his fate.'

In St. Petersburg, 1918, the same enigmatic character 'rode a tank with a sergeant's rank': 'It's so confusing, it's just the nature of my game.' Is he the devil? (the British title of the film is *Sympathy for the Devil*). Or our friend Judas? Or the relentless egoism which, like Steiger's merchant-turned-Commissar in *Dr Zhivago*, always chooses the winning side, just in time? Which earns the old order's royalties while promulgating the revolutionary dream? The contradictions find their likeable, respectworthy, ineffectual compromise in the form of free concerts and fund raising for Oxfam – a compromise no more ineffectual than the foredoomed gestures of extremism …

The dearth of inspiration all too evident in *One Plus One* is linked, no doubt, with this spiritual rarefaction. *Le Petit Soldat* is a nasty, and real, masterpiece. Here the pole of subversive possibility is too distant, too hypothetical, to offer real possibility of betrayal. And Godard is an emotional thinker. Agile as his mind is, it responds to his heart, rather than leading it. One might tend to blame the wordplay's weak, strained quality on Godard's difficulties with English, but the equal and opposite verbal forcedness of *Le Gai Savoir* suggests otherwise. Here, graffiti scrawls include: Stalin-Hilton, Mao-Art, Freudemocracy, Sovietcong, FBI + CIA = TWA + PANAM. (The last isn't so ill-aimed; America's coca-colonisation of England and the world couldn't be more clearly proclaimed than by such commercials as 'The *international passport* to smoking pleasure' or '– means friendship in *any language*.')

Because inertia is its topic, it's no accident that the stylistic conception of *One Plus One* recalls Warhol. Godard planned the film as 'eight ten-minute takes … or possibly ten eight-minute ones'. Both the determined formalism, and the nonchalance of the alternatives, recall Warhol's dry irony. The camera pans slowly, often, it seems, aimlessly, from side to side, preferring, in the *cinéma-vérité* rehearsal sequence, to miss any spontaneously developing interest, rather than seem to hurry to catch it. The film's air of bored emptiness – less conspicuous, less insolent, less easy to like, and, for these reasons only, less stimulating than Warhol's – is nonetheless of a similar order. Over it the commentary superimposes a deluge of verbal concepts, so hypothetical as to be meaningless (it can, after all, be argued that the very processes of thought, memory and hypothesis are schizophrenic – thought involving a 'trace' of emotion broken away from the experience and manipulated and criss-crossed on the mind's equivalent of non-amplified playback). Sometimes, here, the verbal porno-politics are accompanied by visuals which, though at first implying reality (as visuals conventionally do), soon seem problematical (like the Nazi hippies). Symbolic, no doubt, but in a curious way – suggestive of hallucinations, of images which the mind is striving to see as real, just as the revolutionaries' thoughts are striving to make revolution real. With race war now encircling the globe, from Detroit to Malaya, theory has it that black guerrillas should be shooting white women in London now, amidst Jancsoesque calm and submissiveness. Again, theory imposes itself on reality, via kitsch realism (the TV interview, with nature imitating, not art, but commercial art), while commonsense (the girl reporters) out of respect, politeness and sympathy, refrain from breaking down the faith which seems necessary to self-respect. The faith in revolution, in the brotherhood of the black race, there, is as noble and forlorn as Michel's moralistic little parable, to Patricia, about fidelity-in-crime in *Breathless*.

Deploying all the impedimenta of communication (from books through tape-recorders to a-camera-before-the-cameras) the film isn't about communication at all, but about conviction, and about repetition as a means thereto. No-one speaks: everyone reads. The Rolling Stones sequences cover one recording after another of the same number, which the group performs in (fascinatingly) different styles. One Black Panther reads passages from a book which another reads back into a tape recorder. An iron (or safety) curtain of theory has dropped across the world's stage. Life is reduced to footnotes about the theory of life's possibility. The slow bored camera's eye evokes Hal's slow, patronising voice, in *2001*, praising the spaceman's lifelike, but stilted, drawing, which is all the astronaut retains of creativity. Godard, here, is the astronaut – astronaught! – of inner space; not the inner space of the hippies (LSD, macrobiotics, whole-body orgasms) but something older-fashioned, less libidinal, more rationalist: the inner space of a stream of consciousness lacking faith either in emotional drive or in objective correlatives. Consciousness has no aim nor sanction other than a pessimistic idealism, weak as a whim, as soon betrayed as uttered.

A lonely deadness is built into the old order also. The pop group is separated, by sound baffles and head-phones, into the negation of a group: individuals scattered about a labyrinth. Isolated, their pianist plays much like any concert pianist. Little, here, of the Stones' on-stage ecstasies, although, at long long last, Jagger jiggers himself into a private, musical high (celebrating treachery – and celebrating it ironically – so like Godard's double negations), which is like an obstinate, violent flicker of irreducible life, persisting in the Alphaville we call London.

Amidst the intersecting fantasies of politics, art, commitment and being, the final values are thuggery (in *Alphaville*), wistfulness (the scrawler of graffiti – usually Wiazemsky/ Faithfull) and treachery (*Pierrot*); the first a nostalgia, the second uninspired, the third equivocally treacherous and foredoomed.

Just as Bosch shows humans conjoined with, or transmogrifying into, constructions, contraptions, vegetables, animals, demons and other monstrosities, so here Godard's wife, interviewed, as was la Faithfull, by TV, all but becomes a symbiosis of herself with adman imagery and political abstraction (she separates herself by a certain muteness, and mystery …). She knows her Christian name: not Ophelia, not 'Cordilla', but Eve; born Budapest; surname, Democracy. These remarks, disguised as interview questions, and imposed on their subject, evoke the Marcusian line which Godard seems to regard with suspicious longing: 'On LSD you begin to die a little? … Maybe the devil is God in exile? … There is only one way to be an intellectual revolutionary and that is to give up being an intellectual? … Orgasm is the only moment when you can't cheat life? … The Occident is fighting Communism because it is Faustian? … When the novel is dead, then the technological society will be fully upon us? …'

She assents but the remarks are no more her life than the menthol-smart greenery. A similar scepticism underlies, no doubt, the shots of graffiti scrawled on, of all places, pop-coloured cars … The incomplete lettering, and the interposed body of the scrawler, conceal the full text until the last moment, creating a riddle-suspense, concluding in anticlimax. Political names are used like brand names, or in poetico-schizoid conjuration, or like such Burrovian entities as the Nova Police and the Heavy Metal Kid.

All in all, the film is, in about equal proportions, boring in an unstimulating way, boring in a stimulating way, and heavily poignant with numb lost pain. That it marks a moment – or even period – of creative sterility need not be contested. Yet, as one who remained relatively unmoved by the proliferating intellectual notations (too often marginal details) of Godard's most-favoured, mid-period movies, I find this no poorer for being barer; indeed, being monolithic, it is, to me, more moving. One may regret that Godard has recreated, rather than investigated, the curious blankness behind so much talk of revolution now. Yet it's the indispensible complementary movie to the hairy muddle of *If…* (Put those two movies together and a real complexity begins to emerge …)

The Essential Raymond Durgnat

The swing in critical attitude to Godard is disquieting, however. It used to be necessary to emphasise that the Godard cult liked Godard movies for all the complacent reasons, that is to say, as a cleverly styled mirror of contemporary negations and apathies, rather than for their element of disturbed inquiry into them. It was necessary to accuse Godard the stylist, in order to demystify Godard the sage, to expose in Godard the honest artist experiencing all the ravages of alienation, more honestly than most (which is not to say sufficiently honestly for him to qualify as a great artist, except possibly in *Le Petit Soldat*). It is equally necessary now to defend Godard, in artistic difficulty, in something like psycho-spiritual crisis, against a sudden shift to smooth sneers. In the changed tone there seems often more animus than strictly aesthetic considerations would warrant. Godard has, after all, committed the cardinal sin of incommoding the British Film Institute.

What he is doing in a film whose weakness and vulnerability are misleadingly obvious, is not easy to understand. Jagger remarked, 'He was such a fucking twot, but we didn't want to spoil his ego-scene', among equally uncomplimentary remarks about others involved. The remark is too open to be malevolent, and so insolent one would love to agree with it. But if one accepts, on the one hand, *Une Femme Mariée*, and, on the other hand, Warhol's *Harlot*, it is not so easy to dismiss this curious compromise between their aesthetic processes of *belles-lettres* and cut-up, of verbal dexterity and visual nullity, of mannerist subversion of apparent aims. *One Plus One* is an underground movie; as sullen, as uneven, as superficial, as underground movies are, yet also as abruptly beautiful, just as the film's elongated, etiolated architectonics converge on the apotheoses of Jagger and Wiazemsky.

SOURCE: *THE FILMS OF JEAN-LUC GODARD* (2ND EDN, LONDON: STUDIO VISTA, 1969), 178–83

2.10 CUTTING WITH A KEEN EDGE

I'm an addict of underground movies, but also a heretic, in that if you let me loose in underground archives with a pair of scissors and an inexhaustible supply of grindstones I'd vastly love to improve, for example, *The Chelsea Girls*, by cutting it to about 60 minutes on two screens. I'd telescope *Lonesome Cowboys* to a delirious hour or less. (Admittedly, *Harlot* would stay as it is.)

Of course there may be a legitimate place in art for boredom, or relaxed semi-participation. Sometimes a half-hearted half-bored half-derisive involvement with a movie can catch a certain mood. But most underground movies are overlong, for, among some plausible and intelligent excuses there are three which we'd be much better off without. The film-maker is not so much dada with, as gaga about, every square inch of his work, or, if he's more self-critical, of his bearable footage, or, if he's really a still photographer, of his best pictures. The fact that movies are still a costly medium gives every shot an artistically quite irrelevant prestige. There's also the easily refutable, but still popular, myth to the effect that that moving pictures have compulsive powers over people.

After hours of prospecting for gold nuggets in celluloid mountains, I turn with relief to the cut-and-thrust, touch-and-go, bat-it-and-run speed-of-light cinema of Brighton's Jeff Keen. He's been making his mighty midget movies since the '50s, and as so often happens, the lone Englishman beats American fashion to the draw, but, isolated by the apathy around, gets neither credit nor bread. Invaluable as it is, *Catalyst*'s directory of anti-academic art activities carries an over-modest, or maybe discouraged entry which doesn't do justice to the movies. You wouldn't know that they pump images into the spectator's brains till he's juddering to and fro like Bonnie and Clyde in the final shoot-in. As abruptly each movie ends one exasperatedly realises that so much has just happened so fast that only a filmic fandango can be recalled, a state of sad joy, a staccato rainbow existence. The quality of deprivation makes an appropriate after-image, for real beauty always pleases so much it hurts. Many, many years ago Keen began running his movies two at a time, side by side, with an R and B or soul tape. They can be criss-crossed in different combinations, and synchronisations, and at different speeds, and with different tapes, or silent. Each permutation creates a new whole, by which each detail is in itself transformed. Continuous performance becomes continuous re-creation.

The London Film Co-op has a 16mm. reel which I had blown up from 8mm., and Keen's movie-tape road-show includes such gems as *Flik-Flak*, *Pink Disaster Area*, *House of Secrets*, *Virus Scattering*, *Mr. Soft Eliminator*, *Return of Spider Woman* and *Beneath Paramount Skies*. (It's often hard to tell just where one movie begins and another ends, and if, as a result of this delicious confusion, I've invented a title or two that doesn't exist, maybe that's as it should be. A work of art which doesn't confuse us wastes our time.) Amidst a picnic atmosphere, a girl is swathed in polythene. Colour photographs are enhanced with hand-painted colour. From the lower eyelid of a *True Confessions* heroine, there slithers, not a tear, but a cascade of pop icons, catching all the zing, the quick-as-a-flash cornflake divinities of childlike fantasy. That world is restored for us. But the very speed takes on a certain melancholy: 'Nothing lasts'.

There are more disquieting images. A tin toy, crushed into a shape like entrails, and splashed with bright paint, writhes sad coils in heat, blossoms and wilts like a flame-flower, and subsides in charred twists like black shit. An air of heroic futility is summed up by a shot of Jeff Keen pedalling strenuously along on an old pushbike, with a hemisphere of white silk billowing hopefully behind, like a braking parachute on a jetplane. Jackie Keen makes an adorable odalisque for this snap-crackle-mom world in which toys and images dance their dervish dance in the magic timespace of movie cutting. Never has the ultimate wistfulness of the popular arts and 'pop' art together been more convulsively summarised. Such criticism of pop-and-'pop' can be made only from *both* beyond *and* within. Where Warhol's deadpan is a nihilism, the Jeff Keen tempo has, paradoxically, a real tenderness. An auto-destructive undertow is clearly revealed in the sequence where the director-star builds a white framework, paints on it, leans a bike against it, and sets the lot on fire. Even the flames seem fragile …

Keen's memory-, and therefore criticism-defying movies are sensuous and tactile, zany toccatas of sensations for the pores of the mind. They have more permanent equivalents in his exhibition pieces and shortlived verbovisual broadsheet, *The Amazing Rayday* (a collector's item already!) and other publications. Try 14 St. Michael's Place, Brighton, and say you're a friend of Ray Durgnat's.

SOURCE: *TIME OUT*, 21 MARCH–4 APRIL 1970, 27

ANNOTATIONS

FLYWEIGHT FLICKS
[p. 49] For the **Brighton school**, see 'Throwaway Movies' in this volume (p. 95). | **"Pull My Daisy"** (1959) was directed by Robert Frank and Alfred Leslie, adapted from Kerouac's play *The Beat Generation*, and starred Allen Ginsberg and Gregory Corso, among other luminaries. | Keen had photographed the beat poet **Piero Heliczer**'s first film *The Autumn Feast* (1961) when Heliczer was living in Brighton. Heliczer later moved to New York, where he appeared in *Flaming Creatures* and worked with the Velvet Underground. His poetry was published alongside Durgnat's in Michael Horovitz's 1969 anthology *Children of Albion*. | The most likely candidate for the **great American exhibition** mentioned by Keen is the Tate's 'New American Painting', mounted in February–March 1959. | [p. 50] The abstract animators Norman **McLaren** and **Len Lye** came to prominence as adjunct members of Grierson's documentary movement in the 1930s before moving to North America. **Boogie-Doodle** (1940) was made in New York and later released by the National Film Board of Canada; **Colour Box** (1935) was Lye's first film for the GPO Film Unit.

WHOLLY COMMUNION
[p. 50] **Donovan** ('Catch the Wind') and **Bob Dylan** ('The Times They Are A-Changin") entered the British chart for the first time in the last week of March 1965; **Joan Baez** ('We Shall Overcome') followed them at the start of May, during her joint tour with Dylan, as documented in D. A. Pennebaker's *Dont Look Back* (1967). About the time Durgnat's review appeared in May 1966, Dylan began his legendary semi-electric tour and 'Rainy Day Women' reached the top ten. | R. D. Laing, who had by 1965 established himself at Kingsley Hall, brought along a number of his patients to the Incarnation, including the **anonymous, lovely girl** later identified as Jill Molyneux.

UNDERGROUND FILM FESTIVAL PROGRAMME NOTES
[p. 52] The fruit of Whitehead's **Irish safari with the Rolling Stones**, *Charlie is My Darling*, was given a belated release in 2012. | The John Latham **happening** involved, as Durgnat says, the projection of Latham's *Unedited Material from the Star* (1960) on to two performers representing Apollo and Dionysus, each attired in books, getting into a fight, and tearing the books off each other. Latham and Jeff Nuttall almost performed it together at the Albert Hall Incarnation. On other occasions known as *Juliet and Romeo*, it was staged under the title *Film* as part of **DIAS**, the Destruction In Art Symposium, held at a variety of London venues including Better Books in September 1966. | The **destroyed-book, painted relief in the Tate gallery**, which had the central role in *Unedited Material*, was titled *Film Star*. | Keen's **joint exhibition with Jeff Nuttall** was mounted in the basement of Better Books in the summer of 1966. | The **educational film unit** for which Levy made *Time Is* (1964) was the Nuffield Foundation Unit for the History of Ideas, which had strong ties to the Slade; Whitehead also worked there. | Levy's **Ten Thousand Talents** (1960) was included in Amos Vogel's Cinema 16 catalogue; the **Bleecker** Street Cinema was one of New York's major cinephile venues. | Levy won BFI funding for **Herostratus** in September 1962; most of it had been shot by the spring of 1965; and it was provisionally accepted for the 1966 Venice Film Festival. It did not receive the **last snips**, however, until the end of 1967.

ASIDES ON GODARD

[p. 52] Raymond Durgnat, too, was **of Swiss Calvinist stock**. | [p. 53] In Losey's *King and Country* (1964), **Hamp's pain** is that of a soldier on trial for desertion. | Here and elsewhere, Durgnat used **schizophrenic** and 'schizoid' more or less interchangeably. In R. D. Laing's definition, given on the first page of *The Divided Self* (London: Tavistock, 1960) the latter meant 'an individual the totality of whose experience is split in two main ways: in the first place, there is a rent in his relation with his world and, in the second, there is a disruption of his relation with himself' (p. 15). This was the 'sane' position, schizophrenic the 'psychotic'; but as Laing said in the same book, 'it is, of course, not always possible to make sharp distinctions between sanity and insanity, between the sane schizoid individual and the psychotic' (p. 149). Durgnat provided a definition of his own in his review of Bergman's *Persona* (1966) in the December 1967 *Films and Filming*: 'a lack of communication between parts of the same personality' (p. 21). | [p. 55] Conceptual art or **'conceptualist art'** was a new development in the mid-1960s; DIAS was an important landmark in its history, and John Latham one of its early practitioners. | Durgnat provides a paraphrase of the testimony given by **Christine Keeler** during the Profumo trial. Stephen **Ward** was the 'society osteopath' who introduced her to society. | [p. 56] **Malcolm Muggeridge** interviewed **Cardinal Heenan**, head of the Catholic Church in England, for BBC television in April 1966; then only very mildly sceptical, as Durgnat suggests, Muggeridge later converted to Christianity. | [p. 57] **Not that Godard is a 'para'**; nor is he one of **the Paras mushrooming in the grey skies**. In April 1961 a group of retired generals opposed to the French government's Algeria policy attempted to overthrow de Gaulle in an operation that was to involve rebel paratroopers (Paras) landing on French airfields. The plot's failure led to the formation of the anti-independence paramilitary force OAS (paras).

DWOSKIN'S DREAM-FILMS

[p. 59] **Zelda** Nelson also starred in Ron Rice's New York underground classic *Chumlum* (1964). | *Enligt Lag* (1957), described by Durgnat in *Eros in the Cinema* (London: Calder & Boyars, 1966) as 'a long, sober documentary on Swedish prison-life' (p. 58), was co-directed by future *Marat/Sade* author Peter Weiss. | [p. 60] Durgnat described Yōji **Kuri's *Chair*** (1963) as 'a sardonic quick-motion look at human nervous tics and fidgets' (*ICA Bulletin*, August–September 1967, p. 5). It was included in the LFMC's first catalogue alongside Dwoskin's films. | The **Temperance Seven**, a chart-topping semi-humorous trad jazz band, appeared in Richard Lester's *It's Trad, Dad!* (1962). | **Biographic** Cartoon Films was the production company of animator Bob Godfrey, who worked with the T7 and with Bruce Lacey (also a collaborator of, among others, Lester, **Ken Russell**, and John Latham). | In *A Mirror for England*, Durgnat called *The Case of the **Mukkinese Battle Horn*** (1956), a two-reel *Goon Show* spin-off, 'an early expression of the nonchalant nihilism underlying the deadpan parody/self-parody of the best pop art' (p. 176).

LONDON FILM-MAKERS' CO-OPERATIVE CATALOGUE ENTRIES

[p. 60] Durgnat's note on Keen's ***MARVO MOVIE*** is adapted, cut-up style, from the second, 'special motion picture' issue of Keen's broadsheet *Amazing Rayday*, published in March 1965. | [p. 61] Latham's ***TALK*** is thought to be *Talk, Mr. Bard*, completed in 1961 and first shown that year, with Lawrence Alloway's encouragement, at the Guggenheim Museum. *Talk, Mr. Bard* is, however, neither **silent** nor **7 mins** long. | *SPEAK*, on the other hand, though made in 1962 and used to accompany Pink Floyd's early shows in 1966, is thought not to have had its soundtrack added until 1967 – the Floyd's attempt at one was rejected. | Oskar **Fischinger**'s 'musical abstracts', an important influence on **Len Lye's films**, were quite widely shown in Britain in the 1930s.

TONITE LET'S ALL MAKE LOVE IN LONDON

[p. 62] *Oh!* was a verse play by Sandro Key-Åberg, staged by the Traverse Theatre Company in February–March 1967. | [p. 63] Whitehead had filmed Antonioni filming **David Hemmings's purchase of a Spitfire airscrew** in mid-1966. | He recalls (email to editor, 2 December 2012) that Durgnat 'shouted out' in response to his **'tromboning' the zoom-lens** at the film's 1967 London Film Festival screening: 'Stood up and clapped … Sucked him out of his normal shy reticence? Don't know what he shouted.'

ONE PLUS ONE

[p. 64] The **Provos** here means the Dutch anarchist movement Provo. Durgnat had written about both the movement, 'shocktroops of the world layaboutsia' (*IT*, 19 May–2 June 1967, p. 11), and the films of its 'fellow-travellers' (*IT*, 31 October–13 November 1966, p. 7), in the underground press. | Godard went on to use a Sheila Rowbotham article from the left-wing underground paper **Black Dwarf** in *British Sounds*, made for (and rejected by) British television in early 1969. | The **Generals' plot** against de Gaulle was that of April 1961. | [p. 67] In the course of introducing *One Plus One* at the London Film Festival in November 1968, Godard, in protest against the tacking-on of the full version of 'Sympathy for the Devil' to the film's ending, called for a walk-out, punched his producer, was ejected, and snubbed a group of enthusiasts who were planning to show the director's cut outside – hence **incommoding the British Film Institute**.

CUTTING WITH A KEEN EDGE

[p. 67] It is likely that Durgnat made an exception for **Harlot** (1965), Warhol's first sound film, because his friend Harry Fainlight took part in its production. | [p. 68] When handing over the running of the LFMC's screenings to David Curtis, Durgnat recommended as accompaniment for Keen's silent films one **R and B** artist in particular: Clarence 'Frogman' Henry (British Artists' Film and Video Study Collection: LFMC papers, undated letter c. 1967–8). | **Flik-Flak, House of Secrets,** and **Mr. Soft Eliminator** are all from the Cinema 65–LFMC years. **Pink Disaster Area** is probably the twin-screen *The Pink Auto* (1964), which featured **Spider Woman**; none of Keen's extant films seems to have featured her **return**, however. **Virus Scattering** is likewise probably invented; *Under* **Paramount Skies** appears to be the real title of a lost film.

Notes

1. Anon. [Peter G. Baker], 'Underground Movies', *Films and Filming*, March 1964, p. 14.
2. Ibid., p. 15.
3. British Artists' Film and Video Study Collection, Central Saint Martins: Deke Dusinberre interview with Raymond Durgnat, 30 June 1975.
4. Pacific Film Archive programme note, 17 May 1977.
5. Jeff Nuttall, *Bomb Culture* (London: MacGibbon & Kee, 1968), p. 193.
6. Jonas Mekas, *New American Cinema Group and Film-Makers' Cooperative(s): The Early Years* (New York: Anthology Film Archives, 1999), pp. 277–83.

7. British Library, Bob Cobbing papers, Add. MS. 88909/35/2: Letter from Raymond Durgnat to Bob Cobbing, 5 June 1966. 'For wayout film material,' Durgnat recommended in the same letter, 'try Peter Whitehead, 13 Carlisle St W.1.'

8. Dusinberre interview.

9. Durgnat, 'The Underground Movie', *Creative Camera*, April 1969, p. 133.

10. Dusinberre interview.

11. *ICA Bulletin*, nos 172–3, August–September 1967, p. 5.

12. Letter from Peter Whitehead to Andrew Loog Oldham, 30 July 1966, in *Framework*, vol. 52, no. 1, Spring 2011, p. 206.

13. Ibid., p. 207.

14. Durgnat, 'Fading Freedoms/Latent Fascisms & Hippie High Hopes: A Paranoid Guide' (1), *Oz*, no. 11, c. April 1968, p. 22.

15. Ibid.

16. Durgnat, 'Why I Kicked My Underground Habits', *IT*, 9–22 August 1968, pp. 10–11.

17. Durgnat, *Sexual Alienation in the Cinema* (London: Studio Vista, 1972), p. 286.

18. Dusinberre interview.

19. Durgnat, 'Underground Subversion', *Films and Filming*, December 1967, p. 6.

PART 3
IMAGES OF THE MIND

INTRODUCTION

Thorold Dickinson, thanking Faber and Faber for his copy of Durgnat's *Films and Feelings* on its publication in June 1967, reflected on its genesis at the Slade. 'Reading it is like slipping into a flashback,' he wrote to Faber director Peter Crawley. 'I congratulate everyone who has helped whittle down those 400,000 words that confronted me six years ago.'[1] This was no exaggeration, though Durgnat had not so much whittled as chopped. 'I can't really claim to have "edited" him,' recalls his editor Frank Pike, 'but I did spend many hours (probably in pubs) talking to him about the problems the bulk of his manuscript presented to a commercial publisher. It was finally he who came up with the solution of effectively cutting his book in two.'[2] Most of the rest went into *The Crazy Mirror*, Durgnat's book on the American comedy film, published in 1969.

The 1964–5 *Films and Filming* series 'on style in film-making' appeared with alterations – minor except for the expansion of 'Who Really Makes the Movies?' – in the first part of the book. As we have seen, its main thrust was directed against aesthetic essentialism in general and Kracauer's photographic essentialism in particular. For Durgnat cinema was a 'mongrel muse' whose pictorial aspect had been overlooked by the realists. His frame of reference was characteristically wide, but the foreground was occupied by 'such directors as Eisenstein, Sternberg, Dreyer, Pabst, Murnau, Ophuls' rather than the new waves and undergrounds of the 1960s.[3] It was in the last section of the *Films and Filming* series, renamed 'Caligari is Dead – Long Live Caligari' in the book, that he discussed the new cinemas, and the return from realism to expressionism which they portended.

The causes of this stylistic pendulum swing included such technical innovations as 'faster emulsions, simplified lighting, in or out of the studio, and smaller cameras', which together meant that the director's 'personal world' could 'become a subjective, an expressionistic, world' with greater ease and flexibility than ever before.[4]

[The] American *avant-garde* had been developing such effects consistently for many years, but in the popular cinema the most useful milestone is perhaps the opening sequences of Truffaut's *Les 400 Coups*. [...]

The contemporary audience which accepts the 'false-time' jump cuts of Godard's *A Bout de Souffle* and Desmond Davis' *Girl with Green Eyes* is an audience which will take the cinema screen as, not a *literal* reality, but a 'mental world'. So with the 'puzzle worlds' of Resnais' *L'Année Dernière à Marienbad*, Fellini's *8½*, of Welles' *The Trial*, all of which are, in some sense, expressionistic films. Again 'realism' becomes merely a means to an end, a convention which can be accepted or ignored, whichever the artist prefers.[5]

Not all of Durgnat's thesis went into *Films and Feelings* or *The Crazy Mirror*. 'Fake, Fiddle and the Photographic Arts', which expands on his critique of 'photographic realism' and further explores the opposing idea of 'mental worlds', appeared in the *British Journal of Aesthetics* shortly after the *Films and Filming* series ended. Though neither is named, it appears to have been intended to counter Kracauer's *Theory of Film* and, perhaps even more so, Bazin's essay 'The Ontology of the Photographic Image', in which Bazin had argued that the photographic image was 'a mechanical reproduction in the making of which man plays no part', and that the 'objective nature of photography confers on it a quality of credibility absent from all other picture-making'.[6]

In favouring the image's 'emotional resonance' over Bazinian–Kracauerian 'objective accuracy', Durgnat is likely to have had in mind another unnamed theorist, Rudolph Arnheim, the principles of whose 1954 book *Art and Visual Perception* he had earlier wanted to apply to the study of literature. Arnheim, whose study grew out of his earlier works on film, had discovered in gestalt psychology 'scientific support for the growing conviction that images of reality could be valid even though far removed from "realistic" semblance'.[7] There are also traces of Edgar Morin's twin concepts of 'projection-identification' and 'affective participation', used throughout his 1956 book *Le Cinéma ou L'Homme Imaginaire*, also partly informed by gestalt psychology, and in *The Stars*, published in English in 1960 and discussed directly by Durgnat elsewhere.[8]

The references to art theory and art history in 'Fake, Fiddle' also reflect Durgnat's work at St Martin's. History of art and 'complementary studies', the curiously named subject under whose auspices Durgnat was able to teach film, had been introduced to the art schools in the early 1960s on the recommendation of the National Advisory Council on Art Education, chaired by William Coldstream. To gain the new Diploma in Art and Design, students had to devote 15 per cent of their time to academic work, in an attempt to establish parity between art school and university qualifications. As Durgnat wrote in an *Art and Artists* essay in 1969, the British educational elite – the universities, public schools and grammar schools – had historically excluded the visual arts, in part because of the puritan inheritance, and the graft did not 'take' without difficulty.

The nineteenth-century art schools and technical colleges had developed a culture of their own, defined by the 'irreconcilable co-existence' of 'utilitarianism and aestheticism', respectively the ideologies of the design and fine art camps.[9] Neither was compatible with the purpose of the British university, which was 'the creation of a caste of gentlemanly administrators'; and art students who resented their early exclusion from academic education 'on the basis of an ability to verbalise in accordance with the middle class ethos' – i.e. the eleven-plus exam – resented still more their reintroduction to this ethos under the 'Dip. AD'. The ideals of the empirical 'English craftsman syndrome', on the one hand, and unstructured 'artistic megalomania', on the other, died hard, and Durgnat's subjects were 'at best, regarded as a tolerable imposition'.

At the same time, the art schools, unlike the word-bound universities, provided an environment in which film could be studied as a graphic art. Dickinson, inspired by the examples of Sergei Eisenstein – whom he had seen lecture in London in 1929 – and Eisenstein's teacher Esther Shub, had led his seminars through films on an editing machine, shot by shot. Durgnat took up the practice in turn, possibly at St Martin's, probably at the Slade, where he taught occasionally, and certainly at the Royal College of Art. The RCA's Film and Television department, housed in the School of Graphic Design, had links with the Slade, and Durgnat had written for the school's magazine *Ark*, an important

The Essential Raymond Durgnat

forum for the theorists and practitioners of pop art. He began to teach film as part of the RCA's General Studies course in the autumn of 1967.

> Teaching in an art school then put me under heavy pressure to be graphically very specific. While teaching General Studies, I sat in on my colleagues' lectures to bootleg myself a second education. […]

> Around 1965 we started running sequences like John Barrymore's long-distance hypnosis of Trilby in Archie Mayo's *Svengali*, or the ditch-digging sequence in King Vidor's *Our Daily Bread*, and, above all, the Busby Berkeley production numbers in *42nd Street* and *Dames*. We realized that they were visual montages constructed on surprisingly Eisenstein-like principles, even when they used camera movements and in-shot action as the muscle of their 'shocks.' […]

> We ran reels 1 and 3 (in 16mm) of *The Lady From Shanghai* side by side, stopping now the left-hand reel, now the right-hand one, now both together. Just to see or rather *feel* (for it became very kinaesthetic) how the two visual configurations flicked and clicked together.[10]

This second education went directly into his *Films and Filming* series 'Images of the Mind', which began in July 1968 and ended with a long analysis of *Les Amants de Vérone*, the film which had first inspired and frustrated the grammar-schoolboy Durgnat two decades before, in July 1969. The title came from a passage in Béla Balázs's *Theory of the Film*, also quoted by Morin in *L'Homme Imaginaire*, and chiming with Durgnat's thesis, which argued that the camera could go beneath the surface of life and show the invisible by its power to lend 'a visionary and visual character and convey to the spectator that the pictures shown are not those of real objects but of images of the mind'.[11]

The first three parts are given over to what Durgnat described elsewhere as a 'little history of editing', a narrative which culminates in the 1960s with what he had in *Films and Feelings* treated as a new form of expressionism but came to call 'the impossible', meaning the free use of 'purely mental images and continuities', as found in the films of, among others, Marker, Resnais, Fellini and Losey.[12]

In writing this unabashedly teleological account, Durgnat sought to modify and synthesise two influential schools of film history. The older school, represented in Britain by such books as Paul Rotha's *The Film Till Now* (1930), Roger Manvell's *Film* (1944) and Ernest Lindgren's *The Art of the Film* (1948), defined film's essence as creative editing, or montage, and regarded Eisenstein's early work as the pinnacle of the art-form. British documentarists like Rotha saw themselves as carrying on the Soviet line. Dickinson, who had supervised the writing of Karel Reisz's 1953 book *The Technique of Film Editing*, a classic of the same genre, still cleaved to a variant of this view when he joined the Slade, telling *Film* that his lectures dealt with editing as 'the element which in my opinion takes the film as a recording instrument and makes it into a potential art'.[13]

As Dickinson soon realised, however, the montage school had exhausted itself. All sides in the auteur wars agreed that, as Penelope Houston had put it, 'most of the standard text books are useful only for those who still believe that cinema history virtually stops with *Blackmail* and *The Blue Angel*', both early sound films.[14] Bazin's 'The Evolution of Film Language', which appeared in two English translations in 1967–8, propounded an alternative history based on his realist conception of the photographic image, effacing the difference between silent and sound eras. Bazin traced a tradition through Von Stroheim, Renoir and Welles to Italian neo-realism, standing 'in contrast to previous forms of cinematic realism by its elimination of any expressionism and especially by the total absence of effects obtained by editing'.[15]

Apart from his remarks in 'Fake, Fiddle', Durgnat had cast doubt on Bazin's idea that the use of deep focus and composition in depth, techniques associated with Welles and Wyler, 'means that the spectator's relationship with the image is nearer to that which he has with reality', in the first part of his thesis.[16] Conversely, 'Fake, Fiddle' subtly diverges from one of montage theory's founding texts, Pudovkin's *Film Technique*, the main source of the famous 'Kuleshov experiment', first published in 1929. While Durgnat cited the experiment, he disagreed with Pudovkin's assertion that the photographic image was meaningless 'raw material'[17] before its editing into sequence – an assertion that helped sustain the 'prejudice against the "pictorial" element' which Durgnat decried both in Pudovkin's British disciples and in Bazin.[18]

Along similar lines, Durgnat wrote in the fifth part of 'Images of the Mind' that the 'Russian "classics" of film theory were written before gestalt psychology had made its impact on aesthetics, and stand up to modern research as badly as to film practice'.[19] The series is, however, largely a vindication of Eisensteinian intellectual montage, which Durgnat treats as the ultimate origin of the cinema of 'purely mental images and continu-ities' which blossomed in the 'impossible' 1960s. Marking a partial détente with the docu-mentary movement, he describes intellectual montage's 'insidious' survival after the coming of sound in the form of the essay-film.[20] More contentiously, he presents montage as the aesthetic principle of the very films which Bazin had claimed for his own 'diametrically opposed' tradition, including Welles's, Wyler's and Visconti's.

In making this latter argument, Durgnat draws on Eisenstein's notion of 'montage-within-the-image'. As Eisenstein had himself said in 'Methods of Montage', an essay based on the lectures Dickinson had attended in 1929, this notion entailed the 'the appreciation of montage-construction from a "pictorial" point of view'.[21]

Durgnat gives a significant place in his 'little history' to one of his teacher's last films, *Overture*, which Dickinson made to mark the tenth anniversary of the Universal Declaration of Human Rights in 1958, and which he himself described as firmly in the Soviet tradition. Dickinson had, however, more than kept up with his students in their departure from montage-school orthodoxy. In 1963 he gave a lecture, later published in *Films and Filming*, repudiating his earlier remarks on editing and clearly demonstrating the influence of Bazin. Dickinson now believed that 'the widening of the screen and the restoration of deep focus' had inaugurated a new era.[22] 'Montage is no longer the heart and soul of cinema,' he went on: 'it is a valuable element: you can still enrich cinema by understanding the dynamics of editing. But it is no longer the dominant element.'

Yet more strikingly, he argued that such new-era films as Antonioni's *Le Amiche* (1955), slow even for its period, nonetheless exhibited 'a deep appreciation of the montage prin-ciple [...] Selection, timing and emphasis, those three assets of montage, are injected on the floor with the help of the increasing fluidity of the camera.'[23] Dickinson later oversaw the addition of a new section to *The Technique of Film Editing*, written by Gavin Millar, which he regarded as having superseded the original. The new edition appeared, with comments by Dickinson including the characterisation of Eisenstein's *October* (1928) as 'one of the milch cows of the *nouvelle vague*', in 1968.[24] Meanwhile the 'impossible' films Durgnat championed were often included in Dickinson's programmes. 'Images of the Mind' is, among other things, an expression of the Slade Film Department at its zenith.

The Essential Raymond Durgnat

3.1 FAKE, FIDDLE AND THE PHOTOGRAPHIC ARTS

THE CINEMA is often supposed to have a peculiar power of compelling conviction, and this power is frequently attributed to photographic realism. In the course of an interesting piece in *The Twentieth Century*,[1] Michael Elster puts the argument thus:

> The photograph can be the most perfect mimetic image that we are capable of producing. Despite common knowledge to the contrary, the proposition that 'the camera can't lie' has a most strong hold on our minds. We may have seen innumerable examples of trick photography, may have been let into the secrets of the film studio; nevertheless this prejudice remains. It may be that the first knowledge most of us have of photography comes via an explanation of the box camera, in which what is outside the box is transferred, whole and upside down, to the inside of the box by two crossed rays. Whatever is outside must arrive intact inside. Whatever the basis of this prejudice, it surely exists, and just as surely bestows a strong *presumption of reality* on the cinema image. The actor portraying a part on the screen is as truly a part of cinema reality as we are of the reality which the 'Brownie' has transferred to the photo album. This 'belief' in what occurs on the screen as 'real', however much it was staged in a studio, gives to cinema its proverbial power to move and to impress.

In *The Modern Movement in Art*[2] R. H. Wilenski, concerned with underlining the painter's artistic ascendancy over the photographer, writes:

> There are still many people who imagine that the camera can record the forms of physical objects and concrete things and the formal relationships of such objects and things to one another. Both these … activities are in point of fact beyond the camera's powers …. The camera records degrees of light, obstructions to light, reflections of light and reflections of light and shade. It cannot record a house, a tree or a man. It can only record the momentary effects and degrees of light as affected by such physical objects or concrete things. Its records moreover are determined by two accidental physical factors – its own physical position at the moment of exposure, and the angle and degree of the light … but … it cannot record the forms of physical objects or concrete things. …

In other words the common-or-garden black-and-white snapshot is, *vis-à-vis* the 'real' world, deficient in colour and therefore also in texture, in three-dimensional depth and therefore also in volume and mass. Its very fidelity to light-and-shade deprives it of fidelity to form. Thus, in relation to objects-in-themselves, it is at least as much an abstraction as paint-on-paper; while its unselective passivity to light renders it far less easily vivid than painting in suggesting these 'non-photographic' qualities. Wilenski concedes that in its passivity to light 'the human eye considered as a lens records in very much the same way as the lens of the camera'. (Shades of the old art-school dogma – 'there are no lines in nature'?) Nevertheless: 'it was because the camera's records corresponded largely to the purely mechanical part of the average human vision that, when photographs first appeared, the average human being recognized them as records of his own familiar experience and called them for that reason true'. Further, he goes on to contrast (*a*) the purely 'mechanical', or physiological, aspect of human vision, to which the camera corresponds, with (*b*) the psychological selection and emphasis that renders our seeing subjective and turns it into 'perception', with its sense of contour lines, its 'deductive' sense of objects-in-themselves, and so on. To this interpretative, creative aspect of vision the camera, he claims, has no access. It can neither comment nor select. Thus photography renders neither the world-in-itself nor our significant experience of it. It can never be an art. 'The so-called "artistic" photographers of the present day do not realize the character or significance of the camera's records. They are so incurably stupid that they will not leave the camera to do its business; they want it to do more than it can and only succeed in making it do less. "Artistic" photographers fake and fiddle with their negatives and prints and produce hybrid abominations that are not true photographs and not works of art.'

Wilenski seems to me right to attribute 'the basis of this prejudice' to a subjective 'sensation' of reality. Yet I believe it can more exactly be attributed to mutual reinforcement among several factors.

1. Certainly the camera is 'less selective' than the painter. Therefore the spectator, confronted by a photograph, performs upon it the same selective process that he performs when confronted with reality; in consequence it 'feels like' reality. For example, rather than deducing objects from contour lines he 'deduces' contour lines from light.

The photograph's lack of colour may seem as shrieking a distortion of reality as, say, Picasso's infidelities to the human form. But M. D. Vernon makes a significant point in The Psychology of Perception:[3] 'Several experiments have been carried out to discover whether children of various ages seem to attach more importance to the shape or to the colours of objects ....' These experiments, though inconclusive, tend to lend support to 'the view that young children pay comparatively little attention to colour as such when they are concerned in the normal everyday life situation of identifying and reacting to things'. In The Art of Color[4] Johannes Itten suggests that colour is particularly bound up with the emotions. The association of shape with 'identifying and reacting to things' and colour with emotion would correspond to an association even of black-and-white photography with 'reality'. Possibly shape is associated with objects because it is connected with tactile experience (touching, feeling) and with practical action (bumping into, grabbing hold of). We differentiate things by their shapes (even when that shape is deduced from colour), whereas colour is relatively generalized (many things are blue) and fickle (it changes according to the light). Possibly, too, it is because colour 'floats' with relation to objects that it can acquire, as it were, an emotional intensity; it is less burdened with function, already half-way to 'abstraction'. This is, of course, in no way to diminish the emotional connotations of shapes, which, as Vernon points out, children also feel very strongly. Certainly the photograph is in fact inexact about 'true' shape, revealing it only through the pattern of light-and-shade. But we apply to the photograph the same perceptual mechanism which makes for 'constancy of form' in responding to reality. And photographs whose light-and-shade patterns seriously confuse shape get thrown away or used only as 'puzzle' pictures. The camera may be unable to select, but the cameraman is quite capable of selecting what he'll use and what he won't.

2. The camera's impersonality contributes to the subjective sensation of reality. If twelve people with identical equipment photograph a subject from an identical viewpoint, the resultant photographs will resemble one another far more closely than if twelve people with identical equipment sketch or paint it from an identical viewpoint.

The photographs will vary as to tonalities and focuses, but each artist will indicate shape, shadow, texture and so on in different ways, even if 'only' in the calligraphy of their lines. The photograph 'loses' many qualities but there is less 'personal addition'. This may or may not constitute a limitation on the camera's artistic possibilities, but it contributes vastly to the spectator's feeling of reality – of, in fact, the object-in-itself. No 'personal interpretation' interposes itself.

3. To people brought up on photographs the woodcuts of Thomas Bewick have at first a grim, dark, forbidding appearance. Such people have to overcome the appearance of the *medium* before they can read the *picture*. The photograph is not only impersonal, but so cheap and convenient that we are all used to reading reality through it. Sheer weight of numbers has rendered the particular conventions of photography the most transparent to reality – indeed, I would venture to suggest that we are only now at the point when colour photographs are beginning to feel more realistic than black-and-white photographs. The sheer ubiquity of the photographic convention has, I suspect, made many quite realistic sketches, paintings, etc., seem less realistic to us than they would have done to people who had seen few photographs. The more of those cheap Victorian steel-engravings I see the more they carry for me a 'presumption of reality', that is, the more 'transparent' the medium becomes.

4. Michael Elster's flurry of bad suggestions as to why the photograph seems real obscures one very good one. Let's try and clear away these points:

(*a*) Is it still true that people believe the camera cannot lie? I doubt it. Maybe they did in the early days of photography, when double exposures convinced even the thoughtful that 'spirits' were surrounding them; but surely the consequent debates, the innumerable examples of trick photography in still and motion pictures, have done their work.
(*b*) The first knowledge most of us have of photography is not an explanation of its principles but looking at photographs. The (purely intellectual) impact of diagrams of light rays would in any case have been cancelled out by explanations of camera-tricks.

But Mr. Elster's point about our experience of the Box Brownie leads to an important one. The snapshot depends on the existence of a reality to record. We all know photographs can be faked. But we also know, since we've posed for them ourselves, that they usually aren't. On the other hand we know similarly that it's very easy to produce a sketch from memory or imagination or a blend of both. There, 'faking' is so easy that we have to spend years learning to draw accurately. The sensitive artist can hardly bear not to fake. Even in naturalistic drawings he almost unconsciously edits, arranges, improves, 'strengthens' the power-station or moves it so that it balances the tug, and so on. This 'interpretation' has nothing to do with our 'vision'; it is purely formal, resulting from our feelings about both the object and the drawing. In fact by the time the artist has drawn the tug it's elsewhere. Certainly photography was once upon a time so primitive that Paris streets always seem deserted – the traffic and passers-by left no impression on the photographic plate. Even so what struck people was not what the camera didn't record, but what it did. And the need for the sitter to 'watch the birdie' only emphasized the closeness of reality and photography.

Today, still, the photographer's work depends rather more than the artist's on creating or physically modifying the reality which he intends to represent. Certainly the camera cannot comment or select (neither can a paint-brush); but a cameraman can. With lenses, filters, lights, exposures and choice of angle, he can mould what he sees until the play of light reveals the facets and relations he wishes us to see. He can move some way into the artist's perceptual territory. He can work intensively on the negative and the print – work of which Wilenski's 'fake and fiddle' is as gross a misdescription as 'always scribble, scribble, scribble, eh, Mr. Gibbon?' I doubt whether, for example, Man Ray and Moholy-Nagy are 'incurably stupid'. In other words the 'passive' part of photography is often only one phase in a longer process. The photographer selects, say, a face; he walks round it until his angle shows the sunlight moulding the cheekbone; he may set up a regular crossfire of interpretative lighting. He works on the subject rather than on the canvas. He 'stages' a work of art, and then photographs that. Movies are made in a *studio* for this very reason. After the photograph comes the 'fake and fiddle' – and this whole series of processes allows for a great deal of selection, creation and comment.

The principal limit at the moment is the relative difficulty of 'faking and fiddling' with very small parts of the photographic surface – corresponding to, say, brush strokes, or a nervous calligraphy. It is in consequence fair to grant that the photographer is far from equalling the artist in what we might call 'perceptual variation'. He can be as free as the painter over large areas, but he hasn't yet quite reached an interpretative 'pointillisme'. He is at a point, as it were, where brush strokes are meaningless and no photographic impression has yet come to replace the sense of reality-in-itself by 'perceptual realism'. On the other hand he can produce abstracts and semi-abstracts. His inferiority, however important, exists over a limited sector, and even there we seem to be on the verge of break-through. Paradoxically, as we do break through such photographs will have sacrificed their advantages over painting – convenience, ready acceptance by the untrained masses and transparency to the presence of 'reality', that is of the subject-in-itself. Already the more obtrusive 'faking and fiddling' becomes (as with Ray and Moholy-Nagy) the more the spectator feels himself confronted with a canvas rather than a window, with a piece of self-expression to be treated 'like' a painting. Such photographs have sacrificed believability, and are felt to be as 'other' to any reality which may dimly appear through them as some Impressionist paintings. They lose on the roundabouts what they make up on the swings.

At this stage it becomes sensible to call into question the existence of any real difference between the two media – there is painting on canvas and painting on emulsions. Conversely, a painter who sets his mind to it can match the *trompe-l'œil* effects of the best colour photographs. But precisely because of its 'perceptual poverty' photography has retained what many painters have willingly – too willingly? – sacrificed: the presence, the weight of reality-in-itself. Many creative photographs exploit expressive or formal effects only to the point where the photograph still retains transparency to reality. From another angle, the painter's 'interpretation', his evidence of mental processes whether perceptual (Impressionism), conceptual (Cubism) or emotional (Expressionism), often 'dissolves' the subject-in-itself into 'the artist's mind'. 'In itself' means not only its physical otherness but the values and associations which culturally are commonly conceded to inhere in it. Popularizers of Picasso often point out that the distortions in *Guernica* are matched by distortions in American comic-strips – say Al Capp's *Li'l Abner* – in newspaper caricatures and so on. The fact remains that the greater public is baffled by Picasso's but spontaneously accepts and enjoys Al Capp's. These, like de Gaulle's giraffe-size neck, Bristow's two-eyes-in-one-profile, or the fashion-plate mannequin's long legs and huge eyes correspond to ideas and attitudes with which they are familiar, and so set off intuitive responses. Relative to photography the loss in realism is offset by the gain in expressiveness – most photographs of de Gaulle are just interesting, but a good caricature has you laughing and looking twice. The more sophisticated and complex distortions of Picasso are part of a formal game and a perceptual convention with which the mass audience is unfamiliar. The texture of distortions is so rich that no salient points emerge for the audience to seize on. The public is often accused of being so stupid as to insist on the most slavish fidelity to 'photographic' realism. I doubt whether this is so: what it wants is distortions for which it can intuitively feel an expressive correlative. Many colour photographs provide this, mingling a small degree of 'interpretation' (mood, colour used abstractly, formal satisfactions) with the 'weight' of the subject-in-itself. They may be minor works of art, but *pace* Wilenski even minor works of art are works of art. Minor too are those contemporary paintings which the greater public can easily assimilate. Again, the contrast is not one of media. It is the old problem of cultural training. Many of the easily approachable artists of our time work within what we may call the 'caricatural' tradition; they push cartoon-techniques to the point of seriousness or horror. One thinks of Steinberg, Siné, Topor.

A major problem for the 98 per cent of the population who have had virtually no effective education in the visual arts is that on the one hand most of the great 'realistic' paintings in the galleries seem remote because their reality-in-itself is remote (dresses, furnishings, the personal 'style' and implied values of the people, action or objects selected). True, there is the common ground of universal humanity; but people today are not universal humanists and can only grope their way towards that common ground, glimpsing, ignoring, perhaps hating, many aspects of it, because they can see it only through the prism of contemporary culture (which, like all cultures, limits, conceals, interprets, rejects, innumerable human possibilities). The painting's reality-in-itself has only the most muffled resonance. The fatness of Rubens's women is almost as off-putting to our 98 per cent as is the Balinese ideal beauty who was so corpulent she couldn't walk. Only the *occasional* painting strikes through from the past. (*The Death of Procris*, in the National Gallery, for example, is highly approachable.) On the other hand much modern painting, while topical in reference, is concerned with relatively recondite conceptual points which cannot reasonably be expected to interest other than *aficionados*; we can't all spend much of our time looking at ourselves looking. Other painters express contemporary attitudes and experiences, as, for example, Picasso, Bacon and Ben Nicholson, but their styles employ idioms that are to all intents and purposes undecipherable by the uninitiated. When so much celebrated painting becomes obscure then the social channels of communication wither, and those few paintings which could directly appeal to the public aren't brought to its attention or suffer from an *aura* of obscurity. So people lose the knack of exploring paintings, of discovering their configurations and relating them to resonant experience.

Nonetheless the relative facility of drawn distortion gives even the popular artist an important advantage over the photographer. Mass-circulation Italian magazines still carry front-page drawings of news items whose dramatic quality the photographer would find it hard to equal. The overall tendency in popular magazines is to illustrate fact by photographs, fiction by drawings or paintings. Comic strips are occasionally told in photographs, but mainly in drawings (even when they are 'serious' comic strips). It's as if the artist's artificiality suggests: 'We are now in the land of imagination ….' Similarly the hand-made impression of drawings confers a quality of ceremony lacking from even the most opulent colour photograph. It's not entirely for economic reasons that one speaks of 'having a picture taken' but of 'commissioning' a painting. In this sense the artist's medium, with its sense of occasion, is more – not less – emotional than the photographer's.

It is paradoxical that of modern painters so 'obscure' an artist as Salvador Dali should be among those who have the most direct and urgent impact, at least on the middlebrow. The nightmare quality of his paintings is decipherable irrespective of the formal nuances that at best escape and at worse confuse the middlebrow, while his *trompe-l'œil* confers on his subjects a quality of reality-in-itself rivalling the most succulent colour-photography. It may be unreal to have a bicycle in the desert, but it's a bicycle-type bicycle and a desert-type desert and the collision of the two is immediately recognizable as an impossible reality, that is as a dream-reality, with which we are all familiar and which since Freud we admit as significant. In a paradoxical way the *trompe-l'œil* fantasy of Dali and Magritte abides by the rules of nuanced realism, of culturally agreed associations to objects. It retains what the painterly purist may dismiss as anecdotal interest or literary values. But it's a queer anecdote that has no story and a peculiar form of literature that has no words, and I suspect that much of what is scorned in painting as 'literary' can't really be defined as literary at all. For literature has no particular primacy of or monopoly on the exploitation of ideas and emotion; verbal description of, say, a distressed man running is no more final than a picture of a distressed man running. To say that the general public wants literary values from art is really a misleading way of saying that it wants something like resonant experience. And while any artist is perfectly within his rights in saying that for him resonant experience is of no interest at all, it is still true that much art, from religious paintings to Rembrandt's flayed ox, is impoverished by such limitations. Surely the game of art is best played by those rules that maximize its richness and range of interest rather than by minimizing them.

If we admit resonant experience as a legitimate component of pictorial arts, then the photograph's special sphere of competence becomes clearer. More strongly than much painting it transmits reality-in-itself. This transmission can combine with the limitations of the medium to produce a peculiar heightening. The photographs of the American Civil War have the beauty they do because the soldiers, posed, are 'frozen'; there is a strange effect of 'framing', of reverence for these people *as themselves*. They have an elegiac quality. Van Deren Coke offers a striking example in his *The Painter and the Photograph*[5]. He juxtaposes a photograph by Lee Miller of bodies piled on a floor in Buchenwald, and a painting, *Floor of Buchenwald No. 1* (1957), by Rico Lebrun, based on that photograph. Lebrun, a sincere and intelligent painter, has missed over and over again the telling details recorded by the camera's 'passive' eye and substituted conventions of form, of anatomy, of composition. Almost[*] involuntarily he has brought compositional order into a heap of bodies whose horrid eloquence lay precisely in the 'asymmetrical' clutter of thrown-back heads. The photograph reveals that thighs have become thinner than calves, shows the clumsiness of home-made wrappings, stresses the hard pebbles on which the bodies lie. The painter has fattened the thighs, has given the curve of instep a certain grace instead of horrid unnaturalness, has invented neat stitchings which turn the rough wrapping into a conventionalized tramp's patchwork, has lost the pebbles in vague scribbles. Most insensitive of all, he has enclosed the heap of bodies in a tidy pattern of abstract shapes. The photograph lets the heap of bodies bleed off one corner of the frame, so that we sense that this is only part of a huger, an infinite horror.

* For the following comparison I am endebted to Dr. Aaron Sharf.

Lebrun is a sensitive painter. But in his involuntary — and in this case 'involuntary' means mechanical — concern for 'pure form', in his *mechanical* reliance on a certain idiom, he has in fact become blind not to the photograph merely, but to reality. The photographer was not blind. However passive the camera, the photographer chose this 'detail', this angle, this exposure (a wrong exposure would have lost the textural qualities), this composition, this clipping of the frame. The photographer has seen, and shows us, Buchenwald. The painter shows us only a painting: rhetoric. I suggest we can go further. As soon as Lebrun strayed from the idiom of 'nuanced realism' — in which the reality-in-itself is interpreted so subtly that it feels present in the picture — he lost the possibility of bringing the full weight of suffering into the picture. For the horror of this picture was then, obviously, a matter of manipulating lines and forms. He can paraphrase the effect by the formal means Picasso uses for *Guernica* — but this is a paraphrase, rather than looking at reality. And in this sphere the photographer has a head start — provided he can find, or create for himself (*e.g.* in a film studio), an expressive subject.

What discourages the greater public about painting is not any lack of realism but simply the *extent to which* painters obfuscate reality-in-itself by perceptual or conceptual notations, or by formal requirements. Vermeer managed unobtrusively what Bratby manages obtrusively. As T. S. Eliot said, what makes you immortal is what you do behind the public's back — though this doesn't mean that what the public sees isn't art. Immortality is only one way of being alive, and the 'immortality' public is only another sort of public which often doesn't see what the contemporary public sees — which is why we need footnotes, background studies and so on. The greater public wants reality-in-itself and 'style' to compromise and interweave; and they become confused or resentful, as if in the presence of the unreasonably arbitrary, when 'style' begins to obliterate rather than modify reality-in-itself. To put it in another, looser way: if I had the job of popularizing painting, I should begin with certain Expressionists whose work isn't alien to the caricatural tradition; with apparent realists, like Tintoretto, whose 'zoom-lens' perspectives are admirable examples of integrating reality and style; with painters who, like Turner, dissolve objects, but in the interests of atmospheric realism; with painters who work 'through' the human face, body and personality; and with painters of 'dream' fantasy (Fuseli, Redon, Delvaux) rather than with perceptual or conceptual or semi-abstract painters. Other criteria would apply but they are irrelevant to my main point here, which is that it is misleading to oppose painting to photography as if they were ineradicably different genres, like mammals and reptiles. At worst one might oppose them as one might oppose lions to tigers — for here be tigons and ligers. Individual artists and photographers roam the same terrain and hunt the same prey. The painter can match the photographer's *trompe-l'œil* if he wants to (and has the skill). The photographer can produce his distortions and perceptual-conceptual notations if he wants to (and has the skill). For example, one might challenge the conceptual realism of Duchamp's nude descending her staircase by superimposing multiple viewpoints of a set of equivalent photographs upon each other. The film *Geography of the Body* (in effect a series of stills) re-interprets the female nude by extreme close-ups which give it an alien concreteness, and amount to an Expressionist re-interpretation (it becomes a half-hideous, half-fascinating landscape). Reality-in-itself remains. Abstracts produced from emulsions may well be indistinguishable from abstracts produced by brushing, spraying or other processes. In this case photograph and painting are of course equally 'unbelievable', and it's arguable that the flip elegance of colour supplement photography is beginning to be felt as 'interpretative', as a kind of romantic glow in which reality-in-itself is losing its full force, that it is, in fact, the photographic equivalent of 'refined' painting. Our tigons and ligers include, of course, those 'collages' in which painting and photographs are combined. But simply to mingle them is not to sit safely on both stools at once. Into his painting *French Officials Observing Enemy Movements* (1915),[6] the Futurist Carlo Carra inserts a patch of photograph; outnumbered as it is, the photograph can impose no sense of reality-in-itself but can draw attention only to its own sore-thumb texture. But in his album of 'collages', *La Septième Face du Dé*,[7] Georges Hugnet so mingles steel-engravings and photographic details as to create a fascinating warp-and-woof of reality-in-itself and the arbitrary. Each image is a different case. In a photo-collage by Aaron Scharf[8] cutting and placing turns a rose-window into the eye of a rhinoceros; the shock of confrontation would be far smaller without photographic 'believability'. Simply by painting over photographs it is possible to add painterly nuance at its best without losing too much in the way of photographic sense of reality. As usual the future belongs to mongrels; pedigrees have mainly their past. Every year fewer students think of themselves as painters only; their interest and work is weakening boundaries between the genres. Similarly paintings are sprouting struts and pegs and becoming sculptures. The theatre is becoming less textbound and more cinematographic; the film maker is using his increasingly flexible and sensitive cameras less like a 'window in all four walls' and more like a novelist's 'mind's eye'. In a hundred years' time perhaps all the media will be liveliest in what are now no-man's-lands and intermediate territories. Camera and brush will seem simply two tools in the visual tool-kit, to be used separately or together as appropriate to the particular job in hand. Maybe most photography will still be prose to most painting's poetry. But that still won't prove that prose isn't literature.

Meanwhile photography, with its 'nuanced realism' and its contemporary themes, has maintained a genuine contact with the middle- and low-brow. This is not to say that most photographs are inspected as if they were canvases. Often it's a case of look at the photograph, note the message, receive a feeling and – on to the next photograph. It may be maintained that if you don't keep it, it isn't art. The difficulty with this argument is that then neither the theatre nor the ballet become art forms until the invention of cinematography, and until the gramophone record music knew the song but not the singer. Let us amend it to: 'if you don't wish you could keep undergoing it again, it isn't art'. By this definition, certainly, most photographs aren't art. But it also follows that most paintings aren't art; indeed most works of art aren't art. Personally I find that there are films and plays and novels and pieces of music which I don't particularly want to turn to again – I feel I have got their message; but nonetheless I have to concede that they had a substantial effect on me, not simply a temporary emotional effect but something like a revelation of my inner and the outer worlds. And in my thinking about the world they keep recurring as landmarks and guides. If that isn't art, what is?

The arguments brought against photography's status as an art on the grounds of the camera's 'passivity' have, of course, also been used against the cinema. Here similar rejoinders apply. In fact the cinema illustrates even more clearly than still photography one particular corollary of the photographer's ability to select. The famous rejoinder is cited in Pudovkin's *Film Technique*[9]:

> Kuleshov and I made an interesting experiment. We took from some film or other several close-ups of the well-known actor Mosjukhin. We chose close-ups which were static and which did not express any feeling at all – quiet close-ups. We joined these close-ups,

which were all similar, with other bits of film in three different combinations. In the first combination the close-up of Mosjukhin was immediately followed by a shot of a plate of soup standing on a table. It was obvious and certain that Mosjukhin was looking at this soup. In the second combination the face of Mosjukhin was joined to shots showing a coffin in which lay a dead woman. In the third the close-up was followed by a shot of a little girl playing with a funny toy bear. [And in a fourth, not mentioned by Pudovkin here, the close-up was followed by a shot of a nude woman.] When we showed the three combinations to an audience which had not been let into the secret the result was terrific. The public raved about the acting of the artist. They pointed out the heavy pensiveness of his mood over the forgotten soup, were touched and moved by the deep sorrow with which he looked on the dead woman, and admired the light, happy smile with which he surveyed the girl at play. But we knew that in all three cases the face was exactly the same.

In other words the juxtaposition of two photographs creates in the spectator's mind a series of implications, an apparent reality, altogether different from what the camera records. What goes for two photographs goes also for two elements in a photograph. When a movie depicts a character against, or enwrapped in, a picturesque background, the background is not merely a 'place'; it is also simply by juxtaposition – or rather by what the mind does with juxtapositions – the character's mood, or a symbol about him. Many script writers choose their settings entirely in terms of 'mood', or other symbolism. In Orson Welles's *The Lady From Shanghai* the lovers meet in an aquarium and kiss in the darkness, amidst which we see brightly lit tanks containing sharks, an octopus and so on. The setting is more even than an *objet trouvé* – it is a Symbolist poem, recalling the imagery

The Lady from Shanghai (1947)

of Lautréamont's *Les Chants de Maldoror*. Its meaning is further inflected by plastic qualities. The lovers' faces are fitfully illumined by the fluctuating glimmer of lit water, the evil fish are silhouettes, huge in close-up, moving across the screen and blotting out the water-light. Welles *might* have shown the lovers in silhouette, and stressed the texture of sharkskin and sucker – or chosen any number of variations in relative proportion, position or texture, or combination of variations – each constituting a different experience, a different scene. And these differences arise less from any difference in literary or anecdotal interest than from the purely visual changes in texture, rhythm, mass, composition and so on. Hence a documentary film – which works entirely from actual, observed reality – can be as creative as the studio-made film, where the director constructs his own work-of-art to record. Selection = creation. So true is this that it is now usual for films to marry a *created* reality (actors, dialogue, etc.) with a *selected* pseudo-reality (location photography). It is arguable that the photograph finds its true fulfilment in cine-photography. Certainly the natural equivalent to the canvas in terms of emotional weight is the movie sequence – a set of images linked in space and time instead of merely space, with actual movement to set against implied movement and with a musical and developmental structure rather than a pictorial and spatial one.

Michael Elster is concerned with explaining why, if photographs are so realistic, the emotional effect of the cinema isn't overwhelming, why there is a 'second effect, disassociation from cinema experience...'.

> Cinema experience strikes one as being very ephemeral. Here is the contradiction, the impression of reality, the ephemerality of the experience. Ephemeral in the sense that little connection is felt, little relevance seen, between film reality and the outside world .... Separation between audience and performer in the cinema is complete, both mechanically, and, as I hope to show, psychologically ... on the screen we are often transported to environments so strange that, in the absence of a human performer to bridge the gap, no similarity can be found at all. It is this failure by human means that gives the cinema experience, for all its compelling reality, its ephemeral character.

The argument is attractive: the screen reality is so real that it excludes us, and when we emerge from it we exclude it. Two self-contained worlds touch briefly, and go their separate ways. Unfortunately Kuleshov's experience demonstrates that neither the film's reality nor the spectator's is self-contained. Every film is in itself entirely meaningless, just as every novel, every poem, is in itself entirely meaningless; the connexion between the symbols, the elements of thought, can be made only by the spectator. Film and spectator are intimately intertwined; it's a matter of common everyday experience that spectators become passionately involved in films, that they laugh, weep, scream, sweat; and that (as I've confessed to doing earlier) they use films as reference-points for their thinking about the world. I do it *via* Antonioni, Miss Bloggs may do it by joining the Greta Garbo fan club; but both of us are contacting the film *via* emotional resonance. And it's this resonance which constitutes the contact; never realism *per se*. Documentaries may be as realistic as possible in every possible way, and still leave every possible spectator bored stiff; a cartoon film, or a film as patently artificial as *The Cabinet of Dr. Caligari*, may hold him utterly convinced and engrossed. Realism is only one way of arriving at this common experience; the camera is a convenience, and very far from being in itself an emotional Sunday punch. I claim to be a cinema-lover, but I would find 99 per cent of movies inexpressibly tedious.

The Essential Raymond Durgnat

What matters is the 1 per cent (which doesn't lead me to puritanical severity of judgement; I don't mind if your 1 per cent is quite different from my 1 per cent).

Mr. Elster continues:

> The ability to use the camera as a subjective eye, to see the world from a rocket cone, or through the eye of a fly as it were, provided a good peepshow, no more …. All visual tricks and distortions belong to this genre, their effect being to create dirty images. That is to say, images exhibiting the strain, and demanding from the audience the mental contortions of pornographic images.

At this point one may wonder why Mr. Elster should want to compare a striking cinematographic viewpoint with a pornographic image. For what, after all, is so obscene about those newsreel shots of the globe seen from the stratosphere? What Mr. Elster calls strain and contortions I find exhilarating, and what he calls dirty seems to me beautiful. Nor are such shots typical of the cinema's idiom. By and large the commercial cinema makes very little use of 'visual tricks and distortions'. It is extremely conservative and traditional in its determination to preserve prosaic solidity. It would seem that what Mr. Elster calls 'visual tricks and distortions' are in fact all the non-realistic elements of the cinema, everything that goes to create a subjective reality: the angling of shots, the change of viewpoint as shots follow one another across the screen, rapid cutting, camera movements, montage sequences, in fact all those points which textbooks of film appreciation rightly teach us to regard as the cinema's very language, its claim to being comprehensible at all. It would be just as plausible to speak of the 'tricks and distortions … dirty images … strain … mental contortions … pornography' of El Greco, Modigliani, Expressionism, analytical Cubism, Impressionism.

Yet there is a valuable grain of truth in his remarks. His comparison is with the theatre. Here the stars – and all performers by their pre-eminence, by the attention concentrated on them, are in a sense stars – and the characters as incarnated by them – are here, and here alone, in flesh and blood. The stage is only a space, a few indicated effects around human figures. Empty, the stage space is only a presage, a 'tuning up'. The principal weight of emotion is mediated to us through the human figure; we are anchored to the actor's presence, pace and rhythm, his physical constancy and steadiness, from which nothing seriously distracts us. Neo-classical theories about the unities of space, time and action may have been pedantic, but they do have a good hard nub of truth in this 'constancy of physical presence'. (However, subtle outrages against this constancy may actually enhance it. For example, the compression of dramatic narrative against real conversational pace, creating a sense of heightened urgency and significance, and together with their status as the focus of all our attention, turning the stage characters into heroes, demigods, gifted with a divine volatility.) The cinema's advantages over the theatre are familiar enough – its vastly superior spatio-temporal mobility, its battery of close-ups, mid-shots, long-shots and varying angles to emphasize various aspects of a relationship (or quickly establish different relationships), the whole sphere of its pictoriality and musicality. But we can express these advantages as weaknesses. It's because the merely photographic presence of the actors is rather weaker than their unique, physical presence that the camera has to keep punching and weaving and ducking. Certainly we can fill the screen with a dazzling succession of symbols, objects and vistas, but by so doing we also bring about a kind of devaluation. To follow a mile-long shot of thousands of toiling Israelites by a big close-up of the Pharaoh's face, and then *vice versa*, is to devalue both. We can apply something like Le Corbusier's idea of a Modulor. The stage offers a steadier identification with *this* person at *this* time; intensity is created and steadily maintained. The more mobile the cinema becomes, the more this intensity is lost. There is the added interest of landscapes and quick temporal changes, but they too lose the unity. The close-up is only a deliberate equivalent of a process which the theatre spectator performs naturally and unconsciously (and is, in fact, becoming rarer as photographic quality improves). The cinema may be 'supermobile theatre' but only at the expense of being 'splintered theatre'. Each shot disrupts, replaces, cancels out its predecessor. Of course by slowing down its pace and renouncing its fluidity the cinema can acquire something like a theatrical intensity. The longest static take in cinema history is in Welles's *The Magnificent Ambersons*, and runs ten minutes – time enough only for a pretty shortish theatrical scene; in fact with scenes of this length one begins to talk about a play being 'cinematic' in conception. And films which maintain a theatrical 'intensity of presence' can do so only by renouncing the cinema's other possibilities.

The more closely one looks at the cinema's much-vaunted 'realism' the more it dissolves – or rather the more its weaknesses can be seen to match its strengths. The cinema's unprecedented popularity is not, I suggest, due to any intrinsically greater massiveness of impact, but simply to the fact that it requires less training in its 'literacy' than any other art form. It presents its images to the eye just as the mind presents images to the mind's eye. Its narrative form is exactly that of the dream. Hence the ease with which anyone understands its narrative ellipses, its temporo-spatial jumps, its sequences of short scenes. To be popular films do need a linking idea (usually narrative). Only *avant-garde* minorities like the dream-like film; the popular film may have dream elements and overtones but these must be rationalized into a story. In its mind's-eye continuity the film is surpassed only by literature – which requires an understanding of the particular language and perhaps a high degree of literacy; in fact stream-of-consciousness novels are relatively sophisticated. That the camera bestows photographic realism on the cinema's mind's-eye continuity is in a sense entirely accidental. The cinema is exciting not because it is more realistic but because it offers a *mental* continuity. And the link again is the narrative, the idea, that is *resonance of experience*. Its basic affinity with audiences is a subjective one.

By way of coda let us glance at some of the unreal elements in the cinema's idiom.

1. The director can split the screen and show two widely separated actions side by side – Abel Gance used three simultaneous images for epic effect in his *Napoleon* (1927) and Claude Autant-Lara split his Cinemascope image into two for *Construire Un Feu* (1930). The split-screen was used to put two lonely and separated people in their separate rooms ironically side by side in Robert Wise's *Two For The Seesaw* (1962).

2. The flashback is a repudiation of realism. We are now watching what happened twenty years before what was happening a moment ago.

3. The above effects may be combined. Alf Sjoberg shows us Miss Julie aged twenty in the foreground, staring into the fire and remembering, while Miss Julie aged eight opens the door and tiptoes into the room – being thought, but just as real as the thinker.

4. Camera movements may contribute powerfully to the emotional movement of a scene. In the post-war reunion of Truffaut's *Jules et Jim* (1962) the camera shifts restlessly from one character to another; in this dramatic context its ceaseless, fidgety movements lyricize the feeling behind the words of Jeanne Moreau's song:

Chaqu'un pour soi, et hop! parti,
C'est le tourbillon de la vie.

In Ophuls's *La Ronde* (1950) and *Madame De* (1953), however, the camera moves steadily, suavely, through stuffy Victorian décor, releasing the emotional energy compressed by it. But there is no camera *in the picture*.

5. Background music may be out of fashion among critics because of its abuse by Hollywood vulgarians, but its emotional contribution to films shouldn't be underestimated. It can be used creatively – like the ironic zither music of Carol Reed's *The Third Man* (1949). Sir William Alwyn remarked: 'I certainly think music is necessary in films. I can't tell you what *Henry V* was like until the music was put to it. Though I say it myself, I wouldn't have believed it possible that the music could make so much difference. I used to go and see run-throughs of the bits I had to put music to and really I could hardly keep awake for five minutes.'

6. Every story film is dependent on its narrative ideas, on its theme, and the variations on and attitudes to that theme – and all this is nothing to do with photographic realism.

7. If painterly or sculptural distortions are required in a photographic film, the director can provide them by means of make-up and masks, costumes, and décor. The settings of Wiene's *The Cabinet of Dr. Caligari* (1920) integrate painting, sculpture and architecture.

8. In what sense is the epithet 'realism' applicable to: *The 5,000 Fingers of Dr. T, The Thief of Baghdad, King Kong, This Island Earth, Dracula*? Yet all these films have proved themselves capable of moving audiences of *all* intellectual and cultural levels.

9. If people will cry over the troubles of an orphaned baby elephant who learns to fly through the air by flapping his unusually large ears, which is Disney's *Dumbo* (1941), or about the mental anguish of a wooden puppet who wants to come alive but hasn't managed it yet (Pinocchio), both stories being told in cartoon form, then it surely isn't realism *per se* that moves them. In fact it would seem that the unconscious is littered with extremely powerful and persuasive feelings (about monsters, for example) which can't be handled by literal realism because they couldn't possibly happen in reality. Horror, comedy and sentimentality apart, the most complex and strange *univers imaginaires* are rendered with overwhelming power by some of the new school of Expressionist cartoons from Eastern Europe (notably *Les Jeux des Anges* by Walerian Borowczyk (1964)).

10. In *The General Line* (1929) Eisenstein shows peasants rejoicing over the operation of their first cream-separator. Eisenstein's plastically superb sequence, ostensibly

watching it 'through their dazzled eyes', is also an expression of exhilaration in visually plastic terms – whirling, shining – and comes to stand for the fertility of nature – intercut images of bull and suckling calves give the cream a layer of Freudian meaning; it is *mother's* milk. The meaning of the sequence is distinct from the literal meaning. In *Les 400 Coups* (1959) Truffaut tracks past a deserted warehouse with its boarded-up windows, and a cold bleak sky with a pale sun – we seem to be on a landscape of lunar coldness; the closed windows hurt like unseeing, blind eyes.

11. In the days of silent films the irruption of the sub-title didn't break the illusion because sub-titles provided additional, interesting information. Again what matters is not the illusion, but the resonance. In fact the most naïve audiences had no difficulty in relating the seen film, the read dialogue and the 'unreal' music (in the pit), and in weaving these three aesthetic tracks into a coherent organic whole, into one total, integrated illusion. They also cared for the heroine as a heroine while admiring the actress as star ... the apparent illusion is in fact riddled with discrepancies, depends on its discrepancies. Dr. Johnson's remarks on the stage hold good for the cinema: the audience is *both* carried away *and* in its senses from first to last. The mixture of stage and screen in total theatre is far from being the ultimate illusion; it is simply one of several possible mixtures of media, adumbrated in the early days of cinema. In America from 1903 to 1908: 'During the showing of the main film occasionally a lecturer explained the story to the ill-educated and *stirred up excitement* (my italics) 'at the climaxes.'[10] The Japanese clung even more tenaciously to the *theatrical* presence. Initially the audience had difficulty with any film that didn't draw on Kabuki conventions – not because they couldn't understand the cinema syntax but because the cinema was 'like' the theatre and the theatre demanded certain conventions.

> ... different systems were tried; sub-titles, the actors reading behind the screens, phonographs, troupes of actors actually playing the piece while the film was running. None of them had much success. The only system that worked was that of the 'benshis' – the commentator-rhetoricians – for whom the cinema soon became little more than a backcloth for a spectacle of mime, sounds, improvisation and storytelling. During twenty years, this formula had such success that the 'benshis' became the great stars of the silent cinema. This was soon reduced to being little more than an accessory .... [11]

This on the face of it astonishing situation is little more than a variant on the fact that European audiences accepted as realistic acting which was as stylized as that which prevailed on the barnstormer stage – rolling eyes for despair, outstretched arm for 'go', and literal jumping for joy. The model shots and trickwork in early films are often flagrantly unreal to us today; but what registered with audiences of the time was not the obtrusive presence of artificiality but the obtrusive presence of new realisms. The objective accuracy of photography has little bearing on the matter; what's realistic is what's felt by the audience to be realistic and may include the grossest convention and artifice.

By the time it is completed the average film has become something much more than photographs-in-motion. The ordinary feature film dovetails narrative, actors, words, pictures, music, and each aesthetic element intimately influences the meaning of every other. In

Resnais's *Hiroshima Mon Amour* (1959) text read by Emmanuelle Riva is overlaid on a moving camera's view of Hiroshima streets at night; and the director made several essays before deciding which reading speed matched which speed of camera-movement. Only one tempo was right. In matching the curve of music with the movement in the shots, in matching the movement within the shot with the movement of the camera, the film enters artistic territory which has never been broached before and is divorced from simple realism. The cinema is arguably the only *beau-monstre* that beggars opera.

It is becoming evident that in all the arts it is not the illusion as such that creates the resonance but the resonance of experience that creates the illusion. Sub-titles didn't break the illusion because they provided valuable information, *i.e.* additional intellectual and emotional stimulation. What in art we call an illusion is really just a coherent series of emotional stimuli – a gestalt (writing, pictures, music) that sets up a coherent response.

REFERENCES

1. Michael Elster, 'Bodily Distance, Mechanism and Loud Noise' in *The Twentieth Century* (November 1960).
2. R. H. Wilenski, *The Modern Movement in Art* (1957).
3. M. D. Vernon, *The Psychology of Perception* (1962).
4. Johannes Itten, *The Art of Color* (1961).
5. Van Deren Coke, *The Painter and the Photograph* (1964).
6. In Raffaele Carrieri, *Futurism* (1963).
7. Georges Hugnet, *La Septième Face du Dé* (1936), Editions Jeanne Bucher.
8. Aaron Scharf, *Creative Photography* (1965), Studio-Vista.
9. V. I. Pudovkin, *Film Technique and Film Acting* (1954), Vision.
10. Lewis Jacobs, *The Rise of the American Film* (1939).
11. S. and M. Giuglaris, *Le Cinéma Japonais* (1956), Editions du Cerf.

SOURCE: *BRITISH JOURNAL OF AESTHETICS*, VOL. 5, NO. 3, JULY 1965, 270–88

3.2 IMAGES OF THE MIND I: THROWAWAY MOVIES

The 'sixties are an era of cinematic chop and change. Liberated from its tripod and tracks, the contemporary camera can walk, look, listen as lightly as a man. Further improvements in 16mm. may make the 35mm. camera as obsolete as the broad gauge railway; Jeff Keen and others have done important work on 8mm. This bugging-ridden era may bring buttonhole and signet-ring cameras sooner than we think. Ten years from now, movies may be as throwaway as pen and paper.

In the field of fiction films, the dominance of the what-happened-next storyline has been shaken, and the syntax of slow fades, dissolves and establishing shots has become an optional extra rather than a necessity for comprehension. The stilted old documentary has taken on the spontaneity of cinéma-vérité, and a new intellectual dexterity is transforming the cinema from top to bottom.

Simultaneously, the cinema has lost half its mass audience and found unprecedented acceptance throughout a whole generation of students and young intellectuals who are emancipating themselves from the prim snobberies of an old upper-middle-class literary culture. But from the mid-'thirties on, so little new thinking, in this country at least, had gone into writing about movies that as late as 1960 several heavy volumes which were accepted as 'authoritative' could hardly bring themselves to accept the talkie, and others were fixated at a fetishism about cutting and camera-angles. Into this vacuum there poured a sudden torrent of aesthetic theory, sweeping aside old shibboleths and rapidly erecting new ones. New brooms cleared out a great many cobwebs but didn't always know the corner. Film criticism has caught up with the present, but it hasn't yet had time to catch up with the past. In the polemic many of the possibilities and qualities of the older cinema were missed.

This series is, in a sense, an essay at 'reactionary', or at least 'retrospective', film criticism – an attempt to underline some under-emphasised qualities in the 'ancienne vague' style. If so many intelligently-made movies seem rather thin, it's partly, perhaps, because many of the 'ancienne vague' virtues have been too quickly dismissed, or not yet rediscovered.

The Mongrel Image

In an earlier series, I tried to suggest that the cinema was a 'mongrel' form, having various characteristics in common with the theatre, the visual arts, literary forms and music.

'Traditional' aesthetics, however, saw movement and cutting as the essence of 'pure' cinema, which they felt to be superior to 'theatrical' or 'literary' films. But if the cinema is an intrinsically mongrel medium, then movement and cutting can be analysed in relation to all its affinities. After all, cutting is not unique to cinema; as Eisenstein himself pointed out, there is a definite process of cutting from one (mental) image to another in *Paradise Lost*. It may be interesting, therefore, to take a new look at screen editing and relate it to the cinema's 'mongrel' quality.

Film aesthetics traditionally shied away from the cinema's theatrical affinity. It reminds them of pre-Griffith cutting, of the mike-bound talkies of the late 'twenties, of lazy scriptwriters just churning out dialogue instead of thinking in images, of stage actors who haven't mastered the different idiom needed for the close-up. It seems to be a renunciation of the cinema's space-time mobility.

But the stage–screen contrast is only part of the story. There are also important affinities.

To take our weakest point first. The stage picture doesn't have to be a whole (corresponding to the long shot). The spectator's eye follows the actors, and a visually-minded theatre director can manage many 'cinematic' effects (encounters between the actor and space, groupings, etc.). After all, what is that moment of immobility between a good curtain-line and the curtain's fall but a 'frozen frame'?

More important: theatre space, too, can be very fluid. It can be blank pictorially. If the actor wears a coat, it's a street. If he wears a dressing-gown, it's a bedroom. Cabaret and variety make no statements about setting at all. Mime uses neither picture nor words. The basis of theatre is not a sense of setting. It is the presence of the actor.

The cinema is a theatrical art in its use of actors. This affinity brings the two media very close indeed. The cinema's mainstream, the story film, depends heavily on the actor's personality – on physiognomy, on posture, on gesture, on his atmosphere. And both media depend, essentially, on the spectator watching people act things out, 'counterfeiting' emotion. Theatre and cinema are both arts of showing. They are arts of arranging, staging action – arts of *mise-en-scene*. The cinema is primarily an art of showing; even cutting is a way of showing.

In this sense, even the actorless documentary is an art of 'staging'. Merely by placing or moving his camera, the documentary director stages what he sees. Often he stages the actual action (in what the documentarists called the 'reconstructed documentary').

One can put the affinities another way. The cinema is an art of visuals in motion. Apart from current avant-gardes (e.g. kinetic art) the only other arts of visual movement are ballet and mime – both theatrical arts. The Czech 'Magic Lantern' show demonstrated how closely the two media can be interwoven.

There are also 'traditional' affinities, which, theoretically, aren't binding, but are worth bearing in mind in relation to what has happened so far. First, films are usually shown in theatres (and suffer from the small TV screen and the lack of audience reaction). Second, the connection between the theatre and the film has been far more intensive than that between the film and the other arts. The accepted *auteur* of a film is the director, and film direction resembles theatre direction more than any other artistic activity. The list of theatre directors who are also excellent film directors is endless – from Cukor to Eisenstein. Although film direction and painting are both visual arts, there is relatively little interchange between the two forms; and authors become scriptwriters, mainly. But the traffic between theatre and cinema is constant and intensive on all levels.

Most stage–screen differences are, by now, obvious enough. And in the last ten years the cinema has, as we shall try to show, strayed further from the theatre and nearer literature than it has ever done before. It's just because stage–screen affinities are in for an eclipse (and not just on the level of critical theory) that it's worth restating them. Particularly since, as the *Marat-Sade* demonstrates, theatre is resembling the cinema ever more closely – becoming more fluid, more visual.

At the same time, film consists of images, and the director with a sophisticated visual sense can make the most of what, in an earlier series, we called 'pictoriality' and which teachers in art schools have since begun to call 'graphicity' – the ability to cast, and read, sophisticated messages in visual form.

The cinema's affinities to literature are hardly in need of stressing; much criticism has been concerned with plot, dialogue and all the elements which the cinema has in common with the novel, and it's probably still necessary to shift attention to 'graphic' possibilities.

But how have the cinema's multiple – and sometimes mutually exclusive – affinities affected the stream of images that appear on the screen?

The Primitives

When in the Lumière Brothers' programme (1895) the camera dwelt on the cosy family scene known as *Bébé Mange Sa Soupe*, the audience commented not so much on the fact that the people in the foreground had 'come alive' as that the leaves on the trees in the background of the shot were trembling in the wind.

Indeed, through all the items in the Lumière Programme, the stress is not on people in movement but on scenes – the demolition of a wall, a boat leaving harbour, a train entering a station. The camera planted on the edge of the platform shows a train moving diagonally towards and then across the camera – spectators of the time drew back, much as in 1952 they ducked the objects hurled at them in the brief fashion for 3-D films.

This reaction underlines certain differences between stage and screen – e.g. the latter's more convincing decor. But the fact that the difference was so marked suggests that it *startled* the spectators, that is to say, that, in view of the similarities, they were expecting something like a stage performance. Spectators clearly weren't thinking of 'moving pictures' as photography brought 'alive' by the miracle of movement. For then they would have been less startled by the leaves than by baby moving. Another analogy, it seems, was operating. They were sitting in a theatre. The film was to them a 'play', or a music-hall turn, where *of course* the people moved. The miracle was the realistic, moving decor, the spaciousness, the removal of the other three walls.

If this seems strange, it's easy to find a parallel in recent cinema history. When *This Is Cinerama* showed Lowell Thomas in medium shot, i.e. sixty feet high, no one thought, 'My goodness! Goliath in a grey flannel suit!' We automatically took the human figure as our standard of size. Though Lowell Thomas was actually sixty feet high, our brains automatically corrected him to six feet high. It was when we saw the backgrounds and the landscapes that we got the Cinerama sensation – a sensation due, incidentally, not to simple size, but to field of vision. Similarly, in many cinemas, the Cinemascope screen is actually smaller than the 'small' screen – being the 'small' screen topped and tailed. But it feels larger because Scope lenses give better definition over a more extensive field of vision.

From the beginning, the film has been a *theatrical* form rather than an *album* one. Indeed, the cinema was almost strangled in its cradle by the failure of early producers to realise that the appeal of 'moving pictures' as such is brief and weak. By 1902 items of the order of *Waves Crashing Against Rocks* so bored audiences that New York music halls used them as 'chaser' – the last items in a bill – to clear the auditorium quickly for the next house.

The cinema was rescued by the development of its theatrical possibilities. After the Lumière Brothers, its second, and perhaps its real, father is George Méliès, stage illusionist and proprietor of the Theatre Robert-Houdin in Paris, who set out simply to put his stage tricks on film. He made his first films in a little theatre in his back garden – developed it from the photographer's studio, with a glass roof to allow the sunlight through, and a stage at one end. And he defined the film studio as the place where the photographic studio meets the theatre stage. As soon as he had arranged the decor for each scene on his stage (and one scene was on film), the camera was screwed down to the floor facing it, and two pieces of string stretched from under the lens to the corners of the stage. These helped the actors not to wander off the edges of the image (Sarah Bernhardt, later, refused to be so 'cabin'd, cribb'd, confined, bound in' and as a result was intermittently invisible as well as continuously inaudible). Another piece of string was stretched parallel to the footlights to mark the boundary beyond which the actors' feet would be cut off by the bottom of the screen – which couldn't happen on the stage.

The counter-precedents in painting proved ineffective until about 1910. Even here, the pioneer, D. W. Griffith, was a man of the theatre, and he developed the film's resources from within rather than being influenced by painterly analogies. Often Méliès's actors returned to the screen after the story and lined up and bowed to thank the audience for their – assumed – applause.

Méliès's first films consisted of one scene only, but even when his films became longer and ran to a series of scenes they remained tied to the stage 'tableau'. His *La Conquête du Pôle* (1912) shows a whimsical flying-machine speeding past the clouds and planets, and creates a remarkable sense of constant movement by means of moving backcloths of clouds and heavenly bodies. These effects were already a cardinal feature of the 19th century theatre, whose preoccupation with visual realism anticipated the cinema's by over half a century. For example, early 19th century playbills billed the scenes and tableaux rather than the storyline. And the cliché situation of the hero tied to the railway track in the path of the approaching express isn't, as one might imagine, a response to cinematic possibilities. It is the climactic scene of Augustin Daly's play *Under The Gaslight*, first staged in 1867. It's easy to forget just how 'cinematic' the Victorian theatre already was: in many ways the cinema *develops* rather than *innovates*, and represents not a new direction but the achievement of a longstanding urge.

Even when the camera quit the studio for natural locations, it respected the continuity of the theatrical tableau. Edwin S. Porter's *Life of a Cowboy* (1906), a story of cattle-rustling and posse-raising, is situated at a crossroads, which offers a variety of entrances and exits without a shift of scene. 'Cutting' is provided by the screen's edge. A cowboy rushes off to fetch a posse, and the posse rides on a few seconds later – a visual ellipse which solves the problem of accelerating action without interrupting the scene.

That authoritative French film historian Georges Sadoul has persuasively argued that many, if not most, of the editing effects usually attributed to Griffith (e.g. close-ups, cutting on movement) were, in fact, originated by Britain's 'Brighton School' (1897–1910). However, of the cinema's pioneering days, it's probably true to say that if one man hadn't invented whatever was both possible and worth having on Monday morning, someone else would have invented it on Monday night. A race to claim priority isn't really worth running too hard. At any rate, it was only after Griffith either re-invented these devices or applied them to interesting dramatic situations that they took on aesthetic importance. For example, the close-up at the end of Porter's *The Great Train Robbery*, in which a cowboy fires his gun at the spectator, was just a 'gimmick', the 1903 equivalent of Emergo. With Griffith the close-up takes on quite a different meaning, and becomes an integral way of telling the story. Only then can the 'stage picture' give way to the flow of images.

Griffith apart, the screen image remains in the stage picture's leading strings until about 1910. Often the film episode begins with an empty setting by way of introduction; the actors walk on and play their scene; they walk off; and the setting remains empty for a moment – after which the next scene appears, also empty, usually with a title to ease the transition. (Indeed, subtitles often act rather like a curtain.) This kind of syntax is challenged as early as 1912 by Griffith in America, although it's still common enough in films of the early 'twenties, especially in Germany, where the influence of Griffith was retarded by the war.

The general uneasiness about departures from stage protocol persisted even in America as late as 1916, when Cecil B. De Mille allowed the characters in a film to be shrouded in dramatic chiaroscuro. Exhibitors and audiences protested until he came up with a spur-of-the-moment publicity slogan, 'Rembrandt lighting', which proved persuasive. But the analogy had had to be pointed out.

From 1910 on, American directors led by Griffith realised the possibilities of inserting close-ups, mid-shots and long shots into what the audience would realise from the dramatic continuity was a unity. The very strength of the analogy with the theatre allowed the film to break out of the 'theatrical' strait-jacket. The unity of space was only a special form of dramatic unity, which itself was only a special form of narrative unity. In other sequences, Griffith began to intercut from the villain menacing the heroine to the posse riding to the rescue. The individual scene could be fragmented into a 'jigsaw' of places, just as distant places flowed together into a unity. Thus place and time both were flung into the melting pot. And the continuum that links them is the succession of ideas. The screen images become images of the mind, leaping from place to place and point to point.

Elements of spatial continuity remained, and remain, in this new flexibility. Throughout the battles of Griffith's *The Birth of a Nation* (1915) the Confederate army fights left to right and the Federals right to left. This general 'orientational' unity persists today in most film scenes, and clumsinesses may confuse or irritate the spectator, proving that he retains a sense, if not of continuous space, at least of continuous orientation.

Griffith broke the individual scene into so many short, sharp little shots – visual 'cubes' – catapulted on to the screen at breakneck speed. Because their duration on the screen was relatively short, he could play each shot off against the next. The compositions could be made to 'dovetail' or to clash, as could their movements. To recapitulate an earlier example: throughout the climax of *Intolerance* (1916) the automobile with the hero's pardon aboard races the express train with the hanging order to the condemned cell. In successive shots, and also within the shot, the long, heavy charging mass of the express is played off against the swerving little dot of racing-car. The midget racer swerving left to right up and down a hilly road contrasts with the train swinging its long mass right to left around a curve. Prison officials and their victim mount the steps to the scaffold with a petty, bobbing movement, like the works of a watch, contrasting with the steady lunging of the train and the yo-yo boundings of the car. Similar visual 'metronome-and-protractor' orchestrations have since been used to far subtler intellectual effects. Welles's *Macbeth* (1948) provides an admirable example. The 'if it were done when 'tis done ...' soliloquy is spoken in medium shot until 'but that this blow might be the be-all and the end-all here'. And on the 'here' Welles cuts to a close-up, implying immediacy, urgency, the impetuous decision to act.

This 'razor-edge' cutting brings a further question, very much an imponderable that can be solved only on the basis of intuition and experience. How long should a shot be left on the screen? If it's left on too long, after the audience has exhausted all the dramatically relevant meanings, then it is depriving them of further stimulus; they become bored, and their boredom begins to destroy the film's effect. On the other hand, spectators may need time to notice everything relevant in a shot, or to catch its full implications; so it must be left on the screen long enough. Further, some emotions audiences can pick up very fast (e.g. laughter), while others impose a slower rhythm on the material (e.g. sadness). The legend runs that a cutter once cut the first third and last third off every shot in Antonioni's *L'Avventura* and ended up with a beautifully smooth, hard-hitting movie, which he considered vastly more interesting than the original. But Antonioni is undoubtedly right to let his images 'loiter' – the overtones of enigma, of boredom, of the etiolation of feeling, which he produces, and many of the points which he makes by a hypersensitivity to atmosphere and environment, need time to 'soak in'. Too many of his imitators, alas, have much less to say, and their movies would be much less unbearable if cut by the professionals' rule of thumb: cut just when audience feeling has reached its intensest, so that you have a good deal of emotion in 'reserve' to carry forward or pick up again later. Audience feeling reaches its intensest pretty soon after noticing something (how soon depends on the rhythm imposed by the mood). In a thriller, one might deliberately delay the cut from a terrified reaction to the cause so as to increase suspense. The editor also has to bear in mind that a film is meant to be seen in a crowded cinema, where each spectator buoys up his neighbour's emotion; the cutting is often too slow for small audiences (e.g. press shows). Comedies are notoriously difficult to cut and in Hollywood's heyday a great deal of re-cutting went on after sneak previews.

Griffith's influence didn't sweep all before it. After the failure of *Intolerance*, with its paroxysmatic cutting, his *Broken Blossoms* (1919) has a 'proscenium sense' even more marked than that of Lang's *Dr Mabuse the Gambler* (1922). The German cinema, notably, turned its back on Griffithian procedures, and elaborated a different approach to movie rhythms. In Germany, the dominating influence was that of the theatre producer Max

Reinhardt, with his very 'graphic' approach to *mise-en-scene*. The movies of the German cinema's 'golden age' (1919–26) are often slightly archaic in their cutting. Their strength lies in the theatrical and painterly qualities of eloquent decor, lighting, make-up and acting. Fritz Lang (who trained as an architect) and F. W. Murnau (who trained as an art historian) both showed a flair for developing slow, mysterious, fateful rhythms, related less to the cutting of image upon image than to the flowing of movement through space – as we shall try and show in more detail later when discussing Murnau's *Nosferatu* (1922), *The Last Laugh* (1924) and *Sunrise* (1927). For cutting is only one among many methods of producing cinematic rhythms.

Cutting as Keystone

Eisenstein and the Russians were the first to see the full possibilities of Griffith's 'fragmentation' of space-time, and their theory of film, in its earliest forms, emphasised cutting as the basis of film art. Clearly cutting burst in on the 'twenties as excitingly as jazz syncopation burst in on the sweet languors of the Palm Court style.

Indeed, talking about film form brings one up against the same difficulties as discussing music or the meaning of form in any art. The shock power of the close-up, the excitement possible through rapid cutting tempi, and so on, now number among the cinema's coarser effects. But *The Battleship Potemkin* is an aesthetically sophisticated film, because Eisenstein brought to film an eye as 'painterly' as that of the German expressionists. The *cutting* depends on the *showing*.

Thus, as the sailors slumber in their hammocks before the mutiny, their bodies lie heavily, ominously, like over-ripe fruit turning rotten, the tautness of the hammocks expressing the tensions of the situation. (Closely packed, the men lie like the maggots in the meat ….) The compositions are brooding, tense, complicated, suggestive of criss-crossing webs. And the cutting piles web upon web ….

After the first confrontation over the meat, a title, 'Daily Drill Commences', introduces a sequence in which the close-ups of busy hands, the oily ramrods shoved down barrels, the muzzles dripping oil till they seem to slaver, the agitated tempi of polishing – all these movements quicken the repressed animation of the opening sequence, suggesting, in this context, a mutinous seething still held within the bonds of routine. (The same shots could, in a different context, say, a Grierson documentary, suggest 'How busy and happy and keen as mustard our contented Jack Tars are!' But these shots are working in this context.)

As the fugitive *Potemkin* encounters the Russian battle-fleet, a sequence illustrating 'Full Speed Ahead' shows her pistons quivering frenetically, and seems to put us among the viscera of a frightened but determined giant. It is counterpointed by a second visual theme: the cloud of smoke which obscures the sun, turns day to night and leaves only a diminishing wedge-shaped patch of light further and further astern (as the ship plunges ever deeper into the irrevocable …).

The Odessa Steps sequence itself is part of a larger visual complex, introduced by the shots of the small boats clustering around the rebel battleship with their gifts of food. We see the white sails hoisted, fluttering, spreading and stretching under a generous wind, and then furled – a motif echoed in the white animals which they bring, notably, a white-winged bird – while a bourgeois lady, carried away with goodwill, happily twirls her parasol. Later, the whiteness, here so agreeably associated with goodwill, ironically returns, as the soldiers march, with horrible regularity, down the steps. It is as if the whiteness of the town's goodwill were merely an idealistic sentimentality, of which the troops were the other face.

Images of the Mind

Again in *Alexander Nevski* Eisenstein plays on the paradoxes of white – not only are the Teutonic knights conspicuously clad in shining white (traditionally the colour of good) but they die amidst the shining white of the treacherous ice. One can't speak of anything so simple as a colour symbolism, but a similarity of colour is imparted to opposing things, so as (a) not to obscure the key differences by secondary ones, (b) to create the turbulence of ambivalence. In the same way, in *Paradise Lost* – and Milton is always a good comparison to Eisenstein! – Milton stresses the spiritual magnificence of Satan, making him, in many ways, as good as good. This very similarity is a source of tension.

The Odessa Steps sequence abounds in contrasting motifs. Thus the shot of the well-meaning bourgeois lady with her parasol is followed by a shot of a legless beggar hauling himself on his wooden blocks just by her elegant shoes. She doesn't even see him. Her 'goodwill' is only a 'holiday' emotion, and the real conflict is between two forms of brute force – the irresistible troops, and the gun turret of the *Potemkin* which 'stops' the tide of the Steps sequence. Several of the details chosen for close-up seem to have a significance distinct from their melodramatic excitement; notably a close-up of a brooch with a swan, which a woman clutches as she dies, not only echoes the bird passed to the ship for food, but seems to have some further meaning which I don't know.

In terms of overall movement, the sequence falls into two main parts. In the first part, the little armada of sailing ships, flowing from left to right, 'narrows' to the hurling of food along a chain of moored boats. In the second part, the soldiers march, also left to right, their steadiness in contrast to the confused eddying of the crowd, in which Eisenstein stresses varieties of movement – the legless cripple, the bounding pram, the woman who advances against the soldiers. The soldiers are almost completely impersonal – backs, boots, bayonets ….

Cutting isn't a way of 'handling' this sequence. The leaping from detail to detail creates a new reality. Yet this new reality could only be created if the sequence had first been staged. It's a bit artificial to praise the cutting of the Steps sequence without also praising the idea of bringing the soldiers down the Steps.

Cutting is also the briefest and most vivid way of illustrating certain processes. In *Turksib* (1929), dealing with the construction of the Turkestan–Siberia railway, Victor Turin sets out to dramatise, by editing, the springtime melting of snow that turns a river into a torrent. A first shot shows a trickle of water from snowy masses; a second, massive lumps of ice crashing down; a third shows a thread of water creeping along a channel; a fourth shows water now following a more complex, changing course; a fifth shows a broad river flowing steadily round a bend; a sixth, a torrent tumultuously swirling. Each shot introduces a new stage in the process. And this logical progression is far more dynamic than six shots which lacked this ominous quality of steady increase. (Some of the examples quoted in this series are rather stylised, for brevity and clarity in description, particularly where blow-by-blow fidelity to the screen action would involve long explanations of context.)

Narrative continuity is not strictly observed, however. The cut from the first trickle to crashing masses of ice suggests, early on, that this trickle has dramatic possibilities. Without this 'plant' the sequence would begin weakly. As it is, the contrast between an implied threat, and its slow materialisation, is very satisfying.

This 'one shot one idea' can be amplified into a heavier structure. Eisenstein often used several shots to establish each stage of a process, e.g. a crowd gathering. He could do so without falling into repetition because he knew how to play movements off against one another within a shot as well as between shots: the surging of a crowd against architec-

The Essential Raymond Durgnat

tural structures (archways, corners) and against counterpointing elements within the crowd itself (its laggards, its leaders, its hecklers). Thus visual tensions and cross-currents contribute to the narrative, and, by showing certain types in action, can give a full social analysis of the event.

[…]

SOURCE: *FILMS AND FILMING*, JULY 1968, 4–10

3.3 IMAGES OF THE MIND II: EBB AND FLOW

Eisenstein was interested in using cutting to make intellectual linkages of many kinds, and in the 'Gods' sequence of *October* (1928) he used it for the purpose of a destructive critical analysis. A Tsarist General's call to God is followed, first, by a shot of a magnificent icon, then by a series of diverse images of diverse Gods, each less appealing and more barbaric than its predecessor, until, at last, the idea of God is shown to be equivalent, also, to squat little idols and fetishes which resemble nothing so much as clothes-pegs and gas-masks.

The sequence is brilliantly successful, in a poetical way (though obviously not in a logical one; one could reverse the order of the images and suggest that our God is a great improvement on anyone else's – although here again a 'subversive' context or music could suggest that the improvements are all a matter of bluff). But it's something of a tour-de-force and the use of cutting to develop abstractions remains rare, an achievement for virtuosos. The natural method now is some combination of words and images, the former establishing the 'linkages', the latter 'coming in', so to speak, as illustration. Often cutting is relatively cumbersome, simple-minded and unconvincing. Cut-ins of symbolic objects (peacocks and so on) tell us less more obtrusively than a scene tracing the natural development of a situation in its own terms, or the casting of actors whose faces make a similar point quickly, or details of dress or gesture. Thus, if one wanted to make the point of the 'Gods' sequence in a conventional way, one might find some pretext (e.g. war emergency) for having a scene in a museum, and all the fetishes would be a 'realistic' part of the scene. Losey and Antonioni often cut away to statues and pictures. In fact, one could paraphrase the effect without cutting – by a tracking shot down a line of 'Gods' – or, perhaps, the camera zooming across walls and ceiling to bring the faces out of the shadows. Cutting would have the edge, though, at least for Eisenstein's purposes: the suddenness of substitution contributes to the sharpness of parody.

Potemkin-type editing became part of film language generally and featured particularly conspicuously in the work of film theoreticians and documentarists (who were often the same people). The theoreticians wanted to prove that the cinema was a fine art, with its own 'purity', even if the 'passive' camera had to content itself with passively recording reality. And the documentarists tended to take what they were photographing as 'given', as something which they were not creating so much as interpreting. Indeed, a combination of well-chosen set-ups and craftily-applied scissors can turn any reality into something 'created', as Ruttmann's *Berlin* (1927), Ivens's *Rain* (1929) and Grierson's *Drifters* (1929) all demonstrate. All three are little gems of formalist cinema: one watches the patterns, and it is out of the patterns that a dynamic emerges. The irony is that the films survive as examples of decorative aestheticism; none of them says anything worth saying about social reality. They restrict themselves to visual effects, completely lacking the social analysis of the Odessa Steps sequence.

Part of the fascination of *Potemkin* cutting is perhaps that it catches the spirit that had just given birth to futurism and cubism, notably Léger's. Its mood is a bold, hard, urgent one. Its driving rhythms catch the dynamism of industrial tempi. It can reflect cubism's concern with showing an object from a variety of viewpoints all but simultaneously. I don't think it's going too far to suggest that the way in which one image after the other is slotted into the rectangular screen evokes cubism's tendency to analyse objects into regular geometrical shapes. And the movies' space-time continuum is a direct continuation of futurism. Once again, the cinema develops rather than innovates.

Eisenstein's own closest affinities are possibly with Constructivism, for his theories stress, like theirs, the construction of a 'new', in a sense, artificial, but materialistic world, from a 'collage' of the raw material of concrete reality. The cinema medium is very appropriate to the goals of the Constructivists' 1920 Realistic Manifesto, which stressed that volume (a cubist speciality) was far less important in art than movement in space.

As it is, the formal language of cutting can be analysed into four elements. There is the 'collision' of one composition against another – as in Dreyer's *La Passion de Jeanne d'Arc*, and, of course, in Marker's *La Jetée*, which is cut from still images, and shows how cutting can exist as forcefully between static images as between moving ones. Often, again, the static elements of the image can be 'carried away' by bold movement, which becomes the predominating element, so that images can be cut as movement-against-movement (as in the example from *Intolerance*, and in the Odessa Steps sequence). In the films of Jean Renoir, the individual image is often so loose and free as hardly to exist as an entity, and a whole view of man is implied in the camera's continuous movements through 'free', 'continuous' space. In other films again, the composition of individual images is merely not displeasing, or comparatively neglected; yet the central action is strongly and carefully modulated (as in the metronomed sequences from *Our Daily Bread* and *Queen Christina*).

[...]

Shots or Master-scenes?

By and large, Hollywood, preoccupied with stars and stories, turned its back on the subtler and deeper possibilities of editing. The so-called 'montage sequence' abounding in Hollywood films of the late 'twenties or 'thirties, with newspaper headlines zooming into close-up over shots of train wheels and railway lines, were mere devices of little or no creative interest. At their best, they were visual cadenzas rather extraneous to the main action, and perhaps it's not surprising that the most interesting use of flamboyant cutting usually came from specialists (Busby Berkeley, Slavko Vorkapich) to whom the sequences were 'contracted out' and who didn't direct the film as a whole. Vorkapich's dream sequence for Victor Fleming's *Dr Jekyll and Mr Hyde* (1941) includes several admirable visual puns, quite as sophisticated as the Saul Bass sequences in *Psycho*, as when the half-naked body of Hyde's victim 'fades' into a sand-dune which, at his touch, swirls away as in a hot Saharan wind.

Otherwise, Hollywood was more concerned with smooth, unobtrusive editing that would be as 'transparent' as possible (e.g. the centre of interest of a shot should coincide with the centre of interest of the next). And since the early 'twenties, Hollywood's characteristic procedure is to conceive films less in terms of individual shots than of 'master-scenes'. Generally speaking, screenwriters develop a whole scene as a dramatic unity – a master-scene – and certainly bear visual possibilities in mind, but are not responsible for its break-down into shots. This is left for the director and/or cameraman to work out after they have taken into account the contribution of the art director, exigencies of weather, terrain and background, the styles and physiognomies of the actors, and so on. There were excep-tions to this rule: William Cameron Menzies did what is now called a 'storyboard', i.e. a sketch of each scene, for *Gone With the Wind*, and Stanley Kramer had a 'storyboard' for *The Pride and the Passion*. But this was sufficiently rare to arouse comment; it's signifi-cant that the term 'storyboard' is a recent one and derives from cartoon films.

From about 1924 till the 'forties the typical visual structure of a scene would be some-thing like this. It would open with an establishing shot (rather like a 'proscenium' view), set-ting scene and atmosphere. The next shot would be a two-shot of the protagonists, usually in what the French call 'le plan Americain', i.e. head-to-knees, although this gradually tended to give way to head-to-waist. Close-ups would be reserved for the climax of the scene – first a close 'two-shot', then a close-up of each character – briefly returning to the mid-shot or establishing shot to reconnect the climax to the dramatic context. A title or fade would precede the establishing shot of the next sequence. Despite a slightly archaic flavour, this basic technique still served well enough in the veteran Allan Dwan's *The Enchanted Island* (1958). Alternatively, the establishing shot might be a close-up of a detail which sums up the atmosphere or meaning of the scene. Thus, Chaplin or Lubitsch might begin a scene with a glove or necklace and then cut to the mid-shot.

Abrupt though these shifts of viewpoint may seem, they are, in fact, completely invisi-ble to the spectator, who looks through the images, not at them, and has little or no idea where one ends and the next begins. A sense of the image in itself appears only when the film draws attention to it (by quick cutting or elaborate staging) or when the spectator has made a close study of the medium. The spontaneous, 'uneducated' centre of attention is, in fact, the *dramatic* master-scene.

Often all the shots in such a master-scene would be taken from the same angle, main-taining something of the stage spectator's rigidity. But by 1930 most directors were mov-ing the camera through 360°, restricted only by the need for continuity of orientation. And by 1940 or so the characteristic flow of a master-scene would be to move straight from an establishing shot (or to do without it) straight to two-shots (head-to-waist) and then to alternate close-ups which, even if they were, in fact, what are called 'over-shoulder shots', were, in effect, giving the spectator each character's view of the other. By 1950 the alter-nation of reverse angles, efficient though it was, had almost straitjacketed Hollywood style, much as the heroic couplet eventually straitjacketed neo-classical poetry. […]

An experiment in the more complete involvement of the spectator was made in 1947 when in Robert Montgomery's *Lady in the Lake* the audience saw everything through the eyes of the hero, who glimpsed himself only in mirrors, shiny surfaces and so on. But audi-ences participate in films mainly through the emotions of the characters they see, and if a hero's fate is invisible, so are his feelings; thus visual identification rapidly becomes emo-tional exclusion. What the eye doesn't see the heart doesn't grieve over. The 1st person camera can be very effective in short snatches in certain situations (exploring this strange house …) or when sandwiched between what are, in fact, called 'reaction shots'. Many film scenes all but alternate what the hero sees and what the hero feels, merging fact and feel-ing in the intensest of both worlds. […]

Reverse angles: *Citizen Kane* (1941)

Eisenstein's silent films have no individual hero, and, given his subjects, a Hollywood producer would have insisted on writing in a 'Zhivago-figure' to see and experience the whole thing as an individual. This insistence isn't at all unreasonable. For example, I find Wyler's *Carrie* a more emotive film than Eisenstein's *Strike*; and the scene where she catches her fingernail in a sweatshop sewing-machine hurts more than the whole climax of Eisenstein's film. But this Hollywood procedure can become a dogma; in *Strike*, for example, the riot scenes are so shocking that reaction shots could only dilute them (unless they were the reaction shots of the injured and dying, which Hollywood would omit as too 'tragic'). De Mille also tends not to bother about reaction shots, to rely on what is, in a sense, '1st person camera'. The Hollywood dogma is obviously related to American individualism ('If you don't feel it through an individual's eyes, you won't care about its collective meaning'), amounting to a virtual repudiation of the social and the historical as being of interest in themselves. [...]

How brilliantly the 'subjective' and 'objective' view of a character's situation can be combined is shown by these reverse angles from *Citizen Kane*. In the first, *Kane*, from his box, watches his frightened wife on the opera stage, while, in the second, she stands alone, confronted by the threatening enigma of audience reaction. The black space which in both shots isolate her is what she is subjectively aware of. Both shots are, in a sense, 'over-shoulders' – and unusually distant ones – yet also highly subjective. [...]

Liberation from the 'reverse-angle' straitjacket came not through more complete 'subjectivity' but through its very opposite, the visual detachment of deep focus, whereby objects close to and far from the camera are simultaneously in focus. Until the mid 'twenties all films had been in 'deep' (i.e. fixed) focus (like Mum's Box Brownie). But when orthochrome was replaced by panchromatic film, with its better tone values, more light was needed, which in movies couldn't be got by longer exposure since the film has to pass through the camera at a speed which anyway was gradually accelerating (from 16 to 24 f.p.s.; the change was all but complete just before sound came in, and 16 f.p.s. is a grotesque speed for many silent films). This tended to cut down depth of focus. More light could be provided by replacing arc by incandescent lamps, but the latter were noisy and registered on the microphones of sound films; so it was back to arc lights, and, particularly in France, where studios were ill-equipped and lenses often cheap and poor, the result was a considerable loss of depth of focus (which gave French films of the early 'thirties their characteristically white, flossy quality). Sometimes *nothing* is in focus. Toland's new deep-focus procedure reconciled the extreme close-up with clear backgrounds. Initially it required

The Essential Raymond Durgnat

floods of light and tended to harsh contrasts of light and shade, but the sombre mood suited the first two films in which it was extensively used, John Ford's *The Long Voyage Home* (1940) and Orson Welles's *Citizen Kane* (1941).

The movie image thus acquired a new freedom of depth. Now the old 'fragmentation' of a master-scene could be replaced by one shot which, in effect, catches the mood of the whole setting and all the close-ups, and maintains them all simultaneously and continuously. Obviously, the 'fragmentation' of scenes still has some purpose, especially since the close-up attains its lyrical effect not by 'enlarging' the face so much as by ruling out any other element. With deep-focus *mise-en-scene*, the close-up can become powerful, simply because rarely used. But deep focus tends to reduce the number of cuts, and it has a great advantage over reverse-angles in that it builds a scene into a more continuous, consistent, powerful 'mass', a more sustained continuity. The actors, more consistently present, can build up something nearer a *stage* 'intensity of presence'. This is one reason why Fred Astaire refused to allow himself to be filmed Busby Berkeley-style, all cuts and angles, and insisted that the camera follow him round, to preserve the continuity which his dancing would have had on the theatre stage. It's no accident that André Bazin, the first theorist of deep focus and of *mise-en-scene*, wrote a great deal about the 'weakening' effect of too much cutting and about the advantages of the long take, whether static or moving. And the 'filmed plays' of the 'forties – from Wyler's *The Little Foxes* to Cocteau's *Les Parents Terribles* – did acquire a strong intensity. There were fewer cuts inside the master-scene, or more unexpectedly and imaginatively placed, and the master-scene itself could run longer, with not even the illusion of a need for 'fresh air' or 'fast movement' relief – the need for which is a sign of the cinema's inferiority to the stage, not of its superiority.

By 1945 improved emulsions and cameras were allowing deep focus to be obtained without harshness and, as Bazin pointed out, William Wyler's *The Best Years of Our Lives* (1946) features several 'three-tiered' images. The final wedding ceremony is so staged as to fit three dramatic elements into one long 'take', (a) the veteran with hooks for hands struggling to put the ring on his bride's fingers, (b) the settled happiness of the mature couple (Fredric March and Myrna Loy) and (c) Dana Andrews deciding to face the unpleasantness of divorce so as to marry Teresa Wright. The three themes are treated without dialogue, except the, in one case, ironical words of the wedding ceremony. Particularly interesting is the emotional contradiction between these dramatic elements – contradictions even more marked in the earlier shot where two jolly fellows at the bar watch Hoagy Carmichael help the sailor play chopsticks with his hooks while Fredric March, absent-mindedly acting the part of an old buddy, is actually forcing another old buddy, Dana Andrews, to wreck his own love affair. To handle this fantastic amalgam of emotional tones in a 'cutting' style might have had a more obvious irony, but Wyler's simultaneity creates a particular kind of stoicism.

Perhaps the last of the 'theatrical' directors of the 'forties was Max Ophuls; one of the effects of his long tracking and panning shots was to build up the intensity of continuous presence, of continuous mood, and to ensure that the characters were never separated from society but gradually emerged from, and subsided into it again.

The Best Years of Our Lives revealed that American audiences were ready for more complex, 'meditative' attitudes than the rise and fall of single, simple climaxes which had been the Hollywood rule. In France, Jean Renoir had been experimenting with deep focus and simultaneous action ever since *Boudu Sauvé des Eaux* in 1932, but the resultant roughnesses had discouraged emulation. In fact, he soon gave up and came to rely

Three-tiered images: *The Best Years of Our Lives* (1946)

principally on long, lunging tracks and pans instead, the camera following the characters as they moved freely through space. Deep focus, coupled with wide-angle lenses, [...] resulted in a marked slowdown of cutting and an emphasis on arrangement in space, that is, on graphic qualities. In *La Terra Trema* (1948) Visconti brilliantly adapted the 'deep-focus' style to locations, exteriors and neo-realistic subject-matter.

Quite apart from the publicity campaigns, Hollywood's reintroduction in 1953 of Cinemascope (which had been briefly used in France around 1927) was in line with this enrichment of the individual image. However, Hollywood at first reasoned that the visual immensity of Scope would make quick cutting unbearable; after a year or two of visual constipation it was obvious that Hollywood had been taken in by its own publicity, as Richard Fleischer made quite clear when in *Twenty Thousand Leagues Under the Sea* (1954) he cut from a long-shot of a beach to a big close-up of Kirk Douglas's eyes. Nowadays spectators are usually unable to tell you whether the film they have just seen was in Cinemascope or not.

The variety of objects flung at the audience during the 3-D era (1953–4) and the roller-coaster sequence in *This Is Cinerama* (1956) renewed the shock effect of the Lumière train entering its station, and threatened new eras of sensationalist naïvety. But 3-D added nothing to the cinema's storytelling capacities, and soon died, while Cinerama struck an analogous snag. [...] The need to dwarf one's characters has tempted several Cinerama producers into the trap of weak stories and travelogue interest. This more than any other factor has kept Cinerama a marginal form of cinema, though *How the West Was Won* (1962) achieved an admirable interpenetration of story and landscape interest. Henry Levin's *The Wonderful World of the Brothers Grimm* (1962) made the experiment of concentrating on interiors of cottages as of palaces; but this led to many shots of 'gigantic' people, and the 'Modulor' effect applied to shrivel the screen in the spectator's mind.

So steadily did cutting slow down during the 'fifties that by the early 'sixties several thoughtful young filmgoers had a little difficulty in adapting retrospectively to the 'reverse-angle' style of such films as Cocteau's *Orphée* (1950). They found each close-up beginning a train of thought, a 'meditative' concern with the character's feelings, to which the reverse-angle was a premature eruption. That this alteration of style was determined not simply by new technical possibilities but by changing attitudes on the part of film-maker and spectator alike is suggested by the fact that, quite apart from Cinemascope and deep-focus, many American films from about 1950 on began replacing the slick, fast, racy style which had hitherto been the Hollywood hallmark by a rather slow, brooding style, which was described by some critics as flashy, inflated, pretentious, incompetent and so on, but which had authentic purpose. Ever since the early Depression years, Hollywood movies had been geared to relatively simple issues and attitudes on the part of its characters, to which they adopted a quick, matter-of-fact, unsentimental attitude. Hence American movies could, in Howard Hawks's phrase, 'bat it and run'. Often they had to because the material wouldn't stand too much thinking about. For this superficiality Hollywood film-makers weren't solely responsible; they had to match the rhythms and preoccupations of a driving, rather callow society as well as endure the idiocies of the Hays Code and echo American equivocation between puritanism and 'fun morality'. [...]

The artistic possibilities of the trend towards weightier single images were strength-ened by technical improvements in films and cameras, which permitted easy shooting by most degrees of natural light, more delicately shaded tonal ranges, a stronger sense of texture, infinitely more sensitive colours. Thus pictorial qualities were at once subtler, more evocative and more rich, and could, at will, be more realistic or more controlled in their degree of distortion. But where German expressionism, Eisenstein and Visconti owed a great deal to 'painterliness', the 'fifties owed more to the idioms of 'graphic design' – mag-azine photography and advertising. Thus, in Saul Bass's (sub-contracted) credit sequence for Dmytryk's *A Walk on the Wild Side* (1962), the camera follows a cat prowling, a ripple of fur and muscle, suggesting The Secret Life of a Family Pet, along the gutters of the night. In their different ways, such films as Lang's *Tigress of Bengal*, Corman's *Tales of Terror*, Bava's *Night is the Phantom* and Donen's *Arabesque* have reached some sort of climax in the sumptuousness of the screen image.

SOURCE: *FILMS AND FILMING*, AUGUST 1968, 12–17

3.4 IMAGES OF THE MIND III: THE IMPOSSIBLE TAKES A LITTLE LONGER

In the early 'sixties the screen became more fluid than ever in its cutting. The basic rea-son is a profound change in the whole situation of the medium – a change enforced by the prevalence of television (which, despite the protestations of certain theoreticians, is a branch of cinema, not a sister-art), as well as the spread of home movies. Once upon a time, moving pictures were seen only, or mainly, in 'picture palaces', in darkness, with hun-dreds of other spectators, one's whole attention, strengthened by community feeling, poured into them. The weekly visit to the cinema was an event, an entry into a magic world. In terms which aren't at all Marshall McLuhan's, the cinema is traditionally a 'hot' medium, involving one's whole participation intensely. Conversely, if a book annoys or bores you, you just put it down. If a film bores you, you're imprisoned, you writhe and fume.

Now, with TV and home movies, films are frequently watched in semi-darkness or ordinary room illumination, amid the pedestrian surroundings of the home. The sound or brightness may be turned up or down. A little image flickers on the surface of the box. The spectator, once dominated by the medium and its glamour, now dominates it, and often watches half-absently, fitfully, or not at all. TV, and home movies, are 'cool' media.

Moving pictures have become almost as common as print. They compel less attention, less emotional energy, less participation. The spectator who once *reacted*, now *notes*. The medium can become more notional, more cerebral, more 'abstract', in the sense that ideas are abstract. TV plays often move more slowly than films, needing longer to catch one's full participation; theirs are nearer theatrical rhythms than the cinema's; we talk of TV 'plays' even when they're films. On the other hand, other TV genres move very fast, substituting a 'notional' continuity of intellectual interest for emotional participation. Ironically, certain TV commercials, especially the early *Dulux Is A Home's Best Friend* series from I.C.I., move with a speed, freedom and whimsicality rivalling that of the cinema's avant-garde. They can exploit a complete emancipation from continuities of space and time. Theatrical 'continuity' is utterly exploded. Images are flicked or shuffled through like photographs, not just in an album, but in *packs*.

Dick Lester's *The Knack* (1965), albeit adapted from a stage-play, and Fellini's *Giulietta of the Spirits* (1965) apply this mode to the mainstream story film, using rapid transitions from present to past or future tense (the spectator deduces the tense from his sense of continuity), from objective images to subjective images (daydreams, hallucinations), from simple realism to perceptual 'impressionism' and emotional 'expressionism' and even negative or subjunctive images (this didn't happen, this might have happened, this would be absurd if it did happen). Where films once had to choose a style and stick to it (only a few films managed obtrusive transitions), now they could be in all styles at once, since what was looked at was known to be an 'idea' before it was a 'reality'.

In these ways the cinema of the *October* Gods is returning to prominence. Marker, Godard, Lester, Kluge, all like Eisenstein, go off into little 'essays', and move, not from place to place, but from idea to idea. Yet only a few years back, Karel Reisz, in the pages of *Sight and Sound*, was pronouncing Eisenstein's example a dead end!

Well – that's show-business!

The spate of new styles has utterly exploded old dogmas. Godard, bored with the tedious old habits of showing how your character got from A to B, decided, at the last moment, to cut out all linking shots in *A Bout de Souffle*, and proved all over again that you could 'jump' your character from A to B, i.e. make a sudden, unprepared break in 'theatrical' space. Every cut is, in a sense, a jump-cut, and all Godard does is defy Hollywood convention; he cuts with no indication of transition, the character doesn't even mutter, 'Well – it's time I went', or drop some such hint that this scene is over. Thus, the theatrical sense is further debilitated, and the film can become as casual about place as a novel is, or as film-essays had always been. But it's worth remembering that Griffith cuts just as fast, and jumpily, as Godard's contemporaries.

Paul Mayersberg, clearly startled by jump-cuts, has argued that the cinema was a violence-saturated medium, because the cut tore you from one place to another, inflicting drastic shocks on your nervous system. Remarks as hypersensitive as this aren't rare in contemporary theorising. The fact remains that, as every cutter knows, the run-of-the-mill cut is the smoothest, most invisible way of changing place, and no more inflicts violence on the spectator than a sentence like, 'He rose from his chair, shaved, went downstairs and caught a taxi to her house.' There are five 'shots' and four jump-cuts in that sentence, and it creates

The Essential Raymond Durgnat

'From the objective to the subjective': 8½ (1963)

a sense of flow, not of jumps. In the same way, the cinema spectator just doesn't see most cuts, because he's looking *through* the image at what's happening in it. Theories which stress the cutting at the expense of the showing can be very misleading. Most cuts are no more violent than replacing one mental image by another; and this is all smooth cutting does.

Much theorising about 'subjective cameras' has gone wrong for similar reasons. 'First-person camera' sequences, in which the camera pans and tracks round a room, like an eye, rarely seem as direct and natural on the screen as they should in theory. In fact they're a good way of building up suspense, of making the spectator nervous. The principal reason is that most camera lenses have a field of vision even narrower than that of the optic defect known as 'tunnel vision', and part of the weirdness of 'subjective' sequences lies in our feeling that we can't see out of the sides, let alone the corners, of our eyes. *Murderers' Row* brings the fish-eye lens to the storyfilm, but the price in optical distortion limits it to gimmick (or expressionistic) status. The way in which we look round a room is most naturally represented, not by the panning close-up (used to very disorientating effect in Dreyer's *Vampyr*) but by some sort of establishing shot, followed by closer views of significant details or configurations. The cuts paraphrase the fact that, even while our eyes turn, our mind doesn't pan over space, it leaps from one point of interest to another, or from one configuration to another. It's then natural to slip in reaction-shots to stop the cuts from 'jerking' against one another. Or, again, one might represent the action of the eye by 'sweeping' the camera across a room, slowing down to near-immobility at a point of interest, then 'swooping' off again; but even then the camera would create a zip-pan effect not noted by the eyes. Theories that the camera can 'equal' the eyes fall foul of the differences between (a) the camera's and the eye's optical qualities, and (b) the eye's physical movements and the mind's 'editing' of what the eye sees – a process on which gestalt psychology is laying increasing importance. In the last analysis, the cinema is a matter, not of images of the eye, but of images of the mind. Of course, all these effects might be justified by particular moods or situations; our point is that the 'mainstream' cinema is not so hopelessly square and conventional as it's often been made out to be, and that it is often far more natural, flexible and resourceful than over-theoretical improvements.

But such experiments in 'optical literalism' have become less conspicuous among all the possibilities offered by a 'stream-of-consciousness' cinema.

Given this new intellectual flexibility, the cinema is currently exploring a new mode, half-pictorial, half-'abstract', i.e., in a sense, literary – as exemplified by the documentaries of Chris Marker and the half-stories, half-essays, of Godard, his boring sidekick.

Many of these effects are anticipated in Dovzhenko's *Arsenal* (1929) and reputedly are very fully developed in his *Aerograd* (1935). But their current recrudescence is on a much broader front. Through it the storyfilm is acquiring something of the novel's power of discursiveness. And the documentary is experiencing a rebirth. Already in the '30s, Basil Wright's and Harry Watt's *Night Mail* (1936), to some extent, and, even more fully, Basil Wright's *Song of Ceylon* (1934) had begun to move from the 'document' to the essay form, while Thorold Dickinson's *Overture* (1958), a compilation film linking documentary footage from all over the world into one coherent storyline, created a meta-reality, a conceptual reality. It constitutes the link-film between the 'Gods' sequence in *October* and the essay form which, with Chris Marker, comes of age. The sequence in *Lettre de Siberie* (1958), where the same sequence is shown several times over, with different music and commentary, as it might feature in a Stalinist documentary, in an anti-Communist documentary, and in a tourist's home-movie, is both an enquiry into Siberia and an enquiry into enquiries; it becomes, in the end, a philosophical meditation on truth and appearance, the documentary to end all notions of documentary as 'document'. In *Overture*, the image is still 'concrete', in that it gives its sense of lived lift [*sic*] to the overall concept, of co-operation. With Marker's sequence, the image itself is under enquiry, is merely an 'idea', a hypothesis. As it is again, in *Alphaville* (1965), where Godard shows us a road, and talks of galactic space, and we 'feel' a poetic entity – the contrast is a 'montage', in Eisenstein's sense. With all these exciting possibilities to explore, the theatrical aspects of the cinema seem to be in for an eclipse – or, at least, a fallow period. But so long as the cinema depends on acting and acting-out concrete events (rather than on indicating the concrete through words and symbols), that is, so long as it is photographic, it will remain radically theatrical, and Raymond Williams was probably right when in his *Preface to Film*, in collaboration with Michael Orrom, he described the cinema as closest to the theatrical arts (perhaps the two forms are heading for a symbiosis in 'total theatre', a promising cine-sideline, with actors stepping from the screen on to the stage and back again). […]

The neo-theatrical film continues to flourish, not only in the cinemas, but in the avant-garde. One thinks of Jonas Mekas's *The Brig* (1964) – a film record of an actual performance of the stageplay, owing much of its effect to the camera's perpetuation of the theatrical continuity of space. And Steve Dwoskin's poignant *Alone* (1966), though very fluidly cut, dwells so remorselessly on one girl, on her bed, that the film leaves one with the impression of having been shot in one long take.

What we are watching is, perhaps, the cinema's diversification into a variety of idioms. For the cinema's equivalent is not *literature*; its equivalent is *print*. The cinema is not an art form. It is a medium, comprising art forms as diverse as print – i.e., ranging from the stream-of-consciousness novel and concrete poetry. It also includes communicating styles which have no connection whatsoever with art (in the usual sense of the word), or even entertainment, and correspond to journalism, technical manuals or textbooks. Soon, perhaps, such a thing as a 'film critic' will seem as ridiculous as a 'print-critic'. There is no art of the cinema. Long live the cinema arts!

SOURCE: *FILMS AND FILMING*, SEPTEMBER 1968, 12–16

3.5 IMAGES OF THE MIND IV: STYLE AND THE OLD WAVE

In the beginning, film theory had an uphill struggle against the aura of vulgarity surrounding the medium. To the theatre-lover, movies were 'tinned ham', to the connoisseur of the visual arts photography seemed a crude and mechanical rival to brush and pencil, and one Cambridge lecturer in English Literature still talks about 'Wardour Street prose', by which he means the purple-poetic prose of subtitles like 'Came the dawn ....'

Film theoreticians looked around for something that couldn't be patronised, because no other medium could rival it, i.e., the element of 'pure' film. They came up with movement through space and editing. Eventually the chase across the salt flats in John Ford's *Stagecoach* (1939) was advanced as a highspot of film art, because of all the galloping and cutting. It's not very surprising that the intellectual world generally retained a pretty low opinion of movies. For *Stagecoach* may be a beautifully made example of the romantic Western, but it hardly demonstrates the cinema's intellectual parity with the other arts.

Eisenstein's imposing term 'montage' came to be synonymous with editing (and secondarily sound–image overlays), all but ignoring Eisenstein's insistence that montage could exist, not only in the succession of shots but between the different features of one image. He had himself analysed montage as between music and image, and from there it's hardly a step to thinking of montage between music and dialogue, or between one line of dialogue and the next, or between face and behaviour (so that 'casting against type' is a form of montage – and a very important one). Thus, one might speak of 'montage' between Buster Keaton's predicaments and his deadpan response – there's a real parallel between 'Old Stone Face' and Mosjoukine in Kuleshov's soup-plates experiment. And one can speak of 'montage' between the last 'shot' of Bresson's *Journal d'Un Curé de Campagne* – a cross outlined against a plain background – and the commentary describing the priest's death, in words.

Once developed as far as this, the term 'montage' can be applied to any sort of intellectual 'collision' out of which a new meaning emerges. It becomes a way of describing the interaction of any two details, or of detail and context, in any sort of art, or indeed, of any two informational or emotional 'cues'. Thus one could compare montage to a sort of syllogism: given detail *a* (the first cue) and detail *b* (the second cue), then the mind doesn't just add them together, it deduces a third point (*c*).

Or one could suggest a psychological equivalent: the mind tries to make sense of any two stimuli, if they seem to be related, by thinking of a link. Given the Russian situation in the 'twenties, montage theory links with the Marx–Engels–Leninist theory of the world. Western bourgeois philosophy, based on Aristotelian and Cartesian logic, tends to see the world as an essentially consistent place, in which 'contradiction' is equivalent to an anomaly that will have to be explained away. Engels, adapting Hegel rather than Marx, suggested that the world was a place of contradictions, of action (thesis) and reaction (antithesis) and this dialectical 'logic' proceeded with thesis and antithesis producing a synthesis, which in its turn becomes the thesis of a further contradiction. This presaged Eisenstein's insistence that montage was not $a + b = c$, but a versus b produces c.

Which of these formulae is true, if either, belongs to metaphysics rather than film criticism. It's quite arguable that neither formula gets us very far, and that the parallels between Eisenstein's formula and dialectics are altogether superficial. The most useful approach to 'montage' is probably through psychology. The mind will try to make sense of any two (or more) stimuli that seem to be related by thinking of an explanation, link or common denominator, thus reducing several diverse or contradictory cues to one consistent one. [...]

Just as cutting is inseparable from choosing and then arranging the images you cut, so it is inseparable from *mise-en-scene* (Bazin's term for the staging of action in relation to 'dramatic space') and from 'pictoriality' (the staging of the scene in relation to the image).

Indeed, the cinema began editing before it began cutting. In *The Life of a Cowboy* off-screen is a place where space and time both foreshorten. In Méliès's *La Conquête du Pôle* editing is performed within the image. In one tableau, Professor Maboul's flying-machine is first seen, in the distance, flying towards us. Rather groggily, it loses height and plunges behind a ridge in the middle distance. Has it crashed? After a suitable pause for suspense, it reappears, wearily struggling up over the ridge, and then flops on to a foreground glacier. The whole action has been worked out to give visual variety and drama. Later, the airship which may or may not spot and rescue the stranded explorers first appears on the far horizon, sailing sedately from left to right. It disappears off-screen (suspense) before asserting its presence in the foreground.

At another point, a procession of 'futuristic' automobiles rolls across the screen. A large crocodile-snouted racer, sleek, long and low, is followed by a very upright, hansom-cab-shaped conveyance and that in turn by a squarish, steam-spouting contraption. The contrast between the three shapes (horizontal, vertical, square) and the three types is as deliberate and effective a form of montage as playing the dominant shape in one shot off against that of the next. [...]

All these effects are largely questions of *staging*. But if *mise-en-scene* suffered something of a critical eclipse between the days of German expressionism (where its primacy was unmistakeable) and Bazin's analysis of Welles and Wyler, it was partly because the impact of *Potemkin* in the late 'twenties coincided with (1) the crippling effects of early microphones on spatial arrangement, and (2) the limiting effects of shallower focus. The dialogue film suffered from both sets of handicaps, and acquired its reputation as 'unfilmic', which persisted, as dogmas will, long after it had, in fact, liberated itself. In *Boudu Sauvé des Eaux* (1932) Renoir, struggling to retain spatial freedom, resorted to the desperate device of allowing half his image to be out of focus, or focusing on a midpoint between the two halves, or changing focus in mid-shot. But his second solution, of racing, probing camera movements, was less ugly; by 1939 technicalities had improved sufficiently for him to combine deep focus and a fluid camera in *La Règle du Jeu*.

In itself, deep focus is, as we have seen, not new; indeed, there are some 'typically Wellesian' compositions in Stroheim's *Greed*. Nonetheless, the addition of dialogue gave 'Toland-era' films a new dimension. The dialogue could add greater intellectual complexity, and could draw new 'lines of attention' across the image, as in many scenes from *The Magnificent Ambersons*. In both of Welles's films, several scenes are virtually a single take, a synchronisation which is, of course, the negation of cutting. (English critics called the Welles films 'expressionistic', a learned-sounding label which saved them the trouble of noticing what was happening.) One of the most extraordinary examples of *mise-en-scene* is the famous suicide sequence from *Citizen Kane*. At first, from the darkness, we hear laboured, painful breathing, then see the glass and medicine bottle by the bedside. Then we hear anxious queries and knockings at the door, which, at last, is opened, and the family, silhouetted against the light, rush to the bedside. The scene, in effect, opposes the (outsize) glass and the (tiny) doorway; the breathing and the rapping; the sense of a sickroom, the privacy of death and the bewilderment of the living; the reduction of people, in a dying mind, to oppressive sounds and shapes; while the internal visual compression of 'one-scene-one-take' gives a bitter and tragic sense of the claustrophobic mysteries and pressures of a 'house of strangers'. [...]

Citizen Kane (1941): 'one-scene-one-take'

Mise-en-scene was so highly developed already that the coming of Cinemascope added nothing to its resources. In some quarters it drew attention to the possibilities of montage-within-the-image, but those directors who needed their attention drawn to it were obviously not pictorially sensitive enough to do much that was new or subtle. In this respect its real effect was to complicate cutting, especially the slick, quick cutting to which Hollywood had become geared.

When cutting, the editor has to bear in mind that at the end of one shot its spectator's eye may be turned to one part of the screen, and that he has to 'find' the centre of interest in the next shot. The effect has both pitfalls and possibilities, but with Scope's larger field of vision and complexity of detail, the pitfalls, at least, became greater. As Howard Hawks complained about Cinemascope: 'Some people just go ahead and cut it and let people's eyes jump around and find what they want to find. It's very hard on an audience ....' These difficulties could be minimised by storyboarding, but, ironically, the very films in which Cinemascope is most advantageous are those in which the importance of terrain makes storyboarding least practicable: Westerns and adventure films. Nor, of course, does storyboarding suit those directors who work best by responding to actors, and prefer to work to master-scenes. Consequently, Hollywood began exploring ways of minimising cutting; by, to some extent, matching the shot and the scene.

A new rhythm enters the cinema – and an old one returns. In Ford's *Stagecoach* the camera, looking down on the stagecoach from a high angle, pans to discover on the cliff-edge the Indians looking down on it. Thorold Dickinson, in *films and filming*, has cited the contrasted example of Boetticher's *Comanche Station* (1960). The camera holds the little group of horsemen in the foreground and the action fixes our attention to the right-hand side of the screen. Eventually, though, our eyes stray to the left-hand side and there, beyond the ridge, are the Indians – who have been waiting there – how long? In or out of Cinemascope, Boetticher's best films are not only tense, sour stories in their own right, but exhilarating examples of resourceful *mise-en-scene* in the Wyler tradition.

Our few examples can do no more than indicate the vast range of possibilities offered by *mise-en-scene* which, of course, underpins the art of cutting itself. Before the director can storyboard his sequence (whether on paper, on the set, or in the cutting rooms) he has to arrange the action. It affects the choice of locations; Losey has remarked that he and his set designer, Richard Macdonald, unhesitatingly renounce the most picturesque location if it doesn't allow for suitably natural and dramatic staging. And *mise-en-scene* extends, not only to the scriptwriting stage, but to the very basic ideas of a film. No massacre took place on the Odessa Steps. The idea was Eisenstein's. And his later films, of course, illustrate a steady movement away from cutting-montage to *mise-en-scene* and pictoriality. [...]

SOURCE: *FILMS AND FILMING*, OCTOBER 1968, 12–16

ANNOTATIONS

FAKE, FIDDLE AND THE PHOTOGRAPHIC ARTS

[p. 77] As befits the proverbial 'standard work', Wilenski's *Modern Movement in Art*, first published in 1927, went into a fourth edition in 1957. As with the citation from Elster, Durgnat uses it in part because of its typicality. | [p. 78] M. D. Vernon's *The Psychology of Perception*, a similarly 'popularising' book, contains much discussion of gestalt psychology. | [p. 80] **Johannes Itten** was one of the founders of the Bauhaus, replaced in 1922 by **László Moholy-Nagy**. | **Bristow** was a comic strip in the *Evening Standard*. | [p. 81] Saul **Steinberg** was a cartoonist for the *New Yorker*; **Siné** was a satirical cartoonist for his own magazine in France; Roland **Topor**, also in France, for *Hara-Kiri*. | *The Death of Procris*, possibly mentioned because unsigned, undated and of uncertain subject-matter. | [p. 83] John **Bratby**, a British artist of the 1950s 'kitchen sink' tendency. | [p. 84] **Aaron Scharf** was Durgnat's boss at St Martin's, and an important guide in his 'second education' in art. | [p. 88] **Le Corbusier's idea of a Modulor** is, in this context, a means of converting measurements and spatial relationships into the dimensions of the human body.

IMAGES OF THE MIND I: THROWAWAY MOVIES

[p. 92] **In an earlier series**, i.e. the portions of Durgnat's thesis published in *Films and Filming* in 1964–5. | **Eisenstein** discussed *Paradise Lost* in *The Film Sense* (1942). | [p. 93] Alfréd Radok and Josef Svoboda's **'Magic Lantern' show**, first demonstrated at the Brussels Expo in 1958, incorporated actors, dancers, singers, projectors and multiple screens. | Durgnat wrote about Peter Hall's staging and filming of **Marat-Sade** in the June 1967 *Midi-Minuit Fantastique*. | He discussed **'pictoriality'** in the second (January 1965) instalment of the *Films and Filming* series, which became the basis for the second chapter of *Films and Feelings*. | *Bébé Mange Sa Soupe*, aka *Le Repas de Bébé*. | The story of **the leaves on the trees** – derived from Sadoul's *Invention du Cinéma* (1946), in which the observation is credited to the journalist Henri de Parville – is retold in Kracauer's *Theory of Film* and Morin's *Le Cinéma*. | [p. 95] **Emergo** was a William Castle gimmick which involved a glow-in-the-dark skeleton being dangled over the audience. | Durgnat's description of images **leaping from place to place and point to point** echoes an article on 'Film Editing' by Thorold Dickinson's editor Sidney Cole, published in the collection *Film Appreciation and Visual Education* (London: British Film Institute, c. 1944). Cole credited to Griffith 'the realisation that the movie had one unique characteristic: its ability to leap from place to place in space, and from point to point in time' (p. 15). | [p. 97] Durgnat discussed Lang and Murnau **in more detail** in the sixth part of 'Images of the Mind', 'The Restless Camera', published in December 1968.

IMAGES OF THE MIND II: EBB AND FLOW

[p. 100] The **Constructivists' 1920 Realistic Manifesto**, 5,000 broadsheet copies of which were distributed around Moscow in August that year, argued that art should be put in the service of revolution, 'erected on the real laws of Life', etc., and accused the Cubists of mere experimentalism amounting 'to the same old graphic, to the same old volume, and to the same decorative surface as of old'. '*The realization of our perceptions of the world in the forms of space and time*', it went on, '*is the only aim of our pictorial and plastic art*'. | It is perhaps worth noting that Thorold Dickinson also likened montage sequences, such as he was able to insert into films when working as an editor in the 1930s, to **cadenzas** (*Film Dope*, no. 11, January 1977, p. 5). | [p. 101] Dwan's **The Enchanted Island**, already mentioned more than once, was the penultimate film in a staggeringly prolific but almost entirely uncelebrated career that began in the pioneer days of the 1910s. It may have had significance for Durgnat for that reason. | [p. 104] In 'Images and Individuals', the seventh part of 'Images of the Mind', Durgnat credits to Dickinson the view that **La Terra Trema** 'is a major event in screen pictoriality, merging as it does Renoir's informality and Eisenstein's monumentality' (*Films and Filming*, January 1969, p. 66). | [p. 105] In his review of **Night is the Phantom** (1963), published about the same time as 'Michael Powell' (*Films and Filming*, October 1965), Durgnat wrote that Bava had 'resumed the vein opened, and abandoned, by Michael Powell for *The Tales of Hoffmann*' (p. 32).

IMAGES OF THE MIND III: THE IMPOSSIBLE TAKES A LITTLE LONGER

[p. 105] Durgnat criticised **Marshall McLuhan** for his view, set out in *Understanding Media* (1964), that television, as a 'cool' medium, demanded greater participation than 'hot' media like films, claiming, by way of proof, that he was writing 'to the accompaniment of <u>The Avengers</u>' (*Oz*, no. 6, June 1967, p. 29). | [p. 106] 'It is a curious fact of film history', wrote **Karel Reisz** in the February 1951 **Sight and Sound** (p. 415), 'that Eisenstein, who is so often mentioned as one of the most influential figures in the development of film technique, has had so small a lasting influence on the practice of film-making.' | **Paul Mayersberg** was one of the editors of *Movie*. | [p. 107] **Murderers' Row** (1966) was a Matt Helm adventure starring Dean Martin. | [p. 108] **Raymond Williams** argued in **Preface to Film** (London: Film Drama, 1954), that film criticism was 'severely limited in effectiveness' by the bias against the dramatic, condemned with 'terms like *stagey* and *literary*' (p. 1). He also argued against the conventional definition of film realism, preferring, as Durgnat would later, to distinguish between 'realistic in the sense of being part of the normal everyday experience of those by and for whom the film is made' (p. 29); and realistic in the sense of '"producing a convincing effect of psychological reality"' (p. 30). He used the book as the basis of his pioneering lecture series on film at Cambridge in 1968–9, just as 'Images of the Mind' appeared. | **Michael Orrom**, who had been at Cambridge with Williams in the early 1940s, later apprenticed under Paul Rotha and became a documentarist.

IMAGES OF THE MIND IV: STYLE AND THE OLD WAVE

[p. 111] **Howard Hawks complained** in his 1962 interview with Peter Bogdanovich, published in *Movie* and as a Museum of Modern Art booklet. | By **Boetticher's *Comanche Station*** Durgnat means Boetticher's *Ride Lonesome* (1959), which Dickinson cited in his article 'Has the Cinema Grown Up?', published in the July 1964 *Films and Filming*.

Notes

1. Slade Film Department Archive, Box 7: Letter from Thorold Dickinson to Peter Crawley, 8 June 1967.

2. Email to editor, 2 July 2013.
3. Durgnat, *Films and Feelings* (London: Faber and Faber, 1967), p. 36.
4. *Films and Feelings*, pp. 96–7. Cf. Durgnat, 'Expressing Life in Celluloid', *Films and Filming*, May 1965, pp. 47–8.
5. Ibid.
6. André Bazin, 'The Ontology of the Photographic Image', *Film Quarterly*, vol. 13, no. 4, Summer 1960, pp. 7–8. Originally published in 1945 and included in revised form in the first volume of *Qu'est-ce que le Cinéma?*
7. Rudolph Arnheim, *Art and Visual Perception: A Psychology of the Creative Eye* (London: Faber and Faber, 1956), p. viii.
8. Durgnat reviewed *The Stars* in 'Film Goes to the Movies' (pp. 19–20), and mentioned both books in his review of Penelope Houston's *The Contemporary Cinema* (*British Journal of Aesthetics*, vol. 4, no. 2, April 1964, pp. 175–6).
9. Durgnat, 'Art Schools – The Continuing Malaise' (1), *Art and Artists*, October 1969, pp. 7–8.
10. Durgnat, 'Towards Practical Criticism', *AFI Education Newsletter*, March–April 1981, p. 10.
11. Béla Balázs, *Theory of the Film* (London: Dennis Dobson, 1952), p. 145. Cf. Edgar Morin, *Le Cinéma ou L'Homme Imaginaire* (Paris: Les Editions de Minuit, 1956), p. 66.
12. Durgnat, rev. *October*, in *Films and Filming*, March 1970, p. 52.
13. Thorold Dickinson and Michael Orrom, 'The Start at the Slade', *Film*, March–April 1961, p. 22.
14. Penelope Houston, 'The Critical Question', *Sight and Sound*, Autumn 1960, p. 164.
15. André Bazin, 'The Evolution of Film Language', in Peter Graham (ed.), *The New Wave* (London: Secker and Warburg in association with the British Film Institute, 1968), p. 47.
16. Ibid., p. 45; *Films and Feelings*, pp. 29–30. Cf. 'This Damned Eternal Triangle', *Films and Filming*, December 1964, p. 18.
17. V. I. Pudovkin, *Film Technique and Film Acting* (London: Vision Press, 1954), pp. xiv–xv. Originally published as *On Film Technique: Three Essays and an Address* (London: Victor Gollancz, 1929).
18. *Films and Feelings*, p. 36. Cf. 'Truth is Stranger than Fiction', *Films and Filming*, January 1965, p. 46.
19. Durgnat, 'Colours and Contrasts', *Films and Filming*, November 1968, p. 62.
20. Durgnat, 'Spheres of Symbolism', *Films and Filming*, June 1969, p. 31.
21. Sergei Eisenstein, *Film Form: Essays in Film Theory* (New York: Harcourt Brace, 1949), p. 79. A version of the lecture was first published as 'The Fourth Dimension in the Kino, Part II', in *Close Up*, April 1930, using '"picturesqueness"' instead of '"pictorial"' (p. 263).
22. Thorold Dickinson, 'Has the Cinema Grown Up?', *Films and Filming*, July 1964, p. 45.
23. Ibid., pp. 46–7.
24. Thorold Dickinson, 'Introduction to the Second Part of the Enlarged Edition', in Karel Reisz and Gavin Millar, *The Technique of Film Editing* (London: Focal Press, 1968), p. 276.

PART 4
BRITAIN THROUGH THE LOOKING GLASS

INTRODUCTION

Much expanded from the 'Vote for Britain!' series, *A Mirror for England* appeared, after delays, in 1971. It ranged over the years 1945–58, the 'climax period of a middle-class cinema' before the 'combination of proletarian energy and new morality' that animated *Room at the Top* and *Look Back in Anger* shook the old order apart.[1] For the most part Durgnat discussed 'artworks not of the highest textural quality' in order to illuminate the contours of the society in which they were made and seen.[2] As Charles Barr observed, 'so many hundreds of films cannot be held in the mind together. The reader cannot keep up with all the references, nor can he trust the author to still believe all he has written.'[3] Many of the book's critical exegeses were necessarily written from memory, and the result was at times as much memoir as reference work, perhaps most strikingly in the case of *No Trees in the Street* (1958).

An East End story in which a policeman 'wrests a flick-knife from a soft teenage tough and tells him about the bad old days of the grim thirties', *No Trees* was in Durgnat's description the epitome of cinematic Butskellism, with the young ruffian learning that he ought to be 'happy, orderly, grateful' in his 'snug tower block apartment', as provided by the 'brave new Welfare State'.[4] Its writer Ted Willis, later Lord Willis, speechwriter for Harold Wilson, was, according to Durgnat, '*bête noire* of the New Left, appealing as he clearly does to the embourgeoisement of the proletariat'.[5] Durgnat himself found 'old Ted' both complacent about the present and sentimental about the past, and proposed a more clear-eyed alternative, performing an ex post facto rewrite without mentioning that he had worked in the scenario department of the studio where *No Trees* was made, when it was made.[6]

Notwithstanding Durgnat's introductory remarks about 'supplementing the usual textural analysis by a predominantly thematic one' and his conviction that 'many fascinating moments occur in generally mediocre films',[7] the book that followed was, as Barr said, 'suspended between sociology and aesthetics' rather than simply sociological.[8] His oft-cited paragraph on the irrelevance of auteurism to British cinema was followed by another naming Roy Ward Baker, Michael Powell and Terence Fisher as auteurs. Elsewhere Durgnat's auteurism made itself felt by its pointed absence. Of his and Barr's teacher Thorold Dickinson Durgnat wrote that 'most of his films lie outside our time, place and theme. And it's not altogether accidental, for it is precisely this sensitive dynamism that fades from the British cinema generally between 1945 and 1958.'[9]

In Durgnat's scheme, Dickinson's qualities, including the 'ruthlessness of thought and feeling' exhibited in his last British feature *Secret People* (1952), returned to the British screen with Joseph Losey at the end of the decade. 'Not until Losey does so philosophical a stylist appear in British movies. These two exiles, liberal emigrant and Democratic immigrant, are fascinatingly complementary figures.'[10] For the sake of argument, most of Losey's films lay, like Dickinson's, outside Durgnat's 'time, place and theme'. The last line of the book, other than a 'brief sub-chapter on cartoons', ended Losey's story in mid-flow with the contention that *The Damned* (1963), made for Hammer, was 'the last film in which Losey had to work within a form so closely determined by the middle-class traditions which have been our theme'.[11] The best was yet to come.

Durgnat's main point of comparison was the French cinema, particularly the pre-*nouvelle vague* new wave of 'protest films' by Clouzot, Clément, Cayatte and Autant-Lara which he had identified in 1960's 'Look at Old and New Waves'. Thus *No Trees in the Street* had 'the immense merit of suggesting what it fails to be: an epic of the English working-classes, a cross between *The Grapes of Wrath* and *Gervaise*'.[12] Clément's film had played at the Cambridge Arts Cinema in February 1957, the same month *Look Back in Anger* first came to the Cambridge Arts Theatre – a coincidence that may be seen as significant because of the double reversal which Durgnat saw Osborne's play, and the *nouvelle vague* proper, as bringing about.

Since the 1930s, Durgnat wrote in 1965, while '"entertainment" and "documentary"' had been 'antithetical genres' in Britain, 'the French cinema beautifully merged a tender yet caustic feel for human emotion with a militant social consciousness'.[13] The *nouvelle vague* had washed away this latter tendency; but just as 'proletarian energy' departed the French cinema after *Gervaise*, it rejuvenated the British cinema after *Look Back in Anger*. About the time Durgnat's 'Asides on Godard' appeared in 1967, he wrote that:

> Ever since 1962, when I wrote a little monograph on the French New Wave (send only five and six to Motion Publications, 23 Summerfield Road, Loughton, Essex), I've had faint quailing feelings at the prospect of seeing any French film with affinities to that style and tradition. It's not just aversion after an overdose; it's just that most of the directors concerned seem to have expressed themselves thoroughly in their first two or three movies, notably Truffaut and Godard, and they've failed to renew their inspiration. It was only a step from the *temps-mort* to a lack of curiosity about the world around, as if France were less a country with people in it than a set of hypotheses about *ames morts*. Of the French, British, Italian and American cinemas, it's the French which tells you least about French people, and, on balance, I've found English films more rewarding.[14]

The extended version of this theory was worked out in 'Brain Drains: Drifters, Avant-Gardes & Kitchen Sinks', which constitutes a kind of sequel-cum-skeleton-key to *A Mirror for England*. While 'Brain Drains', published in the Cambridge little magazine *Cinema*, concentrates on the evolution of kitchen-sink cinema since the late 1950s, it also provides a sketch of the 'renovated' British art cinema of the same years, including early signs of the British essay-film. Durgnat credited much of this renovation to the emergence of new talent from television, notably Richard Lester, John Boorman, Ken Russell and Peter Watkins. 'TV's Young Turks', which appeared in *Films and Filming* simultaneously with 'Brain Drains' in early 1969, looks at the trend in more detail. Once again, the autobiographical element in Durgnat's view of the film industry – hidebound where television is go-ahead – is unmistakable.

Both essays appeared as the 'Images of the Mind' series neared its conclusion, and are closely related to its central argument. Durgnat had identified Losey and Lester in particular as practitioners of 'the impossible' before he had given the concept a name. Writing in the July 1965 *Films and Filming*, he had described Lester's newly released *The Knack* as a '"mental" world' film, 'one move ahead of Truffaut's *Shoot the Pianist*', which he had in turn discussed two months earlier as part of the pendulum swing away from realism in the last part of his thesis.[15] 'The Great British Phantasmagoria' follows the progress of this British new wave into the mid-1970s, and traces its origins back through Fellini and Marker to Powell and Pressburger.

By the time it was published in 1977, Durgnat had himself joined the 'brain drain' that afflicted British cinema from the turn of the decade, when the withdrawal of US funding 'brought something resembling collapse', as he wrote at the time.[16] Durgnat had crossed the Atlantic in the autumn of 1973, going first to Queen's University in Kingston, Ontario, then a year later to Columbia. Even before leaving he had switched allegiance from *Films and Filming* to New York's *Film Comment*, then edited by the young Richard Corliss. Corliss later recalled that as a film student at Columbia in the mid-1960s 'the three writers I most admired were Andrew Sarris, Raymond Durgnat, and Robin Wood. When Ray became the third of that group to write for *Film Comment*, I felt like Charles Foster Kane after he hired the entire *Chronicle* staff from the *Enquirer:* like a kid with his nose pressed against the candy store window.'[17]

Durgnat published three books in 1974: *The Strange Case of Alfred Hitchcock*, *Jean Renoir* and *Sexual Alienation in the Cinema*, making a total of eleven in the eleven years since *Nouvelle Vague*. Apart from a handful of near-exceptions like *King Vidor, American*, co-written with Scott Simmon and partly based on a book-length study which Durgnat had published in *Film Comment*, they would be his last for a quarter of a century. He took stock in a pseudonymous self-review of *Sexual Alienation*, a piece of writing which registers his dislocation within a transatlantic film culture that had been transformed by the aftershocks of May 1968, though not precisely by its spirit. While slyly claiming affinities with the *maîtres à penser* of structuralism and post-structuralism, it also registers Durgnat's growing rapprochement with a long-disavowed part of his intellectual inheritance, 'Cambridge English'.

4.1 BRAIN DRAINS: DRIFTERS, AVANT-GARDES & KITCHEN SINKS

I

Many French directors move easily between avant-garde, documentary and 'mainstream' (commercial entertainment features). René Clair tackles Dada (*Entr'acte*), documentary (*La Tour*), filmed theatre (*Un Chapeau de Paille d'Italie*). Vigo goes from documentary (*A Propos de Nice*) to the 'expressionistic-impressionism' of *Zero de Conduite* and 'poetic realism' (*L'Atalante*). Carné and Lacombe turn from documentaries to features. Jean Epstein goes from Edgar Allan Poe to documentary (*Mor'Vran*). Renoir works in more genres even than Clair. It's natural, it seems, to be artist, entertainer, documentarist, by turns or simultaneously.

Yet, in England, the same flexibility doesn't apply. Whenever the art current enters the mainstream, it is middlebrow, refined and traditionalist (ex-Shakespeare, ex-Dickens, ex-Maugham). The avant-garde hardly exists, except as a (noncontroversial) conclave within the documentary pale (Len Lye). Documentary is one world, the mainstream another. The two directors (Asquith, Dickinson) whose breadth and depth compare with the French *auteurs* find their style cramped. The industry fears art, vulgarity and the open-minded eye alike, and ventures only cautiously, or under farcical or melodramatic camouflage, out of the upper-middle-class world.

At all events, the '30s documentary is painfully overrated. All but a few keep cautiously within their sponsors' brief: public relations jobs for a series of establishments. Grierson gratifies the Empire Marketing Board, the G.P.O., the Ministry of Information, the National Film Board of Canada. The Lord Reith of documentary intends it to edify, instruct and uplift. An intelligent liberal, he understood that, style being content, aesthetics had impact. He impresses the intellectuals by combining Eisensteinian style with middle-class realism. But, against the vulgarity and struggle which, for French *auteurs*, went without saying as part of life, giving them immediate rapport with audiences and with facts, the documentary opposed a triple barrier: utilitarianism (the village dominie worship of fact), establishmentarianism ('Everything English is a happy harmony'), and a kind of domesticated romanticism (Grierson lyricises drifters, night-mail trains, and trade, as do Masefield and the Georgians). The movement swallowed Jennings – ex-Surrealist, ex-Marxist – without trace. Generally his films are bourgeois-jingoist, and, like *Industrial Britain* and *Song of Ceylon*, just beautiful enough in detail to set my students, rightly, writhing with rage at their serene establishmentarianism. A few of these films (e.g. *Housing Problems*) survive. All in all, the spirit, and limits, of British documentary are those of a liberal, romantic, mystificatory establishment.

When one clears away the critical nonsense with which Grierson set out to fool the highbrows (ipse dixit), and looks at the films, there's no doubt. Time and again, French documentaries annihilate their English counterparts. They have a radical, and a human, rather than utilitarian, tradition; the social background permits controversy. Franju – at once Surrealist and documentarist – is not, as in England he would have been, a lonely eccentric, but a culmination of 'this French school', a French school which evolves steadily from Georges Lacombe's *La Zone* (1928) – BEFORE *Drifters* – to *Loin du Vietnam* – just as *Espoir* and *Baptism of Fire* PRECEDE *Target for Tonight*. The term documentary, appropriate for the English school, is inadequate for the French, which constantly reaches for the *essay* form and craves the significantly broad appellation: non-fiction.

Renoir's *Toni* (1935) and Malraux's *Espoir* (1939) are neo-realist before the Italians. The French documentary shades steadily (via Marker) into cinéma-vérité. Franju, Resnais, Varda, Klein and others move naturally into features. The essay film is brought into feature format and distribution, via Marker, Godard and Klein.

And where does British documentary lead? Its contribution to fiction fossilises into location shooting, stiff upper lip and Ealing England. Jack Lee's *Children On Trial* (1946) hovers on the brink of neo-realism, but the abject evasion of conflict in almost every documentary aborts any English matching of Zavattini. The list of essentially documentary-formed directors is headed by Jack Lee and Philip Leacock. British cinéma-vérité is spiritually and technically a creation of young TV talents. The British essay film hardly exists (outside Levy and Whitehead, who owe nothing to documentary).

II

Free Cinema is the nearest to a transition phenomenon. Lindsay Anderson celebrates the dignity of the workers when they work (*Every Day Except Christmas*) and laments their degradation when they enjoy themselves (*O Dreamland*). *Nice Time* attacks sex and violence in movies (hardly a bold or progressive position) and detects squalor in Piccadilly Circus at midnight. Reisz's *We Are The Lambeth Boys* takes 40 minutes or so to demonstrate that young people's faces are worth looking at in an appreciative spirit and to tell us the *deux ou trois choses qu'il sait d'eux* (their work is monotonous, they're bloodthirsty about capital punishment, full of harmless high jinks and separated by invisible class barriers from public schoolboys). *Momma Don't Allow* is pure botch, socially and aesthetically.

The two critical films are so imprecise as to be misanthropic. The other two are beautiful, as *Song of Ceylon*, that imperial pastorale, is beautiful. As Grierson made a little advance on the 'battle' documentaries (in taking more account of social processes and faces), they have made a little advance on Grierson. The processes don't eclipse the faces; they have reached the stage reached by Mass-Observation in the '30s. Anderson's vehement ambivalence towards the common people, and Reisz's cool, calculated tact, dampen one's enthusiasm a little. We're too obviously in the presence of outsiders to the society they claim to be revealing to us. They're public schoolboys looking the other ranks in the face – respectfully, at last – and that's the source of a moral beauty which is that of a vision. The films have a strained quality, like the love in the voice of a visiting padre: soft, warm, giving, non-responsive, immune, and therefore patronising. Schlesinger's *Terminus* is the only film of this group to look for what it finds, and that is just an interlude in Schlesinger's TV career.

The most moving Free Cinema films are those which put us inside outsiders, and deal with lonely minorities, sometimes of one; Anderson's *Thursday's Children* and *March to Aldermaston*, Robert Vas's *Refuge England*, Lorenza Mazzetti's *Together*. It may well seem as if the working classes function as such an oppressed 'outsider' only – doubly impressive, of course, as an excluded majority. The moral confidence it gives is enormous. Thus it's still a romanticism. Indeed, *Sequence*, the critical magazine founded by Anderson and Reisz at Oxford, denounced the dotage of the British documentary and vaunted (1) the American cinema and (2) poetic fantasy. Its leading articles concern Cocteau, Minnelli, Kelly-Donen, Disney and John Ford. After a working class period, Anderson and Reisz have both shifted back towards a pessimistic left-wing individualism. The tensions between conscientiously radical realism and moral romanticism are extremely brutal. It's easy, and probably necessary, to criticise the incoherence and impulsiveness which, to the unmerciful, may look like bad faith; and to be exasperated by the gruesomely overblown claims made for a handful of merely good, minor documentaries.

Free Cinema's topics had little to offer establishment or commercial sponsors. Trade unions and left wing groups weren't interested in films, or couldn't afford to sponsor any. The cinemas preferred *Look at Life*, *Pathe Pictorial* or *Mining Review*. The older generation of documentarists weren't interested (as Reisz tactfully complained in *Universities and Left Review*). Edgar Anstey at British Transport and others still sometimes produce smart films which the documentarist-critics of the '30s and '40s would have acclaimed, and which no one now notices, or minds. As Reisz remarked, Free Cinema failed. It's not surprising if the struggle through idealism to realism leaves Anderson and Reisz with that experience of confusion which is the real theme of their films. Who doesn't warm to *Morgan*, to *If*....?

III

It's surprising that they don't pursue their quest for realism via TV, for here much of Free Cinema's programme could have been, and was, achieved. To see Michael Ingrams's *Sewermen*, *Street Cleaners* and *Tramps* (all 1956) is to realise just how timid, how remote, even for its time, Free Cinema was.

The British cinema is transformed, not only by TV influences working towards realism, but in an orthodox way; screen adaptions of already proven successes in other media,

Joseph Losey's *The Sleeping Tiger* (1954), Roy Baker's *Passage Home* (1955), both have a sharper sense of class conflict than the later Free Cinema films. But the film which shook the industry was Jack Clayton's *Room at the Top*, financed in the usual commercial way, by an English producer with more Hollywood experience than most. It isn't *Momma Don't Allow* that brings Tony Richardson into the directorial chair of *Look Back In Anger*; it's the fact that he directed the play on the London stage. While the partisans of Free Cinema continued their careers directing stageplays or commercials, the new wave arose via the plays of John Osborne, Waterhouse and Hall, Wolf Mankowitz and Shelagh Delaney; novels by John Braine, Alan Sillitoe, Stan Barstow and David Storey; and a new generation of actors like Albert Finney, Rita Tushingham, Rachel Roberts, Tom Courtenay, Richard Harris, Ronald Fraser, Norman Rossington and Carol White.

The revolution isn't only socio-cultural, it's moral. As a critic pointed out, the new hero (Porter, Seaton) has every trait which made a villain in the older cinema. It's not surprising if, in all this, *auteur*-theory conceptions of calligraphic style take second, or no, place. In just the same way, the great French art mainstream of the '30s represents a deliberate retreat from style-conscious avant-gardery to a Hollywood-type classicism. The *Cahiers* intensification of style consciousness goes, alas, with a drastic narrowing of the social canvas. This isn't to say that style and content can't both be renewed at once; only to say that the novelty of the new British cinema is different in kind from, but not inferior in achievement to, that of the New Wave. The English cinema is now infinitely less class-bound, less bourgeois, more open to society as a whole, than the French, and surpassed only by the Italian.

IV

The stylistic hesitancy is possibly a reaction to an ambient conservatism, checking every impulse, encouraging inner weakness and timid eclecticism. It's arguable that the new cinema is strongest as it adheres to classicism, weakest when it is lured into stylistic innovation. Certainly the best in Richardson is his old-fashioned, Dickensian messiness, his theatrical rapport with actors; and what he borrows from Truffaut is less impressive compared with what he learned from Kazan. John Schlesinger's *A Kind Of Loving* and *Billy Liar* hesitate between cinéma-vérité à la TV and a Renoirian sensitivity. Their weaknesses may arise from Schlesinger's sensitive reluctance to impose himself; the camera is sometimes uncertain whether to emphasise (cinema-style) or to watch (TV-style). The weaknesses are those of richness, recalling, indeed, many Renoir films. Ken Loach uses similar discrepancies of style deliberately, as comment. Reisz uses his camera to whip up energy, so that the hero's confusions and defeats won't be too depressing. *If*, in form and style, has a kind of scatty eclecticism, the challenge of now-it's-true, now-it-isn't, which enables it to appeal to everybody's anarchism while skirting around the $64,000 question: would the rebellion we all crave prove self-destructive, even if we somehow got to blast-off? In the subjunctive, at least, Ford meets Vigo on the playing fields of Eton. It's a tribute to Anderson's spiritual integrity that, from a career which spans yelling 'Stand Up For Jesus!' to filming jingles for Mammon, he distils these ironies, this gallows humour, this auto-criticism, recalling those Eastern European films which can draw on a few hundred years of defeated patriotism. Reisz, a cooler cat, emphasises the outsider's defeat, as well as his self-destruction. After Arthur Seaton, all but tamed by his frigid, semi-detached little girl, comes the sexmaniac of *Night Must Fall* (which might be subtitled: *The Servant*), *Morgan* (every art student's favourite film), and *Isadora* (a boring historical allegory for the hippies).

The Essential Raymond Durgnat

For all its weaknesses, *Morgan* is something of a *tour-de-force*, as probably the only English-speaking film ever to conclude with a triumphant close-up of the hammer-and-sickle.

Visual style apart, many of these films are erratic even on the dramatic level, as if their director has trouble catching the everyday mood, the cultural tone, of the characters. One can criticise innumerable details in *A Taste of Honey*, *The Loneliness of the Long Distance Runner*, and *This Sporting Life*. There are curious lapses in tone or logic in *Saturday Night and Sunday Morning* and the two Schlesingers, *The Kitchen* is torn all ways between Wesker's specific subject (the kitchen), the allegorical subject (the working class failing to unite), between dour realities and the melodrama and eupepsia that substitute thrills for drabness, between Wesker's evident moral ('Socialist kitchens would be less frantic') and more sensible reflections about the nature of restaurant work.

In the event, the Free Cinema radicals are uninterested in the masses except as images for their own discontent. Tony Richardson sheers off to his poetic European limbo, Reisz to his rebels, Anderson to his ambivalent nostalgia. The chore of understanding and exploring experiences other than one's own is left to already established directors, or to those considered infra dig apolitical outsiders. To *We Are The Lambeth Boys*, one may well prefer Clive Donner's *Some People*, or Sidney Furie's *The Boys* and *The Leather Boys*. The mellowness of the Boultings' *The Family Way* is a corrective to movies that portray proletarian life as incessant anger. *The Angry Silence* and *Flame In The Streets* at least acknowledge that collective action is a practical possibility. Peter Collinson's *Up The Junction* catches certain ambivalences in the working class ethos more common-sensically than *The Kitchen*. *The L-Shaped Room* portrays alienation, unfashionably, but truthfully, in terms of squalor and pain. Comic realism, that traditional and adaptable mode, inspires Jay Lewis's *Live Now Pay Later* (how much more subtle than *Nice Time*). Joan Littlewood's *Sparrows Can't Sing*, some happy touches in Michael Carreras's *What A Crazy World*, and of course, Norman Cohen's *Till Death Us Do Part*. To have got from Jimmy Porter to Alf Garnett isn't reactionary in the least; it's a gain in lucidity, for the fact from which the new New Left must start is that Che and Castro are no more the natural allies of the English working class than Mao is Brezhnev's or Brezhnev Dubchek's.

V

Alongside the kitchen sink cinema exists a continuing, and renovated, middle-class cinema, aimed, as often as not, at the American arthouse audience (first revealed by the success of *Brief Encounter*). Kevin Billington's *Interlude*, its style based on post-Lelouch kitsch-Truffaut, is *ersatz*. Peter Watkins's fascinating *Privilege*, Clive Donner's *Here We Go Round The Mulberry Bush*, and weirdies like *Wonderwall* and *Joanna*, belong to the Swinging London brigade.

Here again, efforts at total renovation, à la Godard, simply wouldn't be relevant to what's being said. These films aren't concerned with Godard's reality–unreality games; they are concerned with exploring aspects of social, rather than internal, reality. On the other hand, the ultra-traditional style of Hawks and Hitchcock, with their extremely linear logic, would be equally irrelevant. It's significant that the visual messiness of the British cinema is echoed in livelier sectors of the American cinema (e.g. *The Graduate*, *Pretty Poison*). One may look back to Kazan, whose *Panic In The Streets* and *On The Waterfront*, with their messy, ugly, ethnic faces and backgrounds, were ahead of their time.

The qualities for which documentary stood are now part of the mainstream's repertoire, or, at most, one idiom among many, as in France in the '30s. *The War Game* belongs to the genre of historical documentary, like Renoir's *La Marseillaise*.

VI

Stylistically speaking, probably the most conspicuous English *auteurs* at present are Losey and Lester (two Americans), Polanski (a Pole), Don Levy (an Australian), Albert Finney and Peter Whitehead. If the style of Finney's *Charlie Bubbles* has any affinities, it is probably with Rivette, for its sense of solitude and sectored space, with little symmetries (Charlie's glance wanders from his accountant's face to find a fellow-writer in the background; later, it wanders from that writer's face to find meths drinkers in the background). Whitehead's symbiosis of mind and machine matches, and often surpasses, Godard's peculiar mixture of literary-symbolic reference and eloquent visual blankness. The eye sprouts from the brain and the zoom-lens from the eye. The trombone-slide focus-pulling in synch to the National Anthem in *Tonite Let's All Make Love in London* is one of the most organic pieces of 'post-impressionist' detail since the zooms in Doniol-Valcroze's *L'Eau à la Bouche*; the act of seeing is converted to symbol.

Don Levy's *Herostratus* might be described as mini-Losey (*Time Without Pity* period). It's cut as demonically as with a laser, though whether Levy's Eysenckian theories of association and emotional attack have much validity is another matter. I suspect that the impact of a film which could painlessly lose half an hour or so owes more to the blending of sharp and subtle acting and visuals with crude psycho-social thought than to anything quantitatively new in technique. After all, a cutaway to the hero's psychic icons isn't syntactically different from the memory, hallucination or fantasy flashes in *Hiroshima Mon Amour*, *8½*, *If* or *Pretty Poison*. The leather lady is rather more fascinating in herself than in the fact that she doesn't exist. A traditional film would simply have made her an alternative mistress for the hero, and the film might have been more interesting if she had been; after all, she might well be the *alter ego* he needs, as a masochist's wet dream and with enough life-force for both of them, a splendidly prickly mixture of coloured tart and cool secretary.

After all, our inner and outer worlds aren't always mutually exclusive. The feeling of alienation ends, and the feelings of fun and terror begin, when they overlap. *Herostratus* separates the two, as does, in another way, *Charlie Bubbles*; in neither film could the exterior action solve the hero's problems.

VII

Behind subjective cinema, as behind cinéma-vérité, lies the same technical fact: the lightweight cameras and ultra-fast films which permit shooting anywhere also facilitate *le caméra-stylo*. Furthermore, the absence of slump and war has enabled the '60s to pick up where the '20s had to leave off. It would be a pity if the dogmatic realism which ravaged film criticism from Grierson until Bazin were replaced by an equal and opposite fetishism of style of which Hollywood old-timers like Hawks and semi-solipsists like Godard were the principal beneficiaries. Both cults may be complacent rather than exploratory: the one leading to a nostalgic primitivism, the other to an apathetic nihilism.

One may suspect British cinema to be a major victim of such cults. The society in which we live is, after all, still that of Lambeth Boys, Leather Boys, Billy Liars and Alf Garnetts. The attractions of evasion are all the more obvious. Yet the danger of living mainly inside the congenially cosmopolitan area of one's own head is that ideas develop a life of their own, of which endless doubt and sheer style are the fit artistic image, while emotions and com-mitments revert to the adolescent simplicities of *Rio Bravo*. Certainly any search for new idioms and styles which aren't hand-in-glove with new experiences and emotions will end in pretension. It may be that Losey and Whitehead indicate new stylistic areas for tomor-row's cameras. Meanwhile it's arguable that the 'stylelessness' of the post-*Room at the Top* cinema has the rich healthy and heroic imperfection of Renoir films of the early '30s.

SOURCE: *CINEMA*, NO. 3, JUNE 1969, 12–15

4.2 TV'S YOUNG TURKS

Once upon a time, the cinema never acknowledged the home screen without mocking its tiny size, its unsteady hold and its plethora of idiot commercials, or darkly hinting that its homely quizmasters despised the common people really. Conversely, TV's practitioners explained how distinct the two media were, how TV ought to be 'pure' (i.e. live) and all sorts of other dogmas which just incidentally proved that cinema people ought not to be encour-aged to move in on TV people's preserves.

Steadily, however, TV has not just influenced, but transformed, the British cinema. It has brought a new frankness to the discussion of controversial issues. It has offered an alter-native production structure, with many opportunities for much younger men to be infinitely freer than in the cinema set-up, and it has made lighter equipment and more informal idioms available for the film-maker.

Both sides seem to have muttered to themselves: 'If you can't beat 'em – join 'em!' Cinema and TV are now revealed as different dialects within a common language – dialects which it's quite possible for one person to use alternately, or which don't even need adapting where certain awkward idioms aren't unacceptable.

However, TV's small screen space, and the fact that it is watched in full- or half-light among familiar home surroundings, makes it difficult for TV to match the intensity of the cinema climax, undergone in pitch-dark on a big screen among a mass of reacting peo-ple. The home viewer is less a prisoner of the situation, so finds near-boredom quite tol-erable. Thus cinema films tend to be a succession of climaxes, whereas in TV both peaks and troughs are shallower. In a TV thriller, the action is curter and dryer than in a film, while its dramas accommodate a more thoughtful, brooding style. The kitchen-sink setting (à la *Coronation Street*) comes more naturally, as does homely characterisation. The cinema's larger screen and clearer definition allow for more elaborate effects, and need more care about smoothness. Thus, in the cinema, the workaday TV image seems curiously flat, while many TV directors are, by cinema standards, too content to centre the action in a neutral or messy space. In acting, too, the cinema accepts a more forceful, lyrical style, where the TV director can dwell unemphatically on details. TV directors in their first films frequently veer uncertainly between over- and under-emphasis. From TV, the cinema has relearned a great deal about intimate detail, as about more fluid techniques. It could be argued that the New Wave did little more than use, for the cinema, the lightweight and informal style developed for TV documentary.

The difference in production establishment is vital. The cinema producer's fortunes are more closely bound to profit-and-loss per picture than the big TV networks, and the TV network has various programme hole-and-corners where even an unsuccessful experiment is soon forgotten. By the mid-'50s, the British cinema industry was an old man's, and a craftsman's, industry, in which any new idea was feared and openly hated. It had that deadening 'Yes, but' spirit, where many sectors of TV had a 'Why not? spirit. Once the BBC was stirred from its Reithian slumbers by ITV, Frost and co., it proved again that a central bureaucracy can give vastly more freedom to youthful energy and audacity than Britain's olde worlde businessmen. And whereas the cinema industry was squarely anti-intellectual, TV's new brooms were often university educated, but without being academic about life, an excellent combination. They were afraid neither of being 'highbrow' nor of being vulgar, and there's little need to stress that the deft combination of the two is not only necessary to all serious thought, but also a potent box-office factor. TV (in parallel with *Look Back in Anger*) liberated the cinema of St George from its dragon, i.e. its fear of whatever wasn't middle-brow and middle-class. [...]

Dick Lester, an immigrant from American TV, had already made the short *The Running Jumping and Standing Still Film*, which used favourite Edwardian and Victorian props in a pre-pop-art way. The zany gambolling of pre-1914 gents in parks had a mood quite different from similar motifs in Ken Russell's films, hinting instead at a certain sourness about the smug inadequacy of Britain's spiritual heritage. In their geometrical, pinman way, its Goonish characters, live-action cousins of Goofy and Speedy Gonzalez, evoked a tradition whose activities have degenerated into an ant-like obsolescence.

Lester was, after all, angrier than Osborne, and if his movie oeuvre now deserves a monograph to itself, one can at least sketch its development here. *It's Trad Dad* (1962) and *A Hard Day's Night* (1964) are clearly movie extensions of *Top of the Pops*, sometimes excellent little filmlets; but Lester's readiness to sustain virtual storylessness for feature-length flew in the face of the conventional wisdom. *The Mouse on the Moon* (1963) was a likeable, if low temperature, essay in satirical whimsy, its eccentric Ruritania missing the inspired fantasy of W. C. Fields's Klopstokia. With *Help!* and *The Knack* (both 1965),

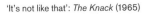

'It's not like that': *The Knack* (1965)

The Essential Raymond Durgnat

Lester joined Malle and Godard as a pioneer of mainstream cinema's movement towards the 'impossible', i.e. purely mental images and continuities. The streak of happy, but mordant, moralising in *The Knack* calls the tune in *How I Won the War* (1967). Rich in allusions and ironies (rainbow coloured ghosts), in deliberate anachronisms (bubblegum cards during the war), in parodies (notably of *Cockleshell Heroes*) and pastiche (of newsreels), and in direct attacks on the audience, its many brilliant moments of immediate appeal are interspersed with ideas which, apart from their denunciation of trite patriotic rhetoric, baffled people. Rather like Losey's *Modesty Blaise*, it uses a kind of visual-symbolic logic still a little denser than most people can follow (or which they can follow only when it expresses conventional ideas, rather than conflicts). Godard, using words, little anecdotes, literary devices galore, and all sorts of highbrow ploys, to present his basically simple mood of cool despair, pleases where Lester and Losey may perplex. But they are resuming the cinematic use of symbols where Eisenstein left off in *October*, and reinventing a kind of expressionism which lacks the too fervid solemnity of pre-war expressionistic drama. [...]

The interesting and, in a sense, solitary figure of John Boorman is best related perhaps to Schlesinger, for his two features, *Catch Us If You Can* (1965) and *Point Blank* (Hollywood, 1967) are both criticisms of cultural emptiness, set in very expensive, and very different, cultures.

In the English film, Dave Clark plays a stuntman who, with the 'Butcha Girl' (Barbara Ferris), flees the cynical world of London ad. agencies. Their mini-odyssey takes them to the beatniks (scattered by army manoeuvres) and a middle-aged couple (Robin Bailey, Yootha Joyce) who have taken refuge in camp nostalgia (for old songs, gramophones, dresses, etc.). The police, hot on the trail of the contract-breakers (i.e. in cahoots with Mammon), burst in on them during a fancy dress ball (the police drive our couple back into reality, the confusions of the 'camp' ball enable them to stay free). Eventually, Steve meets his childhood hero, a Western star now running a ranch as a simple money-spinning proposition. The couple find their offshore island. But, morning and low tide reveal there's no escape – the Mephistophelean ad. agency boss just walked in across the sands.

This little philosophical tale recalls Walsh's *Glory Alley*, Prévert's *Quai des Brumes*, Reinert's *Quai de Grenelle* and Borzage's *Moonrise* in its justification of eccentrics, outsiders and misfits against the social mainstream (even if the beatnik guru's anecdote about cutting a cat in half could seem a concession to the common mass media implication that nonconformity always ends in violence). Lively in its use of space, thoughtful and extremely sympathetic, the film, like Philip Leacock's *Reach For Glory*, seems slightly to muffle its disgust and its tenderness, to move, a little too cautiously, between overtones of the two. Or, if one compares it to Borzage's delicate little lyric, the magic isn't there.

In Hollywood, however, Boorman fulfils the earlier film's promise. *Point Blank* begins where *Catch Us If You Can* left off. The hero, long convinced that money dominates everything, makes his way back into society to get more of it. Another odyssey (*Kill Me If You Can!*), it follows the progress of gangster Lee Marvin as he menaces one member of the organisation after another, for no reason other than greed. And he actually kills none, since an assassination-prone society does his job for him as regularly as fate fulfils Archibaldo's murderous whims in Buñuel's film. This glossy, cold-blooded and satisfyingly nasty tale turns its acreage of sumptuous apartments into a murderous *Marienbad*, a world whose picture windows create envious lookers-in and blind lookers-out, and where the nearest one can get to generous emotions are not hurting the girl who hits one, merely overpowering her, and realising, but only after success, the futility of greed.

Another expert juggler with space is Ken Russell, celebrated for his cultural TV documentaries on Debussy, Elgar, Isadora Duncan, et al. His charming, early short films are less avant- than arriere-garde, for watching *Knights On Bikes* (1956), *The Peepshow* (1956), *Amelia and the Angel* (1958) and *Lourdes* (1958), with their knights, bikes, bathchairs, top hats, deserted stations, sweet little girls looking for angels' wings, bittersweet ragtime and fake beggars, one might, briefly, imagine that Federico Fellini and the Keystone Kops have burst in on the Lewis Carroll world. But Ken Russell is too kind to the Peter Pan in us. Lacking worldliness, this world shows too soft a centre. *Amelia and the Angel* is saved by its lively technique, while the deft and agreeable *Peepshow* has a fine rain of droplets of truth, like the scene in the children's playground, or the lumpy old ragwomen being grotesquely angelic. Perhaps the sternest comparison is with Franju, also a poet of innocence. If one compares Russell's reliance on sunlit nature children or courting couples or gracious house-parties with what happens in the fields of *Thérèse Desqueyroux* between *his* 'angel', Edith Scob, and the bird, one sees Russell is somehow more childlike than Franju, how he slowly works his way to a sadness which may be the end of adolescence but is never quite the commencement of adulthood. Indeed, one may feel that the weakest of his cultural documentaries are the big prestige pieces of which the BBC is proudest, and that his best are those whose subject matter (pop painters, or Bruce Lacey) resists his recourse to the rhetoric of nostalgia.

His first feature, *French Dressing* (1964), was a commercially unhappy hybrid between innocent pep à la Cliff Richard and sad satire of the bleakness of English seaside resorts, presented, alas, in terms so traditionally caricatural as to obviate any tonic effort. Valiantly but vainly, Russell deploys his maestro's sense of space and movement – long piers, roller-skating rinks, marching bands – and crosses Tati-itis with Running, Jumping and Hopping Aboutery. All is lavished on the lost cause of an impossibly tenuous scenario.

Far more interesting is *Billion Dollar Brain* (1967), and not only because it's the second Harry Saltzman production (after the last Bond) to present a too-hysteric America as a bigger danger to world peace than a less volatile Russia. Interlaced with its storyline is a kind of visual-symbolic logic somewhere between *Modesty Blaise* and *Privilege*. A Texan barbecue turns into a blend of Elmer Gantry revivalism and Nuremberg rally, with the fanatical General Midwinter's monogram (M over W) suddenly resembling a swastika. It's all very near *Privilege* in its political fantasy. Politically, the film might have startled NATO-attuned audiences less if the Russians had politely allowed the NATO air force to bomb Midwinter's maverick army through the *Nevski*-style ice, but if the film is in the end less enjoyable than the best of the incomparably less imaginative Bond films, it is perhaps because something cold creeps into the characterisation. So many characters are established as heartless so soon that our interest in the film becomes intellectual-political but not personal-emotional. Perhaps Russell's innocence-idealism mitigates his interest in the states of soul, not always inert, which underlie cynicism, whether on the personal or political plane.

Of the serious realists, Peter Watkins attained fame (or notoriety) as director of *Culloden*, a 'reconstructed documentary' which managed to drag an historical event kicking and screaming out of the history books' cosy atmosphere into the harsh light of reality. The story of its successor, *The War Game*, and how Auntie BBC, scared by the Pharisees, washed her hands, exactly like Pontius Pilate, of the truth, is too well known to need repeating here.

The begrimed, hopeless faces of the firemen cannot but recall the poignant heroism of Jennings's *Fires Were Started*. Watkins's film is the apogee of the documentary style, and

The Essential Raymond Durgnat

The balloon goes up in *The War Game* (1965/6)

the antithesis of the bureaucracy-worship which made the documentary movement spiritually so hollow. As the firemen are swept across the streets by 70 mph convection currents, the commentary informs us that all this happened not only at Hiroshima and Nagasaki but as our dear old RAF bombed civilians at Dresden and Hamburg. This procedure which, theoretically, might break the illusion, the spell, only braces its grip with the steel of fact. It smashes the last barriers which our pathological optimism opposes to reality. This counterpointing of past and present, of visual and intellectual realities, is no less paradoxical and daring than the interlacing of time in Resnais and others. The much-criticised introduction (how World War Three began) seems to me justified (1) for narrative reasons, (2) as just the sort of scenario which is taken absolutely seriously in Herman Kahn-type think tanks at the Pentagon and (3) as setting the whole question of air raid precautions in a wider context. It broadens the theme of universal misinformation, among cabinet ministers as among the men in the street, and it demonstrates the maladjustment of the human race and of its political emotions, which are still in the tribal Stone Age, in this atomic era.

The film's intellectual construction wouldn't have its effect if the 'neo-realism' didn't have its human intensity. It's a matter not only of the incinerated arm which a child holds across its knees, nor of the tremblings of the shell-shocked lining the kerbs, not even of the bucket in which the wedding-rings of the unrecognisably disfigured are thrown (one remembers Resnais's prologue to *Hiroshima Mon Amour*: flesh as source of pleasure, and of infinitely intenser pain …). Maybe because I'm pessimistic, and feel that on present form there's every chance that those large mushrooms will sprout upon a few more countries, possibly including this one, it seems to me captious to be offended by a few less successful effects, e.g. the use of negative to paraphrase the melting of eyeballs.

Most impressively, the film fuses the everyday and the apocalyptic, the familiar and the inconceivable, through a whole range of emotions; the shame in the face of the civil servants who know that all their routines are little more than an ironic deception, the panic of families hiding under the table. The film, like a rosary of such vignettes, evokes the whole vicious circle into which the population would be plunged. An opening shot of the helmet and shoulder of a motorcycle cop frames the peaceful street, while the radio tells of disquieting diplomatic manoeuvres, evokes at once the implacable speed and the confident calm with which law and order will propel us towards the apocalypse. Later, wonderful English policemen are slain by the hunger-maddened crowd, or, bovine-faced, constitute a firing squad for the starving who steal bread. The great danger for cinéma-vérité is to lose its way in a welter of details, but this film is as dynamic in its structure as it is powerful in its details. Yet, even while watching it, it's entertaining to bear in mind that, as a student remarked during a discussion, 'This film is the most dangerous of all, because what it shows is so much more horrible than usual that you think it's showing the truth, and you adjust to it. But the truth – of how people really can die, even from ordinary, almost cosy, things like bullet wounds – is far more horrible than any film has ever shown.'

Though *The War Game* works admirably in the cinema, it lacks the properly cosy home viewing situation. *Privilege* is Watkins's first cinema movie, and deals, appropriately, with show business. It is another essay in the recently flourishing genre which is not so much 'fantasy' or 'science-fiction' as 'anticipation' (cp. *Dr Strangelove*, *1984* and, in a retrospective kind of way, *It Happened Here*). This story of how the City-bureaucracy Establishment take up a Beatles-sized pop star (Paul Jones) and use him as the Elmer Gantry of totalitarian Establishment-worship is hit, below the waterline, as it were, by the difficulty which torpedoed Kazan's *A Face in the Crowd* a decade earlier. How can one show the screen audience worshipping a pop star while appealing to the cinema audience's assumptions that pop stars are just puppets on the strings of public fancy? Watkins, like Kazan, uses every trick of the trade to make it believable, and he convinced me at least sufficiently for every scene to work, to thrill and excite and make a point which one feels is, in spirit, if not in the letter, valid. After all, the Establishment leans on the mass media in every country, and there are plenty of examples in England of the sort of interference *Privilege* supposes (e.g. the secret allegiance of *Encounter* to the CIA, the political preferences in advertising policies, government pressure on the BBC and so on. It's obviously no accident if both of Watkins's films are kept from the mass audience). And it's easy to imagine how, in a crisis situation, all these instances could be systematised, and move in on pop music, recently the freest sector of the mass media (indeed, I rather regret Watkins's concession to anti-pop-music prejudice). But, if this happened, it would happen in a typically English way, and some might feel the movie implausible and paranoid for its borrowings from old-style revivalism and Nazi pageantry (Midwinter was also overdone in the same way). One wonders if Watkins could have found for his revivalism that gentlemanly nastiness, masquerading as concerned responsibility, which he so expertly pinpoints in the pop star's banker backer (and just as Kevin Brownlow hit just the right British note for the Fascist and collaborationist philosophies of *It Happened Here*). Possibly a fuller view of the crisis might have made the hysteric revival of jingoism more understandable. Nonetheless, one can see why Watkins uses the broader effects, or the 'quotes', not only from the Nuremberg rallies, but from *Lonely Boy*, the National Film Board of Canada documentary about Paul Anka, which provides the model for a scene between pop star and agent here. Here, the combination of paroxysmatic scenes, like the 'cop-hate' pop riots (accurate foretaste of Grosvenor Square!), with terse, verbal explanations of the Establishment machinations behind them, have an 'alienation' effect, in the very best sense, better, perhaps, than Brecht's, in that the lucidity co-exists with, and does not need to destroy, the spectator's emotional participation. The brilliantly managed blend of ideology and spectacle seems to have thinned out the human interest – the glitteringly icy moment where Jean Shrimpton discovers Paul Jones's taste for physical, and not merely metaphorical, self-flagellation, deserved something like *The Servant* to lead up to it (though it also convinced on its own). The implication that society's devious rottenness, and not simply private childhood experiences, may be responsible for such perversities of self-hatred is challenging to liberal individualism and rings true; but the film is hollow as to more or less how it happens. As it is, hero and heroine are something between intriguing enigmas and sympathetic ciphers.

Privilege, *Billion Dollar Brain*, *Catch Us If You Can* and *How I Won the War* might be described as 'radical' films, in that they all make radical criticisms of the spirit and workings of society. (This doesn't mean that they're political films; they're no more political than the authoritarianism of Dearden and Relph, or Val Guest, or Anthony Asquith's or the Boultings' liberalism, or the Toryism of Michael Powell or Betty Box, or all those Korda films about how Sabu's smile never sets on the British Empire.) If some of these films seem thin or flawed it is often because they have had to make difficult compromises between the actual semi-conformism of the mass audience, the cinema trade's exaggerated idea of that conformism as absolute, and the idealistic cynicism of young directors sufficiently educated, and in some cases well-connected, to know and to want to warn us just how cynical or irresponsible or self-interested those in power can be, and show how the pressures work (for, knowing this, one can react against them, instead of sinking into a vague defeatism). If certain films are thinner or duller than the theoretically possible masterpiece might be, it is on account of very real difficulties. Losey's early British films were dismissed as 'hysterical' because of his solutions to basically similar difficulties, and Antonioni's heavy emphasis on blank states of mind can be seen as another response to a generally similar problem; the confusion and numbing of feeling, the blurring of conflicts, of character itself, by our particular epoch. *Privilege* puzzled many of the Leicester Square dolly-rockers who'd come expecting a Cliff Richard-type musical, but I think it would be absurd to interpret their silence, in the first half, as a negative reaction to a film whose very real exhilaration lies in its exposé, in agreeably glossy terms, of a system, and helps free one's commonsense from the pious clichés which usually weigh it down. This visually smart and silver film also has a smart and silver ring to it – that of intellectual clarity. [...]

SOURCE: *FILMS AND FILMING*, MARCH–APRIL 1969, 4–10 (MARCH); 26–30 (APRIL)

4.3 THE GREAT BRITISH PHANTASMAGORIA

I. A Mirage for England
During its middle-class consensus – the period of 1945–58, considered in my book, *A Mirror for England* – the British cinema was celebrated for two distinct genres: documentary and phantasmagoria. This rough and ready distinction does make a brisk kind of sense, despite its injustice (which we can't remedy here) to the interesting expressionistic strain of postwar British *film noir*, Carol Reed's ODD MAN OUT and Michael Powell's A MATTER OF LIFE AND DEATH. In its time, the climactic delirium of Reed's masterpiece could seem a last gasp of the pessimistic expressionism of Ford's THE INFORMER and Carné's QUAI DES BRUMES. Similarly, A MATTER OF LIFE AND DEATH – with its very phantasmagoric story of Heaven sitting in judgment on Britain's will to live – could seem a spectacular late entry in the U.S. Depression-and-wartime genre of moral fantasy (DEATH TAKES A HOLIDAY, LOST

Mahler (1974)

HORIZON, HEAVEN CAN WAIT, IT'S A WONDERFUL LIFE). In retrospect, of course, they can also look like harbingers of what is not so much a new genre as a newly flourishing mode. It's by no means restricted to British films, but British films tend to a particular emphasis which we will attempt to indicate.

Certain films stress the proliferation of erotic fantasy at the expense of reality-sense (BILLY LIAR, THE KNACK, THE NATIONAL HEALTH). Other emotional fantasies are steeped in anxiety or regret (SUNDAY BLOODY SUNDAY, THE ROMANTIC ENGLISHWOMAN). Others are politically visionary, whether forlorn (MORGAN) or revengefully self-liberating (IF....). Some psychedelic sagas relate to hippiedom's high hopes (WONDERWALL, YELLOW SUBMARINE, TOMMY). Ken Russell riotously mixes artists' imaginings with what are really little essays in the history of ideas (from romanticism to Nazism in both MAHLER and LISZTOMANIA).

Some films, like John Boorman's LEO THE LAST, develop in as orderly and, in a sense, realistic way as YOU CAN'T TAKE IT WITH YOU. But they are more wistful and sharply aware of their amphibious status as between possibility and pious hope. LEO THE LAST edges us that way by its cadenzas of impressionistic-expressionistic style (the perplexing opening, the wolfish buffet). Essentially, it's in the same "subjunctive" tense as IF...., and Lindsay Anderson's title would fit the Boorman film very well. Boorman's ZARDOZ is clearly visionary, as laden with philosophical ideas as Olaf Stapledon's *Last and First Men*. Its whole attack is inspired by the belief that plausibility matters much less than piling one striking idea upon another, and starting flash fires in the spectator's imagination.

A CLOCKWORK ORANGE is carefully set in a slightly futuristic England – even closer to us than that of 2001, which baffled s.f. addicts by its stress on how little such things as men's suitings may have changed. Similarly, Kubrick's delinquenty film abounds in references back: for all its psychedelia, the milk-bar where nobody can think of anything to do is more like Fifties Teddy-Boys. The result is a sort of social fantastication, a meta-England closer to the virtual present of PRIVILEGE than to the future in FAHRENHEIT 451. PERFORMANCE and DON'T LOOK NOW both turn, or rather gyrate, on axes of vision–metaphysics and reality–unreality, while in Boorman's POINT BLANK an identification figure (Lee Marvin) turns out to be a ghost. Perhaps Ken Russell has most boldly confected a jubilant confusion of photographic-convention reality, mental reality, visual symbol, physical sensation, and aesthetic; the Symbolist movement rides again. But the song-and-dance fight in A CLOCKWORK ORANGE, with its take-off from emotional decorum and visual reality, is another essay in the Russell mode.

Perhaps we can talk of games with reality which amount to Mannerism. Perhaps it's an inverted Mannerism. Schematically, Mannerist painting lunged out from the frame in a sort of strenuous illusionism that asserted and undid itself in paradoxical fashion. But cine-mannerists start from "realistic" photo-movement within the dark and frameless cinema, and then go on to do unrealistic things. Aesthetic attitudes are also involved, as we shall see, although largely through a contrast between the confidently pragmatic British exploitation of aesthetics and a fastidious French nervousness.

The interest in discrepancies between fantasy and reality clearly relates to a common theme in non-fantasy dramas: the undernourishment of subjectivity. Its cause may be British vagueness (A KIND OF LOVING), or manipulation (WEDNESDAY'S CHILD), or complacent materialism (A CLOCKWORK ORANGE), or lack of moral conviction (DARLING), or the enigma syndrome (the innocent family portrait which concludes REPULSION), or mental deficiency (A DAY IN THE DEATH OF JOE EGG).

This link between phantasmagoria and undernourishment is also clear in Ken Russell's best movie, TOMMY. The seed of the poor lad's trauma is parental bad faith; "You didn't see it! You didn't hear it!" they bawl at him in a sort of operatic shock-treatment that propels him into pseudo-catatonia. We're caught up in a variation on the Oedipus complex – only this is more of a Hamlet complex: "My hero father was murdered by my mother and step-father, and now I'll do nothing." Tommy's father's death is a sort of accidentally-on-purpose affair that fairly represents an everyday human mixture of guilt and scruple. Tommy's parents neglect him but are also concerned with him, and the film feels considerable affection for them, despite everything. That Tommy's catatonia is a willful pretense establishes a bizarre connivance in him too. Tommy's complicity helps put Russell's film in a group which includes FELLINI SATYRICON, TEOREMA, and OEDIPUS REX, all of which look at the Oedipus syndrome and clarify facets long eclipsed by Freud's stress on the son's repressed jealousy. For there is also the father's wish to devour the son, the son's willingness to see his mother shared.

II. Alice Over the Rainbow, With Diamonds

The Great British Phantasmagoria involves a mixture of general and local factors. It's not too hard to postulate socio-cultural causes for this quasi-Mannerist phantasmagoria – some common in the West, some particular to Britain. A widespread uncertainty about what's real is recognized in carefully vague vogue words like alienation, future shock, culture shock, the identity crisis of industrial man, and so on. Perhaps older, more rigid cultures did tend to keep doubts quieter – or project them into institutionalized forms like religion, which create one shared, consistent super-reality – whereas complex modern cultures generate a greater diversity of terms in which we only half-believe. From TV commercials to political persuasion we're constantly provoked to think in terms which even their perpetrators know we know are completely idiotic.

If it were merely a matter of truth-versus-falsehoods, the problem would be minor. But we constantly play with various sets of terms and images; we entertain semi-beliefs which aren't obviously sloppy like daydreams, but are only loosely testable against reality. Decision-making processes are long and complicated, and decision-makers may know the results only as abstractions (profit-and-loss, inter-departmental memos, diffuse trends on a graph). We may have ceased distinguishing between this physical world and the next spiritual one. But as our intellectual understanding of this has increased, so has our mental apprehension of it become fragmentary.

Not that the British interest in fantasy is pioneering, unique, clearly distinct, or self-sufficient. In its emphasis on mental images and stream of consciousness it subsumes avant-garde interests (Caligarism, French Impressionism) which had intermittently affected feature movies. Its reflorescence through the Fifties was at first a largely French affair. Marker's LETTRE DE SIBERIE (1958) is extremely important, while HIROSHIMA MON AMOUR somewhat stiffly initiated the commingling of objective and subjective reality which became fully flexible with 8½ Even now, film still has to achieve the intimate intermingling of reality, memory, and "subjunctive" tracks which narrative literature had elaborated by 1900. TV profoundly affected the phenomenological status of movie images. It diminished, domesticated, and devalued (by instant replays) the previous link between moving image and reality. It subjected photomovement to the same contemptuous familiarity as newsprint. Two decades of TV commercials underlined the difference between interest and belief. A new familiarity with plots, and quickness on the uptake, went with a new detachment.

Parallel concerns are clear enough in high culture trends like absurd theater and the new novel. The heirs of Kafka (once thought so obscure) range from M. C. Escher and J. G. Ballard to Borges and Magritte (the last two are conspicuously featured in PERFORMANCE; the same Magritte painting is featured in PERFORMANCE and Lester's THE THREE MUSKETEERS). Even pulp movies freely disrupt chronology, question phenomenological status (the flash-cutting of EASY RIDER), or engineer uncertainty as to what's dream and what's not (as in Jonathan Demme's CAGED HEAT).

A movie like A HARD DAY'S NIGHT doesn't ask for any belief at all. It's not exactly "about" being a movie, but it produces its effects under the assumption that the audience knows "it's only a movie" – that only for a nonsense movie would the Beatles leap about a field like fugitives from a hopping-skipping-and-running-about film. It fulfills, on a pop rather than precious level, the Symbolist dictum that all arts aspire to the condition of music, that they work by developing ideas whose status in concrete reality is irrelevant to a sort of intrinsic logic.

The profound interdependence of subjectivity and objectivity is illustrated by Martin Scorsese's ALICE DOESN'T LIVE HERE ANYMORE, which comes near to the British mode. It has obvious populist/kitchen-sink aspects: its key scene actually takes place in a ladies' toilet. But it opens on a Tara Over the Rainbow tableau which is Alice's Garden of Eden, the impossible dream which she pretends her first marriage is like. The reality with which she finally comes to terms is a bit of a dreamboat affair; I doubt if, for example, John Cassavetes, would have accepted Scorsese's box-office compromise – in tone throughout as well as in its ending. The wizard and his Over-the-Rainbow-land recur, to be renounced, in John Boorman's ZARDOZ, where it's properly human to prefer renunciation, aging, and death to a luxurious immortality as perfect and repressive as Marienbad's. It's not only in Britain that fantasy dissolves into reality. Alice's liberation from her Technicolor blinkers recalls André Malraux's remark that the hidden theme of every worthwhile novel is "Lost Illusions."

For all the overlaps it's probably fair to say that British phantasmagorias have their particular way of dwelling on the rivalry between mental images and reality. The British school tends to be less violent than the U.S. and less cerebral than the French. The characters of U.S. films are less likely to play along with fantasies as such, whether whimsically or cautiously. But they are quicker to take them for granted as true and act on them, so that they become simple assertions. "If you don't have a dream, how're you gonna make your dream come true?" So stories of probably erroneous beliefs like BOB & CAROL & TED & ALICE look more like straightforward drama than like playalongs with fantasy.

The library of *Zardoz* (1974)

In another, but related, U.S. mode, Arthur Penn's MICKEY ONE is essentially a paranoia saga. But it balances its reality sense and its expressionism enough to dispense with the distinct "subjective track" we find in, say, REPULSION. It's as near Bukowski as Kafka. In some other exceptions (FREUD, PRESSURE POINT, ROSEMARY'S BABY) there's still, perhaps, a sense of fighting through the fantasies, of one will versus another, of Jekyll-and-Hydeism. By contrast, Billy Liar doesn't try to make his dreams come true; he's content to walk along with one foot in each world, much as many young Britons since Suez half-believed that Britain was still "great" and half-believed she wasn't.

It's intriguing to compare three treatments of related themes. In THE DAY OF THE LOCUST, John Schlesinger becomes boldly expressionist. THE WAY WE WERE (or thought or hoped we were, till came the crunch) is a straightforward, rather soft drama. And in THE GREAT GATSBY Jack Clayton – who has reversed the general British trend by increasingly abstaining from the Carol Reed-type expressionism quite clear in his own THE BESPOKE OVERCOAT (1955) – uses a kind of impressionism of glossy surface to catch the vulgar fragility of Gatsby's world. Perhaps the technique is too romantico-refined, like Scott Fitzgerald's; Gatsby is, after all, related to Boetticher's Legs Diamond. Fitzgerald is one of those minor novelists whose novels would be much improved by being betrayed. He was too soft a touch for Kennedy-type images.

In contrast with French treatments of similar themes, the British films tend to be less cerebral, less dogmatic, less cold or even schizoid in tone. Whether we think of Resnais, Robbe-Grillet, or Duras, the French style implies a kind of thinning of reality. The British tendency is to endow the mental world with a warts-and-all diversity of detail, much like reality. In the French style, reality becomes the one sketchy mental possibility that just happens to be in some sense real. Their worlds are essentially rationalist, intricate but linear, born of Cartesian doubt, their roots sparse and thin in the compost of human experience. They relate both to the vacuums and solipsisms against which Godard erects his dogmatico-verbal barricades, and to the stylizations that protect so many merely personal films from comparisons with experience.

If the British acceptance of fantasy as such suggests a much more vague, or hesitant, mentality than the U.S. – a too-tactful abstention from the nitty-gritty – it's also rather less paranoid. What it loses by its negative nonaction it makes up by being much less destructive and depressed instead of schizoid. Its lower profile goes with a broader base.

III. The Editor Regrets ….

1. But let's begin our study of the British style at the least obvious place: the turning point of documentary tradition, from affirmation to questioning, in Peter Watkins's CULLODEN (1964). It celebrates the last battle fought on English soil, and is an ironic epilogue to Olivier's HENRY V, where Agincourt represents the fruit of British unity. It's also an antithesis film to the lordly view of history (from BONNIE PRINCE CHARLIE to A MAN FOR ALL SEASONS). As it reverses Olivier's patriotic (and, in its time, natural) delight in realpolitik, so it invents a converse mode of fantastication. The eighteenth-century battle is watched (with the aid of a proper period telescope) by a commentator who addresses the (impossible) camera or microphone and expresses, as if on our behalf, all the attitudes of a liberal, Ealing England. He is a time traveler, horrified to learn the facts of history. Analogous procedures tend to authenticate the science-fiction, or rather society-fiction, of Watkins's later THE WAR GAME, PRIVILEGE, THE GLADIATORS (THE PEACE GAME), and PUNISHMENT PARK.

With their coldly factual commentators, CULLODEN and THE WAR GAME combine documentary lyricism (in the sense of human feeling, not "lyrical" fiddle-faddle) and a kind of technical exposition (like AERO ENGINE, only applied to socio-human mechanisms). Perhaps Watkins is as crucial as John Grierson in the development of documentary. He shows that it has still to offer what *cinéma vérité* cannot: not only the past, but all the non-visual and non-localizable connections that hold the world together.

Although the commentary carefully restricts itself to information, its selection is such that it's fair to say that Watkins editorializes. But whatever Bazin may say, it's virtually impossible not to editorialize; by definition, *all* auteurs editorialize. We really can't expect all films to conform to one particular mode of twentieth-century fiction. Pseudo-objective realism is almost as restrictive as the neo-classical unities of time and space. This is true particularly after TV documentaries have combined the pseudo-objective quality of photo-movement with the direct exposition of unphotographable realities.

To accept John Ford's treatment of the massacre of the Indians in STAGECOACH, while resenting Watkins's treatment of the massacre of the Scots in CULLODEN, is to yield to preferences either in ideology or in questions of temperament and tact. For some temperaments, Watkins falls between the stools of fictional and factual forms; others will feel that he combines the strengths of both. To me his editorializing – with its layers of illusion-expanding commentary – seems more provocative and less mystificatory than Jean-Marie Straub's use (in OTHON) of the merely negative alienation effects of Brechtian theory. Marker and Godard undermine their images by a kind of systematic doubt, and undermine Bazin's faith in phenomenological truth. But Godard continues to brood over it and toy with it and oppose to it little but doubt or dogma. Thus he degrades scrupulousness to solipsism and reduces an interrogation of the image to an inert aestheticism (which, of course, is grist to the mill of pseudo-radical academicism).

The gaps and jolts and discontinuities generated between Watkins's layers of commentary and the image – which thus becomes a *partial* truth, emotive but naive – belong to another philosophical tradition. It is that of Dr. Johnson's answer to Berkeley (Bishop, not Busby); of Hume's commonsense response to his own criticisms of empiricism; and of the simultaneously moral and materialist assertiveness that inspires Marxism to try to change the world instead of understanding (or merely doubting) it. Some things are sufficiently true to be "true," and more significant than others. Action must "bracket" doubt, tolerate it without yielding to it.

A faintly (though righteously) paranoid atmosphere may hover over Watkins's movies. But I don't think this is merely because paranoia is appropriate to politics, where no clear moral code applies; nor because we still, despite ourselves, tend to disassociate our humanist emotivities from the nasty machinations of statesmen. It's also because Watkins hasn't yet taken the final step to what may seem banal but might amount to a new classicism. This would eschew even his scrupulous rhetoric and make straight radical documentaries which, instead of alienation and similar pixilations, would present that careful balance of truths and counter-truths which precludes a runaway lyricism and generates a respect for – and pain about – even the truths most congenial to Fascism. In CULLODEN Watkins comes closer to it than he ever has since. Perhaps the closest film to it is Gillo Pontecorvo's THE BATTLE OF ALGIERS, although a real tension remains between Watkins's humanist sensibilities and Pontecorvo's post-humanist (or post-liberal) apologia for terrorism – and, by analogy, torture, and realpolitik.

2. Dick Lester's HOW I WON THE WAR, a soul-brother of CULLODEN, typifies another idiom of overt editorializing. It takes off from a half-Ealing, half-Goonish plot about a platoon detailed to prepare an advanced cricket pitch behind enemy lines. Any story is completely transformed by adroit mixtures of mordant caricature, strange fantastications, and a kaleidoscope of styles – from documentary stiff-upper-lip to postwar bubblegum cards, from Hollywood blood-and-guts to the lovable dottiness of army farces like TIRE AU FLANC (THE ARMY GAME). A Mannerist interdeconstruction of modes is compounded as the whole crazy quilt of myths, jests, and P.R. lies is jammed up against an uneasy balance of idiocy and pathos and a few spare, sharp intimations of the nitty-gritty. Far from being an antiwar film in the naive and earnest sense, it's an antiwar-is-fun film. Compounding the aggravations of M•A•S•H, MONTY PYTHON, and LES CARABINIERS, the film provoked angry attacks by ex-Desert Rats; it bewildered audiences even as it antagonized critics. Probably the reason is not editorializing as such, but a constant jolting against expectations. (A similar fate was suffered by Joseph Losey's MODESTY BLAISE, which abstained from editorializing, attacked its genre assumptions more subtly, and aroused a bewildered sales resistance to what was sensed but not understood.)

The ins and outs of tact are extremely intricate, and HOW I WON THE WAR is certainly a mean machine. It may owe something to Godard's LES CARABINIERS, but it's principally a crossing of Goon-dada, irrealism à la HARD DAY'S NIGHT, moral criticism as in THE KNACK, and Joan Littlewood's *Oh! What A Lovely War*. Its method of attack is resumed in Richard Attenborough's thorough revamping of that stageplay. The film version editorializes like a newspaper cartoon; thus the rulers of various countries stand on their countries in a map of Europe. Sharing a greater distance from current myths with Godard's LES CARABINIERS, Attenborough's film enjoyed general acceptance – except by the radical left, which followed its usual rule: exasperation at British mainstream, abject tolerance of Godard's nihilism.

It's infinitely regrettable that the box-office failure of Lester's sarcastic trio (HOW I WON THE WAR, PETULIA, THE BED SITTING ROOM) should have forced him back to more covert asperities, like the pointedly cold relationships of JUGGERNAUT. The Four Musketeers are just a quartet of young Blimps in the service of totalitarian intolerance, while Royal Flash is a cad/cadet or Blimp-cum-Bond-cum-Lucky Man surviving in a *ronde* of rigid egoists (Bismarck, Lola Montez, etc.). ROYAL FLASH concludes on an image of idiotic desolation, a bizarre counterpart of Gabriel's end in MODESTY BLAISE. PETULIA apart, Lester is a contemporary heir of René Clair. He has Clair's fantasticated melancholy, and his sense of human relationships as bright, scampering solitudes.

3. In O LUCKY MAN!, Lindsay Anderson adapts the classically Brechtian device of a narrator who, in some not too markedly didactic fashion, keeps giving the game away. What matters isn't the merely negative disruption of the illusion. If it were, we would be forced to talk of alienation effects in, for example, Duvivier's LA FÊTE À HENRIETTE (where each of two scriptwriters keeps twisting the film-within-the-film in the direction of his world-view), or of Olivier's HENRY V (whose disillusions celebrate patriotic sentiments), or Ophuls's LA RONDE (although its sad ironies seep in through the stories as well as through the interventions of its emcee-pimp).

Brechtians have shown curiously little interest in reactionary equivalents of the "alienation" effect. Some Brechtians rather simple-mindedly suppose that the effect itself guarantees an ideologically correct end-product. But what matters is not so much the shattering of illusions by counter-illusions – or contrived and merely phenomenological shatterings of illusions – as what each effect contributes to an overall continuity. If a film's material is interesting enough, the "illusion" will re-establish itself as rapidly and inexorably after every "alienation" as after the opening credits, or as after the jump cuts in BREATHLESS. To affect its context, an alienation effect must come under the normal rules of montage. One could argue that the best kind of alienation effect is a story that opposes our concern for one character against our concern for another, or mixes fear and hope, or combines consequences in ways that shatter comfortable assumptions (as in Losey's storytelling tactics). Indeed, Brecht's whole theory of alienation depends on notions of audience identification and immersion in illusion which are wildly simplistic. They suggest to me that Brecht was overreacting against romantic theory rather than relating to theatrical realities. At any rate, films like Watkins's, Lester's, Anderson's, and Nicolas Roeg's exemplify important equivalent procedures.

We hardly need Alan Price to tell us that Mick Travis, the Malcolm McDowell character in O LUCKY MAN!, has the wrong idea about the people he meets, or that our feelings about them and him should be mixed, any more than we need an overt commentary in SULLIVAN'S TRAVELS (to choose a broadly similar tale of lost illusions). Price acts much more like the chorus in a Greek drama: his is the voice of a hardbitten common sense, about which we can, and do, feel ambivalent in its turn. Price gives the film a sort of musical exhilaration, relaxing it and reassuring us that a disenchanted view needn't diminish our zest any more than it has the singer's. The lyrics also encourage us to think about the film's moral as a pragmatic, philosophic proposition, rather than accepting it as merely the unfortunate but particular experience of Mick Travis. Its apparent "alienation" is a matter of underlining the moral rather than undermining the film.

Price doesn't quite address us directly – he might be performing in a club – but he does come pretty near ex-illusion status. And if one is going to break the illusion in one way, one might as well break it in two. Sometimes the two disruptions, reinforcing each other, work less obtrusively. And so Anderson also introduces pastiche-Pudovkin: small black and white silence. (Pastiche is a running accompaniment of phantasmagoria, for obvious reasons.) Similarly, at the end of YELLOW SUBMARINE, a direct address by the four Beatles (warning us that new and nastier Blue Meanies are on their way to this theater) goes with the switch both from animation to live-action and from a kind of long-shot distance to a multiple-close-shot effect. But whereas Anderson eventually lets Alan Price into the story (with only a pleasant sense of mild trespass), Roeg glories in the distensions of reality in PERFORMANCE's "Memo From Turner" number. This is really a little fantasy-opera where, presumably through Chas's eyes, we see Turner as another gang boss. But here too, I think, we sense a kind of editorializing – if not by the artist himself then by some *persona* appropriate to his film.

4. Ken Russell is another industrious editorializer, but in a very different key. Editorializing is quite clear throughout LISZTOMANIA, from its opening parallels between the romantic piano virtuosi and modern popdom to Liszt's vision of Wagner's music leading to Hitlerism. The romanticism/pop music parallels use a kind of split style (juxtapositions of character-istics from different areas) to achieve what the Eisenstein tradition would have suggested by montage (juxtapositions of complete shots). Russell operates montage (in Eisenstein's sense) at the level of *mise-en-scène*. The contrasts and affinities between OCTOBER and LISZTOMANIA are extremely interesting, insofar as both incorporate battles of ideology, *kulturkampf* insignia, and caricature.

5. Joseph Losey and Nicolas Roeg editorialize by revitalizing montage sequences – by Losey in THE ASSASSINATION OF TROTSKY (where his intended point, waste, remained obscure to everybody) and by Roeg in WALKABOUT (whose broad dichotomy, civilization vs. wilder-ness, is presented with a baldness that forces us to relate *this* story to issues which, because they are general, also involve *us*). Roeg's extremely vivid photography welds the illusion, the generality, and relevance together in a quite straightforward attack.

Schematically, Watkins uses the images to present an immediate, personal experience, the human tense of action, suffering, and pride. The cool, factual aspects of the commen-tary underline the hard, Machiavellian movement of history. In addition, the commentator of CULLODEN and the TV crew of PUNISHMENT PARK are spokesmen for a humanist decency which – though concerned with truth and in no way overly squeamish – is sufficiently "sen-timental" to prefer the Geneva Convention to genocide, and freedom of speech to con-centration camps. In PUNISHMENT PARK the grounds are run on patriotic, Social Darwinist, and B. F. Skinnerian lines; the rigorous trek culls the men from the boys, and its goal (the U.S. flag) associates deliverance with an uncritical patriotism. For his inspiration, Watkins may well have drawn on a notorious instance of the treatment of conscientious objectors in Britain.

IV. Piranhas in a Small Glass Bowl

If Watkins criticizes reality by bringing out its hidden possibilities, Godard criticizes ideol-ogy by exhibiting an impoverished reality. In stark contrast to the British tradition (with its reverence for the texture of reality, which is rich, discursive, and contradictory), Godard sketches in a minimal reality which, unsurprisingly, seems cold, monotonous, dead. The responsiveness of Watkins is replaced by a mere assertiveness, and a desperately willed dogma becomes Godard's ersatz for experience. An imperfect, polluted, but shared reality is denied; and the desired state, still inexistent, can only be dogmatized into existence. In that sense, the readings-aloud from edifying works exactly correspond to ritual recitations of the Apostles' Creed in Catholicism. In TOUT VA BIEN the sit-in languishes, the media intel-lectuals set about deconstructing their subjectivities, and the flag of cohesive anarchism is raised only by ephemeral or defeated confrontations in supermarkets and streets.

It's true that Godard's young have made progress since his LE PETIT SOLDAT: they have inverted his whimsy, privacy, culture, and Fascism into discipline, solidarity, confrontation, and social concern. But for his insouciant relativism they have substituted a kind of moral abso-lutism – a conviction that life is either false or hypothetical, or hardly exists. A stress on language suggests that the only thing one can do with assertion is to assert it – or subvert it. Reality hardly exists outside language, and a recklessness about the former complements a fastidiousness about the latter. The nihilism which in 1960 justified the little soldier's Fascism now justifies the refusal of reality by a mixture of linguistic fastidiousness and radical purism. The antithesis of Godard's radical critique is that of John Berger (the novelist and co-author of three Alain Tanner films), where a dialectic of appreciation and criticism replaces negation and dogma. Ironically, the readings-aloud by a saving remnant in Godard's radical LA CHINOISE match the recitings-aloud by a saving remnant in Truffaut's conservative FAHRENHEIT 451. (It's amusing to imagine Godard as FAHRENHEIT's Montag.)

In its outline, TOUT VA BIEN comes oddly close to a Watkins subject. Precisely according to the Watkins formula, a decently concerned observer covers the strike and is shocked into a commitment whose consequences leave him profoundly changed. Similarly, some basic motifs in WEEKEND would lend themselves to the mordant absurdism of Dick Lester. It is a tragedy of radical aesthetics that attention has fetishized on Brecht and Godard, excluding the wealth of alternative solutions, as well as some instructive comparisons (ONE PLUS ONE/PRIVILEGE/A FACE IN THE CROWD). By failing to realize that alienation is only a form of editorializing (or by using the term to hide the affinity), radical academics cosset their elitism, and hysterically perpetuate the auteurist cult of personality which Marxists should be the first to deconstruct.

If Watkins betrays the anguish of the humanist who awakens from the nightmare of history only to realize that its bloody tumbrels are rattling under his bedroom windows (the L'AGE D'OR vision), the Godardian option is a systematic devaluation of the human cipher. In LES CARABINIERS Godard parodied the Christian sensibilities of De Sica and Zavattini to settle for a misanthropic, almost Célinian, view of "The Universal Soldier." Since then he has struggled to mortify his scruples, to gear his soul for the bloodbaths implied by those rhetorical touches which Andrew Britton criticizes as "dishonesty" in *Framework* No. 3.

Watkins's humanism maintains its liberal scruples alongside a radical disillusionment. Godard struggles to agree (with Pontecorvo on the one hand, and with hard-edge conservatives like Hawks, Fuller, and Siegel on the other) that terrorism and torture are the effective, logical, and natural way of going about the nitty-gritty of politics. While Herman Kahn, Chairman Mao, and Solzhenitsyn assure us that atomic war is eminently thinkable, almost a duty, radicalism hears again the still small steely voices of Machiavelli and Clausewitz, and is not just haunted but more than a little persuaded by the evidence presented in, for example, *The Destruction of Dresden*, *Mass Society In Crisis*, and *The Twentieth Century Book of the Dead*.

Or, rather, we can distinguish two radicalisms. The soft radicalism of the hippie era hopes that de-repression and love are all you need. It took one aspect of liberalism to a literal extreme, and has steadily lost ground to hard radicalism, which thoroughly despises the liberal view that violence is a dysfunction of history. It sees violence as a part of history, which will end only when history ends, with the triumph of the proletariat. For this hard radicalism, not only diplomacy, but everything, is the continuation of war by other means. Makavejev's WR – MYSTERIES OF THE ORGANISM rather uncertainly cleaves to the soft radical view. Oshima is more ambivalent. Godard, in ONE PLUS ONE, can't help getting a little glassy-eyed as Black Power shoots the Swinging London chicks and brings all Enoch's prophecies to pass. But it's quite clear why so many radicals prefer hard-edge conservatives like Fuller and Peckinpah to the moral liberalisms of Costa-Gavras, and opt for alienation (withdrawal of feeling) over involved statements.

In THE DAMNED and KING AND COUNTRY, in THE ASSASSINATION OF TROTSKY and FIGURES IN A LANDSCAPE – in those "lean" studies of totalitarian atrocity which contrast with his "plush" studies of self-indulgence – Losey broods over other aspects of the same nexus. Is terror necessary to efficacy? FIGURES IN A LANDSCAPE is as pointedly abstracted from "psychologism" as the films of Jancsó (or LES CARABINIERS and OH! WHAT A LOVELY WAR), and many Eastern European directors share the sense of dichotomy. On the one hand, consciousness is precious but evanescent; on the other, impersonality buttresses atrocity. Thus Jan Nemec's MARTYRS OF LOVE contrasts with his DIAMONDS OF THE NIGHT, and with Tarkovsky's SOLARIS and ANDREI RUBLEV. THE ROUND UP suggests *The Gulag Archipelago*. Indeed, it might be interesting to compare Losey's severe puritanism with that of Solzhenitsyn, whose journals would climax Losey's "harsh" line as fittingly as the director's Pinter collaboration on an adaptation of *Remembrance of Things Past* would climax his "plush" line. But if the human being is only an ideological machine, as Godard requires him to be, then the real moral of ALPHAVILLE is clear. Godard's Lemmy Caution doesn't come from another galaxy – he's a strayed robot from WESTWORLD.

SOURCE: *FILM COMMENT*, MAY–JUNE 1977, 48–53 (© 1977 BY THE FILM SOCIETY OF LINCOLN CENTER)

4.4 *SEXUAL ALIENATION IN THE CINEMA*

This lavishly illustrated tome sits as heavily on the mind as on the wrists. The author presents it as his sequel to *Eros in the Cinema*. Like its predecessor, it bears the marks of production problems. It covers movies from about 1962 to 1972.

As a sales package it strikes me as misconceived. No doubt the publishers expected that Durgnat's text would satisfy, or at least browbeat, the serious reader. Meanwhile the pictures would attract swarms of nostalgia buffs and soft-core aficionados.

In practice everything has gone wrong. There are too few pictures to turn browsers into buyers. Many of the stills, like those from Losey or Germi films, have no appeal to the nostalgia trade. Some of the handful of hardcore stills show Dr. Muehl's commune at play, and they're likely to offend many serious readers. The text couldn't be more ill-suited for a picture book. *Playboy* will never commission Durgnat.

He has always given the impression of being a loner. He has never mastered the art of writing as if he's by the reader's side, thinking his thoughts along with him. He probably doesn't realize such a tone is possible. He concentrates on thinking the thoughts which his readers have tried to avoid thinking, because they must lead to trouble. Some writers are guides, others are adversaries. Durgnat belongs to the latter persuasion. He generally forfeits what, in the end, is most persuasive: our affection. He may score points against us, but he's always out there, working on us from the other side of the page. He remains evasive even when he tries to be personal. His penchant for switching from one style to another only adds to his remoteness. He's something of a mystery man, and not an altogether friendly one.

His welter of styles makes it obvious why he's so diffident about the auteur theory. He likes auteurs who are also chameleons, probably because he's one himself. Some critics write about film, others about film AND. Durgnat, infuriatingly, belongs to both categories. But of all his books, *Alienation* is most emphatically film AND; occasionally it's AND film.

I would have guessed that Durgnat was a disciple of Arnold Hauser who had also become immersed in psychoanalysis.[*]

Durgnat's heavy interest in Film AND should put him alongside the Marxists, at the opposite extreme from the New Criticism, whose concern would be purely and strictly with Film as Film. Yet in the course of an interview with *Platinum* years ago, Durgnat, with his usual perversity, named the New Criticism as the formative influence on his work – at which the bloodhound slumbering in every literary critic pricks up his ears. Can we produce a cultural composite of our mystery man? First we must look at some critical history.

The New Criticism is now fifty years old. It originated at Cambridge in the Twenties. I. A. Richards reacted against the gentlemanly dilettantism and the gourmet aestheticism which had ruled the appreciation of literature in Britain. He brought a scientific concern for objectivity to reading the words on the page. It very successfully defended literature's independence against the Marxist tendency to make it a subsection of sociology. It rapidly became extremely influential in the U.S.A. There, so its younger critics aver, objectivity became withdrawal from reality. The laboratory spirit became academic remoteness. Under the influence of Southern agrarians, the New Criticism became urbane, elitist, and conservative.

In Britain, however, the New Criticism was taken up by F. R. Leavis. Like Richards, he stressed the text as an autonomous self-explanatory whole. But he welded this stress to the nonconformist conscience, and so to a whole range of moral and social concerns. He made literature central to humanism. Leavis remained a Liberal, but his influence was enormous on the New Left, as well as on Robin Wood, Charles Barr, and the Canadian Peter Harcourt. All have made their debt to Dr. Leavis quite clear.

For Dr. Leavis, the microscopic analysis of a text was never an end in itself. His bent was moral rather than analytical. Often enough he asserted that a text's quality and meanings were self-evident, even where the New Criticism would have showed exactly the opposite. He was uninterested in foreign literature, which was his right. But his influence strengthened the parochialism of English thought in the Fifties. Despite his influence on the New Left, his emphasis on the autonomy of literature left an ideological void. After the glamorous student riots of 1968, this void remained to be filled by radicalism, structuralism, semiology, and the raving Francophilia of *Screen*.

Some English critics had already begun throwing bridges across the gulf between literary interpretation and life. Christopher Caudwell's tragic death interrupted his attempt to combine a scientific impulse like the New Criticism with a sophisticated Marxism. His closest spiritual kin, George Orwell, adopted an essay style, not an analytical one. Raymond Williams, who came somewhere between F. R. Leavis and George Orwell, but to their left, related English literature and social history in four major books whose material remained somewhat remote from contemporary cinema. They may have influenced Alan Lovell's book on documentary and Charles Barr's excellent study of Ealing Studios.

Durgnat's writing never evokes, or acknowledges, Dr. Leavis. He comes closest to the New Criticism when he sets about teasing all the shreds of meaning that he can find in a scene or a style. He does it not only to "thinkers" like Buñuel and Hitchcock, but to lyrical directors like Renoir and Fellini. When he converts lyrical moments into philosophical arguments, his affinities with the New Criticism couldn't be clearer. The strongest influence on

---

[*] Arnold Hauser is the author of a four-volume *Social History of Art*, for which he was much admired by Adorno and the Frankfurt School. – *Ed.*

him has to be William Empson. He's certainly familiar with Empson's work, since he quotes Empson's judgment on Grierson in *A Mirror for England*.

Throughout his circuitous career, from Japan and back to England, Empson remained faithful to another side of the New Criticism. Or perhaps he invented it. At any rate, its scientific objectivity could have led it into his irreverence toward objectivity considered as a radical and militant independence. Empson's battles with C. S. Lewis and the Christian apologists over the meaning in Milton and the morality of Milton's God betray a forceful humanist urge. He's a partisan. And he ventures away from the text in itself to other sciences: moral theology and psychoanalysis.

The gap between text analysis and life continues to bedevil English film criticism. Robin Wood falls back on Leavis's fundamentalism. *Movie*, which sometimes approaches the bland conservative version of the New Criticism, dismissed criticism of a director's philosophy as "impertinent." Peter Harcourt discusses his six European directors finely but in the end seems over-reluctant to resolve their ambiguities. He fears, and probably rightly, that a definite answer will blunt our sensibilities to the living texture of the film. For words on the page often are open-ended. Harcourt's respect for this is an abstentionist version of the New Criticism. He remains almost the only living critic never to have been booby-trapped by unworthy material.

Similar uncertainties permeate American criticism. Mandarin liberals grandly appeal to the superiority of their own tastes. Pauline Kael's irreverent common sense doesn't quite disguise the moral perspectives of a social worker (albeit an increasingly permissive one). In *Sub-Stance* as in *Jump-Cut*, the young scan the horizons in the hope that help is on its way, from linguistics, semiology, anthropology, or any other -ology. Durgnat tries to stay with the New Criticism while reaching out to radical developments in social history and psychoanalysis. Small wonder, then, that the style of *Alienation* groans under the strain of all our culture shocks. He even makes heavy weather of commonplaces. But when everything is called into question, who knows what can be taken for granted?

The longest passage in *Alienation* is devoted to the FELLINI SATYRICON. Durgnat's treatment of the Oenothea plot illustrates his peculiar mixture of radicalism and originality. The beautiful Oenothea humiliates an elderly magician, who takes his revenge by dousing all the cooking fires in her village. He leaves one: a magic flame springing up beneath Oenothea's legs. Durgnat interprets it in the light of psychoanalysis. A father-figure punishes female narcissism by forcing the mother to share her body with all her children. Then he suggests that it's one of the ways in which a woman's unconscious looks on the Oedipus complex. Freud did call it a *complex*, which suggests several ways of looking at it. But one aspect of the complex was allowed to rout all others: Freud's Just-So Story centering on the fraternal horde conspiring to kill the father.

When Durgnat proposes Fellini's version as equally valid, he's virtually using film to rethink orthodox psychoanalysis. He goes on to suggest that the story is matriarchal, radical, and egalitarian, because the Oedipus complex is resolved by a metaphor that presents children as a community's other families. This contrasts with the conservative-hierarchic bias of Freud's narrative.

Elsewhere Durgnat's prose style is nimble enough. But here it labors under the weight of double functions. It's doubtful whether film criticism is a workable framework for such matters. But it's also doubtful whether it can do any sort of job while remaining aloof from them.

Durgnat goes the whole hog, using movies to further his rethinking of psychoanalysis. In so doing he moves alongside thinkers in other disciplines, including Jacques Lacan and

Charles Rycroft in psychoanalysis itself. The special tensions of *Alienation* arise from the interplay of textual ambiguities and radical alternatives. Many readers will find them merely fussy, or positively exhausting. Other readers will find them exhilarating, or recognize the spirit of current culture shock.

In his tenser, more pedantic way, Durgnat shares Harcourt's concern for open-endedness. But he comes very much closer to the structuralists. In *Films and Feelings* he had reduced THIS ISLAND EARTH to one controlling metaphor, with a heavy political slant. This anticipated *Cahiers'* analysis of YOUNG MR. LINCOLN. *Alienation* includes several analyses in the same style.

In other places, however, he has attacked the French school for simplifying content. In a series of articles entitled *Images of the Mind*, he took issue with the Hegelian, and therefore Marxist, concept of the dialectic as a matter of two opposites. In the Hitchcock book, he indulges in little cadenzas of theory. They may not always be completely relevant to the matter in hand, but he wants to upset the way the system-builders make "objective" imply "without ambiguity."

Sometimes he comes very near to using a post-structuralist approach, like Gilles Deleuze. Deleuze's *L'Anti-Oedipe* looks to be the next Paris craze, rivaling Lévi-Strauss and Barthes. He comes very near an atomic view of the mind, seeing it as a "body without organs." It improvises its own temporary, partial structures on an *ad hoc* basis, depending on stimuli from inside and outside alike.

Post-structuralist theory isn't yet completely formulated, so far as I know. When Durgnat turned to montage in *Images of the Mind*, he suggested that the dialectic emphasis on pairs was merely formalist. Syntheses operated in every direction between as many factors as happened to have interacted. This looks rather like a post-structuralist position. Durgnat could have got to it by crossing the dialectic sense of interchange with the unfashionable atomic theory which Bertrand Russell elaborated in his *Inquiry into Meaning and Truth*. However, *Eros* and *Alienation* both quote Georges Bataille, a Hegelian-cum-Surrealist much prized by late and post-structuralists.

Durgnat's book looks really lumbering and old hat if you set it alongside a younger crop of writers on film sex. He hardly mentions Women's Lib, Gay Lib (or even hardcore porn). Yet Molly Haskell, Joan Mellen, and Marjorie Rosen have briskly set about sweeping away all the *macho* hang-ups infesting film criticism. Radical in some ways, they also had the gritty integrity to resist fashion and established wit. They persuaded us all to reconsider a whole genre which we used to laugh at and scorn as "weepies."

Through the glass darkly of *Alienation*, Durgnat looks like something of a debauched and battered uncle to the bright young American girls. He sees THE PUMPKIN EATER as the story of a woman's destruction by complacent male chauvinism. He shares Mss. Haskell and Rosen's concern with mainstream middle-class experience. This concern explains his almost violently unfashionable choice of movies. Would you believe MARTYRS OF LOVE, REFLECTIONS IN A GOLDEN EYE, PETULIA, and De Sica's Sophia Loren period?

In his final chapters, he turns to the Sixties underground. He dismisses Warhol, but admires Jack Smith, Ron Rice, and Kenneth Anger. To discriminate between them he uses the same moral and aesthetic criteria which he brings to Fuller, Losey, Pasolini, and Eric Rohmer. If the book's synthesis remains uncompleted, and most woundingly on the level of its style, the sensitivity and sullen violence of its thought make it Durgnat's most disturbing book.

SOURCE: *FILM COMMENT*, SEPTEMBER–OCTOBER 1975, 62–3 (© 1975 BY THE FILM SOCIETY OF LINCOLN CENTER)

The Essential Raymond Durgnat

ANNOTATIONS

BRAIN DRAINS: DRIFTERS, AVANT-GARDES & KITCHEN SINKS

[p. 117] Durgnat's sense of the split in 1930s British cinema, whereby **Documentary is one world, the mainstream another**, and its cramping effect on Asquith and Dickinson, may have come from the horse's mouth. In *Film Appreciation and Visual Education* (op. cit.), Dickinson described much the same syndrome, writing of a pre-war cinema 'tugged one way by the influence of the living theatre and the other by the reporting of facts' (p. 3). | [p. 118] **Masefield and the Georgians** were profoundly unfashionable poets. | *Baptism of Fire* (1940) was a German propaganda film; nor, the editor regrets, is this the article's crassest passage. | [p. 119] The **'battle' documentaries**, reconstructions of Great War victories, were those of H. Bruce Woolfe at British-Instructional, a leading producer of non-fiction films in the 1920s, later a rival of Grierson's. | According to Durgnat's schoolfriend Brian Hunter, Durgnat himself may have been one of the **lonely minorities, sometimes of one** in *March to Aldermaston*. Hunter spotted him with a banner on one such march, 'in a group of one' (telephone interview with editor, 4 July 2013). | **Reisz tactfully complained** in 'A Use for Documentary', *Universities and Left Review*, no. 3, Winter 1958. | [p. 120] Arthur **Seaton**, as played by Albert Finney, was the anti-hero of Reisz's adaptation of Alan Sillitoe's *Saturday Night and Sunday Morning*.

TV'S YOUNG TURKS

[p. 124] Richard **Lester** had directed a number of Goon-related television series before making *The Running Jumping and Standing Still Film* (1959) with Goons Peter Sellers and Spike Milligan, and, among others, Bruce Lacey. | Durgnat reviewed *The Mouse on the Moon* on release, describing it as 'a jolly jape in the Biographic tradition, a sort of slow-motion tuppence-coloured "Running, Jumping and Blasting-Off Film"' (*Films and Filming*, June 1963, p. 29). | **Klopstokia** is the Ruritanian setting of *Million Dollar Legs* (1932). | [p. 125] Durgnat teased out the **visual-symbolic logic** of Losey's *Modesty Blaise* (1966), notably its 'pattern of sensuous contrasts', in the first issue of *Cinema*, dated December 1968 (p. 2). | **Archibaldo's murderous whims in Buñuel's film** *The Criminal Life of Archibaldo de la Cruz* (1955). | [p. 126] Russell's *Monitor* film on the **pop painters** was *Pop Goes the Easel*, first broadcast in March 1962. His portrait of **Bruce Lacey**, also for *Monitor*, was *The Preservation Man*, broadcast two months later. | [p. 128] There was a violent anti-Vietnam War demonstration outside the US embassy in **Grosvenor Square** on 17 March 1968.

THE GREAT BRITISH PHANTASMAGORIA

[p. 129] The odd couple of **Carol Reed's** ODD MAN OUT and **Michael Powell's** A MATTER OF LIFE AND DEATH was first yoked together by the documentarist Edgar Anstey in Roger Manvell's collection *Experiment in the Film* (London: Grey Walls Press, 1949). Anstey treated them as 'eclectic films' whose claim to a place in his account of 'British experiment' was 'a matter of controversy' (p. 264). 'There remains a danger', he concluded, 'that the foundations they have laid may be more suitable for the erection of a second Hollywood than for a temple of British screen art.' | [p. 130] In 'Genre: Populism and Social Realism' (*Film Comment*, July–August 1975), Durgnat described LEO THE LAST (1970) as 'a spiritual flagship of the late populist line' which 'all but blends liberal sympathies with radical tendencies, the kitchen-sink with T. S. Eliot and the Beatles, Capra with De Sica, populist optimism with social realism' (p. 29). | [p. 134] **English soil** [*sic*] | AERO ENGINE (1933) was directed by Anstey's colleague Arthur Elton. | [p. 138] **Andrew**

Britton criticised Godard in 'Living Historically: Two Films by Jean-Luc Godard', *Framework*, no. 3, Spring 1976. | **Enoch** Powell delivered his 'rivers of blood' speech prophesising 'American proportions' of racial violence in Britain shortly before Godard came to London to make *One Plus One*, which in Durgnat's view predicted much the same thing.

SEXUAL ALIENATION IN THE CINEMA

[p. 139] Kurt Kren's films of the Viennese Actionist Otto **Muehl's** unsavoury activities were, according to Durgnat, among the highlights of the 1966 Destruction In Art Symposium, and became staples of the early London Film-Makers' Co-op. | [p. 140] *Platinum* was a one-off magazine published by the University of Essex Film Society in 1968, its cover adorned by a still from *Herostratus*. In fact, Durgnat told his interviewer that 'I wanted to get away from the English Literature attitude at Cambridge which was very pious and moralistic and a good and convenient place to escape was the local movie houses' (n.p.). | The Canadian **Peter Harcourt** had lectured at the Royal College of Art before returning to his homeland to teach film at Queen's University; presumably he had a hand in hiring Durgnat to work there. Harcourt published *Six European Directors* in 1974. | Candidates for **Raymond Williams**'s **four major books** include *Drama from Ibsen to Eliot/Brecht* (1952/68), *Culture and Society* (1958), *The Long Revolution* (1961) and *The Country and the City* (1973). | **Lovell's book on documentary**, co-written with Jim Hillier, was *Studies in Documentary*, published by the BFI in 1972. Like Williams, Lovell had been closely involved in the first New Left. | [p. 142] **Charles Rycroft** was R. D. Laing's analyst at the Tavistock Clinic when Laing was Durgnat's. | *Cahiers'* **analysis of** YOUNG MR. LINCOLN, a product of the magazine's post-structuralist turn, was published in 1970; a translation appeared in the Autumn 1972 issue of *Screen*.

Notes

1. Durgnat, *A Mirror for England* (London: Faber and Faber, 1970), p. 1; p. 180. Hereafter *AMFE*.
2. Ibid., p. 3.
3. Charles Barr, rev. *A Mirror for England*, in *Monogram*, no. 3, 1972, p. 44.
4. *AMFE*, pp. 58–9.
5. Ibid., p. 57.
6. Ibid., p. 61.
7. Ibid., pp. 3–4.
8. Barr, rev. *A Mirror for England*, p. 43.
9. *AMFE*, p. 230.
10. Ibid., p. 234.
11. Ibid., p. 259.
12. Ibid., p. 61.
13. Durgnat, rev. *Hôtel du Nord*, in *Films and Filming*, February 1965, p. 37.
14. Durgnat, rev. *The Virgins*, in *Films and Filming*, August 1967, p. 23.
15. Durgnat, rev. *The Knack*, in *Films and Filming*, July 1965, p. 25.
16. Durgnat, 'Britannia Waives the Rules', *Film Comment*, July–August 1976, p. 51.
17. Lester D. Friedman, 'The Politics of Editing: An Interview with Richard Corliss', *Film Criticism*, vol. 6, no. 2, Winter 1982, pp. 32–3.

PART 5
CALIFORNIA SPLIT

INTRODUCTION

I

By 1977 Durgnat's progress around the universities of North America had brought him to San Francisco State. At the end of January he wrote to Thorold Dickinson, by then retired, of the house he shared with Tom Luddy and 'various crash-padding friends. Nice & sociable, just what I need after years of a) persona non grata in London, b) stuffy smalltown Canada, c) The Big Apple (or maggots).'[1] Luddy was director of the Pacific Film Archive (PFA), an extraordinary institution attached to the University of California at Berkeley and housed in the University Art Museum. Modelled on the Cinémathèque Française, the PFA had in fact paid host to the Cinémathèque's legendary co-founder Henri Langlois shortly before his death in the month Durgnat wrote home. As Durgnat told Dickinson, who had known Langlois since the Cinémathèque's early days, 'almost his last thing was to discover an early Ford, "The Village Blacksmith"'.

In the spring Luddy invited Durgnat to programme a series of PFA screenings, which Durgnat used to refine and extend the defence of montage that he had first made in 'Images of the Mind' almost ten years before. Titled 'Montage Rides Again!', the series was itself a kind of montage, juxtaposing two branches of a living tradition: the 'Left Bank' group within the *nouvelle vague*, and the underground films Durgnat had seen and shown at Better Books, including those of Bay Area film-maker Bruce Conner. In the autumn Durgnat moved from San Francisco State to Berkeley, and programmed two further PFA series to accompany his classes there: one on 'The Documentary Cinema', the other on 'Films Since 1962'.

The 'Documentary' strand in particular was a development of the earlier series, constituting a history of the essay-film rather than the documentary as ordinarily understood. The term's first programme, echoing Dickinson's first screenings at the Slade in 1961, included films by the Lumière brothers and Dickinson's *Overture*; but also, reflecting Durgnat's experiences in the US, two Manhattan city-symphonies and a film by Les Blank, another of Luddy's crash-padders. The second series favoured British 'impossibilism' and the contemporary Eastern European avant-garde, represented in person at Berkeley by Yvette Biró, whose credits as 'dramaturg' included Miklós Jancsó's *Red Psalm* (1972). Both Jan Němec's *Martyrs of Love* (1967) and Dušan Makavejev's *Sweet Movie* (1974) were introduced by their directors, the latter encounter bearing fruit two decades later in Durgnat's book – one of his best – on Makavejev's *W.R.* (1971).

Around the start of 1978 Durgnat moved to University of California, San Diego to teach in the Department of Visual Arts under Manny Farber. Durgnat roomed with the man he was replacing, Jonathan Rosenbaum, who had come to California after eight years in Europe, including a stint as assistant editor of the *Monthly Film Bulletin*, which had left him 'looking for a way to negotiate my way back to the states and some version of my roots'.[2] The two housemates had earlier collaborated, at Richard Corliss's instigation, on a *Film Comment* profile of Durgnat which Rosenbaum had written and Durgnat completed with an 'Apologia and Auto-Critique'. As Rosenbaum told a colleague, with a nod to the boss, 'we had all the makings of a full-fledged termite colony'.[3]

Farber's closest ally in the department was Jean-Pierre Gorin, whom Durgnat had met in Berkeley and described to Dickinson as 'Godard's Maoist collaborator, now much mellowed and good fun'.[4] Gorin had met Godard when the latter was preparing *La Chinoise* (1967), introducing him to his Maoist friends at the École Normale Supérieure. Later, as the Dziga-Vertov Group, they had made a series of difficult political films, beginning with *Vent d'Est* (1970), which had found a large proportion of their small audience on the American college circuit, not least at Berkeley. It was Luddy who found Gorin a way out when the collective fell apart. Durgnat wrote in 1976 that 'it's impossible to give an idea of how tedious the movies are without making them sound interesting', but had nonetheless shown one of them at the PFA.[5] Gorin recalls him as 'the source of constant, fruitful, often hilarious exchanges. We liked to go up to bat.'[6]

II

Gorin had escaped a post-'May' Paris steeped in disillusionment and acrid with recriminations; viewed from across the Channel, however, the city retained a certain glamour. 'There was', as Colin MacCabe once put it, 'one institution which was shaken by the Wind from the East. That institution, the BFI, was, to my knowledge, the only British institution which was really affected in its innermost workings by what in shorthand we call '68.'[7] As Rosenbaum knew at first hand, not every department of the BFI was shaken in quite this way, but the Education Department, the BFI-funded Society for Education in Film and Television (SEFT), and SEFT's journal *Screen*, in which MacCabe played a central role, were by the mid-1970s collectively embarked on what MacCabe's colleague Stephen Heath famously encapsulated as 'the encounter of Marxism and psychoanalysis on the terrain of semiotics'.[8]

The roots of this enterprise, whose influence on the development of film studies as an academic discipline can scarcely be overestimated, went back beyond 1968 to the aftermath of 1956. Heartened by the popularity of the Campaign for Nuclear Disarmament, the 'first' New Left of E. P. Thompson and Stuart Hall had seemed during its 'brief boom', as Durgnat recalled, to have had the makings of a movement, before it 'ebbed, baffled' in the early 1960s.[9] Its journal *New Left Review* (*NLR*), successor to *Universities and Left Review*, had, however, continued under the editorship of the young Perry Anderson, whom Thompson later caricatured as 'a veritable Dr. Beeching of the socialist intelligentsia. [...] Old Left steam-engines were swept off the tracks; wayside halts ("Commitment," "What Next for C.N.D.?", "Women in Love") were boarded up; and the lines were electrified for the speedy traffic from the marxistentialist Left Bank.'[10]

As Thompson was early to notice, the new *New Left Review*'s historical perspective, which Anderson and Tom Nairn set out soon after taking over, was based on a 'model of Other Countries, whose typological symmetry offers a reproach to British exceptionalism'.[11] The principal Other Country was France, whose 'Class Struggles', in Thompson's parody, 'have been Sanguinary and Unequivocal', and whose 'Intelligentsia has been Autonomous and Integrated Vertically'. This perspective was shared by the journal's film critic Peter Wollen, who had been at Oxford with Anderson – and with the critics of *Oxford Opinion* – in the late 1950s. In an early contribution Wollen charged Penelope Houston with 'failure to understand the critical achievements of *Cahiers du Cinema*' and lamented the 'decadent consciousness' of British filmgoers,[12] a verdict in keeping with Anderson's view of Britain's 'numbed and docile' working class.[13]

The 'non-emergence of a powerful revolutionary movement of the working-class', Anderson argued in 'Components of the National Culture', published in the summer of 1968, explained 'the lack of any revolutionary tradition within English culture', which was characterised as 'mediocre and inert', untouched by Marxism, and intellectually dominated by 'a "White", counter-revolutionary emigration' which only reinforced the natives' empiricism.[14] The one-way traffic from Paris would compensate for this fundamental lack of theory. By 1968, however, 'marxistentialism' was out, and in certain passages 'Components' betrayed a newer influence: 'structuralism'. The use of Ferdinand de Saussure's structural linguistics as a paradigm for other disciplines, pioneered by the linguist and literary critic Roman Jakobson in the 1930s, then by the anthropologist Claude Lévi-Strauss from the late 1940s, had been taken up across the humanities in France by the mid-1960s.

Its ascendancy was faithfully reflected in the *NLR*. Thus by 'Marxism' Heath meant the Communist Party philosopher Louis Althusser, who had subjected Marx to the structuralist method; and by 'psychoanalysis' Althusser's sometime therapist Jacques Lacan, who had done something of the kind to Freud. Semiology, meanwhile, was Saussure's word for the general science of signs, of which he saw linguistics as a province. Such was the mood in Paris, however, that Roland Barthes announced that the reverse was true. Structuralism's main cinematic exponent was Barthes's associate Christian Metz, whom Wollen duly brought to British attention, on the echt-*NLR* premise that 'traditional aesthetics has proved incapable of coming to terms with twentieth century art', in a number of publications in 1968–9, above all in his book *Signs and Meaning in the Cinema*.[15]

Signs and Meaning appeared in a series co-sponsored by the BFI Education Department, in which Wollen was by the late 1960s the dominant personality. The department had in fact been a province of the first New Left before Wollen's arrival, under Paddy Whannel. It was partly in response to Whannel and Stuart Hall's 1964 book *The Popular Arts* that Durgnat, who found it 'well within the safest possible area of received opinion', declared himself for 'the "truancy" theory of art'.[16] Much of *Screen*, whose ancestor journals dated back to the 1950s, was still in the Hall–Whannel vein in the late 1960s; but after a peculiar sequence of events in which a BFI 'Members Action Committee' closely connected to the Education Department tried to oust the governors, the journal was refounded in 1971 as, in Durgnat's words, 'more or less the New New Left at the pictures', edited first by Sam Rohdie, then by Althusser's translator Ben Brewster.[17]

One Althusserian idea with special currency within the *Screen* milieu, because homologous with the *NLR*'s estimation of its own role, was the 'epistemological break', which in Brewster's definition described 'the leap from the pre-scientific world of ideas to the scientific world'.[18] Althusser claimed to have discerned such a break within Marx's work; Wollen identified the same leap in reverse in Eisenstein, 'from the expression of scientific concepts through film' to 'fundamentally unscientific' studies of synaesthesia.[19] *Screen*'s writers used the concept to distinguish semiology from 'the flow of (ideologically complicit) drivel that currently and massively passes as "film-criticism"', as Heath put it in 1973.[20] Paul Willemen, in the same number, voiced his apprehension at the prospect of an English translation of Jean Mitry's *Esthétique et Psychologie du Cinéma*, originally published in the mid-1960s, in the same terms. Whereas 'Mitry's film-philosophy put a full stop after the pre-history of film theory', wrote Willemen, Metz 'establishes a break in the history of ideas relating to the object film'.[21]

Despite this evident commitment to disinterested science, *Screen* had by then already undergone one palace coup, and more would follow. As Wollen remarked from the safety of an American university campus in 1974, 'London's getting to be like Paris'.[22] Durgnat took the occasional pot-shot from a similar distance, but began to engage more closely with the *Screen* tendency after his time in California. Quite presciently, he saw British-Film-Institutional continuity over the 'break', writing in 1978 that 'the country can only sustain one really powerful organization, whose consequent monopoly enables its old-boy network to close its ranks against suggestions from outsiders'.[23] Film studies was on the rise in Britain's new polytechnic colleges, and the BFI was involved in establishing university posts, making *Screen*, with its 'technological-cosmopolitan-academic' idiolect, 'a logical part of the intensification of bourgeois technocracy'.[24]

Durgnat also engaged with its ideas. At the start of 1979 Andrew Sarris told a radio interviewer that Durgnat, who was then teaching at MIT,

> wanted to do a critique of semiotic writers, the people who write for *Screen* and so forth, and the University of California Press decided that the people who are semioticians will not accept the critique, and the people who are not interested in semiotics don't want to read about it at all.[25]

No book ever appeared, but instead a loose series of articles, including a 16,000-word essay on Wollen, 'From Signs to Meanings in the Cinema', and a three-part series amounting to an even longer analysis of Metz's 1974 book *Film Language*, all published in 1982–4 but conceived earlier and condensed to paragraph-length in 'Montage Rides Again!'. One of the Metz pieces, 'Film Theory: From Narrative to Description', makes extensive reference to the films Durgnat showed at the PFA, and a short version of the Wollen essay appeared in the Berkeley periodical *University Publishing* at about the time of Sarris's broadcast. In September 1979, at a conference staged as part of the Venice Biennale and Venice Film Festival, Durgnat, declaring that he would 'adopt the role of public enemy number one', fired off a broadside against 'cinesemiology', drawing on Thompson's demolition of Althusser in *The Poverty of Theory*, published the previous year.[26] Heckled by Willemen and abandoned by the translators, Durgnat walked out, leaving Sarris to offer a defence.

Again the essence of Durgnat's critique was *Screen*'s continuity with what it claimed to have superseded. Most obviously there was the same fealty to *Cahiers du Cinéma*, the same focus on mid-century Hollywood. As Durgnat wrote in 'Film Theory: From Narrative to Description',

> we couldn't agree with Metz that aesthetic theory should, or could, accept as normative – with strong prescriptive overtones – only whatever is most often and most easily done. [...] Theory must understand the deviations, the freaks, the experiments, the tours-de-force, the negations, the one-offs, from which come crucial breakthroughs which the mainstream can exploit and render normative.[27]

More importantly, as Durgnat said at Venice, the recourse to paradigms from linguistic structuralism, whose 'relevance to non-verbal forms are either nil, or entirely subordinate',[28] had not broken with but instead 'exacerbated' British film criticism's longstanding literary bias, which 'often overlooks visual forms and nuances altogether'.[29] His series on

Metz hammered away at the 'radical nonanalogy' between verbal and visual signs, and the elementary observation that 'visual perceptions work along lines radically and forever different from linguistic interpretation'.[30]

The twist in this tale is that in *Signs and Meaning* Wollen had himself diverged from Metz on similar grounds, and initially rejected Barthes's claim that semiology should be seen as a branch of linguistics. As he and Metz both said, the first principle of Saussurean linguistics, the arbitrariness of the verbal sign, could not be used in relation to the visual image without difficulty. Wollen, however, criticised Metz, and Barthes before him, for falling back on to Bazin's ontology, in which the photographic image, far from being arbitrary, reproduced its object unmediated. Durgnat, reviewing Metz's *Essais sur la Signification au Cinéma*, the original of *Film Language*, in the year Wollen's book appeared, also noted that, like Bazin, Metz 'attributes the cinema's impressions of realism to the fact that photography is a matter of direct representation of the world rather than a construction out of signs substituting for it'.[31]

Unlike Wollen, however, Durgnat saw no pressing reason to persevere along the linguistic path, warning of 'a danger in structuralist thinking, the hypostasis of rationalistic patterns and their deracination from specific living contexts'.[32] Indeed, his very lack of commitment to the structuralist cause led him to the provocative argument, repeated in 'Montage Rides Again!', that the photographic image could, after all, be considered as arbitrarily motivated. Wollen meanwhile, following Jakobson's lead, substituted C. S. Peirce's semiotic theory for Saussure's, borrowing in particular Peirce's 'trichotomy' of signs, the indexical, the iconic and the symbolic. The Bazinian image, he wrote, was indexical; the iconic 'represents its object mainly by its similarity to it'; while the symbolic image 'corresponds to Saussure's arbitrary sign'.[33]

This cumbersome apparatus nonetheless led Wollen to conclusions often strikingly like Durgnat's in 'Images of the Mind', written about the same time. Both sought to rehabilitate cinematic symbolism, typified by Eisenstein's *October*, and to champion the iconic – in Wollen's words 'comprehensible by virtue of resemblances to the natural world, yet other than it' – over the indexical.[34] The last words of Wollen's chapter on semiology, the last in the book, were, quoting Gance, '"The time of the image has come."'[35] That time had however passed by 1972, when Wollen added a new conclusion to the book's third edition (the first and second were identical), apparently indebted to Jacques Derrida and the Barthes of *S/Z*, in which he wrote that 'I no longer think that the future of cinema simply lies in a full use of all available codes. I think codes should be confronted with each other, that films are texts which should be structured around contradictions of codes.'[36] There was no more talk of images.

'From Signs to Meanings' is in part an attempt to indicate the passage that was not taken. In Durgnat's view it was not that traditional aesthetics had been proved incapable of coming to terms with the cinema; rather that it had never been attempted because of the 'Parisotropic' Beechingism of the New New Left.[37] Some of the authors Durgnat mentions, such as the Viennese art historians Ernst Gombrich, Anton Ehrenzweig and Arnold Hauser, belonged to Anderson's misdescribed 'White' emigration. Durgnat had said at Venice that Metz and his followers were incapable of 'the kind of halfway adequate visual analysis of images which is an everyday matter in history of art departments', and his critique contains a lament for film studies as practised in the art schools of the 1960s, abandoned by the 'verbocentric' professionals who came later, and all but written out of history in the decades since.[38]

III

One evening in February 1978, Durgnat and Rosenbaum went to see Jonathan Demme's new film *Citizens Band* 'in a movie theater up the coast that had once been a church and still had pews to sit in'.[39] A few years later, Durgnat looked back on the experience as an epiphany which 'crystallised a hitherto vaguer feeling that the American cinema was undergoing another sea-change, into something richer than it had ever been'.[40] Liberated by the break-up of Old Hollywood, which Durgnat portrayed in knowingly old-fashioned terms as a 'formula-ridden' dream factory wrongly eulogised by Francophile auteurists who 'had tried to palm off competent craftsmanship as artistry', Demme and his contemporaries Robert Altman, Martin Scorsese and Jerry Schatzberg were embarked on 'a rediscovery of neo-realism'.[41]

The thought had, in some degree, been fathered by the wish. In 1969, at the end of *The Crazy Mirror*, Durgnat wrote that Hollywood, confronted by the decline of the family audience, had failed to renew itself or address 'minority audiences', and that the time was ripe, 'five hundred years after Christopher Columbus, to discover America; to explore it, rather than land briefly from daydream cloudbanks'.[42] While he later described this as a 'pious hope', he nonetheless found evidence to suggest it was being fulfilled.[43] In mid-1975 he published a long *Film Comment* essay on 'populism', meaning 'movies whose protagonists are ordinary people', based on his Columbia course on the same topic, in which he observed that 'the populist urge is vigorous' in New Hollywood films including Scorsese's *Mean Streets* (1973).[44]

In 'Britannia Waives the Rules', published in 1976, Durgnat claimed that from its investment in British cinema in the 1960s, 'Hollywood could learn the lessons it couldn't assimilate through Vadim and Bardot: how to treat sex more frankly and along with real life. Once the lessons had been learned the money came back home.'[45] Yet his response to *Citizens Band*, '*Mean Streets* in the long grass', seen amid 'a steady diet of English and German art movies – things like *Riddles of the Sphinx* and *Hitler – A Film From Germany*', was real enough.[46] Having sped on the pendulum's swing from realistic to expressionistic, Durgnat now found himself promoting a version of realism against 'ivory tower productions which revolved in ever-diminishing theoretical circles before disappearing up their own lens-mounting (as if the cine-camera could study nothing but itself)'.[47]

In the full version of 'From Signs to Meanings', Durgnat even found himself defending Kracauer's *Theory of Film*, a conversion perhaps inspired by his Berkeley conversations with Yvette Biró, who wrote sympathetically of Kracauer in *Profane Mythology*, a book Durgnat greatly admired. 'Film redeems physical reality because it records it fully enough to preserve innumerable aspects of the physical world', he allowed; and while *Theory of Film* was essentialist in a way Durgnat could not accept, 'for all its flaws, Kracauer's book is Marxist, materialist, existential and substantial, whereas semio-structuralism represents a technocratic, rationalist-idealist, positivist, reaction, abounding as it does in archi-type auteurs, invisible antinomies, Procrustean antinomies and all the metaphysical ills which rationalism is prone to'.[48]

Durgnat's populism was realism without Kracauer's or the documentarists' emphasis on left-wing social consciousness, and expanded beyond their 'narrow stylistic mode'.[49] 'We couldn't follow Kracauer through all his conclusions,' he went on. 'While the advantage of documentary realism is that you can record phenomena whose significance you don't know at the time,' an observation borrowed from Manny Farber, 'fantastication can be symptomatic too (even realism depends on selection amounting to "exaggeration").'[50]

Populism, he had written in 1975, overlapped with realism, but 'may also be socially uncon-scious, morally insouciant (or indeed cynical or misanthropic) and otherwise stylized in its idiom'.[51] So it was that Durgnat could include Altman's 'fantasticated' *Popeye* (1980) within its compass.[52]

The dialectic of 'Popeye Pops Up', published in the spring of 1982, a year after the film's British release, involves more than one surprising reconciliation. Durgnat's new sympathy for Kracauer brought him to appreciate another once-spurned master, Henry James – and not only James. In *Films and Feelings*, fifteen years earlier, Durgnat had written that:

> As recently as my grammar school days, English masters instructed us all in the neces-sity for realistic and deep characterization, logically consistent behaviour, penetrating studies of motive, and that proliferation of vivid detail suggested by Henry James's phrase, 'density of specification'. We were besought to insist upon the 'texture of lived experience', and many of the exegeses we studied had strained to detect such 'density' in such improbable paces as folk ballads, or Chaucer's tale of Patient Griselda.[53]

And, after a close reading of the sci-fi film *This Island Earth* (1955) as a Cold War allegory:

> Our suggestion is that academic criticism is condemned to misunderstand the film, to dismiss it as routine trash, because its psychology is straightforward, its terms melodra-matic, and so on. 'High culture' is preoccupied with what Henry James called 'density of specification' and what F. R. Leavis calls 'texture', with the question 'Does it work on my level?' But such criteria are irrelevant to this as to most movies. The question must be, rather, 'Does it work on its level?' (for people who freely respond to simpler textures).[54]

Now Durgnat used 'density of specification' to extol the realist image without subscribing to realist theory, or to the literary school of film criticism; and 'density of fantastication' for *Popeye*. It was by a synthesis of two hitherto rejected currents of thought from his forma-tive years, synthesised in turn with the findings of perceptual psychology, that Durgnat found a criterion for cinema as both a realist and a graphic art.

Unlike 'From Signs to Meanings' or the series on Metz, the first part of which also appeared in the spring of 1982, 'Popeye Pops Up', which is the clearest statement of Durgnat's critique of cinesemiology, was not published in an academic journal but in the very unacademic *Films on Screen and Video*, edited, as the front page rather strangely (and not very accurately) stated, by Robin Bean. After thirty shambolic yet heroic years, Philip Dosse's Seven Arts empire had crumbled in August 1980, and Dosse had killed himself shortly afterwards. Bean, who had edited the increasingly sleazy *Films and Filming* since 1968, effectively relaunched the magazine with a new publisher, Anthony Churchill's Ocean Publications, a few months later. Durgnat, back from the US and severed from *Film Comment*, had begun writing for it in 1981.

In his essay on *Citizens Band*, also published in *Films*, Durgnat noted that while 'we're seeing the triumph in Hollywood of a realistic urge', Steven Spielberg and George Lucas 'represent an Old Hollywood tendency to insulated, self-referential, formula-ridden, spec-tacular worlds'.[55] This tendency was already in the ascendant, and the perceived failure of *Popeye*, in tandem with Fox's refusal to release Altman's earlier *Health* (1980), led Durgnat to describe Altman's career, in a book published the same year as 'Popeye Pops Up', as 'a classical arch, a perfect rise and fall. But just as the "well-constructed" story has gone the way of the classical genres,' he went on, 'so the rules of the new games privilege surprises, and tag endings which swell into new Acts, so The Robert Altman Story has a good few reels to run.'[56] He might well have been speaking of his own trajectory.

5.1 MONTAGE RIDES AGAIN!

Tom Luddy has asked me to select and introduce a short series of films which depend on their use of montage. It'll make a good chance to see some favorite movies in a new light and juxtapose them with some strange ones. What follows is a brief exposition of what montage means, why it dropped out of cinetheory fashion, and why it needs bringing back in. The series will continue into May. Non theory-buffs are welcome to skip the explanatory sections, which immediately follow, and move straight on to the film descriptions further down – see you later!

What Is Montage? – Originally "montage" is the simple French word for cutting or editing. But through the '20s, Hollywood features and the French avant-garde followed different paths, and the French word wound up meaning something different, at least abroad (in France the two senses co-exist). Hollywood hitched its wagon to narrative, subordinated cutting to it, and emphasized what it called "invisible editing". The fear was that "visible" editing (strongly contrasting compositions, jumpcuts and so on) would draw attention to the image as such, and distract from the story. So visible editing was kept for special purposes, like matching cuts to bridge a narrative gap, or climaxes like the chase in John Ford's Stagecoach (where the story needed the dynamism hard-edge cutting could give but was strong enough to sustain itself over it). Or it was featured in short sharp outbursts, special cadenzas subcontracted out to specialists like Slavko Vorkapich and later Saul Bass. Often a bold montage sequence would bring applause from cinema audiences. But Hollywood was still mistrustful. But from the very early '20s, the French in particular allowed visible editing into the narrative, and loved to let montage off the narrative leash. In some of the avant-garde movies the editing so dazzles your eyes that it dislocates a story which was only a thin pretext for editing in the first place. So "montage" came to mean a sort of ultra-editing, editing that's conspicuously visible, that hits you in the eye; or, at least, generates a special graphic energy and tautness out of the snap and slap of one shot's composition against the next.

From there it was one short step to the Kuleshov–Eisenstein conception of montage as a means of constructing ideas. Instead of the graphic composition of the shots colliding to generate an abstract impression, the content of the shots collide to generate a tertium quid, a new idea that's present in neither separately. And that's the third sense, intellectual montage, often considered crucial in discussions of how much montage matters.

But since a shot often shows more than a single unit or a simple action or idea, Eisenstein extended "montage" to include the relationships between items within a shot, or between the shot and what we think of "its" soundtrack. These relationships could be graphic (corresponding to our second sense), or intellectual (corresponding to our third). And when Eisenstein talks of Milton's "montage" in certain descriptive passages in Paradise Lost, he is, it seems to me, describing as "montage" any sequential presentation of facts or features. There is a close parallel in what the French sometimes called "decoupage" or "decoupage technique", that is, the breaking-down of a master-scene into specific shots (Becker did the job for Renoir on Boudu Saved From Drowning and other

152   **The Essential Raymond Durgnat**

early-middle Renoir movies where he made of assistant director a very important job).

The French talk of mounting where English talks of cutting; and perhaps the French term is better, for editing a film is, after all, a weaving together of fragments called shots. They are mounted into a whole. The cutting, or decoupage, occurs at an earlier stage, when the director is confronted with either a master-scene that must be split up into shots, or an action that he must analyse into shots, or a location into which he as it were 'cuts', with his selection of camera-angle.

And Eisenstein's extension of the term, away from the editing-bench into actual direction and mise-en-scene, is completely correct. For example, John Ford was famous for his ability to shoot a scene so that it could only be edited one way. As his producers complained he edited in the camera. Hitchcock was another. Moreover, a director who has a certain editing style in view must shoot suitable material. Editing can work wonders of transformation, as Kuleshov showed, but normally the shots form a grain that can be very difficult to cut against.

So far we've touched on five senses of "montage": (1) Montage as editing, (2) montage as visible editing, (3) intellectual montage, (4) decoupage or analysis into set-ups and (5) montage within the shot. Once we've allowed the last, it becomes simple and natural to allow two more kinds of juxtaposition. There can be contrasts between blocks of shots (sequences). Thus the very structure of The Godfather Part 2 is pure Eisenstein; past and present are juxtaposed to provoke reflections that transcend any narrative function (even suspense). And so it looks as if "montage" can arise from the juxtaposition of units of meaning of any kind: shots; sequences; features and configurations within a shot; or graphic and semantic units of any kind – graphemes and semes ......

A MINI-HISTORY OF MONTAGEOLOGY – With seven closely connected but significantly distinct meanings for the same word it's small wonder that pro- and anti-montage arguments have tended to extreme positions; either it's the soul of cinema, or it's the original sin.

The Pacific Film Archive's auditorium at Berkeley (Photograph by Jon Winet, courtesy Pacific Film Archive, University of California, Berkeley)

Montage in the first three senses was the mainspring of cinema for Eisenstein, for the English documentarists and for '30s theorists down to Manvell and Lindgren. Their reign lasted from about 1930 to 1960 and the books are still around. But Eisenstein's followers didn't really accept the idea of montage within the shot. As they saw it, montage had to happen around the editing bench. And this encouraged everybody to forget how montage overlapped with decoupage and mise-en-scene.

Early in the '50s, however, Karel Reisz realized that whatever the cinetheorists maintained, intellectual montage had never really caught on. One or two tours-de-force like the "Gods" sequence in October proved it could be done, but only just. And meanwhile most mainstream movies were stitched together by their narrative threads, or, if they were documentaries, by some line of discourse which was more or less clearly stated in the commentary, or explicit in the shots themselves.

Simultaneously Bazin was producing his justifications for the shot, not the cut, being the essence of cinema. When he talked about Wyler's way with deep focus he came within an ace of rediscovering decoupage and montage within the shot and mise-en-scene as montage, of ending the artificial split between "pure film" and the "proto-filmic." But he blew it because being a Christian metaphysician at heart, he was over-anxious to believe that whatever happens within a shot is free and democratic and transcendental and as close to God as the natural world is; whereas montage quickly becomes didactic and artificial. He compared photographic emulsion, which recorded the world the good lord made, to the Holy Shroud of Turin, and he entitled one of his essays: "Montage Forbidden!" In the gospel according to Bazin, God invented the cine-camera, but the devil created scissors.

It's the Struwwelpeter theory of montage. It relegates montage to at best a neutral, negative, self-effacing role. Montage has to be done right, but it can't do anything on its own, it can't add anything much. This shift of emphasis was fortified by a new interest in what could be done within shots. Deep focus. Cinemascope. Camera-movements. Le caméra-stylo. Cinéma-vérité showing reality unadorned and unbetrayed.

Cinesemiology should have set film theory free from this slavish adulation of photography of "reality." For semiology was devoted to paradigms from verbal language, i.e. arbitrary signs. And on that basis it might have recognized that the shot was an artifice from the beginning; even if it wasn't the creation of actors, directors, art directors, and all, the shot took one specific chunk of reality, one specific angle, and selected it for us to study. The cinema, too, was "arbitrary." But cinesemiology was lame from birth. Barthes entertained strange verbocentric prejudices whereby cinema was pseudo-physis not techne. Metz, plunged into despair by his inability to analyse a picture into definite parts, fell right back into the ever-loving arms of Bazin. He considers montage an ersatz, like powdered milk and artificial prostheses. It's a sort of Tristana's leg, an awkward substitute for the Real Thing.

Wollen dissents from them both in Signs and Meaning, but his interest is in visual non-realism rather than montage. So there montage stays, loitering in the cinetheory limbo ......

A Middle Road Theory of Montage. – Let's suppose instead that film has no primary connection with the sort of reality one can photograph. Let's suppose that its primary connection is with one sort of reality one can't photograph: images of the mind. Photography is a means to reaching a mind's eye view, nothing more. And let's suppose that film continuity exists to follow lines of thought, rather than lines of sight. Our minds don't just track, pan and tilt, like our eyes; they also dissolve and superimpose, and again and again they cut. But to say cutting is to say re-editing, that is, bringing together in new relationships. Which

Letter from Siberia (1958): 'where the modern cinema really began'

is to say that the successions and juxtapositions <u>can</u> create out of the images meanings which aren't in the images. The image is female, the context is male. Montage is the connections which create context, which construct a structure.

So montage in that third and crucial sense, intellectual montage, has always been alive and well, and living, before our very eyes. It's never been mandatory or a touchstone of art, as the documentarists implied, but it has always been active, rendered inconspicuous by its quiet usefulness, a sort of family butler who's taken for granted because he's always impeccably there.

But just as the cinetheorists were thinking of burying montage (and murmuring quiet respectful apologies to soothe the ghost of Eisenstein), it burst out once more, in two key movies. In Chris Marker's <u>Letter From Siberia</u> (1958) and Kenneth Anger's <u>Scorpio Rising</u> (1963) montage cuts loose. Fast and loose.

Had we but world enough and time, montage analysis would take a seminar format where we could all slave over a hot Steenbeck, devoting ten minutes or more to analysing each cut, the images that flank it, the way it divides and connects them, the way they slot into an overall context, the way all the meanings of all the shots flow back and forth into one another and around the sequence as a whole, the way the overall structure mixes apples and oranges, cabbages and bedknobs, brasstacks and microsemantics, connotations and cognitive dissonance, dialectics and the logic of deduction, collisions and connections, all done so fast the quickness of the thought deceives the eye and the spectator emerges convinced that he's seen what he only thought of. But a nod is as good as a wink to a smart audience, and we'll be well on our way, brothers, with a brief introduction, ten minutes or so, to each of a series of programmes that will run from April into May and let loose some movies in which montage rides out .....

SOURCE: PACIFIC FILM ARCHIVE, APRIL 1977 (COURTESY THE UNIVERSITY OF CALIFORNIA, BERKELEY ART MUSEUM AND PACIFIC FILM ARCHIVE)

California Split

5.2 PACIFIC FILM ARCHIVE PROGRAMME NOTES

SUNDAY, MAY 1
RAYMOND DURGNAT PRESENTS
MONTAGE IN THE CINEMA (PROGRAM FIVE)
CITIZEN KANE 2:30, 6:15, 10:10

Bazin persuaded half a moviegoing generation that deep focus meant the end of montage. Yet CITIZEN KANE, the locus classicus of deep focus, constantly resorts to montage of every kind – invisible editing, visible editing, flashy matching cuts that jolt through time like jump-cuts, intellectual montage (Kane's wife as he cruelly hears her (a squawking parrot)), montage within the shot (any sense of "free" continuity disrupted by dense shadows from which enigmatic voices boom …). At times (Kane's breakfast-tables) it almost rivals Vorkapich speed. Its cuts are brusque and bold enough to be part of the baroque, its very storyline is sliced into antichronological fragments, it's a labyrinth fretsawed into a jigsaw puzzle. And no good jigsaw puzzle has a one-word answer. Critics hung up on individual psychology could see the revelation of "Rosebud" as two-bit Freud, but far from being the film's core this last twist is just its vanishing-point. For it explains nothing at all, not even the hatred of other people's power whereby he wrecks his chances of his own. Nothing can diminish the dynamism of a movie in which images as heavy and passionate as Eisenstein's meet as fast and intricate a storyline as Hollywood ever devised. It's the last German expressionist movie and it's a source film for '40s film noir (bleakness, flashbacks, misanthropy, pathology). In fact it's the first film triumph of Brechtian epic theatre. For it alienates us throughout (which is what some critics read as "hollow"; we have no rooting interest). The opening flashback and Kane's very monstrosity keep us from identifying with him, and we're given no-one else we care to be inside for long. We're forced to watch and think about evidence of corruption, forced to criticize everybody but never allowed to use anyone or anything as a scapegoat – not even Kane, not even wealth. It's the first Losey film. … And it's a national epic. It's The Man Who Would Be President. It's about the sell-out of Progressivism, the bogging-down of the New Deal. And above all it's a metaphor for the death of the greatest tradition in American journalism and literature, the Muckraking tradition. It's one of the great American subjects, like AN AMERICAN TRAGEDY and DEATH OF A SALESMAN. Criticism's very concentration on Welles the genius has done his greatest movie a disservice, because here his personal, Nietzschean criticism of capitalism gets focussed through a public theme. How mighty a movie this is, connecting COLONEL BLIMP (Britain), with WILSON (another Progressive's Tragedy) and IVAN THE TERRIBLE (or Kane the Hollow) …

TUESDAY, MAY 3
RAYMOND DURGNAT PRESENTS
MONTAGE IN THE CINEMA (PROGRAM SIX)
SON OF MONTAGE – IT'S QUICKER BY MONTAGE 9:00

Montage is the only way to travel; it can get you from Paris to Vladivostok and back in 1/24th of a second. The speed of light, that is. Why isn't LETTER FROM SIBERIA by Chris Marker acknowledged as the movie milestone it is? Because short films still don't get a fair share of the critical whip, because when it appeared documentaries were thought to be an exhausted genre, because when they came back into fashion it was as cinema-verite, which this isn't, quite. And most of all because this isn't anything – quite. There's nothing critics feel more uncomfortable with than a movie that can't be crammed into one pigeonhole and no other. Is this a documentary, or a personal letter, or an essay, or a poet's collage woven out of picture postcards, is it a self-reflexive movie, or a self-undermining movie, is it a Stalinist movie, is its real theme the production of thought itself? Trickiest of all, it said everything Godard said a few years later about the opacity and unreality of pictures of reality, and it talks about those difficulties while also talking about something else – a Siberia which is quite unlike anybody else's .... No, you have seen nothing in Siberia; because Siberia is also the eyes you bring with you (like Marker's) from Paris (which doesn't exist either ...), because every country is what it is thanks to a network of everything else – which for Marker includes Alfred E. Neuman, two Jesuit priests who decided Siberia's history, a horse hobbled in a Culture Park, the American Gold Rush, ragtime pianos and any number of Western movies ....

The famous sequence where three different commentaries give completely different meanings to the selfsame shots of a completely anonymous roadmender did to the documentary what Einstein's Theory of Relativity did to science. It cut the ground from under its feet. This is where the modern cinema really began – the cinema of doubt – somewhere in the middle of Siberia .... Also by Chris Marker, LA JETEE is a montage of still photographs (virtually, freeze-frames) cut together (like jump-cuts) to constitute a strip-cartoon in time instead of space. A ghost from the future seeks to escape his time-looped destiny ... and these powerful images achieve the astonishing feat of stopping film in its tracks without shattering belief. The film that wrecked a thousand theories. "Time must have a stop," said Aldous Huxley. "You Only Die Twice," said Ian Fleming. They were optimists, for maybe you can die, and die, and die, and die, and die ...

TOUTE LA MEMOIRE DU MONDE was commissioned from Resnais by the French National Library. Resnais's tracks and pans, cutting in and twisting round each other, transform the stacks of books and miles of shelves into another planet, as ominous as the library of ZARDOZ. A vast reservoir of artificial realities, it constantly threatens to bury all human life under a flood of knowledge of the past, of visions and fictions, of a thousand and one texts that mimic life, and parisitize it ...

TUESDAY, MAY 10
RAYMOND DURGNAT PRESENTS
MONTAGE IN THE CINEMA (PROGRAM SEVEN)
THE GEOGRAPHY OF MONTAGE – MONTAGE RISING 9:00

Despite KANE, Hollywood slackened up on montage in the '40s. But Hollywood is only the Great Pretender, or rather the Tyrannosaurus Rex, of American pop culture, and the steady click of the scissors only grew louder and louder across the Underground. Willard Maas's GEOGRAPHY OF THE BODY depends on montage by set-up. By means of big-close-ups it extracts nipples, thumbs, palms, toes, earholes and anuses from the visual context, with disquieting effect. And the Dionysio-Surrealist poet George Barker takes it from there. His commentary turns the body-details into long-shots, of deserts and tundras and deltas and the surface of a forbidden planet. Bruce Conner's COSMIC RAY is cut to Ray Charles's "What'd I Say?" and counterpoints it with its own visual pulse, like an extension of the machine-gun rhythms of OCTOBER. It's a jazz battle between its two basic

The hero of *Scorpio Rising* (1963), reading *Li'l Abner*

forms, the wheel (strengthened by numbered leader) and its spokes (a stripper's limbs, a warship's pom-pom guns). A MOVIE, slower, dourer, is a beautiful little reflection on man's virtuoso stunts and structures, and their sea-change into something sinister and strange. Strictly according to Eisenstein, intellectual montage rips details out of context to turn them into metaphors. From Poland, Walerian Borowczyk's RENAISSANCE is almost a companion-piece to LA JETEE; a trip backwards in time, but by a very different kind of locomotion. From a set-up no larger than a man's hand, Charles and Ray Eames's [POWERS OF TEN] takes an eight-minute trip back up and out to the farthest limits of the known universe, and back through his pores again to sub-atomic level. This magical mystery zoom will have you shouting "What'd I see?" And by way of grand finale, Kenneth Anger's SCORPIO RISING, a meditation on leather boys as playthings of the Gods. It's largely structured on symbols and structures, on the warp and woof of one thing with another – blue jeans and blue velvet, Li'l Abner and the Bible according to Aleister Crowley, Jesus amongst the money-changers and a bout of bondage, and a revolving police light that becomes the two faces of a God.

THURSDAY, MAY 19
RAYMOND DURGNAT PRESENTS
MONTAGE IN THE CINEMA (PROGRAM NINE)
THE EDITOR REGRETS – TIME MUST HAVE A SPLICE 7:00, 9:30

Resnais is the master-cutter of '60s cinema. Each and every movie is a different kind of magical montage trip and we chose JE T'AIME, JE T'AIME as his brightest and bleakest film. Resnais is the anti-Ophuls. Ophuls used camera-movements to turn space into time, to waltz himself through Vienna 1900, or Paris a la la belle epoque, in a fond remembrance of time past. Resnais twines past and present around each other so that neither can escape the coils of the other. The present becomes the unquiet grave of all our yesterdays ... And all roads lead to the Palace of Living Death: having not enough past (MARIENBAD), having too much past (HIROSHIMA), altering the past (MURIEL), or, worst of all, having

The Essential Raymond Durgnat

too many pasts (JE T'AIME). I love you, I love you … Resnais's title promises naive romantic fervor, but the repetition proves ominous. A failed suicide agrees to become a guinea-pig for scientists exploring time-travel, and is caught, not just in a given moment, but in an infinite variety of given moments, all variations on one another. And time's winged chariot will never come to his rescue. It's a science fiction tragedy in comic strip images. Everybody thinks of Bergson, and no doubt they're right. But if Resnais, Marker (LA JETEE) and their friend Borowczyk (RENAISSANCE) are all obsessed with time, there may be another reason too: a profoundly Marxist sense of history as the nightmare from which man is trying to awaken. Sartre might have tried to pinpoint individual responsibility (like LES JEUX SONT FAITS); but Resnais doesn't bother, man is only too easily what his local space-time makes him. Ironically enough, JE T'AIME was a good ten years before its time, and its box-office fate began Resnais's seven lean years. People weren't then ready for this quiet mixture of science fiction with a love story as subtle as anything in Rohmer and Rivette. But with Marker's LA JETEE and SOLARIS it constitutes a holy trinity of meditations on the horrors of eternal life.

SATURDAY, NOVEMBER 19
FILMS SINCE 1962:
A PERSONAL SELECTION BY RAYMOND DURGNAT
PERFORMANCE 4:15, 8:00

Warners were sold on a script they can't have read by the idea of Mick Jagger as demon-king of Swinging London. But when their executive finally wandered onto the set and beheld the proto-punk rocker swathed in robes and rouge pushing his natural-born insolence to the point of androgyny (just like a dandy out of Baudelaire), and Anita Pallenberg checking out tripped-out strong-arm man James Fox for nipple-sensitivity, he cried, "Hey, it's all about a bunch of fruitcakes!" or words to that effect. They delayed release for two years and it came out just too late for me to give it the place of honor it deserved in "Sexual Alienation in the Cinema," along with the FELLINI-SATYRICON and Pasolini's THEOREM. And James Fox, who plays its acid-throwing thug, who loves his work too well, got religion soon after shooting, partly, he says, in reaction against the film's bleak view of all the emptinesses and mean-nesses that honeycomb our identities. For hard-rock buffs it has "Mickey Mouth" in blistering form sneering out "Memo from Turner" (and proving yet again that he's the only singer in the world who can give himself a kiss around the back of his own head without even parting his lips). It has a rock-opera-type soundtrack featuring Buffy Ste.-Marie, The Last Poets and other denizens of that imaginary museum, Swinging London. For followers of wild film form it has (a) the sharpest and most lyrical intercutting since Alain Resnais hung up his high-speed scissors and (b) a tracking shot in through the back of Mick Jagger's skull and out again through his eyeball – and a brief meeting on the way with J. L. Borges, as the nowhere man within the man … For nitty gritty, kitchen sink realists its fidelity to a range of English idioms and styles is a treat and a half in itself. As a picture of ego dissolutions it's worth two PERSONAs, as a study in interpersonal relationships it's worth 24 SCENES FROM A MARRIAGE, as a study in traditional English punk rage it's worth seven CLOCK-WORK ORANGEs, as a study in blood and guts it's worth eight Sam Peckinpahs and four Sam Fullers, as a study in decadence it's worth six THE DAMNED and three LAST TANGOs. It stacks up alongside the Pinter–Losey THE SERVANT for ruthless morality (sinisterly transcending morality?) and for expressionist metaphysics it vies with Kafka's

California Split

MAGICAL MYSTERY TOUR. It's one of those once-in-a-blue-moon movies that twist so many themes into so tight a knot that at every viewing it becomes another movie altogether.

SATURDAY, DECEMBER 3
FILMS SINCE 1962:
A PERSONAL SELECTION BY RAYMOND DURGNAT
LISZTOMANIA 4:30, 8:25

If CLOCKWORK ORANGE was Roll Over, Beethoven, this is Up Liszt and at 'em! Ken Russell's fantasia on the life and ideas of Franz Liszt was sulked over by film critics. Naturally, being the low men on culture's totem pole, they're very fearful of being fooled by bad taste. But if J. P. Gorin can salute Kenneth the Terrible as "the most obscene film director on the face of this planet," and directors as diverse as Makavejev, Nemec and Coppola pounce eagerly on every Russell film, just to see what he's dared to do and has done so cleverly, the reasons are splendidly evident in LISZTOMANIA. His most exubaroque concoction ever, even including TOMMY, it's filled to bursting with bravura sequences. Russell boldly mashes together past and present, the 19th century cult of the inspired virtuoso and 20th century rock freak frenzies, until LISZTOMANIA leaves the biopic genre far below its level of symbolic abstraction. Instead it achieves a kind of analysis-by-extravaganza of the Romantic Movement, with its good side (from transcendentalism to "All You Need is Love"), its demonic side (from Wagner to Hitler via Dracula), its sentimental side (Chaplin meets Disney in a country cottage idyll), and its decadence (a production number about Liszt's castration fears brilliantly dovetails Krafft-Ebing with Busby Berkeley). It all comes together in a STAR WARS-type finale where Liszt (contrite but good) zaps Wagner (degenerated and bad) with a well-aimed cluster of feminophallic guided missiles. Well, maybe it all falls apart, rather than coming together, but throughout its long rising trajectory Russell's firework of a film is a splendid sight, a flying melting-pot of culture and ideas.

SOURCE: PACIFIC FILM ARCHIVE, 1977 (COURTESY THE UNIVERSITY OF CALIFORNIA, BERKELEY ART MUSEUM AND PACIFIC FILM ARCHIVE)

5.3 FROM SIGNS TO MEANINGS

I. The Cultural Implosion

We live in Malraux's "Imaginary Museum." For the first time in history, the cultures of all times are simultaneously available, with unprecedented clarity, though still through the glass darkly of distance and reproduction. Our privilege is profoundly confusing. It's less like enjoying a vantage point than drowning in information. As traditional specializations blur, dilate and spread onto neighboring territories, it's difficult to know when they're collaborating or colliding. Knowledge is both exponential and implosive.

Film culture endures these problems in an acute form. It must comprehend a medium more diverse in its elements and cosmopolitan in its roots than any literature of its time.

Like a buffer state in constant civil war, it's begged to be overrun by its neighbors. It's constantly tried to muddle along on paradigms borrowed from other, ill-suited, only apparently more elaborated, disciplines. For example, influential film theories between the wars celebrated "real" or "pure" cinema in ways which, while seeming streamlined and avant-gardist, owed much to aesthetic theories of the 1880s ("pure music," "pure poetry"). They were overhauled by (and partly incorporated into) a stress on social consciousness, replaced, through the 1950s, by "literary content." Both downgraded "pure" cinema into "visual style" in favor of liberal, edifying criteria against which a younger generation was in full revolt by 1960. Some agglomeration of their positions seems to be what Peter Wollen means by "traditional aesthetics," "art cinema," and "realist aesthetics."[*] Latterly, the mutual incomprehension between, on one hand, movements based on structural linguistics (cinestructuralism, cinesemiology) and, on the other, all other approaches, has become notorious.

Surveying ten "decisive" critical books of the 1960s, Richard T. Jameson includes Peter Wollen's *Signs and Meaning in the Cinema*. He remarks that "the work as a whole suggested the possibility of a dialogue between auteurist-humanist types and the semio-structuralists rumbling in the East."[**] It's ambivalent enough to be attractive to everyone, and figures on innumerable academic reading lists. In Blaine Allan's words, it "is still read today as if it were written only yesterday, as a primer for Eisenstein, auteurism and semiology."[***]

Certainly Wollen is the colporteur who first arrived from Paris with the trunkful of wonderful samples which his text displays. Necessary as his reconnaissance was, he leaped to certain conclusions which foreclosed discussion in unfortunate ways. His book remains dazzling, confusing. Always intelligent, always stimulating, it's so brief that positions must be intimated in a shorthand which hides their problems. It piles terms and new paradigms one upon another without having space to define them. No more than a manifesto, but precisely because it's less naked, more erudite, than manifestos tend to be, its network of references to very briefly summarized sources can seem to have met the requirements of discussion. Precisely because it's so telegrammatic, it's hard to know when taking it at its word is fair or relevant. This inhibited the forceful criticisms required if semio-structuralism was to evolve. Hence it dissimulated most of its virtues (a certain responsiveness to difficulties and objections, a moral commitment like a mirror-image of Robin Wood's) and disseminated most of its vices (of which more anon) – for which Wollen can't be held responsible. It benefits, and suffers, from a conjuncture in cultural history; the "low pressure areas" in English-speaking culture which the winds of structural linguistics could bid to fill, as if structural linguistics was the only kind of structuralism in existence.

This text has no intention of being "fair" to a "Peter Wollen" who, after all, and by his own arguments, doesn't exist. It knows only that auteur who, or rather which, can be extrapolated from a text just as "Fuller or Hawks or Hitchcock, the directors, are quite separate from the structures named after them." Perhaps the book's auteur is an "unconscious catalyst," and we can concentrate on our objections while, ungratefully no doubt, taking for granted its skillful avoidance of many tempting traps into which his fellow-travellers and followers sprawl headlong.

The book is first an effect and then a cause of its cultural predicament. It shares with the *New Left Review* of its time (to which Wollen contributed film-auteurist sketches under the signature of Lee Russell) the conviction that English culture was badly obsolete and devoid of effective theory. He summarizes the state of play in British aesthetics by a quotation from Lord Shaftesbury, obligingly providing his dates (1671–1713), as if in

---

[*] Peter Wollen, *Signs and Meaning in the Cinema* (London: Secker and Warburg, 1969; third edition, 1972).

[**] Richard T. Jameson, "In Print," *Film Comment*, 16, 1 (January–February 1980), p. 45.

[***] Private communication with the author.

evidence of stagnation. He clearly implies that only across the Channel had the vulgar-gourmet impressionism which Shaftesbury denounces lost ground in the last hundred years. It's that traditional English, home counties, cry: "they do things better in France."

He believes that "the great break-through in literary theory came with Jakobson's insistence that poetics was a province of linguistics." He cites two books written four and six years before his own and conflates them with the brusque order of the day: "We must persevere along this road."

Earlier, he has feigned shock that "writers about the cinema have felt free to talk about film language as if linguistics did not exist." However, their freedom was imposed on them, given (1) the differences between film and natural verbal language, which is the subject of linguistics, and (2) semiology's notorious silences and prejudices, like the central issue of iconicity, of which Wollen himself complains.

Wollen outlines a different road, implying that it's the same one. "The cinema is not simply a new art; it is an art which combines and incorporates others, which operates on different sensory bands, different channels, using different codes and modes of expression. It poses in the most acute form the problem of the relationship between the different arts, their similarities and differences, the possibilities of translation and transcription: all the questions asked of aesthetics by the Wagnerian notion of *gesamtkunstwerk* and the Brechtian critique of Wagner, questions which send us back to the theory of synesthesia, to Lessing's *Laocoön* and Baudelaire's *correspondances*."

Back, back, back. Even to synaesthesia, which, when Eisenstein goes back to it, Wollen rightly sees is a Symbolist reflux. After this impressive, if outdated, checklist of great topics and great names, Wollen's remarks about aesthetic theory studiously ignore every vital and useful modern text. In film, Kracauer and Morin aren't mentioned, Mitry mentioned only to be rejected. Wollen quite wrongly alleges that only the formalist-constructivist connection around Eisenstein began to come to terms with Modernism. This set of movements is normally dated from the Symbolists (around 1880) down through abstract art to abstract expressionism, around 1960, after which art history begins to speak of post-Modernism (happenings, minimalism, pop art, conceptual art, the current revival of painterly realisms, etc.).

In this astonishing void, semiology can loom as a major breakthrough, especially since for Wollen the New Criticism (1924) doesn't exist either, so that only semiology can teach us to expel the author from the text. Possibly Wollen's unargued dismissal of assumptions that artworks make organic wholes aims at Susanne Langer. Otherwise, Wollen flits from one reference to another. At one moment, Lord Shaftesbury is "the greatest English writer on aesthetics and the semiology of the visual arts" (a judgment as startling as calling Adam Smith the greatest Marxist of all time); at another, Cornelius Cardew is our good example. The unguarded reader may be mightily impressed by casual bytes of erudition, like the (fascinating) remark that Dalcroze Eurhythmics influenced Massine's choreography. But this name-salad can only arouse a thousand complex issues which Wollen has no possibility of properly outlining, let alone solving, hence it's impossible not to turn semiology's disdain of theoryless impressionism against this text. It's more saddening still to see how all this erudition stumbles across none of the aesthetic theories which, for all their flaws and incompletions, have in broad principle integrated all these Modernist and post-Modernist practices with preceding, and mainstream, practices.

It's impossible to say why Wollen should ignore all contemporary Anglo-Saxon aesthetic theory and, in particular, the social-history-based art histories on which modern aesthetics finds common ground with earlier Marxists (e.g. Kracauer, Hauser). It's pertinent that Parisian semio-structuralism was in reaction against the range of Marxist humanisms and critical realisms which runs from Lukács and Lucien Goldmann to the Frankfurt School, Marcuse, and Sartre.

Wollen doesn't altogether forget that the history of high art is that of modernism, and he alludes to the spiritual ferments of Italy, Zurich, Berlin, and above all Paris, melting-pot of exiles from the East, including White Russians. Naturally, he omits London, city of Freud's first triumphs. He relegates the scientific side of the Bauhaus to a parenthesis about typography, and maybe his remarks on avant-garde ideology are intended to reduce engineers to technicians, and persuade us to forget the socio-technocratic thrust of Le Corbusier, Frank Lloyd Wright, etc. Wollen's bias is flagrant. He centers modernism around the heroic age of Russian Bolshevism (adding Brecht).

The fact is that through the 1920s the Bolshevist and bourgeois avant-gardes were both working at full stretch. Abel Gance, an idealist, bourgeois reactionary, working with the poet Blaise Cendrars, beat Eisenstein to super-Griffithian montage (LA ROUE, 1922/3, against STRIKE, 1925). ENTR'ACTE, a Dada film by René Clair and the painter Picabia, beat Dziga-Vertov to self-reflexive, deconstructive, montage by five years. Similarly, the American avant-garde (from 1943 on) is left extremely vague by Wollen until Anger's SCORPIO RISING, which follows Godard, whose pioneering status is much exaggerated thereby. The Parisian avant-garde of the 1920s is epitomized by Léger, Man Ray, Buñuel (none of the "commer-cial" avant-gardists – no Delluc, Dulac, Epstein, L'Herbier, Cavalcanti). Presumably he wants to suggest that modernism goes with progressive attitudes, and that avant-gardes are opposed to the bourgeoisie. Unfortunately, they're opposed to it only by being ahead of it. They're its cutting edge, exactly the reason they're called "avant-gardes."

For film theory as for film history. By centering on Bazin, Wollen can make film culture look like the tail end of a Renaissance-classical-Romantic-realistic amalgam. Thus he can imply that modernism doesn't touch film theory except via Russia and Godard. He liquidates 9/10ths of film culture. […]

The battle between the straw men of traditional aesthetics, and the tin men of Modernism, gives us a clear rooting interest, and it's neatly complicated by aligning Jakobson and semiology with the straw men. The lineage of his assumptions is fairly clear. It goes back, like so much Parisian thought of the 1960s, to Jakobson, who recuperates Peirce, and Lévi-Strauss. Barthes intensifies its "euphoria of scientificity" (as he later dismissed it). That, not scientific, but technocratic, spirit inspires Wollen to assign Godard the role rela-tive to film which Robbe-Grillet was supposed to have performed in literature (his novels, and indeed films, are textbook cases of non-communicating interrogations which defy non-modernist "recuperation" and deconstruct themselves as an incentive to deconstruct-ing everything). The excitement of Paris, 1968 privileges Althusser and Kristeva, whose rationalism affords a pretext to abolish the historical-materialist-sociological Marxisms which number among the targets of 1960s linguistic structuralism. It pervades *Cahiers* Mark IV, *Cinéthique*, and *Screen*, and its notion of a clear division between traditional aes-thetics and modernism is symptomatic of its inadequacies.

French literary theory had stagnated since Symbolism, and the only real contact English cinestructuralism had with English aesthetics was via F. R. Leavis, whose indifference to theory was notorious, and, to a lesser extent, via the New Criticism, to which Wollen pre-sumably refers when dismissing "organic whole" theory.

To accept this schema is to omit the mainstream evolution of Anglo-American aesthetic theory. Modernist theory appears very early (e.g. with Wyndham Lewis). In 1923 Ogden and

Richards publish *The Meaning of Meaning*, whose very title conveniently indicates the convergence of metatheory and self-interrogation in its materialistic communication theory and its structural approach to semantics. Just like Jakobson later, they opt for Peirce over Saussure, whom they trenchantly criticize, and they help establish aesthetics as a hybrid of philosophy, logic, semantics and psychology. While the variety of these disciplines precludes any neat list of names like that on which Parisian structuralism fetishizes, and while it clarifies rather than conceals the real difficulties of theoretical integration, it obviates sleeper-holds like that with which structural linguistics paralyzed semiology. In 1924 Richards's *Principles of Literary Criticism* is aggressively, though prematurely, materialistic. Aesthetic theory slowly but surely catches up with modernist practice, until by, say, 1945 mainstream aesthetics accommodates both the "traditional" and "modernist" functions, and underpins the formulations in this text. By the mid-1950s it has outlined the incorporation of gestalt and post-gestalt psychology, providing the bases for the books by Arnheim, Ehrenzweig, Hochberg and Meyer mentioned below. (Ehrenzweig further crosses them with Freudian theory, which was accepted by English culture far more swiftly and thoroughly than by French.) Gestalt theory involves a powerful sense of structuration, and this theoretical mainstream has broad affinities with Jean Mitry's *Esthétique et psychologie du cinéma* and the theoretical summaries of Jean Piaget (*Structuralism*, *Main Trends In Psychology*, *Main Trends in Inter-Disciplinary Research*, *Insights and Illusions of Philosophy*). Other inter-disciplinary areas are explored in Susanne Langer's *Philosophy in a New Key*, Gregory Bateson's *Steps to An Ecology of Mind*, Anthony Wilden's *System and Structure* (of particular interest for its criticisms of Piaget, Metz and Lacan, and for metatheorizing the highly critical stance also exemplified by Jonathan Culler's *Structuralist Poetics* and Philip Pettit's *The Concept of Structuralism*).

This mainstream thoroughly overlaps with Marxism in its joint concern with social history. Thus two Marxist-social-materialist texts, Arnold Hauser's *A Social History of Art* and Kracauer's *From Caligari to Hitler*, number among its most influential formulations. Wylie Sypher's *Rococo to Cubism in Art and Literature* will serve as an example of how far mainstream aesthetics has moved from synaesthesia and simple correspondences in correlating transactions and equivalences between the media.

By 1960, aesthetic theory, far from lagging behind Modernism, has become so efficient that it's *driving* aesthetic practice as much as it's following it. The very malaise of art derives from the extent to which it does no more than interrogate its own codes, in a curious replay of the Symbolist solipsism of 1880–1900.

The correlation, however broad, of avant-gardes and progressive tendencies is unconvincing. For avant-gardes relate to social-professional specialization as well as to less stable kinds of social fragmentation. Further, avant-gardes often turn Fascist, or conservative, or feed back into the mainstream, without extremism. Interesting as the long-neglected Russian avant-gardes are, avant-gardes are a pan-European phenomenon, whose peak, if anywhere, was Paris. The French avant-garde features of the 1920s coincide with France's social stagnation and exhaustion; the American underground with the End of Ideology. Of the leaders of the French New Wave, only Godard (and Marker, an older, committed leftist, whom Wollen all but excludes, presumably to showcase Godard) closely relates to Paris, 1968. Truffaut remains Conservative, while Chabrol is – what? – smartass-supercilious-aloof? (Wollen is indignant at his neglect by critics.) If the New Wave relates to a revolution, it's not to 1968, which followed it by nine years, nor even to the Algerian War and its aftermath, a much more likely candidate though less attractive to intellectuals; but rather to the onset of the French national technocracy, Eurocapitalism, and *le défi américain* (which pours through the pages of *Cahiers* into Wollen's favoring Hollywood with hardly a mention of French, English, and Italian industry developments). While the coming of sound and industry consolidations must indeed have contributed to the avant-gardes' eclipse in 1930, the massive social violence of the period (national revolutions) cannot be overlooked, since it also propelled poets like Auden and movements like Mass-Observation in the general direction of social consciousness and mass-society-documentary. The British documentary's symbiosis of realism, montage and a certain populism was not only highly creative, but an appropriate prelude to the war to come. To dismiss it as "conservative" is to suggest *either* a rigid association of avant-gardes with radical progressivism, *or* elitist enigmas (if everybody can understand it, it can't be avant-garde). But why shouldn't the avant-garde periodically rejoin with the main body? Why shouldn't agit-prop aim at a mass public?

The fact is that where Bolshevik aesthetics stopped, aesthetic theory in the bourgeois West moved on, proving ever more restless and resourceful, resilient and sophisticated, self-reflexive and self-critical, accumulating the discoveries of avant-gardes as they came and went. Many of these avant-gardes were both anti-bourgeois and ultra-bourgeois, precisely because capitalism is dedicated to progress, i.e., manipulation, analysis, resynthesis, deconstruction, the "destruction" of the old by the new. Moreover, modern art applies, adapts and integrates these experiments in the avant-garde laboratories and applies them to its wider publics. Just as the British documentary sustained intellectual montage when Eisenstein had to abandon it, so the Bauhaus philosophy dominated the design of London Transport stations (and even its stylized underground map provides an excellent example of the signifier achieving a functional autonomy from the signified). It's only too easy to catalogue what bourgeois capitalism doesn't do and contrast it with what a hypothetical Socialism might do.

Let's be clear that for nearly two hundred years capitalism has been in the business of permanent revolution, i.e., progress so hectic that it's an endemic alienation effect, "culture shock," "future shock." It's capitalism which pushes agit-prop to the virtuoso sophistication of certain TV commercials, which may be dazzling montages, or routinely achieve double-back-action ironies well beyond the reach of Brechtian theory. Capitalism is thoroughly rationalistic, analytical, cerebral, and quick to be psychologically violent; to manipulate people as if they were (Deleuze's phrase) "desiring machines" which must be uncoupled from any "organic unity" their psychology might require and plugged into an impersonal schizo-system. It's closer to Dziga-Vertov's (Stakhanovite, i.e., industrializing) fragmentation than to Eisenstein's homages to emotionality. However, to talk as if the intensification of modernist interrogation could only benefit the left is to fall into every trap posed by the system. Wollen observes that Hollywood has resisted traditional "art" (his inverted commas). But his thought develops an intriguing ambiguity; it sounds as if it's by fighting *against* a *popular* Hollywood that the film avant-garde will retain its advantages over other avant-gardes. The complication is symptomatic, for PENTHESILEA and RIDDLES OF THE SPHINX pointedly reject everything *popular* about film.

Though Wollen criticizes naively realistic theories of the cinema, he grants Bazinism a near-monopoly of important film writing for maybe twenty years. He criticizes romantic auteurism, yet prostrates himself slavishly before *Cahiers* (whereas its auteurism had assumed that American directors possessed all the privileges of the European "art" directors). This astonishing dismissal of non-Bazinist writing follows the general postulation of "antinomies" from which sophisticated (and Marxist) positions are systematically excluded.

Similarly, only one kind of auteur theory is possible; not to admire Hawks's work is to assume some "existential distinction between art films and popular films." Yet Wollen concedes that distinction in his previous sentence and in his reasons for dismissing Welles! Worse still, his antinomy excludes auteur theories which would (a) accept Welles alongside Hawks, Ford, Boetticher, etc., (b) prize his films as an interrogation of theirs, and/or (c) admit Welles to a pantheon excluding Hawks. Wollen's pantheon is debatable at its edges, but its core seems to comprise all the reliable old troupers: Hawks, Ford, Hitchcock, Fuller, Sirk.

In Paris, *Positif* had maintained a counter-emphasis on those liberals and dissidents (Wilder, Welles, Sturges, Brooks, Aldrich) against whom *Cahiers* and Sarris were prejudiced, by the association of critical films with a "liberal" art cinema. *Movie* had taken theories of the end of ideology seriously enough to edge from center-and-right to plumb-center. Wollen's pantheon shuffles back to the right, a move camouflaged by an attack on the MacMahonists. It's unaffected by Wollen's concluding volte-face, whereby Hollywood, though not monolithic, is "an implacable foe." An all-interrogating modernism might have turned to his friends and fellow-travellers in Hollywood. But his withdrawal of interest from extending auteurism can only build this right-and-center bias more solidly into film culture. It's *this* selection from Hollywood which should be "defended and safeguarded." Indeed we mustn't for a moment take our eyes off it, for it "provides the dominant codes with which films are read and will continue to do so for the foreseeable future," and even avant-gardists and theorists cannot "simply turn their back on Hollywood."

Yet by 1969 there were clear signs that Hollywood was evolving a new spirit, a new populism, which constituted, amongst other things, the succession to neo-realism, but shorn of Rossellini's mystical realism. The seminal film is Cassavetes's SHADOWS (1959). Watkins's CULLODEN (1964) owes little or nothing to Godard and a great deal to the British documentary tradition; in its wake, films by Dick Lester, Nicholas Roeg and others evolve their dazzling syntheses of intellectual montage, realism-and-symbolical discourse, and non-Hollywood fictional styles. Once again, an antinomy (modernism-Old Hollywood) has excluded the variety of intermediate positions which can hybridize and develop into a new mainstream. Once again, the model of "binary oppositions," taken from structural linguistics via Lévi-Strauss, has sabotaged thought. […]

II. Que Viva Eisenstein!

After his Introduction, Wollen devotes the first of his three chapters to Eisenstein, "the first, and probably still the most important, major theorist of the cinema." The competition for "most important" is severely limited; only Bazin is summarized at length. Wollen is concerned to explain why Eisenstein failed to produce a coherent, scientific theory of film – why he failed to become Jean Mitry, as it were. Brevity precludes a balanced account of Eisenstein's ideas of montage, and much of his space goes, not to Eisenstein's theory at all, but to his career and times. The structural principle guiding Wollen's otherwise bewildering selection of detail and evaluation is immediately apparent: incongruity as incoherence, culminating in the phrase "half-industrial and half-music-hall" which Wollen thinks summarizes "the curious artistic admixture of the time." He doesn't seem to mean the 1920s in general, since he links "most of the works of the *avant-garde*" with "a dismal mixture of theosophy, Worringer, Frazer, bits of Bergson, even Bradley, and so on," excepting only "the early collaboration between the Russian linguists and Futurist poets" and the Surrealists who "made an effort to understand Freud" (which is inaccurate; they borrowed from him). But Wollen wants to reduce whatever happens in the West to "dismal" attempts; and one wonders what happened to Freud, Einstein, Heisenberg, Riemann, and the across-the-board input from logic and science into avant-garde activity throughout the 20th century. Again, "bits of Bergson" become a lot more formidable when we remember how they link with the intrinsic evolution of 19th-century realism to generate the stream-of-consciousness movement in literature – often firmly contexted in social realisms.

Wollen's Eisenstein suffers from a master-antinomy: a split between scientific aspirations (which were bound to be frustrated by Bolshevism's scientific crudities) and an unscientific emotionality, such that Eisenstein settled for a science cruder than it need have been. This ravages *The Film Sense* and *Film Form*, throughout which Eisenstein attempts to "shore up, scientifically and intellectually, an art increasingly preoccupied with emotional saturation, ecstasy, the synchronisation of the senses, myth and primitive thought ('Folk images equal human knowledge,' he said, apropos of *Que Viva Mexico!*)."

Wollen's "shore up" clearly implies that all these preoccupations are a way of intellectually falling down. However, we don't share Wollen's certainty as to where scientific, intellectual, and "merely" emotional operations begin and end. Far from exhibiting Eisenstein's remark about folk images like some nadir of irrationalism, we would compare it to Lévi-Strauss's stress on the complex structures of "savage thought" and to Freud's wry remark that he was fated to discover what nursemaids had always known. Moreover, Lévi-Strauss's system of binary oppositions (for all its flaws) constitutes a plausible case of montage (collisions of antithetical ideas), which is why so many Marxists thought that Lévi-Strauss was adding another string to their bow. Similarly, if you can understand Freudian theory, whether (partially) theorized by Freud himself, or (comprehensively) by Edward Glover, you have acquired a sense of system which constitutes an *authentic* structuralism (as against borrowings from structural linguistics, which can't explain a different field). Arguably, Freud is more structuralist than Lévi-Strauss, more dialectical than Engels.

Freud deeply interested Eisenstein, probably because both men assumed (a) that emotions were psychic structures, and (b) that the scientific intellect is ready prey to obsessions and psychodramas of every kind. Hence it's difficult to be interested by Wollen's old-fashioned, pre-Freudian, rationalist dichotomy, "heart versus head." Which is straight out of St. Thomas Aquinas, via Platonism on one hand and Cartesianism on the other.

We may well wonder why Eisenstein's sense of structures of thought merits pejorative comparisons with alchemy, and why Wollen prefers Brecht, whose dreary, high-art didacticism needs no science at all. It's even more startling to find that no breath of censure attends relentless old tearjerkers like John Ford, Douglas Sirk, or the New Left's other Hollywood heroes: Hawks, Hitchcock, and the arch-emotionalist Sam Fuller (on whom Wollen edited a startlingly acquiescent book). The sad fact is that this whole generation of "rigorous" young Marxists drop their critical guard to knee-level when faced with these old Hollywood maestros of lower-middlebrow kitsch. The New Left is a softer touch than *Movie*; confronted with Hollywood in all its bourgeois glory, Wollen has nothing Marxist to say. At best, the wilderness/garden antinomy he sees in Ford might link with a Marxist emphasis on the means of production. But instead of going beyond Nash Smith's supposedly "magisterial" *Virgin Land*, we're edged *away* from questions about the *ownership* of the means of production. Ford's highly emotional (and genuinely beautiful) mystification of the West, Fuller's virulent McCarthyism, provoke no protest. Maybe Wollen deliberately relegates his Marxism to a low profile. However, many students assume that *Signs and Meaning* asks Marxist questions about the cinema.

Wollen may well be trying to understand Eisenstein, but he effectively finishes him off; *Screen* will focus on a theoretician about whom Wollen's book has little to say: Dziga-

The *October* gods

Vertov. Otherwise, Wollen's description of Eisenstein's predicament admirably evokes the enthusiastic confusion in which Bolshevik avant-gardes were wallowing when Comrade Stalin threw his monkey-wrench into their works. But the central social fact behind Eisenstein's reversion to a crude Behaviorism and a crude dialectic is that even with such sops to OGPU, Eisenstein very nearly followed Meyerhold into the GULAG Archipelago. Wollen is severe on Eisenstein's supposed psychodrama, on Marxism's jejune state, on a Bolshevik "frenzy." But Stalinism appears only as "philistinism," and is grotesquely diminished by the comparison to McCarthyism. Omitting the Stalinist terror, which penetrated every corner of intellectual enquiry, Wollen (a) divorces art from social history, (b) "blames the victim" in the tradition of a sociologically innocent Freudianism, and (c) deploys auteurism to the advantage of Hollywood traditionalism and the disadvantage of modernist innovation.

But let's take the other option. Let's be severe on Ford (as above) and look for structure in Eisenstein's work. Certainly, Eisenstein's stories aren't very interesting on the narrative level. The "binary oppositions" in POTEMKIN are the ones you first thought of. But Eisenstein's graphics are already a set of structures, and semio-structuralism's problem is how to analyze pictures (as Metz made plain). Wollen implies that learning how to interpret pictures is a project for the future, which would mean that so far no one has understood the visual arts, from Rembrandt to *The Beano*.

Yet semiology would find its life much easier were it to learn from modern aesthetics, for example, Arnheim's *Art and Visual Perception*, Ehrenzweig's *The Psychoanalysis of Artistic Vision and Hearing*, and Julian Hochberg's section of *Art, Perception and Reality*. Eisenstein, like a large percentage of the human race, thought pictorially in terms of change and movement, so that we can add Leonard B. Meyer's *Emotion and Meaning in Music* to our list. All these works can easily be coordinated with Eisenstein's notion of montage, by the way.

Wollen sees, and it's a great insight, that Eisenstein's departures from narrative (the OCTOBER Gods, Kerensky's steps and props) anticipate Godard's non-narrative (or only vestigially narrative) cinema of symbolical ideas. Our point is that Eisenstein's narratives "shelter" symbolic structures which are revitalized, energized, by their graphic/plastic intricacy.

Wollen nearly sees this structuration when he comments on the pressure of biomechanics throughout IVAN THE TERRIBLE. But he dismisses the same thing in NEVSKI as "heroic postures" and deprives them of any semantic input, *à la* Godard, from similarities to icons. Even Ivan's acting is merely "strange, distorted." Yet the acting in IVAN is based on kinaesthetic, muscular, tensions; and tensions, by definition, are structures! But a simple application of the books prescribed above, easily adaptable to moving and changing images, is all we need to read IVAN in the terms in which Eisenstein saw it.

As for OCTOBER, it analyzes swiftly into a structure of statements about organization. The Tsarist regime speaks through architecture (palaces, rooms, statues, streets) and interior design. The Bolsheviks have words (orators, banners, pamphlets). But organization isn't just communication; weapons are statements too. Machine-guns poke their snouts in and speak (we *see*, by cutting, the rat-tat-tat); bourgeois petticoats swirl like anti-banners, their parasols are used like bayonets. Kornilov's Cossacks have Islamic prayers inscribed on their weapons; they're met by agitators; everything finishes in the "language" of dance. Even if OCTOBER without Trotsky is like *Hamlet* without the Prince, the structure survives to exalt the film's astonishing anticlimax. For OCTOBER culminates in the massacre (of mis-led women and cadets) that didn't happen. Sure, some wine-bottles get smashed, but, as Nietzsche said, "A little revenge is more human than no revenge." Otherwise, a really popular organization is magnanimity, whereas "law and order" is all kinds of chaos: massacre, flight into nowhere, crazy defiance.

Isn't that as interesting as the garden/wilderness antinomy which Wollen pursues through Ford? Isn't it the same antinomy; the palace is a garden, the rabble is a wilderness. There's a twist, though: the terms reverse. The palace is wild disorder, the rabble a decent order.

Taken in the same way, IVAN THE TERRIBLE is as complex as YOUNG MR. LINCOLN, with which, indeed, it rather interestingly twins, for, as *Cahiers* noticed, Lincoln's stare is rather *terrible*. God looks through both men. Whence another irony. If the structure of LINCOLN is to be ana-lyzed in terms of narrative, it's unlikely to be Ford's. Rather it comes from a cross-breeding of American ideas which is engineered by whatever pooling of talents (committee) decided on the script. Insofar as the structure is Ford's, it must involve purely visual structures and the weighting which they inflict on the narrative's connotations. You can't perform a Lévi-Straussian analysis on Ford *qua* Ford until you can perform a structural analysis on his images.

Similarly, you can't perform a structural analysis of IVAN until you've done (among other things) a structural analysis of the architecture and the clothes (and how they relate). When you've done that, Eisenstein stops looking quite so soft and hazy; he's very disci-plined, very hard, very sharp, and that quite astonishing control transforms the lyricism into something else. Eisenstein was surely right in trying to be that only apparently incongru-ous thing, an engineer of emotions. For emotions are attitudes, decisions, ideologies.

The absence of any terms of visual analysis from Wollen's book (other than Metz's declaredly unsatisfactory tentative) condemns it to be broken-backed. Eisenstein wanted to extend montage from *collisions between shots* to *collisions between items within two shots* and (anent NEVSKI) *collisions between aural and visual elements of the same shot*. He did-n't quite, clearly, reach the ineluctable corollary; that you can have montage between visual elements within the same shot (even an immobile one).* But he reiterates the existence of montage in literature (where the shots are highly problematic). He doesn't quite divorce montage from cutting (in theory, though the practice is clear in POTEMKIN), and "pure film" theory of the 1930s followed him, for much the same reason, an assumption that editing was film's main source of dynamism. It couldn't risk the assumption that *mise-en-scène* involved contrast, collision, tension, and was the continuation of montage by other means.

When the 1950s end of ideology gratefully soaked up Bazin's anti-modernism, it dis-seminated also his mismatching of the shot with reality, with the natural, with the raw. It forgot that *mise-en-scène* is manipulation just as montage is. The interaction of

---

* Although it now seems that he took this step in his classes, and described *mise-en-scène* as "hidden montage." Cf. Vladimir Nizhny, *Lessons With Eisenstein* (London: George Allen and Unwin, 1969), pp. 138–9.

Bazinism and auteur theory produced a paradoxical notion: the image carries both raw reality and the auteur – but the auteur doesn't speak through the *mise-en-scène!* The heritage of "literary content" asserted itself: the auteur was in his script and his script's themes. Visual style edged in, briefly, now and again.

The term *metteur-en-scène* rapidly became pejorative (even though it is the ordinary French word for "director"!). Wollen sees that very little in a film is "raw" reality, that the natural is *always* thoroughly cooked (simply by being selected). [...] The camera doesn't imitate "raw" nature (as Barthes supposes); it cooks it. The camera is a cooking machine, and what goes in natural, comes out artificial. The two aspects of selection are well known; photography is only moderately realistic; and selection both intensifies and recontextualizes. Where there's a cooking machine there's bound to be a chef, who for his part is busily interfering with nature too – plucking the feathers, mixing the sauces. Every amateur with a Box Brownie has known enough for a hundred years to become a *metteur-en-scène*, to "direct" Granny, and make her an actor playing herself, by telling her to (1) tidy her hair, (2) stand near the azaleas, (3) watch the birdie and (4) say "Cheese." It's not unreal – cooked meat is still meat. It's just not raw. [...] This permits his spirited, and altogether effective, rebuttal of Bazin, Metz and Barthes. Resoundingly he justifies artificiality. [...]

Yet if Wollen's spirited defense of the cinema's artificialities had borrowed just a few propositions from modern aesthetic theory, he could have considered film as being, first and foremost, "visible thought" (or rather audio-visual thought), including, but not restricted to, what Arnheim calls *Visual Thinking*. Photography is a mechanically convenient (and cheap) form of it, but it's essential to begin film theory from the animated film (which Wollen rightly wants us to do). The next step is to begin the theory of photography, not from its means, but from its aims – the photograph succeeds if it's a clear diagram of something. Indexicality is subordinate to iconocity. Film theorists rarely remember that handmade illustrations are more accurate and clear than photographic ones (blueprints, scale drawings, etc.), and that photography depends on a photographer who spots the moment when reality is "exposed." Never reality in toto; merely one or two things he knows about it. One still photograph is already montage. [...]

Unfortunately, Wollen takes it for granted that ideas of realism must be conservative and propagandistic, that nothing significant links Joyce with Balzac, that modernism is the negation and never the extension of realism in the sense of an exploration of reality. He follows Parisian structuralism in its attempt to obliterate the numerous, necessary and intimate links between realisms and Marxisms in their assault on bourgeois conventions and rationalist idealism. Hence Wollen can't dissolve the Eisenstein–Bazin antithesis which has been making an idiot of film culture for twenty years, despite Gozlan's pulverization of Bazin's arguments, part of which appears in Peter Graham's *The New Wave.*[*] It's not simply that Bazin's Exhibit A, CITIZEN KANE, constantly slams in cuts so dynamic and intellectual that Eisenstein would have waved his cap in wild applause and hugged Welles like a soul-brother. Bazin's worst omission is even more influential. The whole British documentary movement was founded on the symbiosis of (not just neo-) realism with montage. Cavalcanti and Grierson are completely clear, completely lucid. Grierson talks about "the creative treatment of actuality." He knows that what he is doing is agit-prop. If film culture had possessed itself instead of chasing after the latest Paris fashions, the paralytic antitheses like Rossellini–Eisenstein, Bazin–Eisenstein would never have arisen.

[*] Gerard Gozlan, "In Praise of André Bazin," in Peter Graham, ed., trans., *The New Wave* (London: Secker and Warburg, 1968).

Wollen swallows Bazin's insinuation that montage rather faded away. However, it is conspicuous in films of the Bazin years: CITIZEN KANE, Franju's LE SANG DES BETES and HOTEL DES INVALIDES, Marker's CUBA SI! and LETTRE DE SIBERIE (a crucial film), Resnais's TOUTE LA MEMOIRE DU MONDE, and HIROSHIMA MON AMOUR (whose time-slicings depend on montage, are pieced together intellectually, and take in symbolic shots and optical effects in the line of the 1920s avant-gardes). But Wollen doesn't theorize montage, and it's difficult to see how he could, once he has preferred semiological paradigms to Mitry's "logic of implication" and Balázs's "current of induction." For montage relies on patterns of expectation (i.e. implication) and surprise (contrast, collision). These patterns depend on knowledge of the world, and lead on to a constructivist theory of reading, whereby the first shot (or element) suggests a hypothesis (i.e. implications) which the next corroborates, falsifies, strengthens or weakens. Discrepancy, i.e., collision, surprise, provokes the replacement or revision of the hypothesis. It's hypothetico-deductive empiricism, much simplified.

Just as the structural linguistics which underpins both what Paris thought structuralism was, and semiology after Barthes subjugated it to linguistics, couldn't deal with history, and so hoped it had, so it couldn't deal with knowledge of the world, with the means whereby we construct it, and with those semantic operations which stand outside *langue* and determine what selection *parole* must make from *langue* to be meaningful. This knowledge of the world is largely (but not exclusively) socio-cultural, thoroughly interpenetrated by natural processes. It decides which propositions are accurate, idiotic, nonsensical, metaphorical, or usefully approximative. *Langue tel quel* knows no difference between "All cats are grey at night" and "Lunar unicorns prefer Camembert to Relativity Theory," between "Macbeth hath murdered sleep" and "Colorless green ideas sleep furiously." Metz's discussion of "grand syntagmas" never stumbles on montage. All it can discover is "contrast," whereas in montage contrast is only a preliminary to some new connection, revision, continuity. For Metz's linguistic categories don't know much about semantic operations. How can they? They're designed to operate *obliviously* of most implications and the cognitive operations they require.

Montage pushes beyond semiology to semantics via a second route. A juxtaposition, or collision, between shots, or signs, has no sign, since it consists of a juxtaposition between signs. The question of how to handle the juxtaposition resembles logically the famous question of whether a sign is a dyad (signifier/signified) or a triad (a signifier, a signified, and their relationship).* If we prefer the triadic form, then the question "Where does the relationship, at the moment of reading, exist?", then the answer has to be: "Not in the text, but in the spectator's head." Immediately logic is respected, texts become incomplete and thoroughly vulnerable, as both Barthes and Eco admit, to "the pleasure of the text" (which is really the pleasure of the reader). The problem of idiosyncratic, competing and inter-subjective reading falls from a theoretical to a practical one, reading becomes a constructivist operation, and cognitive psychology takes its rightful place in aesthetic theory.

What is true of juxtaposed signs is true of juxtaposed codes. If film is not a heterogeneous code, it's because it involves heterogeneous codes, and since all interpenetrate none is complete. Wollen sees that texts may be destructive of the codes used in other texts. And romantic aesthetics stressed that new ideas can destroy *idées reçues* and art emphasizes contradictions. If *ideas* are to be criticized, then codes must be *retained*; for how else will the ideas be reached, and shown to be false? It's not just an academic question, of whether we shall call conventions a special case of code or code a special case

* Anthony Wilden, *System and Structure* (London: Tavistock, 1972), pp. 265–8.

of convention. To destroy all codes would be to paralyze thought. How do we decide which codes to destroy or retain, if not on the basis of certain ideas? The famous degree zero is as specious as "impartiality."

Wollen juxtaposes two different propositions as if they were one. (1) Film is a *gesamtkunstwerk*, combining many kinds of discourse and code. (2) Film theory must begin by modelling itself on structural linguistics. He nearly sees that structural linguistics is so restricted to language per se that it cannot cope with anything else. Unfortunately, the champions of semiology haven't even been able to understand why so many theorists (Mitry, Henderson, Britton) firmly divorce the two propositions, or treat structural linguistics as a province of linguistics, linguistics as a province of semiology, semiology as a province of semantics, and semantics as a hybrid between logic, sociology and cognitive psychology.

SOURCE: *FILM READER*, NO. 5, 1982, 300–23

5.4 POPEYE POPS UP

I. Altman Through the Looking Glass

POPEYE sketches a story to paint a world. Its details are its core. It stretches its soul across its skin.

It's about Popeye having biceps like kitbags, calves like pistons, a mutilation that looks like a wink, and red hair like Captain MacWhirr in Conrad's *Typhoon*. It's about Olive Oyl's lanky-legged gait and splay feet in Goofy boots, about her spaghetti lines, onion face, and vinegary frailty. It's about a burly burger-chef who twirls a spatula and rolls his leery eyes behind delicately lifted fingers. It's about a burly villain sucking his thumb while snoring, and about Popeye seeking his kidnapped fosterbabe by putting a message in a baby-bottle and pitching it down a slipway like a ship.

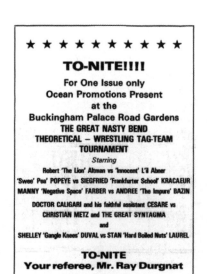

The townsfolk strut and tumble around the screen in a choreography that splits the difference between dance and activity, acrobatics and just gesture (Biomechanics Rules Okay). It's a whirligig of detail that's hose-piped around the screen and desynchronised just enough to distend and boggle our visual gestalt and whisk us into a Happy Land which Lacanians call the Imaginary and which mainstream aesthetic theory calls, after Ehrenzweig, 'gestalt-free perception'.

Strangely liberating for some, rather frightening for others, depending on temperament and expectations, it explains why some spectators sit through *Popeye* in a sort of euphoria, while others react like Mavis Nicholson interviewing Robert Altman on BBC Radio 4:

It was a strange film to get into, if I might say so, because I found the first five minutes alarming. I mean it's like going into Hell, quite honestly. The set is so strange and the people are grotesque. And then you sort of acclimatise yourself, I find I did … and what it has on me is a very strange effect, I still semi-dream about it.

Its first shot of the grainy-gleamy sea is perfectly realistic, but, like the real sea in certain moods, it's luminous and magic. But not just pretty: it edges towards the carefully unreal, creak-and-plastic sea in the *Fellini-Casanova*. It consolidates what's really a new movie idiom, one which evokes the widely shared delight among painters in strange realism: Photo Realism, Magic Realism, Super Humanism, and the Brotherhood of Ruralists' neo-pre-Raphaelite delight in the details of the physical world. Conversely, rock album covers love to interfere with photographs, by graphic enhancement and fantastication, and Helmut Newton carefully stages photographs to be as 'unnatural' as paintings. While fine art painting is coming in out of the cold of half a century's increasing abstraction, movies seem to be resuming *Caligari*-era struggles against the limitations of photographic realism. Labs permitting, we can expect them increasingly to explore subtly 'estranging' development and printing technique, and every other means to 'painterly' interpretation.

The sensation of equivocation continues with a real bay, strangely shaped as any art director's creation. Within it nestles Sweethaven, whose spires and gables, the shocks and planks, suggest Disney Gothick but stop well short of it. It's still too accentuated to be likely; it splits the difference between a cartoon, with its carefree connotations, and the nightmare-tinged vista of *Our Town*.

Essentially a theatrical set, it takes full advantage of film detail (from the camera's changing viewpoints) and film space (which surrounds the characters, and us, like a living-space, instead of being remotely tucked away behind a proscenium). The characters are just as amphibious. Robin Williams achieves a cartoony character by an attention to detail worthy of Kazan or Cassavetes. Far from reducing live actors to cartoon outlines (the great temptation), Altman engineers hybrids, where flesh and blood people *occasionally* do the impossible things cel-people do *constantly*, but keeps its too, too solid kinaesthetics. There's an odd lashback when Bluto chews a coffee-cup. It feels like a cartoon absurdity although it's a music-hall-type trick. On the whole, though, what began as a cartoon edges towards a Dickensian solidity (albeit fixity).

The film is two-and-a-half-lens dimensional. Idiosyncrasy a-go-go makes it an all-dancing bas-relief. The musical ensembles are strange conjunctions of disparate activity, with everyone doing his own thing at right angles and with back turned to everyone else. There's little of the unison parade, performance, or personality-projection which musical numbers usually enshrine. More often there's a sort of acrobatic introversion, and Popeye wanders through the crush like an Alvin Ailey dancer. He's worse than rejected, ignored. It all verges on Eccentric Theatre, and the Bolshevik aesthetic of the 1920s.

II. From Delirious Realism to True Grittiness

POPEYE is a long-shot film. It's an ensemble canvas, and like certain paintings it's crowded with the fantasticated details children love. There's a double fantastication: the crowding and timing would be hyper-realist even if the details weren't. Wherever the eye grazes something ensnares it. It's a high-definition world as well as a half-unreal one. It's caricature, but stays solid.

Tenniel and the Victorian illustrators of children's books knew how richness of detail could give fantasy a reality effect. Early comic-strip artists exploited that strategy when they crowded their panels, which burst out of the frame (asserting their 'reality' by challenging the form). Relatively speaking, movie cartoons have offered very impoverished detail as imaginative pasture. TV's partial and apparent animation represents a nadir of media exploitation of children's tolerance. Their cyclical narratives (even *Tom and Jerry*) swiftly become thin through reflex stereotypy.

Popeye follows the other strategy; live-action textures revive the hand-made image. The heroine in Altman's *Images* wrote for children such *cherished* stories (actually written by the film's star, Susannah York). A rising generation of book illustrators, notably Nicola Bayley, have paralleled the fine-art convergence of painting and photography. The medium (or rather the process) matters less than weaving a world which detail makes 'realer than real', solid and delirious. Somewhere along the line, lessons may have been learned from (on one hand) psychedelic art (bright detail, however fantastic, is hallucinatory, i.e. realistic) and (on the other) Tolkien endowing fairyland with epic form and moral *gravitas* by the sober *respectfulness* in his style. It's like a homespun answer to sci-fi plastic. But ginormous space fleets are as amazingly elaborate as Archigram architecture.[*] Their every nut, bolt and turret has blueprint precision. To borrow Charles and Ray Eames's distinction in their very beautiful *Toccata For Toy Trains*, George Lucas fuses the accuracy of the *model* with the fantasy of the *toy*. Each image has a curious way of being in long-shot and close-up at the same time (it pulls your attention between ultra-steep perspectives, extravagant outlines and details). Vastness and minutiae stun disbelief. Photographic realism has nothing to do with it, being merely a process of transmission for a series of magic-realist constructions. *Popeye* relishes texture, almost as if it's out to rival the new pop-up books of Jan Pienkowski.

In a curious way, a new fantastication is recreating that Victorian solidity of the imagination which seemed almost extinct. In Disney's cartoons it peaked with *Bambi*, but it's carefully nurtured through his live-action fantasies like *The Absent-Minded Professor* and *Mary Poppins* (which accordingly was championed by some Parisian Surrealists). In that respect the Disney acceptance of Altman's angle on *Popeye* runs true to their best form.

There's only a fine line between two approaches to fantasy. Literalist realism is content to neutralise disbelief in fantastic events, by special effects which make flying horses move as naturally as horses, or dragon hides look as realistic as elephant hides. But *Popeye*'s ultra-realism combines literalist elements with enhancements and deviations. It goes for hallucinatory vividness rather than photo-type realism – or on top of it. The two kinds correspond to the model and the toy, and, as the Eameses hint, the model corresponds to a spiritual climate where correctness normally clips the wings of the imagination. It neutralises scepticism but can't create. Its reign meant that when fiction turned to fantasy it often had to hide behind the magic prefix 'science-'. 'You'll believe a man can fly' is merely illusionist. But, if *Superman* stays at the merely realist end of the stylistic spectrum, *Star Wars* sits in the middle, and *Popeye* opposes to it, not a *realistic fantasy*, but a *fantastic realism*. Like many such 'oppositions', each extreme is impure. The comic-strip simplicity of *Superman* is too poised, posed, stripped, not to be a little unnatural, and this gives it just a smidgeon of an unreal vividness. All fantasy involves realistic elements, and all realism involves ideas and connections which are visually as unrealisable as hypotheses and fantasies (the former being a special type of the latter). Hence our spectrum is

[*] A happy misprint: 'architexture'.

The Essential Raymond Durgnat

indicative not definitive, and though it can't be used to categorise, it suggests how apparent 'oppositions' arise from different combinations and proportions of common elements.

Film styles have encouraged the change. Vastly improved techniques have permitted such clarity of detail that, with *Pirosmani* in Russia, *Barry Lyndon* in England, *The Tree of Wooden Clogs* in Italy, and *The Long Goodbye* in the USA, directors everywhere have relished their new ability to number the streaks of the tulip, to cherish the hues of a bowl of fruit on a sunlit table, while keeping their distance, structuring a tableau, enwrapping the story in the scene. Whether or not there's a painterly quote (like the Friedrich rainbow in *The Duellists*), the visual 'syntax' can be closer to painting-with-movement than to 'classic Hollywood syntax'. (Not that montage is forbidden: but the new elbow-room for pro-cinematic mise-en-scène would allow a one-setting, one-set-up, one-take, feature movie all the visual variety it needed.) The new painterliness spans the spectrum, from a newly sensitive realism to the 'sculptural' constructions of the *Fellini-Satyricon* and the *Fellini-Casanova*. Which aren't so far from the Altman–Jules Feiffer *Popeye*.

The enwrapment of story by scene is aided and abetted by a new narrative terseness, allusiveness, discontinuity. It must owe much (as Hawks suggested) to audience-saturation with plots, so that a detail or fragment can now say what used to need an expository scene. And it may owe something to a certain lessening of hero-centred lyricism by a new sense of uneasy relationships – with social spaces, and processes, and others-as-aliens. At any rate, 'the story' is now more readily seen as a strand in a social canvas, and there's some evidence (though that's another article) of a new American sense of social cross-sections and interweaving loneliness.

Time was when directors usually had to shape everything around the dramatic flow. Now they can be more discursive, untidy, tangential, and work to the *scene* as well as the *thrust*. Once the director had to pace, space and structure almost as rigorously as a dramatist. Now he can work in much more of a novelist's sprawl. And old 'plot logic' has allowed steadily more room for *patterns* of details, which echo one another across a slower, looser drift of events.

There's a kind of plot 'pointillisme'. In *Nashville*, for example, Altman need only dwell on a man with a violin case for us to have prewritten a whole scenario: he's got a machine-gun or a sniper's rifle in it, and who's he gunning for? Then second thoughts provoke a rewrite: there'll be a twist on the twist, and something very different or even nothing in it. Eventually we get a twist on both twists: there's a *small* gun in it. A classically ironic structure, but far briefer than old storylines would have to be. Other things can use the space.

The *Popeye* narrative is braided through such surprises. When Olive Oyl too petulantly pushes open a door, will her inertia propel her through the window directly ahead? No, in a kind of delayed ricochet, she'll collapse onto the bed, but after intervening chat and for a different reason altogether. The pioneer of such shaggy-dog distensions and reflexive, anti-yock, chuckles is Jerry Lewis, whose *The Ladies' Man* (1961) looks ever more detail-environmental, magic-realist, and proto-Altmanesque, as its 21st anniversary looms.

III. Against Photography

POPEYE straddles a notorious rift. Most film theories emphasise, if only by puzzling over, the continuum film–photography–reality–realism–illusionism–persuasiveness. This tends to weigh against artificiality, against the non-realistic film. And although film culture (like film-goers) is much more eclectic, theories tend to be purist. Whether documentary-based, neo-realistic, photo-ontological like Bazin, reality-redemptive like Kracauer, or semiological like Metz and Barthes, they revolve around reality-effects and make artifice look suspect.

Since Metz and Barthes start from verbal language, with its arbitrary codes, their logic should have pushed them on to rehabilitate the artificial in film. But just because their paradigm proved helpless to analyse images, and the ideas which arise from images, and also because they ignored obviously relevant sciences like cognitive and perceptual psychology, the cinesemiological project surrendered, however reluctantly, to vague notions of 'photo-realism'.

Since about 1930, a variety of factors favouring realism of one kind or another (the social struggles of 1933–45, the excitements of documentary, neo-realism, and cinéma vérité) have rather overwhelmed the contrasting theoretical tradition. This assumes that film is powerful for resembling the audio-visual displays of dreams (Surrealism) or stream of consciousness. Film is 'realistic' because its display is like the mind's display. However, the stress on mental vividness also suggests a sort of hallucination (like dream) or illusionism, which both risk reintroducing realism. And 'realism' is always a weasel word. It encourages all sorts of confusion between external reality, physical reality, the visible aspects of reality, those aspects of visible reality which are local enough to permit photography, and the photographable aspects of those local realities; not to mention any type of display which reminds our perceptual system of how it scans external reality; and the fact that some elements of visible reality are more important to us than others.

Film culture as a whole continued to be highly sceptical of 'photo-reality' theory, whose implications would have banished or marginalised too much, from *Caligari* to Disney, from the star system to auteurism, from background music to the calligraphic camera, from Méliès to Busby Berkeley, from the decorative tradition of the Nazimova *Salome* to *Popeye*.

While this weight of evidence was so decisive that resort to theory was felt to be unnecessary, the irritation with 'photo-reality' theory bred an excessive irritation with theory in general. Perhaps theory should start from the fact that film is discourse; i.e., a reality which constantly sends us back to *another* reality, in relation to which it's a non-reality. Moreover, photography is a process, not a form, and the types of form which the process produces miss most of reality. The prestige of photography is established by (a) its convenience and by (b) talk about it! While this isn't the place to outline the arguments, they would involve *separating* film, photography, realism, reality, illusionism and persuasiveness so as to see how tenuous their links really are. While photography is of particular convenience to film, it no more defines it than oil paints define painting. Photo-reality theory regularly forgets the superior accuracy and clarity of painted drawings, which are routinely preferred not only by technically minded admirers of aircraft, automobiles and machinery, but, for rigorously realistic reasons, by botanists, zoologists, and doctors. Painting had achieved trompe-l'oeil long before photography, and computer simulations achieve admirable compromises between a reality-effect and a diagrammatic clarity, achieving a sort of 'magic realism'!

Hence films are not interesting for the degree of realism of the image (for many completely realistic images are completely boring, while others are so unclear, or so untypical of their subject, that they feel completely unreal). More important is the quality and relevance of the ideas which the images *suggest* (and they routinely suggest more than they 'contain'). For some ideas a visual reality is necessary or convenient. For others only a *sufficient* degree of realism, or *some* realistic aspects, are needed. And then reality is conveniently acted, staged, or faked. From this angle the 'essence' of film is not photography, but the studio, i.e., the construction of a situation which presents reality visually or in performance. This *can* be done by going to reality itself; a location is a special type of studio. But reality is usually cooked ('Say cheese'), or selected, so as to create the sort of clarifi-

The Essential Raymond Durgnat

catory display which is what a studio exists to provide. A *real* object on a rostrum or photographed through a microscope (as in scientific nature documentaries) is *reality*, but in a virtual studio. Similarly, photographs are normally rejected unless they have some quality as a *diagram* ('it's a good picture of her').

The *diagram* shades into the *performance*, and the visual aspects of film shade into the performance aspects (hence film is so close to theatre that movies had trouble escaping from it). 'Photo-reality' theories flourished on this (exaggerated) reaction against theatre, and against photography's early temptations to poor imitations of painting. But film is a performance art first, and photography and reality are optional. Often artifice is necessary for the clear *display* which images and performance share and which discourse requires. Thus film is essentially a discourse in audio-visual *display*. The discourse suggests ideas which are outside ('behind') the display. The method of perception is entirely different from the *reading* of the verbal *text*, and its 'syntax' (scanning-structure) is dominated by the right half of the brain, not the left half. The failure of linguistics-based semiology was inevitable on those grounds alone, although perceptual psychology inexorably implied it from about 1950.

Once the idea of display subordinates 'photo-reality' (important though that is), films which, like *Caligari* and *Popeye*, graft the unrealistic onto the realistic, cease to seem artistic 'monsters'. They're a completely natural procedure, so natural that children accept them quite as easily as they accept documentaries.

The documentary movement first associated realism with social realism, to a degree from which film theory has had difficulty escaping. It was Bazin who rather separated them again, because, though he was very excited by De Sica's and Zavattini's neo-realism, his 'photo-ontology' starts from the Holy Shroud of Turin (which, incidentally is an entirely non-photographic image, since light is not involved). Bazin opened a wedge between realism and social realism, but increased the stress on photographic *process* as confused with photographic *image*.

Bazin hardly touches on positive artifice, but tends to depreciate it. His restrictions on montage can seem to condemn most *weakenings* of reality, as interference or subtraction, rather than construction and clarification. Similarly, he subordinates mise-en-scène to a photographic feature (deep focus) and rather peculiarly groups it with reality rather than artifice (thus bracketing Wyler with Rossellini!). But it's simpler to see montage as a normal function of discourse, along with other ways of selecting and arranging (a) mise-en-scène, and (b) camera set-ups, 'snipping' a picture 'out of' the world.

Bazin isn't puritanical. He likes low-profile artifices which don't jar with reality, he is intrigued by striptease and the omnipresence of Jane Russell's *unseen* bosom throughout *The Outlaw* (with its stress on the invisible it becomes a kind of Bresson film). But Kracauer is more puritanical. Or, at least, he's more influenced by an (historical) opposition: of Hollywood studio and glamour and daydreams versus locations, neo-realism, and materialism. He doesn't rule out artifice altogether, but he likes it to be realistic in detail and reality-istic in spirit. Thus tap-dancing may be unrealistic in terms of a particular diegesis, but at least it depends on a realistic representation of a real body's physical movements. Wouldn't both Bazin and Kracauer have been fascinated by *Popeye*?

Kracauer's argument reads more pompous than it really is. Behind it there's a Walter Benjamin-like wish to assert mechanical reproduction against old fine-art snobberies. There's a distaste like Alison Gernsheim's for arty-farty photography. There's a fascinating cross between the rationalist-moralist Marxism of the Frankfurt School and the spirit of

California Split

the New Objectivity (a movement which painterly realism should make fashionable again any moment now). But because his argument is more rigorous and remorseless than Bazin's meditations, its weaknesses can hide its qualities. He underestimates the extent to which the human mind can see and remember what the camera can only record. Yet actors, costume designers, set dressers and art directors can not only construct a realistic artifice, but construct an artifice which is different from, but as rich as, reality, and which uses those differences to clarify what visual reality cloaks or omits. Deviations from – even outrages of – realism are a natural and convenient way (often more convenient than montage) of rendering the invisible visible. The reality we see *out there* consists largely of *ideas in here*.* We quickly see what we expect, and, conversely, what we see programmes our expectations. Perception and cognition are inextricably intertwined, and the *interfusion* of the visible by the invisible means that all visual discourse is first and foremost 'visible thought'. To this realism, like representationalism, is merely contributory. Since vision allows for all sorts of distortions anyway (like the 'constancy of vision' which ensures that we see a table as rectangular even from all kinds of odd angles), visual distortions are often perfectly natural to use. They belong 'in' reality just like the ideas we have about reality, and that's why visual artistic distortions can seem 'realer than real'.

All signs – whether pictorial or verbal – depend on *associations* which are quite distinct from the form of the signifier, and quite distinct from the denotation of the signifier. They belong with description, with 'knowledge of the world', and with Mitry's 'logic of implication' as the semantic cement of film images. Semiology has had great difficulty in understanding that, since film is not a language, its meanings can't be divided into denotation and connotation, and that, just as linguistics is a province of semiology, so semiology is a province of semantics, which is a province of psychology, which, like everything else, is condemned to be inter-disciplinary, and can't be autonomously rigorous.

Kracauer over-reacted against a tendency for artificial films to be satisfied with a visually rather empty texture – either because they aimed at dream-factory glamour, or a merely rhetorical universe, or a grand lyricism; or because *building* a richly-textured world quickly becomes more expensive than markets will bear. As it is, fantasy usually co-opts realistic techniques (location settings, carefully matter-of-fact reactions, etc.), just as *Popeye* co-opts its strange sea and cove.

But it belongs to that small but delicious genre of films which achieve a reality-like density of caricature. One thinks of the Panama-Frank *Li'l Abner*, of *Red Garters* (where the houses of a Western town are built in outline alone, a single idea which nonetheless generates a continuous fascination), of the Victor Fleming *The Wizard of Oz*, of the Dr. Seuss *The 5,000 Fingers of Dr. T*, of the Busby Berkeley production numbers in *Small Town Girl*, and many moments in other films, from *The Wiz* to Renoir's *Little Match Girl*. But of all these films *Popeye* comes closest to matching neo-realism in the density of its fantastications, which somehow retain an ontological realism. They generate a sense of liberation which intensifies the film's vitality, so that it's Hellish for some, euphoric-delirious for others, or silly or difficult for others again. Thus, in another BBC discussion, critics complained

---

* In Wittgenstein's terms: 'seeing-as'. But perceptual and cognitive psychology abound in examples of a process only philosophers find difficult. The theoretical mind is slower still. But the logic of these examples is that connotation, far from being fickle and elusive, leads us to shared *and established* associations and elements in descriptions which involve knowledge of the world and the logic of implication, that is, a semantic theory. It's elaborated in my article 'The Quick Brown Fox Jumps Over the Clumsy Tank (On Semantic Complexity)', *Poetics Today*, Vol. 3. No. 2, Spring 1982.

The Essential Raymond Durgnat

that it was *neither* a proper cartoon *nor* properly real. Indeed, Popeye's huge arms made one critic so uneasy that he became haunted by the notion that poor Robin Williams had been ruthlessly pumped up with steroids. This led to a brisk argument about whether one *could* discern the join between the actor's real arms and the sculpture parts, with suggestions that it was the film's *duty* to show us that the muscles were artificial, and not a horrifying deformation.

The more normative response is probably to enjoy (a) the graft of artifice and realism, and (b) Altman's spotting that the linearity of the comic strip, far from excluding, actually left room for, a lovingly elaborated fairground-baroque populism. Fleetingly, *Popeye* evokes Murnau, another expert in dreamlike locations, artificial super-realism, and *uncanny* symbioses of the two. Sweethaven oddly blends realistic spaces with a sort of Toytown space, just as, in Murnau's *Sunrise*, the train ride from deep forest to city centre is all the more lyrical for cutting-and-compressing visible-real space. The shanties and slipways of Sweethaven have a kind of 'accordion' topology.*

While film theory regularly opposes fantasy and realism, or at least treats them as distinct modes or genres, film practice is far more nuanced. The moment such a cleavage appears, it becomes rewarding to bridge it! *Caligari* is a fascinating case. It was written for a normal realistic treatment, and it would work very well if given it. As it is, it depends on the spectator's *inability* to distinguish the real world from the madman's mental images. Throughout the film, we have to assume that the distortions are an anti-realistic convention. Only *in extremis* do we get a 'justification' from a realistic viewpoint. But we never needed that justification to believe the film. On the contrary: our assumption that this is an unreal idiom is vital, to camouflage the big twist, that all this has been a hero-narrator's crazy opticity. The film can only work because we spontaneously accept the wildly unreal as an equivalent of the real.**

It's a fascinating case of an extra-diegetic feature suddenly becoming an intra-diegetic one. It also illustrates the dangers of separating the two and thinking that the term 'diegesis' is any clearer than 'the action'. Odder still, the 'realistic' framework is nearly as unrealistic as the 'mad' sequences, so that their 'realism' is entirely notional, and *Caligari* is expressionistic even when it pretends not to be. There certainly is a difference in style between the two parts, but it's a matter of mood (stability), not realism.

Much German expressionism has a strong social-critical interest which relates it to neorealism. *The Last Laugh* is a perfect Zavattini-type story (the doorman is de-classed without his uniform, just as *The Bicycle Thief* needs his bike). Kracauer sees how close to Zavattini's thinking Carl Mayer's was. We badly need a counter-history of film 'styles' and 'genres', one which will stress their hybridisations, their dialectic, instead of their differences and antinomies. Every style, every story, is an agglomeration of features, just as our normal thinking weaves together elements from every 'level'. Similarly, Altman's way with *Popeye* is very like his way with *McCabe and Mrs. Miller*. There, he takes the Western, and neo-realises it, in a Viscontian (or rather, Bologninian) way. In *Popeye*, too, he particularly cherishes ambience, atmosphere and information. He doesn't overdo things with picturesquerie unbridled; there's his usual underplaying, restraint, even *surliness*. The film becomes a very consistent, very steady, but quite mind-boggling fusion of cartoon, myth, neo-realism and reality-effect by fantasticated detail. Since caricature notoriously shades into expres-

* Which stills can't catch. It depends on how cutting and camera have kept us moving, how background moves in relation to foreground, etc.
** It's true that *Caligari* is often impossible as well as plausible, whereas *Popeye* is more often implausible than impossible. But the two categories are fascinatingly interfused. Sometimes the impossible is plausible!

sionism, and Sweethaven has its 'Nasty Bend' side, we conclude with the astonishing equation, Altman = 1/3 x Segar + 1/3 x Zavattini + 1/3 x Murnau. Which may seem incredibly double-jointed and triple-brained, but it's less impossible than it sounds, for there's nothing monstrous about hybrids. They're as everyday as mongrels. It's the pedigree animals that are so unnatural that they have to be strenuously segregated.

IV. The Negative Space Shuttle

WE HAVE proposed that the core of film is 'audio-visual-display thinking', not 'photo-reality', and that 'density of specification' (Henry James's term) hits what 'illusionism' misses. And this leads straight to the thrust of Manny Farber's 1979 MOMA lecture.

Briefly, Farber proposed looking at movies for the richness of their concrete details of the world, for the kind of physical-experiential weave through which painters work. This has its psychological (and therefore social) extension, including the sort of temps-mort which enriches Renoir's work *Toni*, but which permeates cinema irrespective of 'art' or auteurs.

From this perspective, the intensity of Leonard Kastle's *The Honeymoon Killers* would come, not from its psychology (it hasn't any), and not from its dramatic structure (it's too cool to need much suspense and we feel only a rather distant, caustic, pity for the victims), but from the fact that it's a fresco of bare, standardised motel rooms, of lives without families or friends, of the oddity together of the lovers' physiques, of a fat woman's whim to pick at chocolates.

Farber compares the vapid voids of this film of affluence with the warm faith suffusing Frank Borzage's Depression-era *Man's Castle*. The cooking stove with its gas cylinder, a moveable shrine of domesticity, is as sacred an object as the wife's nonchalantly held prayerbook, or a gesture which reveals that, for her, Heaven is *up there*; it's physical too. Whether casually or not, the film stresses a now almost forgotten feature of the times: the transparent curtain which divided the black jazzband from the white singer.

Farber suggests that a Hal Roach two-reeler, *Spanky*, paints a far more vivid picture of '30s neighbourhood life, its obsessions, anxieties and mores, the physicality of coins and bills, than the most 'serious' (pious) art films of the 1930s, and that *this* will fascinate, not only social historians, but lay spectators, for catching the texture and spirit of a long-gone time for living, for living another set of human possibilities, in a way which criticises and makes strange one's own.

Given these preoccupations, the distinction between art and non-art would dissolve, the auteur and his philosophy become a deus ex machina, or background extra, and the film's world would cease to be metaphoric of a private vision, but recover its rich autonomy. Figures of style would remain just as significant, for conveying, not merely an auteur's 'sensibility', but, far more important, the style, the texture, the experiences which many people shared and constitute a way of life in its relation to the material world. As Farber's choice of *Spanky* suggests, such details can be reconstructed, without neo-realism, can accommodate distortions of various kinds.

Thus Farber sharpens Kracauer's underlying thrust, and much of Bazin's drift, but frees them from their crippling photo-ontologisms. It accords with Renoir's respect for artifice, and his scrupulosity in describing realism as 'a *detour* through the real'. It frees social realism from liberal pieties, and for Marxists it recharges the social realism which Lukács rightly opposes to Brecht's preachifying. It links certain documentary interests with temps-mort theory and it constitutes a perfect apologia for Altman's fascination with textures – material, social, psychological.

The Essential Raymond Durgnat

V. Popeye Versus Raging Bull

THE POPEYE comic-strip looks like a cinch for camp and nostalgia. Or Sweethaven could have been a populist Heaven, a grassroots heartland. Camp apart, a strain of fantasticated nostalgia always runs through popular art, from Al Capp's Dogpatch to W. C. Fields's Klopstokia (in *Million Dollar Legs*: on such a team, Popeye would have the million dollar biceps), from Snow White's male-bonded seven dwarfs working and washing in their cottage to Pepperland.

Isn't Popeye a sort of Sergeant Pepper, a seafarer who returns from some Nowhere-Man's-Land, some sea of holes, only to find, that 'Liverpool' has become the sequence of 'all the lonely people', that Sweethaven has been renamed Nasty Bend and lives in terror of a Commodore whom they never see (another kind of Nowhere Man!!) and whose side-kicks are Bluto and a WASP-type taxman?

In a sense, Altman's film is Al Capp sharpened up by Preston Sturges, with a Hal Roach aesthetic to cover the middle ground. Broadway wit apart, Sturges had strong demotic interests, and a fine ear for vernacular idioms, rather like the line everybody remembers from *Popeye*: 'Wrong is wrong, even if it helps.' It's a socko line but you could study it forever. It's anti-camp because only its form seems simple-minded. And though Popeye doesn't see the joke, it's not on him. It's on all the smoother ways of saying the same thing. It's something to do with the way a big abstraction is so swiftly followed by that entirely personal 'helps'. It's a toe-stubber, but not a debunker. And it gives wrong its due, because it doesn't pretend that help isn't help, as more philosophical phraseology like 'expediency' would do. Weirdest of all, 'help' suggests that the world is a place where aura help [*sic*] isn't all that unusual. It's poignant, instead of sentimental, because Popeye doesn't overlook pain and rejection, he *decides* to: 'Thirty years of grudge is enough.' Reading the *Popeye* cartoons, it never occurred to me that he'd lost an eye, I thought it was just quizzically shut. But Robin Williams's physique suggests a prequel: 'How Popeye Lost His Eye'. He asserts a tardy, precarious, reconciliation. He's never as foolish as he is.

Sweethaven evokes the curmudgeonly or melancholy solitudes which haunt *Our Town*. It hasn't the terrifyingly existential cemetery, and if its texture thins out and the cartoon formula takes over once we get to the cove, perhaps it's because it isn't a nitty-gritty-land. The soul-fight over the spinach is bracketed by the fist-fight, rather than vice versa. The skeleton–spinach–octopus combination hasn't the eeriness of its plant, which, very symmetrically, is bones, carrots and fish. 'After six weeks of carroks, me eye sike got so good I cud see through walls! See da fishes on the bottom of da oceang. After ten weeks of carroks, I cud see thru flesh – look a man thru his bar bones! Ya can go too far wit a good t'ing. Even eye sike.'*

The idea of opening up hidden things has a happier twist, though. As the Commodore opens his treasure-chest, it turns out to contain valueless souvenirs – pious relics – of Popeye's infancy. Will his gaze turn to fury? – No, it doesn't, and Pappy has weirdly combined Popeye-hatred with object-fetishism. Luckily it includes a can of spinach, the one thing patient Popeye still can't stomach. It'd be only too easy to get very Freudian, especially with Olive Oyl simultaneously trapped inside the bell of a red ventilator (and giant octopus tentacles sneaking up her kicking legs). But the box with its trumpet is more like the childhood toys of Borowczyk's *Renaissance* than the *Chien Andalou* box, with its adult trinket. It's about realising, through fetishes and nostalgia, the preciousness of transient states (like childlikeness) despite (and even including) their mean side and their nuisance value.

* Dialogue from the Richard J. Anobile movie-novel. (Avon Books, 1981, $9.95). There seem to be variant versions of the film in circulation, with conspicuous cuts between the British press show and release.

When Popeye wants to show his father 'wot a fine figger of a orphink I growed up into', he adds 'widdout one whit o' his help whatsomuchever'. And the last part isn't a knocking clause — it's a tribute to his father's fibre, some of which he gave to Popeye himself.

Often comedy depends on the same distance as nostalgia, and if the two modes go well together (so that comedy is as much forgiveness as criticism), it's because comedy's tolerance is its counterpoint of tragedy's pain.

VI. The Spinach of Wrath

AGAINST the *California Split*, the Sweethaven ensemble. In *Three Women*, adult orphans, in *Popeye* 'Even a orphink needs a father and a mother'. The women drift together and share out parent–child roles; in *Popeye*, 'I came here looking for my father and now I'm a mother'. In *A Wedding* an ensemble of people nervously put their role-repertoire on display. But Popeye's 'I yam what I yam and that's *all* that I yam' is more — depressive? defiant? modest? — than 'that's *what* I yam', which is the usual version, or recollection, of the lyric.

The Commodore, as Popeye's wicked father and spitting-image, isn't only a '50s-style Oedipal-father-cum-alter-ego, but is '70s-style sociological with it, like the patriarchs dominating Peyton Place and Dallas. At least he came by his hating 'fair and square', in a phrase which, like a reminiscent line in *The Empire Strikes Back*, rings of Senator Hayakawa's celebrated 'We stole it fair and square', about the Panama Canal. Similarly, the octopus shares a sicklier shade of green with spinach, which saves Popeye *in extremis*, not through macrobiotic magic but through something closer to the tonic persecution celebrated in that Country & Western song 'A Boy Named Sue'. Ideologically it's a short step from rearing kids tough to speaking loudly and carrying a big stick, and Popeye's Innocence Regained is partly about America not hating itself despite a heritage of violence, both externally and domestically directed. It celebrates an archaic anarcho-conservative populism, which treats Blutos and Taxmen just the same, but 'Don't think I blame ya, cause I doesn't' (to Bluto) and 'Nothing personal' (to the Taxman). Popeye could easily be quietly mad, one way like Harry Langdon, another way like many Altman characters, or for that matter, Scorsese ones.

Sweethaven has been compared to a frontier town, and Popeye to the lone cowboy who cleans it up. But Altman isn't very given to the frontier thesis, and Sweethaven rings much more general, a sort of collocation of small town and urban waterfront. Its wrecks, slipways and shanties suggest the strange wooden staircases that dominate, not only Sternberg's *The Docks of New York*, but Harry Langdon's *Three's A Crowd*. Popeye is, not a nomad and a born loser exactly, but, like Steinbeck's 'hairy ape' and Sternberg's stoker, or the brawling crew of *The Voyage Home*, he belongs to melting-pot, manual-labour, America, and with all its beggars of life and bums, its ad hoc families, its flotsam-and-jetsam children (*The Salvation Hunters*, *The Kid*, *The Champ*). Conversely, Olive Oyl would dearly love to be a Magnificent Amberson, and a touch of Agnes Moorehead shrillness is in her already. But she permits Popeye to carry her luggage everywhichway, and she's spunky enough to marry beneath her and to know that Bluto isn't above her, but just huge.

In *The Great Comic Strip Heroes* Feiffer celebrates the Superman generation of caped crusaders. But Popeye is *also* a subhero, from an earthier and humbler generation. Superman, like a plastic amalgam of God and cop, descends on malefactors (who tend to speak fractured English) from a great height, like a guided missile zapping most forms of disrespect to city skyscrapers. Whereas Popeye has survived from the rude, crude, dock-and-bowery America, which disappeared as Mickey Mouse scampered upmarket from hot dog seller or tugboat skipper (like Spanky's people) to suburban householder. No doubt the cartoon

Popeye owes his commercial survival to his least interesting traits (Mickey Mouse sweetness plus the punch Donald Duck desires). But Nasty Bend is a social structure in which Popeye makes both ancient-and-modern kinds of sense. It scrambles everything up rather like Al Capp's Dogpatch. But where Al Capp is politically conscious, this is America with that capital K, which stands for Kafka, Krazy Kat and the Kommodore. Indeed, it was the old, chaotico-bureaucratic, Ellis Island, America which inspired Kafka's America (and Sternberg's China).

Now that sex has the Seal of Good Housekeeping, it's junk food which flies the flag for funk, self-abuse, and animality. The 'Everything is Food' number upfronts the gastronomic flavour of the names. Olive Oyl, Wimpy, Sweet Pea, Ham Gravy, Oxblood Oxheart is an intriguing recipe, and should certainly appear on the menu of every Movie-Meals restaurant. It's food for Lévi-Straussian thought, and all the more nourishing for having all those non-food names by way of roughage. The names fall into categories? And what hidden meaning lurks behind 'Bluto'? Maybe there's an American explanation; maybe it's brute + Pluto (not so obscure, being the name of a planet and Poe's *The Black Cat*). Or maybe it's meant to sound like some patent food or brass polish or washing blue starch – the sort of non-food substance that children think about eating and drinking and that sits within smelling distance of foods in corner stores. At any rate, it all mixes a sort of salad à la melting pot, in physical-pungent terms suiting Altman's taste for physical textures . 'You are what you eat' is far too spiritual, too fastidious, for this cram-it-all-in America. Life's a goulash soup, which so mixes the bitters with the sweet that we all keep having to throw up.

VII. Biceps Over The City

LI'L ABNER, another powerhouse innocent, is more complacent than Popeye. Dogpatch isn't a School of Hard Knocks, but almost an AFL-CIO suburb, done as the lazy Deep South, just as the Flintstones do Suburbia as the Stone Age. Al Capp's New Deal mind gears Dogpatch to socio-political pixilations whose Exhibit A is The Schmoo, a parable about the means of production. Popeye's spiritual ecology is more archaic, closer to Krazy Kat than the Marxist Brothers, although 'Popeye Joins The Union' might make a fun two-reeler (after all those '70s union pictures, from Scorsese, Ritt, Widerberg, Schrader, Ashby …).

The anti-system streak in *Popeye* is something else. The system is corrupt, and Olive Oyl is exempt from every kind of tax (no doubt even Tax-Exemption Tax, Catch 1040). But this personalised favouritism extends the film's real waveband, the quality of private life, which is Feiffer's and Altman's common stamping ground. There's a skew-whiff overlap with Woody Allen (*Sleeper* being another fantasticated society). *Three Women* has a Woody side to it, and Feiffer's *Carnal Knowledge* and *Little Murders* hit their targets in a mean-mother way whereas Woody aims off to either side (farcical or solemnly Bergmaniacal). Altman's discursive style conjures up shifting spaces between dialogue, like the mental slits between comic-strip panels.

If these silences occasionally evoke Antonioni, his ethereal schizo-drift is replaced by something much more down to earth. Antonioni is cerebral and ascetic whereas Altman, however Antonionian his characters (*Three Women* is near *The Red Desert*), keeps the score in a beady-eyed, bar-room way. Antonioni is born under an air-sign, Altman under an earth-sign. An Antonioni–Altman–Allen spectrum isn't strange at all. Not only are they all As (for Alienation), but modern cinema is dominated by an unnoticed genre, the film of low-plot psychosocial observation; critical, compassionate, ironic.

As the three women make, or fake, a family together, their life together smacks of carefully restricted role-playing more than commune conviviality. Warmth seems to have been lost with, or behind, the parental generation, somewhere in the Sweethaven from which *this* Shelley Duvall never quite escapes – and just as well, for she finds *both* her healthy dose of alienation (with Popeye), *and* her parental responsibility, within it. When she and Popeye bicker over the baby's sex under a parasol beside a boat, the scenery sketches a sort of open-air home, like life with the Joads, or a De Sica couple. The lumber-mill repeats it later. For Altman (as for Renoir) a home is defined by two bodies, or two minds, being seriously together for a while for some reason. It's their jostle and tangle which is Man's Castle. Buildings quickly become webs, and don't keep empty space out, so that Altman's films abound in unusual knottings or clearings of space, as indoors stretch like outdoors and exteriors coil round people like interiors.

Popeye ends oddly; Bluto (who keeps seeing red – *la vie en rouge*) turns yellow. It's as if neither the repulse of Bluto, nor the family romance, can be taken home and spread around. Sweethaven really has become Nasty Bend, which may be just 'a nasty bend' that America, or we all, have to turn. Or maybe each name is as true as the other, just as *Our Town* is infiltrated with our aliens (the dead). A town by any other name …

VIII. Dada Knows Best

THOUGH critics often look for *demonstrations*, art, like thought, works by suggestions. Hence films rarely complete a structure, but mix parts of many structures, and can't be analysed in terms of any one. Altman's films cut across all the familiar genres and the Big Themes just by keeping close to the personal. They keep juggling sets of little details, little means, little expectations, which entertainers have always understood, but onto which Antonioni, with *The Red Desert*, and Buñuel, with *The Phantom of Liberty*, really begin loading the main weights once entrusted only to plot points. Altman, too, is interested in these 'little things' and the enigmas that can result. But his interest is more descriptive. He contemplates the mix of motives, disguise, and 'suspended' emotions that make up life but do nothing in the story. Old Hollywood would write a scene to establish that a character has several wide parameters and several possibilities. Altman just watches him walking towards somewhere. And it's not a Western-type walk; it lets us look at all kinds of detail about him; it's like a Henry James descriptive paragraph. Henry James without words is a very interesting kind of *display*.

When Altman cross-cuts between (a) Popeye looking at his Pappy's picture, and (b) Bluto, furious at his curfew-defying window, advancing towards it, the sense of parallel action à la D. W. Griffith fragments two ways. As Bluto *first* clambers down the poop-deck, *then* strains at a rowboat, *then* lumbers up the shore, the night-pictures counterpoint the suspense. And not only Popeye's mood, but the 'Me Poppa' gag, *also* break the build-up, so that we forget-and-remember what a plot-type comedy would have built up into a con-tinuing advance. The syntagma disrupts itself. The gag becomes merely the cherry, or rather the olive, on a moodpiece which juggles two melancholy nocturnes (Bluto's cheated effort). We're somewhere between Edward Hopper's lonely nightscapes and René Clair's roof-and-windowscapes (which were also poignant for containing caricatures who strangely feel like characters – which is puppet-theatre magic). Nonetheless the mood-piece refuses a European sort of lyricism, because American muscle ripples through it.

By retexturing a familiar sort of slow slapstick gag, Altman gives it a sort of extension-and-discontinuity. It's a kind of gestalt I've never seen before, but it goes with the pointil-liste economy of the New Narrative. With many more details to intrigue us, it's less clear which will become narrative and which won't. And even though emphasis or repetition sooner or later sorts us out, the initial uncertainty 'equalises' plot and non-plot in a carefully confusing way. Old Narrative could exploit such ambiguity too, as when the 'plant' made the plot-point arise in a 'natural' or 'logical' way. Indeed, the detective story depended on burying the clues amongst the circumstantial details, i.e., the descriptions buried half the plot. But though details could always move from one 'level' to another (because a plot isn't a level at all; it's a dotted line), there *seemed* to be clarity (in detective stories you knew the rules). The New Narrative fragments the plot, and thickens the details, and your interest is spread across the surface in a stranger, fuller, way.

In *Three Women*, a bright little corner of a dress, trapped in a car door, flutters like a distress signal, yet says nothing clear (like the flags on the ship in *The Red Desert*). So *Popeye* is full of *incomprehensions*, from Popeye's sotto voce mumble to the very poignant gag where he talks to and kisses (i.e., treats as a present person) the photograph which turns out to be only the words 'Me Poppa' in graffiti. It's a semiotics joke. 'The picture is not the person' is followed by 'Denotation is not depiction'. The first has an exact analogy in Semantic theory ('the map is not the territory') and the second has an exact predecessor in the celebrated telegram sent by Rauschenberg ('This is a portrait of Iris Clert if I say so'). The overall joke has other components too: photography-jokes are intersected by time-jokes. 'Hello, Poppa. Soon you and me, we'll be togedder: thirty years ain't dat long! Besides next Wednesday's our anniversary.' The present tense ('Hello') collides with lifetime-type time (thirty years ago), which collides with eternity-type time (thirty years is 'but a moment in my sight'), which collides with local-type time (next Wednesday), which collides with children's-birthday-type time (anniversaries are special even if they're no different). Thus mechanical time is thoroughly discombobulated by Bergson-type duration. It's a capsule version of Resnais's favourite theme, of being true to yourself despite time-splits. It's about *l'amour fou* for your father and keeping the faith, baby, which comes through − details − like the beatific smile spreading over Popeye's face, despite the tight mouth, the forehead vein, the lost eye, the fractured English, and all the other damage that gets done to losers.

Is this gag Altman or Feiffer, or what mixture, who can tell? Whether or not it makes a genius-size gag, its incongruities depend on very fine semantic tuning. It's quite hard to analyse out, but intuition operates effectively at subliminal levels, it probably registers every wrinkle and certainly monitors some nuances strongly enough to feel like laughing. Ten-year-olds will get it, and not only that; at the London magazine screening, 20% of the critics were suddenly awash with tears.

Similarly, it's mildly interesting that Popeye has slung a hammock over the bed which Olive praised to the skies and promptly flattened. It's so consistent with being a sailor man that it's just a little-smile environmental detail, a non-yock gag. But humour isn't an ingredient that exists *in* a gag, like the alcohol flavoured with something else. It's generated by the not-too-serious collision of the serious ideas.

At one extreme, Popeye tells his father's picture, 'Stay alive, that's all I ask', and that's a gag because it's so pessimistic that it makes no demands, it's got No Expectation (Rolling Stones title). At the other extreme, Olive fusses over (or under) her fanciful hats: 'It's ugly! I think it's a conspiracy! Why would they manufacture deliberate ugliness unless they wanted me to look ugly! If we find that out, we find out everything!'

Nice contrast of philosophies: Popeye's bedrock existentialism, no paranoia. Olive: natural vanity, paranoia. The film is a peculiar alternation of the intricate and the lapidary, each sharpened by juxtaposition with the other. Olive's speech splendidly sums up the conspiracy theories (Who Shot J.F.K.? − Kafka's Father Did), which weirdly yet naturally mix egocentricity with a sense of systems gone haywire. But there are also good reasons for it. Olive's petulance isn't merely an anti-mass-production snobbery joke, and a conspiracy theory joke, it's also a self-reflexivity joke, for we know who the Great They is – it's her director, who wanted her to look so odd, and whose in-film physical type is Bluto. Asked about his fondness for featuring Shelley Duvall, Altman replied, 'I just like the way she walks across a room' (or words to that effect). And it's a perfect reply, and the key to his whole aesthetic. You just watch, but with an intentness that yields to you that person feeling herself in that room and seeing that room around her self.

The same displacement rules Popeye launching his baby-bottle. A bottle *for* a baby becomes a bottle *to* a baby; launching a ship *with* a bottle becomes launching a bottle like a ship; a particularly important bottle *needs* launching like a ship; somehow the baby will read the message, and so on. Neither metaphor nor metonymy, it's a true recombination of ideas and a thoroughly structuralist gag, got at by lateral thinking.

Few of the gags are tight like that, some are fussy and completely pointless, like 'Oxblood Oxheart' (galumphingly repetitious name), calling a boxing venue 'Max and Sons Square Garden'. They're jokes of no-jokes, little Shaggy Dog mini-stories, and dislocate the verbal texture just as the phoney wigs and whiskers dislocate the visual texture. Hal Roach is the past master of such subliminal infra-gags, their locus classicus being the *County Hospital* 'Hard boiled eggs and nuts!'

P.S. – All these jokes are on me. First, I'm confusing jokes with little grotesqueries which cheer you up but aren't quite jokes. Second, there is a point in 'Max and Sons' – it *debunks* 'Madison', or, at least, it substitutes someone much less grand. And you can get a fix on the eggs-and-nuts joke by imagining expecting to bite on one and finding it's the other and by remembering the missed-out courses. How poorly the serious mind gets the picture, compared to the laughing mind!

IX. A Homage to Hal Roach

NOT only the Laurel and Hardy comedies, but the Charley Chase and Edgar Kennedy two-reelers, all cherish the sub-gag grotesquerie, the mindless oddity: Stan and Ollie just standing there together. Ollie knocking his hatbrim back or rolling up his tie, Edgar Kennedy's slow-burn subsiding into a temps-mort, the Three Stooges' lumpen-cretinism. It's a vaudeville art (or craft) which becomes weirdly highbrow in W. C. Fields. The Joe McDoakes comedies are their final fling, with the gags quickened, to not lag too far behind *Tom and Jerry* speed, which is much more abstract, more impatient. The cartoons are about impulse, the two-reelers are about the aggravations of the everyday.

When the Taxman apologies to Olive Oyl for not recognising her from behind, it's a physique joke in the Laurel and Hardy tradition, like all the straddle-kneed postures which Altman concocts for, or with, his leading lady. *Popeye* owes very little to cartoons and much more to two-reelers, which he's either remembered or reinvented or both, and, in either case, improved (but not uplifted). He thoroughly revamped them, roughly as he revamped TV situation comedy in *M*A*S*H*. He elaborated the texture, levelled the jokes down towards it, and recharged everything by the bittersweet infra-drama which predominates over the comedy in *A Wedding* and *Nashville*.

But other pixilations of genre then follow. *A Wedding* is 'sophisticated comedy' in having that social setting and subtlety and being very funny, although it's often also dramatic and too true to be funny. But its operation is very simple. It's like being able to walk all round a function, to get into the attic and behind the scenes, and enjoy the privilege of a long and thoughtful look. Hence it keeps evoking direct cinema (say, Wiseman's *Model*), while retaining the

The Essential Raymond Durgnat

richness of fictional structure. Michael Ritchie's *Smile* makes the continuity quite clear. Apparently disparate genres can be opened out onto one another by straightforwardness.

One might look on *A Wedding* as a New Narrative descendant of sophisticated comedy à la George Cukor, and lower-class screwball comedy like Hal Roach or W. C. Fields. But much '30s comedy sits uneasily within the usual classifications, like 'sophisticated', 'slapstick', 'screwball'. Sturges and Capra are often – what? – populist, political? *Christmas In July* and *The Miracle of Morgan's Creek* weirdly mix Hal Roach with Paddy Chayefsky, and enjoy it. Similarly, *Popeye*, Altman's 'naivest' subject, has a very sophisticated writer, whose comic strips are highly 'sophisticated comedies', and whose *Carnal Knowledge* becomes savage (and finally obscene), like plastic-age Stroheim.

All this may seem very complicated if one assumes that genres are *moulds*, allowing only minor variations to films which nonetheless exist 'within' them, or that thinking is condemned to follow coded paradigms which it takes arduous 'deconstructions' to analyse and escape. But even non-auteurist entertainers often think like *authors*, that is, they follow their particular story wherever its logic leads, enjoying its changes and switches of mental set, cutting across genres as if they didn't exist, or being intrigued by equivocations and allusions. And even when they do work to formulae, they often think of formulae as *ingredients* rather than *moulds*. They're not churning out jellies but cooking a stew which can mix all kinds of shapes and flavours (expectations). *Here's* a soupçon of cartoon, *here's* a chunk of satire, *now* a solid mouthful of drama …

Altman isn't the only director to show how old genres have dissolved, and that tough new hybrids have appeared, that can crystallise and dissolve again quite freely, so that, more than ever, not only a logic of recombinations, but a no-genre fluidity, is the order of the day. Altman subverts, not only genres, but expectations generally, without losing the coherence necessary if a new authenticity is to break old grooves, ruts and moulds altogether.

SOURCE: *FILMS ON SCREEN AND VIDEO*, APRIL–MAY 1982, 18–23 (APRIL); 20–3 (MAY)

ANNOTATIONS

MONTAGE RIDES AGAIN!
[p. 153] In semantic theory, **graphemes** are the smallest units of written language; **semes** are the smallest units of meaning. | [p. 154] Roger **Manvell** was a highly influential figure in British film culture in the 1940s and 50s, a prolific writer, editor, broadcaster and lecturer. In an interview given at about the time of this essay, Durgnat credited Manvell's popular 1944 book *Film*, against which he had rebelled as a young man, with 'guts, drive, presence and decency' (*Rouge*, no. 8, 2006, n.p.). | It was Peter Wollen who criticised Barthes for seeing cinema as **pseudophysis not techne**, that is, essentially, for reducing cinema to a recording instrument and undervaluing its potential for rhetoric and symbolism, in *Signs and Meaning* (p. 147).

PACIFIC FILM ARCHIVE PROGRAMME NOTES
[p. 156] '**Losey**', Durgnat wrote later (*Cineaste*, Spring 1981, p. 43), 'does to *everything* what *Citizen Kane* does to "freedom of the press."' | [p. 157] **parisitize** [*sic*] | [p. 158] **RENAISSANCE is almost a companion-piece to LA JETEE** in part because their directors Borowczyk and

Marker collaborated on *Les Astronautes* (1959); Borowczyk's wife Ligia appeared in *La Jetée*. | Anger's leather boys are **playthings of the Gods** as in Eisenstein's *October*, a comparison made at greater length in *Sexual Alienation in the Cinema*. Anger's first movie experience was a double-bill of *The Singing Fool* (1928) and *Thunder Over Mexico* (1933), the unauthorised version of Eisenstein's *Que Viva Mexico!* In 1950 Henri Langlois gave him footage from the same project to re-edit according to Eisenstein's script, the result of which was shown at the Cinémathèque Française and attacked by Jean-Luc Godard in the *Gazette du Cinéma*.

FROM SIGNS TO MEANINGS

[p. 161] **Blaine Allan** was a former colleague of Durgnat's at Queen's University. | [p. 162] The **two books written four and six years before** Wollen's were Jakobson's *Essais de Linguistique Générale* and Hjelmslev's *Prolegomena to a Theory of Language*, the latter actually from 1943. | It is likely that Durgnat gives the seminal date of **the New Criticism** as **1924** because that was the year I. A. Richards published his *Principles of Literary Criticism*. | [p. 163] As well as being Richards's collaborator (and many other things besides), C. K. **Ogden** was the author of *Opposition: A Linguistic and Psychological Analysis* (1932), which Durgnat treated as a critique of binarism. | [p. 164] Piaget's ***Main Trends In Psychology*** (1970), Durgnat explained later ('Theory of Theory – and Buñuel the Joker', *Film Quarterly*, vol. 44, no. 1, Autumn 1990), left the reader in no doubt that 'thinking, from perception on up, is pluri-structuralist, in co-ordinating structures (visual, verbal, acoustic, etc.) radically and systemically different from each other, sufficiently loosely and flexibly to accommodate constant "re-view" of constantly changing input' (p. 44). | Meanwhile Piaget's ***Main Trends in Inter-Disciplinary Research*** (1970), in Durgnat's gloss (rev. Metz, *Psychoanalysis and Cinema*, in *Film Quarterly*, vol. 36, no. 2, Winter 1982–3), took on 'Jakobson's assumptions of the dominance of thought by language' (p. 60). | [p. 167] Durgnat in fact contributed a chapter to Wollen's **startlingly acquiescent book** on Fuller, published in 1969. | [p. 168] Durgnat elsewhere ('Through the Looking Sign', *Quarterly Review of Film Studies*, vol. 8, no. 4, Autumn 1983) supplemented the reading list headed by **Arnheim's *Art and Visual Perception*** with, among other titles, Gombrich's *Art and Illusion* (1960), Arnheim's critique of the same in *Towards a Psychology of Art* (1966) and Ehrenzweig's *The Hidden Order of Art* (1967). | [p. 169] **Metz's declaredly unsatisfactory tentative**, as cited by Wollen, was an 'interpretation of a famous shot from Eisenstein's *Que Viva Mexico!*. | [p. 170] It was Eisenstein himself, according to Wollen, who saw the continuation by **Joyce** of 'the line commenced by **Balzac**'. | **Gozlan's pulverization of Bazin's arguments**, echoed in Durgnat's Slade thesis (*Films and Feelings*, pp. 29–30), was originally published in *Positif* nos 46–7, June–July 1962. | [p. 171] Durgnat borrowed the **"Colorless green ideas sleep furiously"** argument from Noam Chomsky's 1957 book *Syntactic Structures*. | [p. 172] Brian **Henderson** was the author of *A Critique of Film Theory* (1980). | Andrew **Britton**'s 'The Ideology of *Screen*' appeared in *Movie*, no. 26, Winter 1978–9.

POPEYE POPS UP

[p. 173] It is no accident if *Popeye* **edges towards the carefully unreal, creak-and-plastic sea in the *Fellini-Casanova***; the two films were shot by Giuseppe Rotunno, responsible for a number of other Fellinis as well as *Carnal Knowledge* (1971), also written by Jules Feiffer. | [p. 181] **Al Capp's Dogpatch** was the setting of *Li'l Abner*. | [p. 182] The **'hairy ape'** is probably the stoker protagonist of Eugene O'Neill's 1922 play *The Hairy Ape*, a favourite of Steinbeck's. | [p. 183] The **'70s union pictures** include *Boxcar Bertha* (**Scorsese,** 1972); *Norma Rae* (**Ritt**, 1979); *Joe Hill* (**Widerberg**, 1971); *Blue Collar* (**Schrader**, 1978); *Bound for Glory* (**Ashby**, 1976).

The Essential Raymond Durgnat

Notes

1. BFI Special Collections: Thorold Dickinson, Box 47, Folder 2: Letter from Raymond Durgnat to Thorold Dickinson, 31 January 1977.
2. Jonathan Rosenbaum, *Placing Movies: The Practice of Film Criticism* (Berkeley: University of California Press, 1995), p. 61.
3. Ibid., p. 68.
4. Letter from Durgnat to Dickinson, op. cit.
5. Durgnat, 'Britannia Waives the Rules', *Film Comment*, July–August 1976, p. 59.
6. Email to editor, 7 January 2013.
7. Colin MacCabe, *The Eloquence of the Vulgar: Language, Cinema and the Politics of Culture* (London: British Film Institute, 1999), p. 154.
8. Stephen Heath, '"Jaws", Ideology and Film Theory', *Times Higher Education Supplement*, 26 March 1976, p. 11.
9. Durgnat, 'Fading Freedoms/Latent Fascisms & Hippie High Hopes: A Paranoid Guide' (2), *Oz*, no. 12, c. May 1968, n.p.
10. E. P. Thompson, *The Poverty of Theory* (London: Merlin Press, 1978), p. 35.
11. Thompson, 'The Peculiarities of the English', *The Socialist Register, 1965*, p. 312.
12. Lee Russell [Peter Wollen], 'Culture and Cinema', *New Left Review*, October 1963, p. 114.
13. Perry Anderson, 'Origins of the Present Crisis', *New Left Review*, January–February 1964, p. 36.
14. Perry Anderson, 'Components of the National Culture', *New Left Review*, July–August 1968, pp. 3–57.
15. Peter Wollen, 'Cinema and Semiology: Some Points of Contact', *Form*, no. 7, March 1968, p. 9.
16. Durgnat, 'Film Goes to the Movies', *Film*, Winter 1964–5, p. 25. Durgnat reviewed it at greater length in *Views*, no. 8, Summer 1965 ('The Impotence of Being Earnest', pp. 76–80); and in the June 1965 *Books and Bookmen* ('Pop Culture', pp. 72–3).
17. Durgnat, rev. Simon Clarke *et al.*, *One-Dimensional Marxism*, in *Film Quarterly*, vol. 34, no. 4, Summer 1981, p. 43.
18. Ben Brewster, 'Glossary', in Louis Althusser, *For Marx* (London: Allen Lane, 1969), p. 249.
19. Peter Wollen, *Signs and Meaning in the Cinema* (London: Secker and Warburg in association with the British Film Institute, 1969), pp. 57–69.
20. Stephen Heath, 'Introduction: Questions of Emphasis', *Screen*, vol. 14, nos 1–2, Summer 1973, p. 9.
21. Paul Willemen, 'Editorial', in ibid., p. 2.
22. Gerald Peary and Stuart Kaminsky, '"Structuralism Implies a Certain Kind of Methodology …": An Interview with Peter Wollen', *Film Heritage*, vol. 9, no. 4, Summer 1974, p. 24.
23. Durgnat, rev. Charles Barr, *Ealing Studios*, in *Film Comment*, July–August 1978, p. 74.
24. Ibid.
25. Al Auster and Leonard Quart, 'Confessions of a Middle Class Film Critic: An Interview with Andrew Sarris', *Cineaste*, Spring 1979, p. 14.
26. Durgnat, untitled entry in *The Cinema in the Eighties* (Venice: Edizioni 'La Biennale di Venezia', 1980), p. 28. Durgnat, following Thompson, had called Althusser 'the most Stalinist of the French bourgeois mandarins' (ibid.). It was apparently this passage that upset Willemen. Perry Anderson reassured readers of his response to Thompson's book, *Arguments Within English Marxism* (London: Verso Editions, 1980), that Althusser was no Stalinist but a Maoist, which Anderson considered 'perfectly defensible' (p. 110).

27. Durgnat, 'Film Theory: From Narrative to Description', *Quarterly Review of Film Studies*, vol. 7, no. 2, Spring 1982, p. 127.

28. *The Cinema in the Eighties*, p. 28.

29. Durgnat, rev. Peter Wollen, *Signs and Meaning in the Cinema*, in *University Publishing*, no. 6, Winter 1979, p. 15.

30. Durgnat, 'Film Theory: From Narrative to Description', p. 111; p. 115.

31. Durgnat, rev. Christian Metz, *Essais sur la Signification au Cinéma*, in *British Journal of Aesthetics*, vol. 9, no. 2, April 1969, p. 212.

32. Ibid., p. 213. 'If it's a fascinating book to grapple with,' Durgnat concluded, 'it's not only for the intellectual exercise; the margins of this reviewer's copy are covered with comments which would need a very much longer review.'

33. Wollen, *Signs and Meaning*, pp. 122–3.

34. Ibid., p. 137.

35. Ibid., p. 155.

36. Wollen, *Signs and Meaning in the Cinema* (3rd edn, London: Secker and Warburg in association with the British Film Institute, 1972), p. 173. The first and second editions took their cover image from *Herostratus*; the third used a still from *Vent d'Est*.

37. Durgnat, 'Culture Always is a Fog', *Rouge*, no. 8, 2006, n.p.

38. *The Cinema in the Eighties*, p. 28.

39. Rosenbaum, *Placing Movies*, p. 68.

40. Durgnat, 'Hollywood Turns to the Citizens Band', *Films on Screen and Video*, December 1981, p. 8.

41. Ibid., pp. 8–9.

42. Durgnat, *The Crazy Mirror: Hollywood Comedy and the American Image* (London: Faber and Faber, 1969), pp. 246–8.

43. Durgnat, *Durgnat on Film* (London: Faber and Faber, 1976), p. 13.

44. Durgnat, 'Genre: Populism and Social Realism', *Film Comment*, July–August 1975, p. 23; p. 28.

45. Durgnat, 'Britannia Waives the Rules', p. 51.

46. Durgnat, 'Hollywood Turns to the Citizens Band', p. 10; p. 8.

47. Ibid., p. 8.

48. Durgnat, 'From Signs to Meanings in the Cinema', *Film Reader*, no. 5, 1982, p. 312.

49. Durgnat, 'Genre: Populism and Social Realism', p. 24.

50. Durgnat, 'From Signs to Meanings', p. 312.

51. Durgnat, 'Genre: Populism and Social Realism', p. 24.

52. Durgnat, 'Hollywood Turns to the Citizens Band', p. 11.

53. Durgnat, *Films and Feelings*, p. 180.

54. Ibid., p. 268.

55. Durgnat, 'Hollywood Turns to the Citizens Band', p. 11.

56. Durgnat, 'Foreword: The Man With No Genre', in Norman Kagan, *American Skeptic: Robert Altman's Genre-Commentary Films* (Ann Arbor: Pierian Press, 1982), p. xiii.

PART 6
LOOKING BACK

INTRODUCTION

I

In the autumn of 1980 Durgnat came back to Britain, and back to the Royal College of Art. He was hired by Christopher Frayling, head of the RCA's new Department of Cultural History, partly to teach film-makers, by then becoming established in British art schools, and 'partly to teach a general history of film which will be open to the entire College'.[1] His first year coincided with the 'MacCabe Affair', in which the broadsheet public was gripped by the story of the Cambridge English Faculty's refusal to promote Colin MacCabe, an assistant lecturer in addition to his *Screen* activities, because of his advanced post-structuralist views. In the melee that ensued, Durgnat found himself allied with his old adversary Lindsay Anderson, who had launched a parallel attack on BFI-sponsored film theory in the *Guardian* when the affair was at its height.

Again adopting the role of 'public enemy number one', Durgnat reformulated his Venice critique, recently published in the American magazine *Cineaste* as 'The Death of Cinesemiology', in a series of articles in the non-film press.[2] The film-cultural establishment circled the wagons. In *Framework*, a little magazine which had given Durgnat space before its effective takeover by the BFI, Peter Wollen wrote that the MacCabe affair had been 'foreshadowed by Durgnat's malign call for a struggle against semiotic infiltration of the universities and cultural institutions',[3] while Paul Willemen observed in the same journal that 'Durgnat has been dusted off and paraded like a Blimpish Colonel in Thatcher's PIP Squad', PIP standing for 'Plain-clothes Ideological Police'.[4]

It was therefore brave of Richard Combs, editor of the *Monthly Film Bulletin*, to invite Durgnat back into the institutional fold. The *MFB* had recently been expanded to include feature articles, and, as Combs recalls,

> when I asked him to write, it was because to me he was a luminary of the biz (*Films and Feelings* had inspired me to start writing), and I naively assumed he was generally so regarded, whatever the political fault lines in film writing that had developed over the past decade or so.
>
> I soon discovered otherwise.
>
> The negative vibes came from different directions and for different reasons, though I won't exaggerate and say I was ever leaned on not to use him.[5]

By a combination of enmities old and new, Durgnat managed to rouse the BFI to an unaccustomed unity of purpose. Combs, however, stood his ground, and became, in the years before the *MFB*'s absorption into *Sight and Sound* in 1991, Durgnat's best editor; later they became collaborators on a series of projects published and not. Durgnat had not benefitted from the absence of proofreaders at *Films and Filming* in the 1960s, nor from the bloated wordcounts available to him in the 1970s. Combs's *MFB* imposed a newfound concision, as well as basic subeditorial control.

Durgnat made his second *MFB* debut with a tribute to Stephen Dwoskin, a colleague at the RCA at the time. While Dwoskin had, many years earlier, fallen out of favour under the post-Durgnat regime at the London Film-Makers' Co-operative ('because I kept subject-matter'), he had come to be championed by 'B.F.I.-type radical academics', as Durgnat put it, who saw in Dwoskin's use of looks-to-camera a guilt-inducing critique of voyeurism, scopophilia and the male gaze.[6] Durgnat's 'Skeleton Key' is in part an attempt at recovery. As Dwoskin told him in an interview, 'They're very possessive about me now, though, Ray. They don't want heretics like you writing about me.'[7] 'Cooped in a Co-op?', published later, contains Durgnat's reflections on the path taken by the LFMC since the late 1960s, and on the institutionalisation of the avant-garde.

At *Films on Screen and Video*, then at its short-lived successor *Movie Scene*, and finally at the *MFB*, Durgnat became a regular reviewer for the first time since the 1960s; but much of his work in the 1980s, particularly for Combs, was retrospective, revisiting what he called in a 1990 review of *8½* 'art-house cinema at its peak, i.e. its evolution between 1958 and 1963, (a) from social phenomenological realism to explorations of mental process and subjectivity, and (b) from predominantly dramatic narratives to a modernist poetic'.[8] As with the Dwoskin piece, Durgnat's third bout with Godard draws on a personal connection, this time with Jean-Pierre Gorin. His essay on the 'Left Bank' film-makers, on the other hand, is a somewhat belated engagement with a group he had hitherto treated only sparsely, despite their collective place in his personal pantheon.

II

Elsewhere, too, Durgnat risked assimilation. In his introduction to the collection *All Our Yesterdays*, a landmark in British cinema studies published in 1986, Charles Barr called *A Mirror for England* 'a book too idiosyncratic to be smoothly absorbed into the critical and scholarly tradition, but one which has had a pioneer's influence'.[9] Proximate evidence included Julian Petley and Andrew Higson's chapters in the same book, which together, more than twenty years after 'Standing Up for Jesus' and 'Vote for Britain!' projected a super-Durgnatian image of British film culture in which the 'documentary-realist tradition', still hegemonic decades after the movement's demise, was seen to have banished from the earth a 'Lost Continent' of fantasy counter-cinema whose greatest exponents were Powell and Pressburger.

The Archers' absorption into the Anglo-Franco-American canon in the late 1970s and early 80s had begun in earnest with a retrospective at Tom Luddy's Telluride Film Festival in 1977, at which Powell was presented with an award by Martin Scorsese. Durgnat was at once vindicated and left feeling slightly uneasy. 'The urge to over-"auteurise" P & P', Durgnat warned in Ian Christie's book *Powell Pressburger and Others*, published to accompany the NFT's P & P retrospective in late 1978, 'could lead one to celebrate the film's virtuoso *strangeness* at the expense of its middle of the road, down to earth qualities, and the massive shot of *realism* in its "poetic realism".'[10] His longest work on the

Archers, which made the sources of his ambivalence plainer still, appeared not in any British publication, but for a French magazine he had long admired: *Positif*.

At the end of 'Standing Up for Jesus' Durgnat had emphasised its left-wing credentials; but *Positif*, first published in 1952, was also the bearer of the Surrealist line in French film culture. It was this aspect of the magazine that led it to champion British horror films, especially *Peeping Tom*. In 1962 *Positif*'s publisher Eric Losfeld launched from his Left Bank bookshop base a sister magazine, *Midi-Minuit Fantastique* (*M-MF*), which was entirely given over to this tendency, and named after the disreputable cinema where *Peeping Tom* had had its first Parisian screening.[11] Durgnat noticed its first issues in the *Motion* 'Companion', treating the first, devoted to Hammer director Terence Fisher, slightly sniffily, but crediting to the second, titled 'Vamps Fantastiques', 'a properly ecstatic and uncritical tone towards all morbid fantasies'.[12]

M-MF's co-editor Michel Caen noticed in turn the 'Companion' from the land 'which is to necrophiliacs and sadists what Carpathia and Transylvania are to werewolves and vampires' with greater generosity, praising Durgnat and Johnson's 'mise en page soignée' and their cover, 'on which Barbara Steele, very obviously bearing the devil's stigmata, seems to whisper "come and kiss me, you will die, but we will know together eternal life"'.[13] With the next issue, published in September 1963, Durgnat became the magazine's London correspondent, a position he held until 1967. His contribution to *Positif*, which coincided with Powell and Pressburger's first retrospective at the Cinémathèque Française in early 1981, thus marked – along with those to Britain, the RCA and the BFI – another return.

Towards the end of that year Durgnat revealed in an 'about the author' note that 'A forthcoming book is on Michael Powell.'[14] None ever materialised, but 'The Prewar Bs' and 'Remembering Michael Powell', published a decade later, suggest what might have been.

6.1 *ABOUT JOHN FORD*

"This book," declares Lindsay Anderson, "is the record of an enthusiasm, an obsession, that has lasted for over thirty years." When Plexus asked him for his study of Ford's work, abandoned by the BFI twenty years before, he extended it to embrace the previously unobtainable movies and Ford's subsequent career.

His new appraisal traces the tensions between (and within) Ford's genius and his subjects, his professionalism and his poetry, his temperament and his collaborations. He movingly describes his various comic–cruel–sad encounters with Ford, over twenty-three years, and elicits incisive testimony from collaborators who range from Henry Fonda and Harry Carey Jr. to Frank Nugent and Willis Goldbeck. The book's 385 photographs, including many beautiful frame-stills, furnish persuasive evidence for Anderson's pivotal concern: to rescue Ford as *poet* from Ford as *auteur*.

It's an intriguing opposition, especially from the critic who, in *Sequence* around 1950 (well before auteur theory was a gleam in *Cahiers*' eye), championed Ford's "service" films, and traced his vision as an evolving whole. Anderson's (and Gavin Lambert's) concern for films as "poetic vision" broke the cultural stranglehold of a certain "liberal" priggishness. But now he offers another "recall to order," this time towards readings which movie makers, poets, and moviegoers can share, and away from the merely theoretical Ford constructed (or rather extrapolated) by auteurists and structuralists from Sarris to Wollen.

His book is terse (in a wartime British way), rich, and haunting. Straightforwardly assertive, it generates a montage effect between different angles, epochs, and testimonies. Its *Citizen Kane* (or Admiral Ford) effect is possible because Anderson, too, has reconciled an uncomfortable vision, a practical professionalism, and a craftsman's awareness that poetry comes, not from some preprogrammed psychothematic structure, but from suffering and adventure, complicity and contingency. He watches Ford's films with a very sharp eye for the subtleties that distinguish an authentic resonance from showbiz routine. As rare and strange as Anderson's films have been, his position at the Royal Court Theatre, and his collaborations with David Storey, have made him a heavy presence in the London theatre.

Working with actors is preeminently a matter of style and its finesses, before, or without, the thematic cataloguing, and other academic semi-abstractions, against which Anderson rehabilitates the value of an artist-craftsman reaching, with his best integrity, a common reader. He implies also the centrality of distinctions (not absolute, but practical) between art as testimony about real experience, the cruder affirmations of myth and ideology, and the formulae of mere entertainment. Crucial, therefore, is the "microcontent" which distinguishes Ford's best movies from those which share the same broad issues or themes, but are flawed, routine, uninspired, or arthritic.

Anderson's evaluations can't be "proved" rigorously or objectively, but for excellent reasons. First, modern semantics, though far in advance of semiotics, is still inadequate to high-definition texts. Hence the arts are ravaged by reductive interpretation into those big, obvious themes whose hollowness Anderson sardonically exposes; or by assumptions that narrative "logic" is an auteur's philosophy in storybook form. I regret that Anderson passes in silence over Ford's Vietnam stance, which I predicted from the films, and which contrasts with Anderson's own involvement with Joris Ivens. But there's no logical contradiction between our emphases, not just because our purposes differ, but because not even a perfect semantic theory can penetrate the normal ambiguity of texts, especially poetic ones. Hence Ford speaks equally to Bolsheviks like Eisenstein and Donskoi, and to conservatives like Kurosawa and Wayne. After all, opposite ideologies may solidly resemble one another, in many crucial blocks and contradictions of experience.

The coarsening of specific, and therefore complex, situations into "big" themes is compounded when academic formalism degrades style-analysis, by fetishizing on certain obvious features of film form (whether they're "dynamic montage" as in the Twenties and Thirties, camera-movements as in the Fifties and Sixties, or alienation effects and camera-as-look as in the Seventies and Eighties). This can only disrupt the interaction between *all* the elements in play (formal, mental, ongoing context, spectator-contributed). Anderson's theatre-honed sense of an "acting picture" in *My Darling Clementine*, with its choreography of pauses, may well be "impressionist," in the sense of being more summary than descriptive and more commendatory than analytical. But his finger points to where the treasure lies, and trying to go further, in words, risks schizo-detail and false precision (since visual meaning is verbally indefinable). In contrast, Wollen's "shifting antinomies" have no way of gearing into a visual or formal-structural finesse. They're a vast improvement on some earlier auteurisms, but don't even match the "Eng. Lit." attempts to link quality with complexity and irony of fifty years ago. Actors' and pictorial styles are so problematic that I wish Anderson had thought aloud about Ford's craftsmanship, especially his *reliance* on actors to give what *they* knew how to give, versus *his* contribution via lighting, placing, pacing. And I wish he had talked with Ford's lighting cameramen. Fonda's tale of the first take in *Mister Roberts* hints that maybe Ford was very much a pictorialist, like Maurice Tourneur.

The Man Who Shot Liberty Valance (1962)

Where so many auteurisms risk extrapolating a nonexistent, merely tautologous, Ford out of accidental, trivial, or very vague thematic similarities, Anderson, a practical man, understands how the means of production of "texts" include the man who drinks or fumbles and the times which change. Hence making movies is entirely unlike plotting recombinations on some thematic-formalist computer. Making art is making meaning, which only exists historically. It's what a text and a reader do together – with the artist thinking ahead. Those interminable debates about the exact, correct, profound meanings of art should warn us how minor, exotic, and normally irrelevant such meanings, if they exist, must be. What more often communicates is the *surface* of a movie (its story as a local-physical predicament, its moods and details as a wavelength of experience). For many spectators, their sense of authenticity is decisive; and Anderson's from-the-text deduction of Ford's decline is corroborated by fellow-craftsmen from Wayne to James Warner Bellah.

Anderson echoes Leavis when he attributes the New Scholasticism to "sociology and aesthetics" (whereas I'd diagnose too little of either). Sometimes his curtness evokes his appearance in *O Lucky Man!*, where he swipes Malcolm McDowell smartly over the head with his copy of his script, saying, "Smile!" Only here he says: "Prefer!" If he's as curtly confident about what true poetry is as my old Latin teacher (another demon book-swiper) was about what correct syntax is, it's normal that testimony and dogmatism should use the same language. Discussion exists, not only to eliminate or "settle" such differences, but to explore and cherish them: to see movies through eyes which will never be our own.

Anderson opened all our eyes to something in the military films, even if only *They Were Expendable* calms my qualms for long. My preference for Ford as "poetic realist" embraces *The Long Voyage Home* and *The Informer*, and I feel with Dudley Nichols's Ford rather Frank Nugent's. I can't bear *The Quiet Man*, but weep all through *The Last Hurrah*, God help me. The lighting of *Liberty Valance*, and the physical movements of the Wayne–Stewart combo, fill me with physical unease (like the way the women sit in *Seven Women*). In *Young Mr. Lincoln* I admire the plot-logic's fine distinctions, but the actual issues are pure crackerbarrel; only Ford's touch and Fonda's face wrap them in religious truth. Often, when Anderson and I share a love – of *Clementine*, of *The Sun Shines Bright* –

we shade them differently; to me they're death's door films, as bleak as funerary art. (Anderson's link of Ford with Wordsworth is very helpful: Lake District peaks vs. desert mesas). Like Anderson I relegate the auteurists' masterwork, *The Searchers*, to a lower level, on which Sam Fuller's *Run of the Arrow* goes well beyond it. (Curious that Ford, no mean hater himself, botched his one film about a hero who violently hates.)

Unlike Anderson, I see the Dodge City satire in *Cheyenne Autumn* as a state-of-the-nation lament, adumbrating *Britannia Hospital* as an anguished *Carry On*. But mine is rather a "second-degree" response, like my being moved by the rest of the film because its very creaking makes its liberalism more poignant, hardbitten, and obstinate. If such responses have certain limited purposes, their consistent *programmatique* would entail the triumph of mediocrity, and the post-modernist impasse of the Sixties, when a soupcan was as sensitive as Rembrandt, and turkey farms became pantheons.

Actually Anderson's eye is as generous and understanding as it's discriminating, and he discerns the maturing or fading poetry in the non-canonical films. His rehabilitation of Ford's "conservative" virtues, like duty and sacrifice, which the structuralist ideology would undermine, in its alienated fashion, makes his book a complex challenge. Appropriately, since Ford's bedrock humanism is spiked with contradictions: liberal–conservative, populist–loyalist, Catholic–WASP, anarchist–militarist, peasant–puritan, demagogue–pietist.

Every normal classification (genre, nationality, ideology) would rule out any affinity between the two men: the Irish-American and the Scot from British India, the Victorian-of-the-Twenties and the New Left Oxonian of the Fifties. If it weren't for Anderson's testimony, we'd hardly dream of making the connection.

Perhaps the missing link between the two men is Kipling. True, Ford schmaltzified *Wee Willie Winkie*, (just as Huston's *The Man Who Would Be King* is weirdly weak-kneed). It's Ford's service films, however, with their garrison families and Indians, their groping for rule as trusteeship, their officers and rankers, which transpose the British Empire's Northwest Frontier to America's Southwest one. Anderson takes Kipling's title, *If....*, for a subject which is almost "Post-Christian Soldiers In The Service of Their Revolution," while *Britannia Hospital* dissects a Britain from which the morality of *If....* has gone.

Another affinity hints at the underground channels that render bourgeois "decadence" so flexible, so resistant. Catholicism (Ford) had its Calvinist moments: the ideal Calvinist was "a monk in the world," like the very name, Judge Priest, like the widower Lincoln and the celibate Earp. Puritanism adapted to imperialism is a Kipling theme; puritanism *and* imperialism is a Ford theme; puritanism *after* imperialism is an Anderson theme.

Most importantly, perhaps, the two men relate via Poetic Realism (*floruit* 1935–1949). Ford's style forms slowly (as Anderson shows) through the decade preceding it, Anderson's through the decade following. Ford approaches it from *outside* social realism – via the silent Westerns and via a populist expressionism borrowed from German art films and Twenties theatre. In *The Grapes of Wrath*, a marvelous realism-expressionism hybrid, he converts Steinbeck's *naturalist* novel into an American masterpiece.

In a sense, poetic realism fulfills that older, too quickly dismissed, art-populist expressionism, ballasting it for the largest possible public, in tune with that long, collective crisis which linked the Depression, the Popular Front, and the "People's War." That crisis kept Poetic Realism terse and melancholy, non-divisive and humanist – albeit *film noir* pointed to its corrosions. Against Fifties grey flannel, Free Cinema revived it, achieving, first, an alliance of documentary-eye with a wider sense of poetry, of popular anarchy. Then came *This Sporting Life*; it's populist expressionism in plain clothes, and it's kitchen-sink *noir*.

If.... envisaged a revolution; *O Lucky Man!*, acquiescence, at least pro tem; and in *Britannia Hospital* the same actor becomes Structuralist Man, a recombination of used parts, twice beheaded ("the abolition of the subject").

If Ford evokes a crisis of humanism amidst some Irish and American alienation, Anderson traces a crisis in left humanism. In a probably clumsy article around 1963, I feared that Free Cinema's afterglow of crisis-collectivism, and even its Fordolatry, might blunt and blur new realisms. I didn't foresee that Swinging London would queer the New Left's pitch and that a younger left would take Structuralism's anti-humanist turn. Still, Free Cinema lives: Anderson took it to Poland for *The Singing Lesson*, John Berger and Alain Tanner rethought it for bourgeois radicals as the Sixties sagged into the Seventies, Karel Reisz's *The French Lieutenant's Woman* nobly reasserts a subversive-moralist romanticism, Ford à la feminism. Left humanism's fellow-travellers range from *Man of Marble* ("*Don't* film the legend!") to *The Lacemaker*.

From the mid-Sixties the Structuralist Ideology condemned its left wing to think either deconstructively (i.e. anti-poetically) or in terms of corollaries from an abstract, inexperienced theory. Like the mills of academe it is "conceptual rather than intuitive," and Anderson rightly treats it, not as another, newer-than-New Left, but as a machine for scholars who expect bureaucratic status. *Britannia Hospital* suggests a sequel: *Britannia University*.

This isn't jeering: the contradictions are real, obstinate, heavy with consequence: after *O Lucky Man!, The History Man*. They reappear throughout *About John Ford,* insofar as any deconstruction of the words such as they are would show only an extremely Conservative value-system (and some non-bourgeois conservatives have fascinating positions). Instead, it acquires a formidable complexity and precision from Anderson's whole oeuvre. In 1963 I feared that "Print the legend" might overwhelm "Print the lot." How wrong I was.

SOURCE: *CINEASTE*, JUNE 1983, 56–8

6.2 A SKELETON KEY TO STEPHEN DWOSKIN

Outline for a Text Not Written

1. 29/8/82: received R. Combs request 1500 words re S. Dwoskin & suggestion of note format.

2. Usual disclaimers (e.g., point-of-pin schema, built-in auteurist slant, etc.).

3. Q: Why are Europeans so positive re SD's work, British largely negative? (Check startling funding data with SD.) Working subtitle for this section:

DWOSKIN AS THE ABOMINATIONS OF LEVITICUS
(cf. Mary Douglas, *Purity & Danger*, 1966, Chap. III.)
SD as monster, i.e., transgressor of established categories, namely:
(A) SD's NYC culture shifted to G.B. eludes both geocultures.
(B) G.B. avant-garde sub-culture operation polarised as per P. Wollen's two avant-gardes: **(i)** ex-painterly culture, **(ii)** neo-Bolshevik sectors (Straub, Godard, Jancsó). But PW's Category **(i)** sidles past SD (presumably as non-Marx, non-semiotics-based) to substitute

M. Le Grice–P. Gidal. *But* their post-modernist materialist structuralisms fear and exclude almost all painterly formalisms (including subsequent post-post-modernism). Hence:

(C) British difficulty with SD's fine-art culture (mainstream-to-p.p.m. semantics).

(D) Mistheorisation by Lacan-based theory distorting "the look" into voyeur-formalism. Hence:

(E) SD scapegoat for new feminist puritanisms.

Re **(A):** Establish SD's psycho-formalist representationalisms (between expressionism, Matisse, magic realism).

Re **(B):** Note inadequacy of painterly/political antinomy, since multiplicity of avant-garde thrusts in *each* medium must be compounded by film's multiple-medium gestalt. Praise hybrids (dialectic, compromise, multi-functionalism, over-determination).

Re **(C):** Contrast painters (as optical–tactile–kinetic) with readers (abstract, blind, non-pictorial, linear rigidity of reading-stare).

Re **(D):** Criticise 'scoptophilosophy', indicate origins in British culture-structures breakdown.

Re **(E):** Propose friendly alternative to feminist-puritan readings. Cite SD quote on passage from seeing to being, then formulate alternatives re seeing/knowing as **(i)** dominance for/vs. **(ii)** sharing/caring response. (Beware anti-humanist denials of possibility of communication.)

4. Career outline. *W s/t:* LONESOME ROAD BLUES

Pose problems re alternative groupings of films. **(A)** Periods or sets? **(B)** Thematic evolution or interweaving; schizo-separations or separate but non-schizo growth points in convergence? **(C)** How far is evolution internally driven ('organic' growth) or externally (socio-cultural context?). Stress this article uses only one taxonomy (alternative recombinations of other selected factors equally viable).

5. 1st period (1961–5) and subsequent similar shorts, *W s/t:*

THERE WAS ONE GREEN BOTTLE …

Person/actor (NB. hybridity) like bottle in still-life.

Message-in-a-bottle claustro-mutism.

From minimalist monologues (e.g., *Sleep*, 'dance' of stop-motion sleeping feet) to duologues (affinities: S. Beckett, A. Warhol, Y. Ono, W. Borowczyk's *Rosalie*, *Gavotte*).

Alone (1963). Double stasis (camera, Zelda) in (a) space, (b) time. Duration-distortion. Pedal point time-binding. Mahler? Arhythms like atonality? How SD and Ron Geesin (music) devised the Chronomatograph.

Chinese Checkers (1963). Sitting-down dancers. SD always super-sensitive re fingers (kinetic tactility vs. limb immobility?). Hypnotic web of eye and limb movements interwoven with (no, interpenetrate with) camera-calligraphy. Rather: camera-choreography. Soho-loft bleakness (suddenly conspicuous light switches on wall) vs. sudden fantasy faces, like the Clown-Birds of Paradise.

Psycho-formalism problem. Are looks into camera **(A)** direct-address to 'male' (objectifying) spectator-fantasy, **(B)** direct-address to 'female' (identifying) spectator-fantasy, **(C)** direct-address to social-distance-spectator (accusation/appeal), **(D)** in-diegesis reverse-angle 1st-person p.o.v., **(E)** all the foregoing at different times or sometimes ambiguously in different balancings? If **(C)** or **(D)**, then subject is interpersonal interaction (including negotiation/communion/seduction), temps-mort, micro-Renoirism. The formalism serves bedrock/baseline/tragic humanism.

Triptych of socio-sexual desolation: **Naissant** (1964), **Moment** (1969), **Take Me** (1968). 1920s "Birth, copulation and death" become, respectively, 1980s birth, masturbation (copulation aborted) and failed seduction (desire dead, imagine: Krapp's Last Reel, Waiting for Coming; NB. Make other sad jokes to lower tone of article: type of alienation effect). Humiliation of women, accusation of cameraman: Information Man as Inaction Man.

6. From Soliloquies and Duologues (or doubled soliloquies!) to (**W s/t**): INTERLOQUES Essays in 'happening' aesthetic. Semi-controlled 'laboratory conditions' for direct-docu-men*t*ary (*ment* from French "mentir", "he lies").
Me, Myself and I (1968): drab, undressed twosome; **Central Bazaar**: exotic, dressed-up 'encounter group'.

7. W s/t: BREAKING THROUGH THE FLESH BARRIER
Relate SD to G. Bataille (from Surrealist and permissiveness angles), W. Reich (body-psychology), general 1960s libidinology.
Times For (1970) loving. Camera follows boundary-layers, edges, of bodies, spaces, touch, orifices. What sex is your eyeball? tongue? instep? fingertips? nipples? Limbs and looks wound around like skeins of wool. Aquarium of bodies commingled, degenderised, desocialised, hyperfantasised into insubstantiality.
Dyn-Amo (1972) or times fo(u)r dying. After *Times For* pattern (1m + 4f), *Dyn-Amo* = 1f + 4m. (Is this contrast an implicit statement about male/female worlds? e.g., female com-petition vs. male bonding? Possible, but equal likelihood of more archaic, still inarticulate psychostructure behind contrast.) *Dyn-Amo* starts with macho female (Jenny Runacre in pre-*Jubilee* gear) and moves through progressively more castrated women to climactic crucifixion. Men sexless too: like lumpen-space insects from W. Burroughs, C. Wilkinson (*I Was Hitler's Maid*), the s-m obsessions of Robbe-Grillet.

Un(re)solved aesthetic problem, rendering these nearer-to-narrative films *less* compre-hensible than earlier lyrical tableaux. This is divergence/interference between **(A)** SD's late-modernist pictorial thought-thrusts, **(B)** situation-in-time, and **(C)** 'hot' dramatic given and potential with narrative/moral movement. Amalgam easily read as self-indulgent irresolution plus fetishising, objectifying deviation/insistence.
Central Bazaar (1976). Frustrating situation plus cornucopia of props (clothes, cosmet-ics, jewels, i.e., para-epidermal body surrogates) frustrate gender, pixilate sex, chip at iden-tity. The gay and the flustered, the rough and the passive. Carola Regnier's compassion/discomfiture/concern for dignity (Mother of Mercy + *Mädchen in Uniform*). Shining exception: upbeat little Asian pearl. Personae exasper-evapor-ated in fantasy-block-fantasy no-win truth-game. Daisy chain of 50s bleak-o-sleaze (W. Maas, *Geography of the Body*), 60s psychedelia (R. Rice, *Chumlum*), 70s interactionism-as-power (N. Roeg, *Performance*), 80s schizo-unisex (Deleuze–Guattari, *L'Anti-Oedipe*). **(i)** Opening table-laying sequence, exemplum of SD's constantly moving telephoto shots restructuring 'clas-sical' perspective, e.g., flattening of candles, calves, rejigging of angles of sides of table. **(ii)** Elements of stanza form in variorum repetitions. **(iii)** Telephoto focus enhances colour-flux effect. **(iv)** Multi-layer music: palimpsest-montage.

8. W s/t: DAUGHTER, LOVER, AUTONOME
SD's Carola Regnier period. Two streams. **(A)** Expansion from preceding monodramas, and 'implosive' happenings, to dramatic structures. Movement still uncompleted: tandem

lyricisms, shifting perspectives, re-entrants and disruptive criss-crosses. Between a 'dramatic cubism' and (old-fashioned, classical) multi-perspectivism.

(B) Autobiographical emergences.

(A) Impersonality: **Death and Devil** (1973). Wedekind not 'performed' but revamped for post-formalist, feminist, mentality. After *Dyn-Amo*'s 'neo-primitive', 'theatre eye', frontality (counterpointed by cinezoomography), this pro-poses some less unconventional mobile-impersonal vantage points. Odd effects as of early talkie. (NB. Offer checklist of SD's various camera procedures.) Problem: disparities of theatre/painting, scene/narrative, dialogue/dramatic structure, awkward except for spectators equipped with both state-of-the-art cineliteracy and post-modernist painterly eye.

(B) Autobiography: **Behindert** (1974). Active Actor, Effaced Director. C. Regnier, composite epicentre of **(i)** all the females in *Dyn-Amo*, and **(ii)** the 'centrifuged' males in *Central Bazaar*. Unique somatic acting/being: she goes from sharp-and-light to swamped, choked, knotted, saturated with self-frightening fury.

SD spares only the odd glance at himself as himself. This foreshortens potentially classic drama of:

His male sexuality + masc. gender + disability-enforced infantilism + Ginsberg-era looseness

vs.

Her female sexuality + functionally bigenderised autonomy + unfearful compassion/curiosity + Germanic probity/tension.

The Silent Cry (1977).

Female infantilism matching *Behindert.*

Feminist metaphor and/or neurotic case history?

This completes SD's trajectory towards other-identification.

Camera places *spectator* in girl's place, thus exposing her/him/it (NB. The "it" is no joke: spectator gender neutrality/androgyny not rare) to his own direct response (unmediated by *different* screen ego) to screen father, screen lover, etc.

Psycho-semantic problem: Q: Does SD's effacement of hero(ine) behind camera-eye relate to structuralist "abolition of the subject"? Q: Does SD's personal disability correspond to social-actual neurosis due to current British culture-structure; the 'body-snatcher' theory of the bourgeois hegemony ("Oh, Doctor Lacan, bourgeois culture structures me so tightly that even film reviewers are thought-police constructing us! And only you, me and post-structuralism know what's going on!!!").

9. *W s/t*: I THINK THEREFORE I SEE (AND VICE VERSA)

Consider SD as characteristic late modernist in uncharacteristic medium. Working after deconstructionist phase of bourgeois culture (Freud, Heisenberg, logical atomism, etc). In synch with 80s reconstructionist phase (old avant-garde separatisms negotiating new symbiosis with mainstreams). A trajectory of true modernism. Pre-modernism: What The Painter Saw. Impressionism: from What The Painter Really Saw to I Think I See How I See. Post-impressionism: I See As I Think. Fauvism: I See As I Please. Abstraction: I Make As If I See How I Think. Conceptualism: I Think Instead Of Seeing. New Realism: I Re-Realise It's Real!

SD: Camera-onics paraphrase 'hand-made' painterliness. Not 'hand-held' but hand-woven. SD achieved lyrical symbiosis 1961. Outstanding problematic: reconciliation of dramatic dialectics and visual 'cubism' which normally requires one-person p.o.v. (Just as analytical cubism tended to monochrome; cf. J. Berger, *The Moment of Cubism*.) Where cubism copped out, may film stay on the case!

Outside In (1981). Cubist title. Multiple-idiom movie (cp. Godard, Makavejev, K. Anger, etc.). All the Isms: intimism, realism, symbolism, vitalism, esp. Rabelaisianism. "Put Me Among the Girls". Good-Time Movie (contrast Le Grice–Gidal ingrown formalism, Gidal's mastur- bation film). Digress for several paras. on Merdelle Jordine as anti-Grace Jones: painter vs. art groupie, aggression vs. elusive change, monolithic vs. mercurial, fist-head vs. hawk- eye, stab-glance vs. hummingbird-glance. Relate with feminist strategies. If too long, make separate article.

Imagine these last three films as treated by Mike Leigh (indignity, humour, non-u, dis-grace, micro-faces).

Jagged-edged, infinitely fertile marriage of post-post-modernism & mainstream.

10. W s/t: A TIGHTLIPPED OPERA, OR THE BRITISH SOMATONE VIEWS
Long eulogy on harsh beauty of Gavin Bryars's music, music-as-sound (anti-concrete music), silences, reiterated chords as time-stoppers, bedrock pulses. Ontological music.

SOURCE: *MONTHLY FILM BULLETIN*, NOVEMBER 1982, 252–3

6.3 COOPED IN A CO-OP?

The London Film-Makers' Co-operative celebrates its 25th anniversary with a slate of new films at the London Film Festival, where it's subsidised by the Japan Foundation, Canada House, Channel Four, Cable London PLC, and, via the BFI and the Arts Council, the Tory Government. Its programmes adorn the Tate's yuppie-bright brochures. Meanwhile, back in the darker, starker, atmosphere of the LFMC's theatre/studio/laboratory/offices (42 Gloucester Ave, NW1), its retrospectives recall the dedication and infighting, the joyous explorations and scowling cultural struggles that now inspire, now bedevil, avant-garde subcultures.

No terms quite fit: avant-garde, parallel, oppositional, underground, independent, exper- imental, artists' and yes, home, play ducks and drakes with one another. The very name 'LFMC' means, by now, British Moving Image Artists Co-operative (BMIAC?). It's not quite a Co-op in the narrow sense of shared profits and concerted effort; more a cross between institute, umbrella, and interface. It's traditionally torn between two tendencies: one pragmatic, eclectic, catholic, the other militant, sectarian and narrow-minded.

Such tensions underlie Cordelia Swann's NFT booklet note: 'The LFMC was founded in 1966 by a group of artists and film-makers whose modernist (romantic) premise, similar to that of 20s Soviet film, was that the films to be made should be interested in new visual perceptions and that these would form a new art practice which would challenge main- stream film and offer an alternative film culture …'. Fair enough, but it slightly concertinas LFMC history.

The 1966 Co-op was a response to American (not Soviet) models, and related upsurges (beatniks, bebop, Humph's, folk and skiffle, an Albert Hall poetry reading, psy- chedelia, flower power, the Arts Lab, the *Oz* trial). I wrote a third of the LFMC's first cata- logue with one hand while writing for *Oz*, *IT* and *Movie*, and teaching 'bourgeois' art history, with the other. The general *zeitgeist* was non- (but not anti-) academic, a late bloom of Bohemia-and-backwoods counter-culture, reinvigorated by popular affluence; apolitical anarcho-libertarian, Come-all-ye. Its modernisms were already mainstream and unconcerned to challenge 'Hollywood' (recently rehabilitated by *Cahiers du Cinéma* and the *Nouvelle Vague*, against the left). That *zeitgeist* stirred the art-school sit-ins, and, in parallel, the student riots of Paris '68; but they were taken over and 'interpreted' by a second wave, primarily academic, a convergence, or criss-cross, of currents: 1) a riptide of art-school modernisms (minimalism, conceptualism, assorted specialisms); 2) educational liberalism radicalised by political romanticism about Uncles Castro, Ho, Mao, *et al.*, and soon afterwards, Recession; and 3) linguistic structuralism, semi-Leninised, as per Gramsci and Althusser, by a new New Left, attractive to 4) academicism which, like bureaucracy, lives on state subsidy.

The two waves were easily confused, then as now. Briefly, Wave 1 saw culture as an 'open field' whose systems and signs were rough and ready indicators, not definers, and *ad hoc*ishly adaptable. Wave 2 thought a dominant ideology had so closed most minds to diversity as to require subversion (for which 'challenge' was a regular euphemism). The Co-op, like *Undercut*, its 2nd wave magazine, and *Afterimage*, were modernist, not Leninist, while over at SEFT *Screen* was more Leninist (in the foregoing sense) than modernist, but they shared an academic, formalist-literalist 'opposition' to 'bourgeois culture'. They often portrayed it in its GCE O and A level terms, overlooking its real-life operations, in its Pop art terms (Monroe *à la* Warhol), ignoring literate-civilised Hollywood (Katharine Hepburn *à la* Tracy–Cukor), or as political melodrama (Hugh Gaitskell As A Famous Monster), ignoring the extent to which all politics, cultural included, are structurally ironic.

The main difference, though, was local-situational. The LFMC's first Chairman was Harvey Matusow, an American ex-Communist, famous there for having denounced umpteen Comrades to HUAC, and then recanted (cf. V. Navasky, *Naming Names*, John Calder 1982), and notorious here for a found-footage film called *The Enchanted Pot*, so stunningly boring it alienated every potential supporter of the LFMC. Matusow having disappeared, soon after the LFMC's tiny kitty, I got hiked in as its Hon. Chair by a desperate Committee, which included Bob Cobbing (the concrete/graphic poet and manager of Better Books, who made it a poetry centre, and the LFMC's first pad, until its move to the Arts Lab), Ron Geesin (sound artiste extraordinaire), Philip Crick (progressive arts theorist), Simon Hartog (our friendly neighbourhood Trot, now a mini-mogul at C4-associate Large Door, named for Buñuel's *L'Age d'Or*), and Steve Dwoskin (still avant-gardening today, like that other Grand Old Man of the avant-garde, Jeff Keen, regrettably too far away in Brighton).

Our '67 catalogue featured famous names: Paul Bartel, Bruce Conner, Hilary Harris, Hy Hirsh, Ian Hugo, Kurt Kren, Jack Smith, John Latham, Michael Nyman. Antonioni, visiting, was impressed by *Castle One*, a mixed-media piece contrasting a filmed light-bulb and light with the real thing (a fine test-case in phenomenological semiotics). The BFI was rigorously indifferent, no discussion, end of story. Friendly responses came from Dilys Powell (later of that arrière-garde magazine *Punch*) and *Films & Filming* (with its theatrical and showbiz sales). More ad agencies than art schools joined. True, antiporn crusaders could have had us in the dock, as well as *Oz*, though we were permissive, not vicious. (All very different now, with the NFT running Gay seasons a gogo, and quangocrats well aware how subsidies buy bricks in the wall of cultural-educational power.) English film-makers, poorer than American, were still, as Dwoskin said, loners, not joiners, having little to share with a Co-op or one another. Clearly a film Co-op needed not our motley crew, mostly part-time amateurs from adjacent fields, but tightly organised gangs of filmwise fanatics who would route their own careers through their avant-gardes.

From around 1970 art-school interest gave the avant-garde its institutional basis. Appointed by Freddie Gore, RA, to St Martin's, Malcolm Le Grice's first friendly remark quite threw me, like Tweety-Pie feeding Sylvester the Cat a stick of dynamite. Didn't I think illusionistic, fictional films were sinful, encouraging people to believe what wasn't true? Simply put, it encapsulated the aggressive puritanism behind 'the Art-School Film' – 'Abstract Film and Beyond' (Le Grice), 'Structural/Materialist Film' (Gidal), 'Formalist Film', 'Concrete Film', 'Self-Reflexive Cinema', 'Cinema Degree Zero'. All well-adapted to student exercises, and various student hostilities to art history, whose richness and diversity may indeed confuse one's own agendas. Though as Gore rightly, but sadly, told one particularly supercilious batch, 'You're not art lovers, you're art haters ...'. Through the 70s a sub-sidised, quango-academico-bureaucratic subculture grew. At the Arts Council, Rodney Wilson, Ian Christie and others maintained the catholic traditions of modernism, but at BFI Production highbrow agitprop ousted avant-gardism; gradually pure-film formalism domi-nated the Co-op, until, to cite Ms Swann's tactfully tortuous prose, 'with the oncoming gen-erations, other film-makers were allowed to admit that they did not exist within a political and cultural vacuum devoid of influences from different areas of film, music, literature or art'. (Dare I add life outside art, e.g. 'bourgeois' science? And weren't political blinkers part of the problem?)

Some artists approach meaning by thinking about form, others invent forms by start-ing from meanings, most weave between the two. Form *tel quel* is a specialisation like any other and, as in music, no line divides the exercise from the work of art. Almost equally beautiful and formally studied, are Dwoskin's lyrical-Lesbian-erotic *Chinese Checkers* (Wave 1) and Le Grice's *Berlin Horse* (Wave 2), although the latter evokes articulacy less than archaeology, its formal landslips burying biomeaning, its systematic variations suggesting/refusing normal semantic flows. But formalism easily spirals from phenomenological exploration into ever-decreasing circles, especially when exacerbated by fear of a 'bourgeois ideology' which never was (just as it easily confuses Foundation exercises with fundamental research). In socioFreudspeak, 'bourgeois culture' is the fathermother, and killing your parents maims your own fertility; better to salute them and move on.

Hence innovatory initiatives, pure forms included, passed to non-purisms, a Wave 3: computer-paintboxes (bourgeois technocratics?), rock promo videos blithely free of 'clas-sical Hollywood syntax', the New Romantics around Derek Jarman, the 'neo-painterliness' of P. Greenaway and, theorywise, Arts Council-type catholicisms reflowering under the green fingers of Al Rees and Michael O'Pray. Mainstream and avant-gardes turned out to overlap, more to mutual advantage than in cultural struggle.

Around 1960 an education-information-image-explosion began thoroughly confus-ing/interfusing structures, in every medium and sphere. For a decade now, rock videos have routinely deployed 20s modernist forms: stream-of-consciousness, Dada, energic pulsations like Futurism, collages, alienation effects, impossible spaces, expressive abstractions. Modernisms didn't 'end'; they transformed and merged with the mainstream, as avant-gardes should, thus precipitating post-modernisms: some, like Wave 2, opposi-tional; others, like Waves 1 and 3, complementary. Who dares prescribe what an optimum synthesis would be? As, in the new 'mixed economy', sponsorships complement subsidies, should the LFMC 'go with the flow' and assume more 'agency' functions? Can it, without imperilling that independent spiritual space which 'co-op' stands for?

SOURCE: *ART MONTHLY*, NOVEMBER 1991, 24–5

6.4 JEAN-LUC GODARD: HIS CRUCIFIXION AND RESURRECTION

The Seven Ages of Godard

Let's slice the life so far into seven periods – or rather, an order of emergence of styles, for each prevails for a while without excluding the others.

1. 1950–1960: Godard's first decade: apprentice writings and 'short story' films. Sketchy and bold.
2. 1960–1965: New Twists to Old Narratives: from *A bout de souffle* to *Pierrot le Fou*. The quest for a personal morality (more Malraux than Sartre). Exemplary text: Bogart. As the quest fails, so …
3. 1963–1967: Narrative collapses into episode-and-essay, a belles-lettrist lyricism of schizo-sensibility. Virginia Woolf for a tower-block, lumpen-bourgeois time. Sensitivity and parody. Exemplary text: none; philosophy, sociology, all are 'nihilised'.
4. 1967–1969 (*La Chinoise–One A.M.*): From Old Sensibility to New Texts. Can the New Man's Mind mirror Lenin-to-Lacan?
5. 1969–1972: The Dziga-Vertov Group: Film Form as Social Form. "I Observe, therefore I Act." Exemplary texts: Mao + Althusser.
6. 1974–1979: Retreat to the Videobunker. A revolution in ever-diminishing circles.
7. 1979–1985: Euroculture Rides Out. Godard's seventh era resembles his first, but that cult of clear action yields to oceanic feelings of Romantic art and myth. E.T.s: Beethoven, Bizet, the Bible.

After noting the dialectic of action and reflection, the latter being richest in the 'lush' style of the seventh age, we turn to longitudinal slicing by some major themes.

Ruling Passions

1. Les Héros sont des Zéros

Belmondo's first line in *A bout de souffle* is: "Okay, I'm a cunt". Godard is the first insistent ignominist in French films. Though not the only one: confrères include Claude Chabrol, Jean-Pierre Mocky (doyen of the school), and Old Wavers Jacques Tati and Luis Buñuel. Godard's Belmondo heroes have driving passions and superior skills, complete with hamartia and grace at the close, as per classical tragedy and Hollywood-Mosfilm. But already they point towards the universal imbecility-and-pain of *Week-End*, Godard's Cinema of the Absurd. Not even Third World spokesmen scowling into camera are spared! The caricatured gay in *Sauve qui peut* upset some sensitive souls, but is true to Godard's rude form: he dishes it out to himself-as-himself in *Prénom Carmen*. The antithesis of ignominism is Romanticism, expressed by the successive E.T.s. Whether Godard 'closes' the synthesis is the kind of problem that reveals the weakness of Marxist dialectics.

2. Fight a Crooked Fight

Many Godard heroes are intellectuals who are also freelance crooks. They're spiritual family with foreign legionnaires (*Le Petit Soldat, Les Carabiniers*). But then they start signing on the party lines of revolutionary brigades, i.e., the foreigners' legions, the Third World. Demob (or sabbatical?): circa 1980.

3. A Skein of Syllogisms

A: If art is only lies like truth; and if facts are only truth like lies; then, before life, lies, facts and truths can coincide, we need …

B: a revolution, what else? The Little Red Book can lead us to the Higher Marxematics, but …

C: If only the texts attest to reality, how can we test the texts? Godard, who is as meaning-hungry as he's obsessively sceptical, keeps bouncing off the text/reality interface. All of which exacerbates what follows:

4. Ideas Against Form; Ideas About Form; Form Without Ideas

Godard's always erratic forms bespeak problems which deserve a long book. And not a homage, but a medical book. Especially since the neurosis (or is it psychosis?) is not personal but cultural.

He gets into it because (a) he's more verbal-abstract than visual-sensuous, and (b) his inspiration is not only improvisational but impulsivist. It comes and goes in short pants, as ideas flash through his mind, obliquely to visual continuity. Which hardly fits feature-length structures requiring craft reliability and moment-by-moment novelty. And, by one of life's little ironies, by the time he was wriggling free into essay-type free forms and any-length counter-cinema, his inspiration was drying up.

Godard is very sensitive to visuals, sufficiently to disregard some mere conventions of craft. But Old Wave craftsmen were probably right about *A bout de souffle*: the continuity was such a mess that he *had* to slash it into jump-cuts, for only drastic avoidance could obviate surplus confusion. The producer of *Le Mépris* has revealed how, a third of the way into shooting, he asked Fritz Lang to give the young genius a severe talking-to about continuity. With detailed explanations of how it works. And Godard accepted from his heavy godfather what he continued denouncing to mere mortals. Sometimes, it's true, you don't need to know your craft, ignorance of old conventions can even clear the way for more functional-ergonomic forms. But sometimes you desperately need your craft; it's a taskmaster, demanding new ideas or generating shared ideas while you fine-tune strange ones.

If Godard's combination of brilliance and incompetence dogs his first periods, it's logical that it should become an issue in his self-reflective stage. But he approaches the question of form without confidence, with ambivalence, with deep suspicion of the meanings he supposes are built into it. He approaches it with an animus against using it. The 20s avant-garde revelled in form, so that *Un chien andalou* is not just the antithesis, it's also the apotheosis of continuity editing. It goes beyond it because it knows it so well. It knows exactly how to play one implication off against another, with the utmost finesse. The 60s structuralists are inhibited about form: they want to inspect bourgeois forms from a platform outside them. But radical culture is as dependent on bourgeois culture as Marxism is on rationalism; it has no outside platform. So Godard, in sync with structuralism, becomes neurotic about form. As if all forms were hopelessly polluted by bourgeois conventions. As if non-bourgeois ideas had no power to dictate and devise forms. As if only bourgeois ideology had a phallus. Alas! Writing degree zero came to mean: thought degree zero. And auto-deconstruction became auto-castration.

The happy fact is that form is a subject exactly like any other. You can treat it just as neatly, briskly, locally, progressively: you can "bat it and run", as Howard Hawks advised, whether you're telling a story or pursuing an analysis. One reason why the forms of language don't determine our thoughts is because they allow so many alternative formulations. Formulation (*parole*) overrules, outflanks, outwits form (*langue*). Marx did it, texts like this do it. Moreover, Marxist ideas must precede Marxist critiques. For deconstruction depends on the previous invention of alternatives, not vice versa. Godard, far from painfully preparing a newer, purer language, was refusing to use the appropriately impure languages with (not within) which so many directors (from Chris Marker's magic *Lettre de Sibérie*, way back in 1958, to Jean-Pierre Gorin's magic *Poto and Cabengo*, 1979) were pushing cinema forwards. To be sure, no one possesses a language which can guarantee immunity from error; but no such language can exist; even logic is at the mercy of its assumptions. That's why linguistics-based structuralism was so paralytic. It could neither invent a new language nor solve any problems in the old.

In *A bout de souffle*, and in fits and starts thereafter, Godard knows his subject so well that he can let it prompt form for him: every little eddy and nuance leaves its mark. But once he becomes afraid of form, and refuses it, then he stares and glares at it, suddenly slashes at it, as if to deface it. He dawdles, doodles, ruminates, lashes out, rivets his eye on the lens instead of keeping it on the ball, loses himself in a *Blow-Up* tennis match. To think you play against form is to think you play against the net.

5. Pirouette with Crazy Pete

From Drama to Soliloquy: The first two features have a fine bourgeois narrative, that is, a dramatic dialectic. But slowly this sense of life as dialogue collapses into soliloquy. Anna Karina's face flattens into lyrical blanks for hanging Godard's silent pauses on, a physiognomy for remembering Dreyer and Bresson by. Slowly the labyrinth of echoes, the anxiety of influence, the maze of connections without substance, the schizo-circuit diagrams, become unbearable. A spirit–flesh–form unity is desperately desired. So Malraux yields to Mao (action in communal form), aestheticism to structuralism (its mirror image).

From Action to Reflection: The breakdown of narrative, far from being a radical breakthrough in some bourgeois Chinese Wall, is a reversion to man-of-letters, High Culture practice. The famous author keeps a journal, a pot-pourri of impressions, reflections, apothegms, piecemeal observations. And publishes it in formless segments and fragments. When inspiration fails, travel broadens the mind. Agit-tourism takes over, impressionism and self-reflexivity infiltrate disciplined reportage. Godard's world cruise takes in two trips to Paris, the U.S.A., Britain (well, Brixton); also stopping at Palestine, Italy, Mexico, Mozambique, Lausanne. Happiness is a revolutionary express. But every country becomes the interior of Godard's mind, just like every Sternberg studio set is really Anatahan.

From One-Liners to Graffiti: Godard was always a great joker, the dissident answer to Woody Allen. Or Ivor Cutler. The Seventh Python. Take Belmondo's throwaway mutter to himself (or is it direct address to us? Well, same difference): "Cars are made to go, not to stop, as Father Bugatti used to say". That line comes on so casual, but oh so slickly splits accelerators from brakes, and makes movement, as essence of car, into a crazy extreme and a categorical imperative. Also it links two types of macho: youthful impatience, fatherly wisdom. So, long before *L'Anti-Oedipe*, it's a textbook schizo-structure.

Often humour, e.g., wordplay, stresses form against meaning; i.e., it plays off semiotics against semantics. As Godard's inspiration congeals, formalism supervenes. The camera looks blankly at graffiti and subtitles like graffiti … even the actors' faces are graffiti … slogans are written across lines of parked cars, so that the words will all drive off in different directions. If alien structures hegemonise the commanding heights of your psychic economy, then the rest of you is condemned to a guerrilla existence, like the dispirited cripples in *L'Age d'or*. Your only weapons are graffiti, jokes, slogans, cryptic emblems.

After Anonymous, Godard is surely one of the great graffiti writers of all time. (The bourgeois take over yet another folk form.) The medium has ignominist tendencies: "I'm just A. Non on a blank wall, and if you're reading this, you're probably wetting your trouser leg". And like Godard, graffiti operates easily in a mode considered unbelievably sophisticated by High Culture literati: equivocations between parody/pastiche/subversion/homage, in a word: alienation, but incorporating triple-back-action spring-loaded action-reaction mechanisms. Of which the antithesis (there's always an antithesis) is: the slogan. The Order of the Day. Easily backsliding from categorical imperative to dogmatic repetition.

If Godard's influence on radical-academic culture leads it deeper into élitist mystifications and inverted aestheticisms, it's hardly his fault. He followed his nose and no one had to follow him. But it's time to deconstruct the whole disaster. Structuralism, like the Titanic …

Sympathy for the Angel

That was the bad news, now for the good news. As a true poet, Godard led the field, as the 60s entered twilight worlds, where reality shades into hypnagogia. *Week-End* (1967) goes further than *The Milky Way* (1969) in reviving the focus-losing drowsiness of *L'Age d'or* (1930). *Les Carabiniers* (1963) did everything already. He also set the pace in setting up notional scenes, symbolic indications of other actions and abstractions. 99% of the normal movie budget goes on getting merely circumstantial details right, or at least, not conspicuously wrong. But if you can get audiences to accept a symbolic sketch, a sort of live-action cartoon, like Low's or Vicky's (with pangs not laughs), you can slash your budget by 90%: to UB 40 proportions, in fact. You can also get straight into intellectual, abstract cinema, without routing everything, as Eisenstein thought you would have to, through the forms, fuss and bother of montage. Not that Godard invents non-realism, as some highly amnesiac denunciations of bourgeois realism suggest. But he does a great deal to diversify, widen, cheapen it.

Dr. Dziga and Mr. Vertov

Dziga-Vertov was an inspired constructor of new forms for new men. His self-reflexive streak accepts, affirms film form, for its joyous openness to a dynamic semantic. Many a 60s formalist, oppressed by Brecht and Barthes, read his montage as primarily alienation-and-deconstruction. Which reflects a curious split in the Dziga-Vertov Group. Godard now claims that the hard-edge politics was all the other guy's doing. But it seems more likely that Gorin was the optimist, the enthusiast, the investigator, the reconstructor, and Godard the critic, the tragedian, the tunnel-visionary.

For Godard solo, in *Week-End*, the revolution boils down to cannibalism, steeling yourself to a horror greater than bourgeois horror. And who wouldn't reject the racist-sexist-psychotic black panthers in *Sympathy for the Devil*? But with Gorin to cheer him up, as in

Tout va bien, the revolution is a sit-in, it starts now, even if our neighbours don't know the words beyond the first verse. Gorin is Dziga-Vertov's son and heir, while Godard throws his spanners in their works, just as slyly as he sabotaged bourgeois humanism. Gorin's solo flight, *Poto and Cabengo*, is D-V's spirit, reincarnated in 60s forms, enriched by Les Blank's camera-eye (itself schooled by fleshly love: of blues, of garlic, so that here libraries feel as free as fields …).

Old Metronome-Head Meets the Woman of Bronze

An early sign of mental blocks breaking up was Godard's long text-and-design for *Cahiers du Cinéma* No. 300, May 1979. It's a fine contribution to the undersung and impure arts of book design, mise-en-page, montage-cum-collage and verbo-typo-picto-pagino-graphics. Guttenberg strikes back. It's a better film than most of his films.

No Chinese uncles here, except perhaps Uncle Alf Hitchcock, and he gets put in the dock. In the name of Solidarnosc, Godard settles accounts with his too-long time as a desert father. He rehabilitates traditional fiction forms (front cover). He utters some healthy brutalities about avant-garde supersensitivities ("Duras = Pagnol"). Some fine infamies about *Cahiers* cults of yore ("Hitchcock's style glosses Kim Novak's face into a pair of buttocks"). Godard's picto-text is a love letter to another face, another cinéaste. Far from being a monolith, she's a mover, all long legs and hand-held. Far from being a sphinx of objectivity, she's a documentarist within a fiction. She's Krystyna Janda in Wajda's *Man of Marble*. "About whom", Godard complains, "all the critics are silent". But for him she's "Janet Leigh in Stalin's Old Dark House".

Now what's so salutary about the Eastern European cinema if not that it's a classic *and* a Socialist cinema, that it's Lech Walesa not Louis Althusser, that it's flesh not text, and action against structure? So here's Krystyna striding and sharp-eyed (no more glazed paralysis) leading an investigative cinema (no more mirror-formalism) to ferret out the facts (no more theory-solipsism) of an individual's life (reconstitution of the subject). So here's the Eastern European cinema, about which all our semiocrats are so strangely silent. There's even sympathy for the peasantry, the bourgeoisie – those families, those interiors, on pp. 4–8, aren't they French and/or Polish, just like the iconography of Boro's *Dom* and *Renaissance*?

The Enchanted Studio

The first revolution was an American girl (Jean Seberg). The second revolution was a Chinese Uncle. And the third? From Uncle Wajda it ricochets back West, to all our great-godfathers. The great paintings, operas, musics. Can we capture the radicalism of passionate spirits?

Sauve qui peut, the first in the period, re-stresses modern ignomiy. But its realism has more heart than, say, Chabrol's *Les Bonnes Femmes*. It's a sympathising story of 9 to 5 folk. It stays with them. And like the Jane Fonda picture, it's about everyday sadism and counter-sadism. It's an upfront picture of power. So Godard is genuinely interested. He follows through, he keeps it local. It's *The Night Porter* but stripped of fancy dress. Somehow too its tower-block tangles, its remote-control rules, suggest *Salò* up to date. It evokes Pasolini's strange symbiosis of energy and freeze, of neo-romanticism bursting under the surface.

Sure, it ends sadly: the boss-man links his office workers into a coldly nasty meccano of naughty bits, a schizo-association chain-gang. ("Put another franc suisse in, every office ori-fice …") . But that schizo-sex tableau is countered in *Passion*. The studio sets, like spiritually charged pictures, lure us into nostalgia for what we never had. Okay, so we can walk around to the back of the flats, where the illusion ends and carpentry takes over; we can throw the model out of scale just by standing in the middle of it. But still they call us to an exaltation which they almost ... can't quite ... but if ... somehow ... This revolution would start in all those bourgeois places: romanticism, *Sturm und Drang*, Méliès and Delacroix, museums.

These replicas transmit rather than degrade the originals, and indeed the original subjects, that is, their states of soul. Passion survives a double remove. Godard's own film makes a third. And the overall relay of parody and homage sounds like our cue for some tricky theory. First, as Professor Freud has shown, all mythical subjects represent the Primal Scene. Hence the Lacanian formula for *Passion* would have to be:

$$\frac{G}{PS \left(\dfrac{r}{o}\right)\left(\dfrac{H}{P}\right)} = VB$$

Where G = Godard, PS = Primal Scene, r = replica, o = original, H = Homage, P = Parody, and VB = Virgin Birth. The equation decisively corroborates our earlier linkage of formalism with fixation on purity. Godard's overwhelming question is: can any language guarantee immaculate conception without becoming unspeakable?

And very precisely, Godard's latest film does for the Virgin Mary what its predecessor, *Prénom Carmen*, did for a gypsy whore. The opposition confirms the impeccability of our structuralist con-pute-eur. (For a computer is not a phallus; it's what Lacan thinks bourgeois woman is; it accepts the assumptions your desire places in it.) *Prénom Carmen* incorporates the simplest forms of self-reflexivity: Godard presents himself as/ridicules/defends/ everybody's gaga sugar daddy. It's St. Joseph's part: the godfather who isn't God's phallus. It's also a finely balanced mirror-stage. And a parody of Truffaut as everybody's father figure in *La Nuit Américaine*. For Godard's mind is like Zelig's face: a parody of whatever's in the vicinity. As for the Virgin Mary film, it's Godard's version of certain scenes in *The Milky Way* and *The Life of Brian*. As the cinema has become more Godardian, Godard has become more accommodating. It's practically *Oedipus at Colonnus*.

In a sense, it's a remix of Godard's Belmondo, always craving a mixture of moral passions and romance. (All of us are lying in the sprocket holes, but some of us are looking at the stars.) It's pat in sync with the current romantic revival (Herzog, Wagner, Coppola, Syberberg, Conan, Carmen x 4). It's easy to be sardonic about the Romantic Vampire, but Godard's counterpointing it with ignominism makes a refreshing variation. Less for what he says about it than for what it gives him. It's hardly a matter of masterpieces (and isn't interesting discourse enough?). But it's good to see Godard's mind all cranked up and tanked up, quivering to go, like a Disney biplane.

No doubt he'll hit cloudbanks again. He's too much the escapologist to stay on course. Especially after twelve years on the cross, where Mao and structuralism converged to fix him. He has to be fickle, for his are the reflexes that can juggle an egg and a cannonball and a lighted candle and a live hedgehog, while playing "The Flight of the Bumble-Bee" on a harp with the other hand.

SOURCE: *MONTHLY FILM BULLETIN*, SEPTEMBER 1985, 268–71

6.5 RESNAIS & CO.: BACK TO THE AVANT-GARDE

1. Polemics and Poetics
This essay re-explores the early documentaries (1949–65) of the 'Left Bank group': Alain Resnais, Chris Marker, Agnès Varda and William Klein (who often worked on one another's films), plus Georges Franju. Harbingers of the New Wave, their tightly integrated socialism, humanism, high culture and poetic formalism contrasted with (a) the 'modern bourgeois' ethos of the *Cahiers* group and (b) post-New Wave formalisms, anti-humanisms and agit-propisms. This essay thus constitutes a 'positive' complement to the deconstruction of Godard (M.F.B., September 1985). The Left Bank documentaries equally contrast with 60s Vertovism, Robbe-Grillet's auto-deconstructive texts, Straub/Huillet's and Akerman's concretist-minimalisms, 'degree zero' neo-primitivisms, etc.

2. Two Generations, Two Strategies
Both movements respond to the 50s 'information explosion'. The Left Bank strategy parallels the 'positive' structuralism (modern science, Piaget, Goldmann) whose multi- and interdisciplinary convergences synthesised 'reality' as networks of forces, as a pluralism of connections. The later, linguistico-literary structuralisms were 'negative', fixating on separated structures (languages, codes, ideologies), fetishising differences into oppositions, and emphasising separate (monolithic) ideologies over the interactive shiftings of thinking.

This 'skeleton key' to Left Bank creativity emphasises, and recommends, its rigorous integration of elements: a 'critical poetry' mainstream; a solid materialism (non-naive realism); a Wittgensteinian emphasis on the limits of discourse; virtuoso movie craftsmanship; and a non-academic avant-garde drive. This synthesis of thriving traditions marked a qualitative change in movie language and agenda; avoided the pseudo-problems that subverted radical formalisms; and remains an almost dauntingly rich basis for reconstructing socialist modernisms.

3. Two Historical Epoques
I. For the French left, the 50s were nightmare years. Massive colonial wars triggered near-civil war and nationwide terrorisms. The Communist Party staggered from the Stalinist Big Lie to EuroCommunist bewilderments. After the failed struggle against German rearmament came paranoias about Gaullist repression. "La planification" (technocratic reorganisation) triumphantly renovated a bourgeois-dirigiste system. Affluence and Coca-Colonisation set about softening up the 'solid working-class'.

II. In contrast, the late 60s combined widespread stability, prosperity, technocracy. Proletarian affluence tamed the French Communist Party, and a dissident student lumpenbourgeoisie preferred alien ideals (Uncles Mao and Ho) or alienating ideas (Althusser). From this strenuous, yet tenuous, distance, the native culture could seem a homogeneous hegemony, unconscious of its crucial contradictions, and incapable of critical self-reflexivity.

4. Two Cultural Predicaments

I. The Left Bank found the feature film industry almost closed to young talent. It found itself penned within the shorts-and-documentaries ghetto; the equivalent of not B but Z-films (mitigated by festival-critical kudos and small state advances for 'quality' product). Censorship was exceptionally heavy (until alleviated by de Gaulle's anti-Americanism). Marginalised but not alienated, the Left Bank group synthesised the disciplines of craft and market and High Culture literary accomplices like Raymond Queneau, Marguerite Duras, Jean Cayrol, Jorge Semprun, Alain Robbe-Grillet.

II. The 60s radicals were more alienated than marginalised. Entry into film/TV had never been easier, nor equipment and distribution cheaper. Censorship almost evaporated; film found newly diverse markets. Somehow these convulsive changes provoked the new, academic-radical culture to a cultural rejectionism: scornful of impurity, debilitatingly sceptical of existing and impure forms and meanings, their only accomplices were politically compatible theorists. Godard's *chinoises* study edifying tracts like Calvinists dreading that their bourgeois formation has predestined them never to receive that amazing grace. Or militancy is degraded to simplistic hard-sell agit-prop.

5. Style as Substance

Left Bank films are the children of Bresson and Queneau. Bresson, for rigorous formal concentration and elliptical continuity; Queneau for the systematised caprice, the stream of ruptures, the sideways skip that reveals tangential networks. Where Bresson's intensity remains monotonal, lyrical, the Left Bank uses it for brevity, swift change, switches of latitude, parody, pastiche, modulations and ruptures of mood, topic, genre. Whence its plurality of discourses; it's a non-Bazinian cinema.

Similarly with its intensive use of montage with voice-over. As Eisenstein argued, montage expedites abstraction, concepts; juxtaposition becomes interaction; images, colliding, 'extract' aspects from, or propose new connections for, each other. The stream of images underlines process, change, transformation. The voice-over adds the agility and abstraction of words; vastly expedites exposition; and can swiftly emphasise selected aspects-and-connections of the images. Richly textured ('realistic') images don't clog this speed; on the contrary, they propose *more* aspects for this abstracting process.

Far from resounding like the 'voice of God', the voice-over is simply the voice of thought. Left Bank voice-overs routinely speculate, hypothesise, change their mind, doubt, and interrogate what they see. Transcending commentary, they fulfil the normal functions of words and thought. Spoken word, printed word, images, music, sounds weave their separate 'lines' around and through one another, like a jazz of phenomena, converging, diverging, cross-checking, destabilising …

In the documentary section of *Hiroshima mon amour*, the voice-over opens as dialogue and continues as thought-track – a conspicuously subjective interior monologue, permeating flashbacks and 'objective' shots alike, it interrogates, brackets, suspends images in contestation and hypothesis.

6. Franju's Poetic Realism

Far from being tied to bourgeois apron-strings, 'realism' fully accommodates social criticism (e.g., Zola's accusatory Naturalism) and left-materialism. It's appropriate that Vertov the Stakhanovite and Vigo the anarchist shared cameraman Boris Kaufman, whose direct cinema becomes formal-structural in *Man with a Movie Camera*, poetic-symbolic in *A propos de Nice*.

Vigo pioneered poetic realism, whose populism and melancholy atmospheric is social-critical in Vigo, Carné, Daquin, Allégret. Franju's documentary *Le Sang des bêtes* (1949) is poetic realism (at times, direct cinema) + 'double-vision' concentrations on particular scenes, actions, details. A butcher wades in a sea of blood as he sings "La Mer". A virtuoso craftsman hacks a hanging carcass in two as the town-hall clock strikes twelve. Gentle nuns beg the offal. Barges move with a 'social' fatalism.

The film's dialectic is: Zola (bestiality of proletarian life) ↔ Vertov (non-idealistic dignity of labour) Carné ↔ (tender and melancholy populism) ↔ Vigo (abstraction into symbolic language). Formalism-wise, Franju invents (or rather discovers) the elegiac freeze frame (*Monsieur et Madame Curie*, 1952). Method-wise, Franju's successors include Anger (cleaning the bike in *Scorpio Rising*), Makavejev (W. R.'s museum, the mass therapy sessions).

7. Resnais's Pictorial Unencyclopaedia

Resnais's *Guernica* (1950) transmutes the documentary 'genre' into – belles lettres? the essay? The little boxes of genre theory can't contain discourse when, as here, it deploys its natural versatility …

Resnais's film is realistic as to its first-level subject (Picasso's "Guernica" and other works). It's non-realistic as to its second-level subject (the events at Guernica) and as to its third-level subject (the inhuman shapes of panic and of menacing non-feeling in man). Isn't its fourth level a protest against German rearmament?

Perhaps the same protest permeates *Nuit et brouillard* (1955). Its first level is the concentration camps; its second, the human experience therein; its third, the inadequacy of documents, the evanescence of traces, its makers' and our foredoomed struggle to comprehend those long-gone moments of truth. It's about the anguish of collective memory, of communication, of information; of semiotics when *both* the objective signifier *and* our imaginary response are inadequate to the signified, which is a subjective *and* collective, social-historical reality …

Toute la mémoire du monde (1956) discovers a complementary horror: an over-abundance of semiotics. As the all-tracking, all-cutting camera relentlessly drives through these labyrinthine shelves, the 'information explosion' becomes exponential, a chain reaction. Knowledge, thoughts, documents, multiply their meta-worlds, relativise one another, and terrorise the living. Isn't the later, radical determination to impose a rigorous semiotic order a drastic *triage*, a defence reflex against this deluge? Against this 'China syndrome', Barthes fetishised those Japanese neon signs which could seem blessedly void of meaning.

Accompanied by Queneau's pataphysical verse voice-over, *Le Chant du styrène* (1958) follows a plastic bowl along the production line, and the stream of time, but *backwards* to its amorphous origins. This genetic destructuration leads from consumerist banality to nature's chaos, and narrative reversed ceases to be narrative. It's Genesis Lost.

The 'information explosion': *Toute la Mémoire du Monde* (1956)

Resnais's features mostly follow our period. But let's just flash-forward:

In 1959, *Hiroshima mon amour* will combine a documentary about documentation (museums/ruins/films …) with its subjective correlatives (repression/fetishisation) and its moral correlatives (political idealism masks personal trauma; flesh/identity is fixated as indexical trace or it reverts to amorphousness through atrocity – or through pleasure …). *L'Année dernière à Marienbad* (1961) will present a pseudo-world, forged (in both senses) from mental constructs plus film itself plus spectatorial logic … In *La Vie est un roman* (1983) separate spheres of thought/discourse/style will fail to rendezvous and pool their genes (genres) … *Mon oncle d'Amérique* (1980) will be a parallel montage, between Laborit's psychology and case histories which transcend, resist its limits …

La Guerre est finie (1966) will devise for images a future-hypothetical tense (Yves Montand imagining faces for the fellow agents he is about to meet). *Je t'aime, je t'aime* (1968) will invent the looped-subjunctive mood, when a man is trapped in a sequence of alternative states, in parallel universes, each merely a trivial variation on the others …

Resnais's early films, steeped in resistance stoicism and 50s left-pessimism, are elegantly harsh, like Tarkovsky's. His later films have been slighter, sweeter. Too gently radical, perhaps? Or akin to Renoir's remark: "I'm getting old, now I play Mozart"?

8. Agnès Varda and the Womb with a Kino-view

L'Opéra-Mouffe (1958) is slum life seen through all the senses of a pregnant woman; and through the senses poeticised, intellectualised. Hence those complex and delicate verbal and visual puns. Thus, Opéra-Mouffe = Opéra-*Bouffe* + Rue *Mouffe*tard. A pregnant belly resembles vegetable produce piled on a stall, or sliced open; the embryo is 'shown' as a chick marooned in a drinking glass. Answering that insistent question, "Who will (s)he be?", various hypotheses are insinuated by present faces: poor, tired, dead-drunk, mad …

9. Chris the Magic Marker or, how to Tap-dance Along with Uncle Vladimir …

Chris Marker's pseudo-personal, political super-travelogues explore Peking (1955), Cuba (1961), Israel (in 1960, when kibbutzim collectivism still impressed the left), a meta-U.S.A. (1959). *Lettre de Sibérie* (1958) is a kaleidoscopic epic-pastorale, and a summit of Socialist poetics. Refracted through Vertov's kino-eye, Eisenstein's scissors, and Vigoesque symbolics, this far-off land becomes an Erewhon. Voice-over: "This could be autumn in Ermenonville or New England, were it not for these telegraph workers, booted like Michael Strogoff, performing at the altitude of trapezists the gestures of shoemakers … If one of these climbing Cossacks were to absent-mindedly reel in his line, he would roll up a ball five thousand miles long …". It's a Tex Avery idea, and not many minutes have gone before this film bursts out into a cartoon pastiche of cartoons.

Marker's swift shuttle of images and thoughts is goaded by a 50s convergence/collision of consumerism, Communism and pre-industrial traditions. Here, women construction workers meet King Kong; here, an old-style folk song to charm the reindeer, that all-round raw material, inspires a Bolshevik TV commercial to sell the spectator Horn Flakes; here, Siberia's history begins with fresh-frozen pop-up mammoth meat, and ends with a project to rename constellations after its forest animals. A sequence of road-menders is four times repeated, and is transformed by three voice-overs: the Stalinist commentary, the anti-Communist commentary, and the civic-practical commentary; concluding with a vindication of compilation films over *cinéma vérité*.

The problematics of Leninism vs. liberty inspire some discreetly coded discourse about socialist society versus wild-animal nature; about reindeer races where the losers are merely the last to win; about film-makers who fear an unreliably tamed bear less than the policeman sent to protect them from it. It's not just the flashing thesis, it's the cogitative agility, the montage of surprising ideas, that construct it. This is one of the few political films whose semantics one can analyse forever.

In *Loin du Viêt-Nam* (1967), Marker will organise into one beautifully organic argument diverse and highly individual episodes by Resnais, Varda, Godard, Joris Ivens, Claude Lelouch and William Klein. Both the letter form (being personal and informal) and the political statement (being collective and pluriformal) share multi-perspectivism. Both allow conventionally separated, seemingly incompatible genres, moods, topics, tones, visions, thought-lattices, semantic-fields, to interlace or collide obliquely, to cross-check or interpenetrate. Marker watches his film's form break down, go mad, disintegrate into violence/silence, à la Bataille.

Marker rejoins Resnais with *La Jetée* (1962), a trapped-in-time-twist tale told in stills. The static forms, as conspicuous as they're expressive, become strangely transparent in this freeze-frame-like tragic-strip. Its post-World War III tortures reflect Cold War jitters less than latent Eurofascism …

10. William Klein, the Radical American

At the *chosiste* end of Klein's spectrum: *Broadway by Light* (1958) evokes his still photography genius. It starts as a suite of moving stills, strange or too-close or bled-off shots of neon signs, whose broken, enigmatic or non-meanings construct a schizo-paranoid, Martian-lizard landscape … (Klein, Resnais, Varda, Marker: all masterly still photographers).

At the fantasy-artificial end of Klein's spectrum, *Mister Freedom* (1968) is a live-action political cartoon. Its pastiche *film noir* (Eddie Constantine-style) becomes straight socialist polemic. Delphine Seyrig plays La France ("I'm only a whore in the service of capitalism"), torn between Mister Freedom, Moujik Man, Jacques Occident, Christ Man and Chairman Mao's China, who is acted by a long, floppy inflatable. All this transforms the language of political cartooning into serious metaphor, while the fine detail of dialogue, plot twist and décor allow precise and effective argument. Not so much a satirical fantasy, more a political scenario. Between the two, the torrent of terrifying faces and voices in demo and counter-demo in *Loin du Viêt-Nam*.

Postscript

Occasionally, Gorin–Godard emulate the Left Bank style: *Pravda* is their "Letter from Czechoslovakia", their best political travelogue; *Letter to Jane* is their 'road-menders' sequence'. But, by and large, aren't such 60s radicalisms the last gasps of socialist culture, garrotted by a bourgeois-academic theory-ocracy?

SOURCE: *MONTHLY FILM BULLETIN*, MAY 1987, 132–5

6.6 AIMING AT THE ARCHERS
[TRANSLATED BY YVONNE SALMON]

I. As the left turns, or, Gone with the (discreet) Wind of the bourgeoisie

While left-wing criticism has known its moments of terrorism, the bourgeois trend has ultimately prevailed. It has finally come to accept, more or less, the directors whose stars rose thanks to the influence of a transatlantic *nouvelle vague* and to *Cahiers* and Co. Sam Fuller's anti-red hysteria, Douglas Sirk's reformism via Technicolor-and-water, Howard Hawks's Nixonism (the sheriff and his men), Capra's petit-bourgeois populism and the paleo-capitalism of the young Roger Corman are not only tolerated but ignored. It is not just Détente, it is an Entente Cordiale – or Moral Disarmament. Here it is tempting to see nothing more than a semiotico-Jesuit strategy: the gloss converting the text, reducing it to raw material for the critical surtext which henceforth becomes its true meaning …

We therefore wish to maintain a certain ambivalence when the same logic appears at last to rehabilitate a too long despised English cinema. It is a matter of particular concern that Althusser's followers, who want to «depoliticise» Michael Powell, call Thorold Dickinson, his antithesis in the ideologico-genetic structure of English cinema, a «vicious» ideologue. The latter was the grey (or rather red) eminence of the ACTT in its heroic age; Powell boasts of never letting himself be unionised. Thus one purges one's fellow travellers in order to celebrate a likeable Tory, patriot and imperialist.

Our affection for Powell's work is left unscathed by this «confusionist» recuperation. But we must warn that the sometimes subtle ideological emblems of perfidious Albion may elude foreigners, especially thirty years on.

II. Le citoyen fantasque

1. The Life and Death of Colonel Blimp. In the political iconography of 1939–1945, Colonel Blimp (the invention of cartoonist David Low) symbolised an entire military, imperial, paternalist and oppressive class. It's the field marshal in *Oh! What A Lovely War*, it's Michael Hordern in *How I Won the War*. This was the closest to Marshal Pétain that England could offer. P & P (Powell and Pressburger) make him a Colonel Bramble or a Major Thompson

whose flaw would amount to an innocent loss of contact with social reality (a foretelling of P & P's own careers). This choice was the result of both box-office calculations and propagandist imperatives. Although it did not prevent the wrath of Churchill, who undoubtedly felt targeted, the film remains a political polemic intended to redeem, to the point of absolution, the establishment which was ultimately dismissed in the elections of 1945.

2. **A Matter of Life and Death** celebrates the Churchillian dream: a love match between the United States and the United Kingdom. The faded utopia from which our young poet-pilot must escape cannot fail to evoke the political controversy of the era. While it was the flippancy of a (French) aristocracy that led us here, a grey and dreary socialism threatens England under Labour rule. Ever the gentleman, Powell admits that socialism does not lead to the tyranny of *1984*; indeed he celebrates the «good Prussian» of the German tradition. But it is in the name of imagination, love and life that the film's hero fights the minimisation of man to which socialism, heir to utilitarianism via the Fabian movement, leads.

3. **The End of the River.** 1947. England is losing her economic hold over South America. Here we celebrate an imperialism on which the Conservatives and Labour could agree: without flag or army regiments, but still capitalist and paternalist. Sabu, the «good Indian» (child subject) of Korda's films, shows how these Indians, migrants from the interior, would be saved from ignorance and exploitation by the good graces of a *Sanders of the River*-style colonial administration. While it is acknowledged, albeit belatedly and in passing, that such things as «responsible» unions do exist, here a union both revolutionary and corrupt is singled out. In any case, wasn't it indigenous exploitation which drove the Indian from his village in the first place? The film is a celebration of «enlightened» and «English» employers.

4. **The Queen's Guards.** In the aftermath of Eden's Suez fiasco, Powell celebrates the efficacy of officers from the most snobbish English regiments when faced with the Arab world. At a time when films by Asquith, Cardiff, Val Guest and Leslie Norman were dealing with anguished questions of military ethics, Powell recounts how the youngest son of a military family manages to exonerate his older brother from a shameful accusation (that he had allegedly killed an unarmed prisoner).

5. **They're a Weird Mob.** This McCarey-esque comedy celebrates a Tory vision of Australia, the land of open, virile and joyous capitalism. An Italian journalist cheerfully accepts his temporary demotion to the world of manual labour. As in the work of Vidor, another poet of manual labour, racism and the class system quickly surrender to the strong, likeable and well-adapted pauper.

6. **Sebastian.** It's James Bond on Carnaby Street.
We don't hold a grudge against Powell for being a man of the right. We like him all the more since he does not conceal it. He is neither a high priest of tradition (which he respects), nor a «business is business» fanatic. And all these «ideological» films include other themes. *Black Narcissus* is *The Nun Who Would Be Queen* (and behind Powell, there is always Kipling, although Powell softens both his sense of mission and his Puritan self-criticism). *They're a Weird Mob* celebrates a bourgeoisie both enterprising and human, close to that celebrated by Pasolini in his «Trilogy of Life», but without meanness. This is the best of all worlds, today.

The Essential Raymond Durgnat

III. Alice in red shoes-land

In *A Mirror for England* I classed Powell as a romantic whose Achilles heel was a lack of conviction. I should rather have spoken of particular films as romantic, in the sense that they aimed at the supposed romanticism of the middlebrow public. It is a romanticism which knows how far to go too far. Powell gently but firmly rejected the «nostalgia» for the demonic which I attributed to him (based on his Austro-German officers, *The Red Shoes*, *Hoffmann* and *Tom*).

While romantics are often uncomfortable with themselves, that is to say, in their own society, Powell is very much at ease. His is a well-balanced romanticism, at once romantic and pragmatic. The highly unusual mix of calculation and impartiality which shocked critics and paralysed audiences of *Peeping Tom* in fact came from a serenity, a tolerance, a quiet curiosity. Powell speaks of the film as though he let himself be seduced, naively, by the crypto-structural ingenuity of Leo Marks's screenplay; perhaps he underestimated the need for indignation which Hitchcock satisfied in *Psycho*. While Powell realised the structuralist agenda before its time, he also achieved a de-moralisation more complete than even the partisans of degree zero thought could have imagined.

But Powell achieved this by a different route: through the prosaicism of fairytales as believed in by children (and not as analysed by Proppists).

English critics had already spoken of a «morbidity» in *The Red Shoes*, with its emphasis on the bloody feet of the ballerina after her suicide. But the production team had only realised Andersen's anti-sentimentality (as had Renoir). Hein Heckroth is said to have asked several children what they would like to see if the story were filmed, and they all replied «When they cut off her feet.» In fact, a compromise was reached between fidelity and good taste: the executioner is transformed into a steam locomotive. But there was enough blood to satisfy the child in every adult.

When I attributed a Viennese gaiety to Pressburger, Powell replied, choosing his words carefully: «I think our films were fantasy on the part of Emeric, taken seriously by me.» But this might be the seriousness with which we are supposed to tell fairytales to children, the seriousness already found in *The Thief of Bagdad*, the artistic orientation of which Powell

The Red Shoes (1948)

attributes to its scenarist Miles Malleson. Pressburger, with the freshness that comes from exile, may have provided him with less clichéd, less generic and more serpentine fantasies.

Is Powell's «Daemon» the benign demon of cinema? He acknowledged seeing everything in terms of cinematic potential. But if Mark, the Peeping Tom, is the Caliban of this obsession, Powell would be the Ariel. Cinema is not his red shoes, but his flying carpet. He loves to play with special effects, like Renoir in his Vieux-Colombier phase. He is a «bricoleur» de luxe. While he can sometimes evoke Gance, in that he has a stop-at-nothing cinematic scope, Gance's monumental lyricism is foreign to him, and he has an un-Gancian sense of humour. Likewise, Hitchcock's infinitesimal (and transcendental!) calculations elude him. Sometimes he manages to synthesise both of their spirits, sometimes he falls between two stools. His professional virtuosity supports his imagination «to the letter», or rather «to the eye». Where the average film-maker would step back, on the grounds that the spectacular alone should hold the viewer in a trance, Powell rushes in, calmly, with a certainty as to how to «craft» the thing. And this crafting is as much psychological as technical and formal.

It is this spirit of poetic craft which renders Powell more similar to Hitchcock than to Gance. However, it is sometimes evident that Powell lacks Hitchcock's middle-class background, the class that best represents the «convergence» of public tastes. Powell has a more affluent, more cosmopolitan background. Hence his fate as a cinéaste «maudit».

IV. A trajectory which fizzles out

1. Powell began with ten years of intelligent routine work. One notes in particular *The Edge of the World*, a Flaherty-esque (and sometimes Epsteinian) documentary, which nevertheless renounces neither fiction nor optical phantoms. The mix of genres and complex scenes already demonstrates his strength, together with a gift for the «inner avant-gardism» which he shares with Hitchcock, Asquith and Grierson–Cavalcanti. Like them, Powell designed effects which are really (and not merely conceptually) evocative, and which do not interfere with narrative economy.

2. The collective effort of the «People's War» led Powell, hand in hand with Pressburger, to the pinnacle of public favour. Ian Christie's dossier of official criticism from the time, while very interesting, might lead us to underestimate the prestige – diffuse, but decisive in terms of creative freedom – that Powell derived from the trilogy of national self-criticism that comprises *Blimp*, *A Canterbury Tale* and *A Matter of Life and Death*.

3. After the war: doubt. *The Small Back Room* and *Black Narcissus*, a diptych on the psychopathology of English «teams» (scientists on one side, nuns on the other), explore the national effort towards domestic recovery, concurrent with imperial retreat. The former film gives us an intense, intimate drama: a complex realism, bordering on expressionism. The latter offers a subtle, exotic, ethereal drama bordering on decorative mysticism, that is to say the crisis of the subject.

4. With *The Red Shoes* P & P pursue the second option. A choice which proved fatal in the long run. Doubtless they were influenced by Rank's triumph with *Brief Encounter* in the «cultured» American market, which Hollywood had left hungry. But their rather fragile romanticism turns into escapism (which must be distinguished from the aestheticism of *The Tales of Hoffmann*).

There were high hopes for the new alliance between P & P and Korda. But the 1930s impresario had little sense of the more intimate and contemporary subjects which Ealing, Hollywood and Rank were able to offer a now more advanced public. Along with Goldwyn and Selznick, who also lost their footing, P & P were led into an obsolete romanticism which they knew how to illustrate but not how to resuscitate: Baroness Orczy for *The Elusive Pimpernel*, Mary Webb for *Gone to Earth*.

5. Rather like Renoir, in the uncertainty of 1947 Powell set his sights on another culture. He hoped to found a consortium with a few painters (Picasso, Graham Sutherland) and poets (Dylan Thomas). Spectacular aestheticism would have most probably prevailed over illusion. But the career that follows is an uncertain one. The beautiful traditional fresco of *The Battle of the River Plate* succeeds at passing, without anticlimax, from naval battle to diplomatic intrigue. *Peeping Tom* sank a career in which commercial successes, always rather patchy, had become few and far between. Moreover, the English film industry no longer looked to American art-houses. So it was exile: the theatre (whose artistic problems greatly interested Powell), Australia and TV.

One might see Siberia from here ... I see a certain ambivalence rather than a curse; I think that Powell was equally happy to amuse himself, be active, or do nothing. Although the thought of movies obsessed him, the red shoes did not drag him to the studio-cosmopolitanism of the Hollywood of the time. Even if he was the exotic bird of a grey cinema, he was also too English to want to Americanise himself.

V. The auteurist thread in the tapestry

Is the main thrust of the Powell psychodrama the reconciliation of son and father (which here includes the elder brother)? Even when the father is stupid or evil, he remains a hot-tempered child. Sometimes the father figures are multiple and spread out (which weakens, rather than strengthens, the patriarchal theme). The paternal network is complex. Colonel Blimp is a prodigal father to the younger English generation; but Blimp himself has a father-brother, his fiercer and more logical alter ego: the Austro-German officer played by Anton Walbrook. For the English pilot in *A Matter of Life and Death*, the father is the brain surgeon; for both the pilot and surgeon the father is the heavenly judge with Old Testament Hebrew traits; and for the American prosecutor the father is England in the age of the American Revolution (which he believes to be unchanged). If Blimp must renew himself under the iron rule of the son, Peeping Tom never escapes the paternal bosom. He watches «the mother», and kills her, in her many forms, but without feeling any emotion towards her. His crimes are impersonal and obsessive, passionless and pitiless. The captain of the Graf Spee commits suicide («Oh, that was right, dad, that was brave»). Yet the wicked Caliph of Baghdad is forgiven nothing.

This generally harmonious arrangement is duplicated on the social plane. It is Tory, but without rancour. Without being capitalist or traditionalist, it bets on the regeneration of the upper-middle class. This optimism extends to nature, whose barbarism can be taken in small doses (the Celtic fringe transforms the capitalist Wendy Hiller in *I Know Where I'm Going*). The most dangerous social realm is inner space. Blimp, Peeping Tom and Sammy Rice go astray in a half-willed, half-inflicted solitude. At the same time, Powell reveres eccentricity. Sometimes in «uncles», often in women, we find signs of androgyny (but without the guilt and sadism which Hitchcock attributes to «filial» transvestism).

Powell's social perspective is that of the individual shared (without being torn) between the imagination and the team. The hero is «engaged», but any anxiety or Sartrean questioning is absent, since the object of his engagement is the team of friends. And where Sartre directs his inquisition against romantic and bien-pensant minds, sparing only criminals (Genet), Powell the «technologist» is the senile father who likes to cultivate the childlike imagination.

VI. The boy who turned Technicolor

On three occasions Renoir dedicated himself to the «little theatre». The Grand Theatre of Michael Powell offers us variety, elaboration, luxurious and bizarre virtuosity in the same vein. For both of them, realism is achieved by means of special effects. Which does not mean that realism is just a special effect like any other.

However, Powell plays out only very English scenes, as though to form a «binary opposition» to Renoir's novel *Les Cahiers du Capitaine Georges*. Unlike Capitaine Georges, Blimp wins his beloved, and there is no nostalgic yearning for prostitutes. Powell's fetishes would instead be red hair and piercing eyes, in short, the Celtic woman.

The English, who adroitly conceal their tensions behind mists of compromise, fascinated Renoir. *La Règle du Jeu* could be perfectly transposed to the English landed gentry (although it is a working upper class, less well-defined than the French aristocracy). It was to make an insidious example of him that the heavenly messenger of *A Matter of Life and Death* is a French aristocrat who lost his head in the Revolution of 1789. Renoir's title itself aptly encapsulates the strengths and weaknesses of a cinema of which Powell would be the brilliant and fragile crystallisation. It is the acceptance of the *règles* and the *jeu* − life as a cricket match − which makes British cinema a Laodicean cinema, neither passionate nor cold, neither romantic nor cynical, neither … nor … [*]

If team spirit can undermine the «austerity» of English film-makers, it can also bestow upon them chameleon-like interests. Powell is a chameleon who knows how to invent new combinations. To the hybridism of *The Edge of the World* we can add that of *The Small Back Room*, a realist-expressionist *film noir* on the «stiff upper lip». He goes from the fantasy trompe-l'œil of *The Thief of Bagdad* to the anti-illusionist fantasies of filmed ballet, recalling the spectacular aesthetics of Méliès, Dziga-Vertov, Busby Berkeley, the American musical and Jerry Lewis's *The Ladies' Man*. *Bluebeard's Castle* has a crystalline fluidity whose simplicity is gently brutal. In *The Tales of Hoffmann*, whose diversity of cinematic styles brings «centrifugal» treasures, he achieves the symbiosis of an overloaded set with staccato montage, and explores the many and varied dialectics of the illusion-spectacle with the casual mastery of a private joke.

Sometimes Powell evokes that other chameleon, Laurence Olivier. Speaking of the satisfactions of acting, Olivier said that the most delicious moment is when one moves the audience while feeling absolutely nothing oneself. Powell's boldness is «semiotic» in the sense that for him the content is a pretext for the spectacle. But to pick out a «deconstruction» would merely produce a tautology; Powell knows, and says, what he means. Such an analysis of the mechanism would be unnecessary since its parts have never ceased to be visible. Powell gives us a striking proof of what Brecht seems never to have understood:

---

[*] Hence the sarcastic remarks of the young Truffaut, whose subsequent films reproduced everything which he criticised in English cinema. His themes are fear of a passion which we no longer know how to depict, a moralism which preaches prudence, and adorable children. If *La Nuit Américaine* lives, it is because it deals with team spirit and stoicism. It is a film very much in the Ealing style (*The Cruel Screen!*?) where Truffaut himself replaces Jack Hawkins as captain of the «ship».

The Essential Raymond Durgnat

that the bourgeois aesthetic is no victim of illusionism, but is instead an aesthetic which rightly considers that every new idea or vision should cause a «Verfremdungseffekt».

At the same time the spectacle needs signification (a pure spectacle would be a signifier without a signified, i.e., in-significant). Speaking of the speech in *Blimp* in which Walbrook attributes Nazism to the frustration of unemployed officers, Powell observed: «It was a beautiful chess move by Emeric, of which I was never really convinced.» Which is to say that Powell does not confuse rhetorical tricks with reality. And if sometimes he loves a trick without a direct link to a familiar context, one must take into account the gap between Powell's cultural background and that of the mainstream cinema audience.

The opening of *A Matter of Life and Death* pans across the cosmos (already a charming «alienation effect»). A very calm voiceover speaks directly to the viewer. A blazing star: «Someone must have been messing about with the uranium atom again … ». Finally, we find ourselves close to our sun: «Reassuring, isn't it?» This coolly ironic voice, like that of an angel-father, knows us well. The play of alienation and disalienation is rather complex. There is no need to disalienate ourselves from the scariness of endless and infinite spaces. But to think of them is already to have them in our heads.[*] Since man is only relative to the universe, the universe is only relative to man. Humour is pragmatism's insolent response to the absolutism of objectivity. And this «relativity» orders the film. If the heavenly messenger is heralded by the smell of fried onions, it is only to ground him in concrete reality: the absolute must submit to its scale. «Relativity» also inspires a heterogeneity of terms (a tear, a rose, historical debate, scalpels, etc.). The symbolism is more poetically accurate than one would think at first glance. If the stairway to heaven is an escalator, it is because automation evokes an impersonal mechanism, that is to say historical inevitability − which is not a Marxist monopoly; the English had anticipated the decline of their empire from the moment of its inception. (From Kipling comes another theme of heavenly debate: was it possible that the English had lost the moral seriousness which defined their way of life?) The tear on the rose, the sentimentality of which was so criticised, is placed alongside the scalpels of the team of surgeons. When the intended surgeon is killed in a motorcycle accident, it is not a question of the hands of fate, or some other metaphysical pessimo-paranoia. The dead man is replaced by another team which is more or less as competent, and he continues the struggle in the afterlife.[**]

John Ellis wants to eliminate all references to reality in the film, to see only reflection on (or by) the spectacle. But these references are part of the drama and suspense, and so part of the spectacle itself. In arguing that Powell sought to short-circuit all consideration of content in the mind of his public (i.e. market), Ellis himself eliminates not just the public life of the artist, but also precisely those socio-economic systems which Marx considered so important. Being elitist, Marxists of this kind want to suppress the masses and dethrone the text in the name of the-artist-for-art's-sake! The new criticism would like to isolate, in order

[*] The universe is merely a balloon, since space is curved. Coincidentally, the autobiography of David Niven, the film's star, is titled *The Moon's a Balloon*.

[**] We can identify a very eclectic and perhaps not accidental symbolism. Towards the start of the film the English surgeon amuses himself racing an American jeep on a country road. He wins, but flirts with disaster. Later the English ambulance is delayed because the phone is cut off. The surgeon goes to find the ambulance − and crashes straight into it. It is a cross-dissolve of ideas (a winding plot typical of P & P). Speed + jeep/speed + ambulance: Anglo-American rivalry, English «muddle» … According to dream logic, this is indeed a «défi américain» to the heart of England, albeit disguised as English deficiency, and a mundane kind of deficiency at that − not something that one could reasonably be blamed for.

to strengthen, certain trends which it believes to be zeroising, whitening, deconstructive, etc. But, once isolated, these trends can only function in a vacuum, being deprived of the material which allows them to function, and to be observed while functioning.

However, «bourgeois» cinema has never ceased to count on the scepticism which underpinned Coleridge's insistence (c. 1800) on «the willing suspension of disbelief». Since the viewer only very rarely forgets that this is a spectacle, alienation is a constant. And realism can only be a mental phenomenon of which trompe-l'œil (cinematographic or otherwise) is only a tertiary cause. Besides, the form/content relationship does not resemble the signifier/signified relationship according to Saussure, but instead resembles the dialectic between two texts, one of them on screen, the other in the mind. This would explain, without mystifying difficulty, both perpetual misunderstanding (Eco) and perverse pleasure (Barthes). For the utterance, albeit attributed to a text, only seems to reside there thanks to the collaboration of the viewer, that is to say by mental projection (Morin). These are the commonplaces of bourgeois praxis, whose flexibility affirms the «thousand flowers» of modernism. And this diversity gives Powell's cinema, with its formal daring and dramatic sparsity, the air of a schizo-machine. While he never exaggerates (hence the terrible serenity of *Bluebeard's Castle*), sometimes he plays a game whose triviality is sickening (*Honeymoon*). For our part, even when we cry with one eye about the excessive sparsity of material, the boldness of this sparsity can achieve a rather pleasing freshness.

VII. Symbolist cinema

In practice it is never easy to separate self-reflexivity, spectacle, art-for-art's-sake, decadence, aestheticism, Symbolism and theories of art as the free play of the imagination. Powell is the perfect technician, «illuminated» by poetry and addicted to aesthetic Symbolism. The spectacle reveals itself as such, but the glamour of this virtuosity quickly spreads to thought, which becomes yet more contagious. With Powell, the obviousness of the spectacle enhances the imagination-for-imagination's-sake.

Thus, spectacle and reality only separate in order to revalue one another. The poet backs the pilot, the aesthete backs the patriot. So we accept political engagement with neither Sartrean disgust nor the enthusiasm of the poet-soldier Rupert Brooke («Now God be thanked Who has matched us with His hour»).

But Powell would perhaps say that *Marienbad* lacks the smell of fried onions.

The major differences between the imaginary and the real (between thought and skull) are symbolised by the brain surgeon's camera obscura. He is removed from the village, all the better to spy on it, and to spy with a paternal and poetic love so terribly lacking in the technician Peeping Tom. But if the two worlds only separate so as to rejoin, they must at the same time engage in adversarial debate. We find the same dialectical heterogeneity when the poet-pilot's friends struggle with him against his private Thanatos, giving his imagination all available means: tears, scalpels, historical evidence, legal-metaphysical arguments, etc.

Powell represents a current of English thought which may seem too pragmatic to be philosophical. But since this mode of thought begins by rejecting both Cartesian definitionism and Kant's separation of realms, it quite naturally achieves the functional equivalent of a dialectic. Hume's scepticism makes possible a «transferability of effects» which hierarchical binarism prevents, and which is formulated not in terms of a synthesis of action/response, but instead in terms of a compromise between multiple heterogeneous

The Essential Raymond Durgnat

factors.* Here can be seen the influence of Britain's «laissez-faire» social history, just as the coming unification of Germany was the secret paradigm of Hegel, and French bureaucratic systematisation is for Cartesianism.

Powell's philosopher would be A. N. Whitehead, or perhaps F. H. Bradley, the English Hegelian who preceded him. Powell's eccentricity lies in turning his attention to the «breaks» and «levels» of European schematicism, «pixilating» them as if for fun. And let us not forget Pressburger, from whose country came the logical positivism which is so closely tied to English empiricism and American pragmatism. The triumph of this anti-metaphysical current coincides with the metaphysics of *A Matter of Life and Death*. Here Powell–Pressburger are at play, just as the logical positivists love to quote *Alice in Wonderland*.

VIII. The man with laser eyes

Black Narcissus «blocks» Bresson in the same way that *Peeping Tom* overtakes Lévi-Strauss. But Powell also frees himself of anything that renders English cinema opaque to foreign eyes (and to young English intellectuals). His work displays some basic principles which are generally blurred by conventions (which, incidentally, are merely the principles of a certain social praxis). The tepidity, greyness and even the «anti-auteur» astylisation of a certain British cinema, come from the consciousness that these social conventions, albeit absurd for the individual, are also categorical imperatives, upon which the society which moulds this individual depends. One submits to it with a stoic but ambivalent determination. This cinema is more Sartrean than it may seem, although the antisocial and nauseating solitude (just like Pascalian terror) is assuaged once the critical spirit is softened by team spirit. Too often, this critical spirit is suppressed altogether; but the instability of the synthesis resurfaces from time to time.

One can only imagine Powell's take on Kipling's *The Man Who Would Be King*. If Powell reveres Kipling, it is perhaps because he recognised a spirituo-patriotic «commitment» all the more arduous for containing an internal antithesis: Puritan self-criticism. Powell goes as far as dissociations, without emphasising contradictions whose interplay makes Orwell in Burma the «guilty conscience» of Kipling in Afghanistan (or of Rumer Godden in Tibet).

It is understandable that on one hand Kenneth Anger and Martin Scorsese (whose social realism does not preclude aesthetic and dramatic interest), and on the other the self-reflexive «aliénistes» of Brechto-Althusserianism, find themselves in accord over Powell by detaching him from his social context. But just as we would do a disservice to the fecundity of Hollywood if Sirk were favoured to the detriment of the many other directors of critical dramas, we would likewise impoverish Powell, and the workings of his spectacle, if we also denied the presence of this emotional and ideological «greyness» onto which he projects his Technicolor fairytales. His thinking fascinates because of the juxtaposition of cloud and crystal, dissociations and slippages.

---

* The dominant continental philosophical traditions (hermeneutics, dialectics, rationalisms and structuralisms), as opposed to Anglo-Saxon, or more precisely Anglo-Austrian empiricisms, share a tendency to separate the world into discrete facts and compartmentalized disciplines.

But Powell's «baroque» heterogeneity signals the opposite trend: in his work, segregation is so obvious that it actually facilitates the reintegration of the semi-autonomous disciplines which grand systems prevent by their rigidity. As a technician, Powell borrows the bricoleur-and-bisociation aspect (as Koestler put it) of scientific research and laboratory work, where it is normal to move from one system to another.

IX. The camera obscura of Dr Powell

As Renoir père would have advised, Powell follows the currents of this collective thinking as overdetermined by the whole English dia-synchronic structure. If it had (only just) avoided civil war between 1780 and 1945, stability came at the cost of personal emotions. A nation of «centrist» compromise is also a frustrated nation; it represses individual aggression, whose availability in American ideology makes the latter so accessible.

Hence, ultimately, the fate of the quartet which promised so much in 1945: Powell, Lean, Reed, Dickinson. Lean quickly became a fastidious (and ostentatious) painter of clouds, which are to him what the mesas of Monument Valley are for John Ford (a formulation which would reopen the Lean case: à bas *The Quiet Man*, vive *Ryan's Daughter*?). If Reed was the leader of English *film noir*, his «sincere» pessimism ultimately corroded his style. Before going into exile Dickinson made two films whose biting morality was hardly «English». And Powell's optimistic, frivolous and crystalline cinema also became a victim of this 1950s crisis of the subject, which hit the cinema of a nation doomed to stagnation particularly hard.

This work, whose weaknesses never bore us, includes some exemplary moments where the dialectic between spectacle and content generates a rich and strange synthesis.

1. The Life and Death of Colonel Blimp.

«Citizen Kane versus Colonel Blimp». – This is the English «establishment» criticising itself, as *Citizen Kane* criticises American progressivism and *Ivan the Terrible* criticises Stalinism. This was the era of self-examination, using flashbacks narrated from the present with all-pervasive amnesia, and a restrained yet fatalist expressionism. Powell surprised with a colourful, jolly, pleasant film, full of changes in subject, tone and dramatic perspective.

«Colonel Blimp's Private Joke». – Each of the soldiers is carefully named (already a tribute to the common people) as they prepare themselves for the manoeuvres which will humiliate and awaken Blimp. Among these names, some evoke the names of the film crew which appear on the credits. This self-reflexive osmosis, bringing the shooting of the film into the film, suggests social transformation, an opening to democracy and a weakening of the auteur-Führer principle.

«The Death in the Kaleidoscope». – If we don't recognise in *Blimp* a virtuosity equal to that of *Kane*, it is because its de-structuring of tone, time and methodology, though more flexible, is less consistent. When the Blitz kills Blimp's faithful batman, his death is presented as follows: (1) A flash, sketched comic-strip style. (2) A black screen, noise. (3) The announcement in *The Times*, inserted by Blimp. (4) The Home Guard still going through the debris.

The semiotic alienation of (1) contrasts with the Bressonian subjectivism (both blind and noisy) of (2); the closure apparent in (3) precedes a return to a more realist trope which is nevertheless brutally and elliptically elegiac.

2. A Canterbury Tale.

«An Episcopalian Romanticism». – The English feared that the demands of total war would eventually threaten their identity (where does moral repugnance end, where does the fear of a democratic «detraditionalisation» begin?). This is a constant theme for Humphrey Jennings, and one which Powell transposes into fiction.

A falcon soars from a medieval hand, and the cut transforms it into a Spitfire. Twentieth-century people come to Canterbury without knowing that they are pilgrims. But the good Anglican God (neither Puritan, nor Catholic, and therefore eclectic enough to bless the entirety of a rather pagan Commonwealth) nevertheless gives to each the modest miracles which were all that one could dare wish for within the limits of English propriety. The cinema organist (!) in a conscript's uniform plays 'Onward Christian Soldiers' on the Cathedral's grand organ. The squire, tied to the past, pours glue into the hair of English women who go out with the «Yanks» instead of going to his magic lantern screenings (a motionless pre-cinema). The taste for paradox derives from a Heraclitean ideology: everything turns into everything else. The transformations are expressed via a screenplay whose twists and turns and juxtapositions astonished even Chris Wicking, the new champion of the «poorly constructed» screenplay, forty years later.

From the patriotic and pre-neo-realist documentary of the time, P & P borrow only what it takes to «naturalise» a symbolic thought. The masses turned their noses up at a film which is perhaps too bourgeois, too «nice», too «reasonably» mystical. Also, perhaps, the English working class was neglected (while they took centre stage in *Waterloo Road* and *Millions Like Us*, among other films). P & P too plainly favoured the Yanks, who were in reality too rich, too predatory and too close to English women parted from English soldiers.

3. A Matter of Life and Death.
«An Orpheus Without a Princess». – *A Matter of Life and Death*, or *Les Jeux Sont Faits* for a nation which has known neither civil war nor defeat. America was also doing some soul-searching of its own, by means of heavenly judgments – *Heaven Can Wait* for hedonism, *Where Do We Go From Here?* by *The Skin of Our Teeth* – and, later, *It's A Wonderful Life*, the most troubled of them all.

It's a cinema of symbols, film «blanc» (or rose-pink) versus «realist» *film noir*. While Jennings cites Shakespeare in *Words for Battle*, Powell's poet-pilot leads the debate *after* the battle. The *jeux* are never *faits*. Everything and anything is used to sabotage the stairway of destiny: tears, roses, ping-pong balls, radio broadcasts brought to us by a dead friend, hippos, accordions, Cleopatra's noses …[*] It's not as frivolous as all that. It reflects the precariousness of the summer of 1940 (and P & P have a fine ear for the connotative repercussions of the poetic symbols they want to incorporate as narrative aids).

England has to defend herself before two successive juries, the first drawn from the races it has colonised, the second from those same races blessed with American citizenship. At the time none of this seemed «serious», it was all light-hearted. But the Third World was already judging the First (following the precedent of Kipling in *Gunga Din*, of course).

To the prophetic logic of the New Testament, Spengler and Marx, we oppose casuistic suspense and the gamble, that is to say history experienced pragmatically, as drama. We hope, we play the game of life and of death, we reel off the words which l'élan vital whispers to us … If everything is unreal, nothing is …

4. The Small Back Room.
«The Small Black Room». – The other dark room where black and dark grey become colours …

5. Black Narcissus.
Michael Walker noted our use of the term «melodrama» in respect of *Black Narcissus*. The

---

[*] «Oh time, stop your racket …» But be careful: eternity is the antechamber of death. P & P inhabit a Bergsonian universe; we ignore mechanical time (tradition, digression, achronology, a contemplative awareness of duration, cyclical structures) to honour instead a duration which can only be human if one resists frivolous pursuits, solitudes and absolutism, in favour of friendly engagement.

young critics expand the meaning this word at the expense of «drama» (initially to avoid the Hollywood terms «soap opera» and «women's picture»). We define as «melodrama» any drama in which the psycho-dramatic action is rather heavy handed, and which includes shocking scenes (murder, etc.). Although *Black Narcissus* culminates in melodrama, we do not deny that the sparsity of the drama opens up into a melancholic, meditative lyricism. It is not that far from the philosophical drama of Renoir's *The River*, adapted from the same novelist, Rumer Godden. But we think rather of David Lean (it is a slow film, airy, told with white, passive, determined female faces …). We can also think of Bresson (restraint, secrets, modesty, detachment), but a Bresson in Technicolor, lost amid the Sternbergian décor. This formalism, at the same time finely honed and brightly coloured, recalls that of Murnau and Lang, but does not mimic them in the least. The most casual details are precise and complex: the mule between David Farrar's manly legs, while rendering him ridiculous, reveals the animal-in-the-man: wilful, insolent, sincere. The exotic prince (Sabu) finds the perfume which gives the film its title … in an Army and Navy Stores shop in London. We underestimated this film in its time, when it suffered from its proximity to a glut of coldly romantic subjects. It is now recognised as an example to follow. P & P coupled a sense of spectacle with a philosophical poetry: the traditional recipe of «little theatre» cinema (for example, Bergman's *The Magic Flute*). We can believe neither in the film, nor in its beliefs; but from its schematicism springs a *vital* naivety…

6. The Tales of Hoffmann.

«Le Sang d'un Cinéaste» (here we recall Cocteau …). *The Tales of Hoffmann* is a film of modest budget whose sets suggest a blockbuster. It is a triumph of literalism over realism. One recalls the plastic stormy seas of *Fellini-Casanova* (and Casanova ends up becoming the Colonel Blimp of eroticism …). It is a Chinese box of a spectacle. When Hoffmann sings the story of Kleinzach the hunchback, we discover him among the figurines adorning Bavarian beer mugs. But while the figure «should» be a puppet, P & P use «live action»; and when Kleinzach leaves the mug, we see its exterior clearly, the dents corresponding to the shape of his back. It is a «literal» and not «realist» detail, which mesmerises us by revealing a «coherence» *within* the spectacle and the intelligence *behind* it. It is an anti-vitalist dissociation; but one must be Heraclitean and see the «separations» which the film likes to deploy, only to violate them straight away. Likewise, heavily baroque sets rub shoulders with slick parquet floors, unadorned and very much of the studio. It is not merely a concession to the dancers; rather, these are the contradictions which reveal the spectacle as such. In opera, as in fairytales, illusion couples with the viewer, who ceases to be a mere voyeur because his heart is made complicit. In this «Gesamtkunstwerk» the supposed illusionism of «photo-cinéma», heightened by the ballet interposed therein, submits to the rule of opera, the *beau-monstre*.

We are not surprised that Anger shows such admiration for Powell; *Hoffmann* is *The Collapse of the Pleasure Dome*, it's *Gondola Rising*. It is an anti-Bazinian cinema, Kracauerian-despite-Kracauer, a dream built out of interpenetrating spectacles, a lucid dream in which we remain asleep just for the pleasure of dreaming. It is pure cinema, an anti-literary cinema, of which we can recall nothing once we have left the screening room, and which we can only talk about by re-viewing the images on an analytical projector – in anticipation of the videotape …

SOURCE: *POSITIF*, NO. 239, FEBRUARY 1981, 22–33, INCORPORATING REVISIONS FROM ITS REPRINTING IN ROLAND COSANDEY (ED.), *RÉTROSPECTIVE POWELL & PRESSBURGER* (LOCARNO: EDITIONS DU FESTIVAL, 1982), 66–83

The Essential Raymond Durgnat

6.7 THE PREWAR Bs: REWARDS AND FAIRIES

1. The Electrical Everyday

An out-of-work car salesman sets about cutting his landlady's tablecloth into a boiler-suit for a ragged Cockney urchin. Standing the little boy on the table, he drapes the rough-cut around his shoulders. Gracefully flowing, it leaves one shoulder, and a patch of bottom, bare. The boy has "become" a Diaghilev faun. (*Something Always Happens*, 1934.)

Misled by *The Phantom Light* (1935), a ship heads for hidden rocks. In slow-cranked shots, strenuously rowed lifeboats lunge towards it. Meanwhile, the ship's "sparks" hands a message to the cabin-boy, who strolls with it to the captain, who takes it, opens it, and reads it, and silently ponders the choice: between the officially sanctioned light, or the mysterious wireless warning. Powell's style emphasizes, enjoys, the measured masculine movements, the boy cheeking the sparks but waiting on the awesome, kindly, preoccupied skipper. Enclosed in wet black oilskins in night space, the men's faces *beam*. It's pure Kipling: hierarchy, duty, decision, *inner* light.

Such "transfigurations" of workaday worlds into *inner* romanticism key my fascination with Powell's prewar Bs. The faun stance (an auteurial "quote," presumably unrecognized by the characters) emblemizes free spirit coexisting with commerce. The ship's crew glow with nonalienated, though strictly capitalist-hierarchical, relations. Diaghilev, Kipling: same difference – art and navigation, equal enterprises of the spirit ....

Because Powell's Romanticism is adventurous, it's not subversive. Because it's versatile, it's not escapist. He relished headline realities. *Red Ensign* (1934) discusses undercapitalization in family firms, recommends quasi-Keynesian investment plus Imperial Preference (protectionist quotas), to kick-start Britain out of slump into competitiveness, and champions financial dealings so shady our hero gets six months' jail. The motor-car salesman is bored with mere capitalism ("selling things I haven't got to people who don't want them"), but he keeps his hawkish wits sharp by charming and tricking everyone, from waiters to widows. What finally fires his enthusiasm is the sighting of the roadhouses along the new "arterial roads": i.e., the new consumerism. In a boardroom *coup* he unseats his father-in-law-to-be – who takes it with a businessman's tolerance.

Powell's romanticism invokes Apollo, not Dionysius; it's passion, but *une passion disciplinée*, practical, icily resolute. The salesman's jack-of-all-trades tailoring job conjures forth the faun. Respect, not emotion, rules the cargo ship.

Kipling and Diaghilev were spiritual godfathers to many of Powell's generation and background (Georgian gentleman-farmer/county-town lesser-Establishment/Empire-building stock). The B films brood, by plot or by eye, on changing roles for that class ethos, as "the vortex of commerce" engulfs the declining gentry, shakes up business/family/money relations, spreads U.S. ideas. Powell's gentleman-farmer – and military – eye for the human, especially male, figure, and its stances in spaces, is the kernel, or constant, of his kaleidoscope of styles.

2. Everything Old is New Again

My second interest in the prewar Bs may, alas, be limited to a highly exclusive, and steadily shrinking, club: Englishmen of a certain age, whose memories of the Thirties these flicks refresh. But it's not just nostalgia, for they're *witness*, to "The Way We Live Now" as it then was. Powell's gimlet eye, tight rhythms, and delight in digression inspire vignettes, *temps-morts*, and trivia to speak volumes in a flash. The era's accepted classics (Hitchcock, documentary …) tend to moralism, social or ethical, of which Powell's "goldsmith's chain" of cameos are bracingly free.

Crown v. Stevens (1936), a Simenon-type murder tale, dwells on the servitudes and grandeurs of the shopkeeping trade. Cockney warehousemen switch between informal discipline ("Oi oi oi, less lip and more work from you, young lamp-post!") and jokey salutations imputing hierarchy to mates ("'appy days to Your Worship!"). Our hero's girlfriend opens her own dress shop (conspicuous Thirties things, often woman-owned); at closing time she's keen to get away, and coax some self-confidence into her painfully shy young man; but a rich, fussy old lady pins her down to selling. The sharp clash of mental *rhythms* stresses impatience disciplined vs. touchy insensitivity, independence offering servile attention. Two squanderbug wives have a nice cozy chat about extracting money from their mere hubbies, and needle each other in sugary tones; their Marcel-waved hair and artificial silk blouses and ornaments glisten and ripple with delectable energy. In a chemist's shop, a lady customer whispers her order in the assistant's ear – a risqué, though censorproof, touch.

The Stevenses' maid is a grotesque: humpbacked with undernourished humility, lanky lips all over the place, nerves furiously a-twitch with inhibited initiative and defensive stupidity. Thirties Bs made domestic servants comic; Powell's acid and patrician eye broods over a half-stunted, half-defiant class. *Her Last Affaire* (1935) features a sharply observant maid (Googie Withers, the Boadicea of British film, and a fit sparring-partner for Joan Crawford). What the nob 'tecs need to know, she doesn't say, till asked; the effect is of fine, proud, devastating indifference.

Our ambitious young hero, to clear his father's name and so unblock his own career, blackmails a Cabinet Minister's faithless wife; the shock gives her a fatal heart attack. Finally, her stern but long-suffering husband persuades the young man to let the whole sordid story stay hushed up. Which brings out – and unsentimentally – the logic, forbearance, and humility in oldfashioned, upperclass, "patriarchal" codes of honor. It's more understanding, therefore interesting, than retro-exposés of "Establishment hypocrisy" like *White Mischief.* For "the past is a foreign country, they do things differently there." Most retro-radical denunciations of WASP "roots" are as grossly moralistic as missionary denunciations of twisted heathen ways. This film says it for today's students' great-grandparents. The Thirties "classic", i.e. "advanced," plays don't (why not is another essay); so this stagey old fossil, complete with creaky melodrama, cheapo sets, and odd bursts of Powell style, has its place in art as witness.

3. The Once and Future Powell

It's 1935, and His lazy young Lordship can't think of a reason to get up in the mornings. But an American heiress, with democratic pep and business brain, gets him going. They open a clinic where the idle class can come and get *work*-cures. The erstwhile slugabed tears into a dozy old buffer – not only a Colonel Blimp lookalike but also, like Blimp, humiliated by a young toughie. *Lazybones* gives its post-1943 spectator an uncanny shock, of déjà vu-cum-flashforward. Even the family crest behind the credits says "Looking Backward Looking Forward" ….

Similarly, the tailor-made faun of 1934 "pre-echoes" the nude goatherd (on an English beach!!??) in *A Matter of Life and Death.* Many such auteurial motifs are made strange by the diversity of Powell's styles and genres, by his constant sense of changing times. His

The Essential Raymond Durgnat

Romanticism stems from that paradoxical thing, a *tradition of change*, some deep abiding spirit mutating through different zeitgeists, ideologies, mental sets.

If Powell's "rise and fall" is a three-act drama, the prewar Bs are Act 1 ("The Vortex"). Act 2 is war/postwar team-unity. Act 3 is retreat, or advance, into Private Worlds (a dream-delirium ballet, a lonely cameraman renting out his father's house …). In four of these films, the merits relished above occur cheek-by-jowl with:

4. "A Load of British Rubbish"

This nigh-proverbial phrase was inspired by bottom-drawer British B films 1928–1938. So my fourth pleasure risks being mistaken for Camp, or that perverse principle, "It's so bad that it's good." It's neither of those, but it *is* "For Connoisseurs Only" – which should cover most readers of FILM COMMENT.

Of Powell's surviving Bs (all mentioned here), *Red Ensign* (*Strike!* in the U.S.) and *The Phantom Light* (Celtic-fringe detective-Gothic with a comical Cockney and Murnau atmospherics) were top-notch Bs. The rest were "Quota Quickies." QQs arose thanks to legislation supporting British movie production from Hollywood dumping and restrictive practices. It spawned sub-cheapo flicks, some screened only to cinemas' morning cleaners, no paying customers expected. British Warners made the best QQs, but for more than three takes on any shot Powell needed the studio head's exceptional permission.

Whereas Hollywood Bs involved conveyer-belt efficiency, formula series, and solid consistency with proven markets, British QQs were wildly inconsistent in every way. Normally limited to a market one-fifth U.S. size, they were more like one-offs handcobbled in fly-by-night sweatshops. *But*: their stories might come from middle-class plays, or crime novels, and involve, or inspire, much sharper truths than Hollywood stereo-pulp. *But*: this wider material further pixilated their minuscule budgets. So flimsy sets and flat lighting commonly give everything, even faces and bodies, a cornflake-packet-cut-out look. The shots resemble outline diagrams more than illusions inspiring the suspension of disbelief. They live up, or down, to Godard's allusion-without-illusion and Coppola's video-storyboards. Which is already interesting.

Hasty blocking-out and no rehearsals entailed the utmost roughness. *Lazybones* – runt of the litter, shot in 13 *nights* – abounds in continuity bloopers, as Powell tries *nevertheless* for the latest "syntax" (fewer establishing shots), or chances a daring line-cross. In one shot a player set to exit left wheels right and crosses camera so close and out-of-focus her form dissolves into dandelion-puff spreading on the breeze. Eyeboggling deficiencies sit cheek-by-jowl with opportunistic virtuosities, e.g. a calligraphic "travelling" following Sara Allgood through a courtyard and two rooms.

With that semi-illusion, like a continuous alienation effect, upfronting form and craft *tel quel*, these cocktail salads of clumsiness, solid craft, and sudden brilliance goad close and recherché analysis. They're first-rate discussion-pieces for film theory. And they challenge one academic assumption after another: that film pace can be split into syntagmas (doesn't that travelling make three separate spaces one?); that taboos existed on looks into camera; that narrative entails structural rules of point-of-view; that something called "classic Hollywood syntax" flows from something called "bourgeois ideology" and lacks any basis but convention ….

SOURCE: *FILM COMMENT*, MAY–JUNE 1990, 28–30

6.8 REMEMBERING MICHAEL POWELL

I was all set to give a little talk on Powell at the National Film Theatre. Having prepared a startling topic – would you believe Powell vs Pasolini? – I beheld the subject of my lecture sitting in the front row, calm, curious, affable, mischievous.

I'd known him only from his films. But just to meet an auteur in the flesh promptly kills some ideas stone dead, starts off others, and sets your mind reconfiguring the two or three things you had previously construed. Like Olsen and Johnson in *Hellzapoppin'*, I tore whole pages out of my script and extemporised away until my last sentence, which was "… and I don't know quite what to make of that". My presentation ended well before time, for once, and Powell basked in the lively discussion and the thunderclaps of ideological struggle rolling over his head. When I dug up my old theory of his fascination with the demoniac, he just replied, "No", in a placid, firm, definitive way, like the stonewall "Why?" made famous by David Lean's Powell impersonations. Later, he said quietly, "Some of my work was once compared to …", and he paused, head lifted as if listening afar, mouth half-pursed, half-cherubic, like a rose, "Kipling …", enfolding the name with, not bated breath exactly, but a dropped tone of awe and satisfaction, as if in the presence of the stern master, he the loyal truant.

In a restaurant later he embellished a story recounted in *Million Dollar Movie*: for *Gone to Earth*, Korda had suggested faking the foxes by unleashing corgis with feather dusters tied to their tails. Powell chortled for what felt like five minutes, continuously, but evenly, highlights gleaming on his rosy cheeks, a physically beautiful balance of freshness and control. Clearly he was thinking through the visual nuances of the scene, emblematic, somehow, of his inspiration.

We met a few times more, once in Finnish Lapland at the Festival of the Midnight Sun. By then, his sight was so bad that Thelma Schoonmaker had to describe for him the food on his plate. To introduce his films, he'd memorised the steps down to the stage. As the blurred warmth of the lights fell across his face, his performance, immaculate and precise, reached out like a grandfatherly embrace, spare but efficacious.

He had just begun unleashing in Anglophone critics the sorts of affection that Renoir tapped in *Cahiers du cinéma*. It's as if each generation loves, in a selected grandfather, the traditions it deplores in its fathers and simultaneously revels in the discovery of new freedoms in the very things its own fathers rebelled against. Though things aren't quite so simple now, since the intervention of Marxism, which has had contemporary grooves of academe deploring the 'national culture' with a passion worthy of a better cause. Often theorists rationalise their guilty pleasures by presuming Powell's art to be 'subversive', or by seeing *Peeping Tom* as a demonstration of cinema's sado-scopic drives (as if that made bourgeois culture more guilty and themselves less), or by investing Powell's appearance in a film about Aleister Crowley with overblown meaning, so as to surround him with sulphur.

His first volume of autobiography, *A Life in Movies* (1986), established everything that was antithetical about him: his deep roots in an Edwardian-cum-Georgian gentleman-farmer's life, his man-about-town hedonism in the 30s (so unlike the disapproving poets), his wartime patriotism, and his post-war exoticism. Powell was, is, a *de luxe* avant-gardist, individualistic within a national cultural spirit: like Old Vic/Sadler's Wells theatre/ballet culture, like Gance, like Dreyer. Which makes him all the *more* interesting, and all the *less* stereotyped.

From 1950 he seemed to fall between an old and new spirit, and in *ALIM* (his love of acronyms is contagious) one sensed him groping as to which reader to address and therefore what to say. *ALIM* was one-third film book, one-third travel adventure and one-third personal rumination. Indispensable overall, wonderful in parts, it woolgathers all over the map, needing a bland but drastic editorial job, like David Lean's book on *The 49th Parallel*.

One feared for the second part, *Million Dollar Movie*, entirely dictated and bound to tackle its author's decline and fall, a thorny topic which could have led to all kinds of schmaltz, evasion of libel and every other showbiz ploy. But Powell's second shot lands in, or near, the gold. It centres squarely on the films. It's tightly edited on the whole and perhaps *improved* by dictation. For film, like drama generally, is much closer to spoken culture, to 'spinning a yarn', which is a performance art, than to written texts which are not time-based.

Despite its cheapo title, *Million Dollar Movie* bears rich witness to artists at work. The lean years after 1951 turn out to have bristled with fascinating projects, as Powell all but brought off a fusion of cinema and highbrow modernism. Here we have Powell and Stravinsky matching each other's quotations from Dylan Thomas; Powell plotting collaborations between Massine and Matisse, between Graham Sutherland and Georges Simenon, even between Marks & Spencer and Israeli national leaders (for an intellectual-national epic about Chaim Weizmann). Here we have Sir Thomas Beecham bustling The Archers through Offenbach; Powell and Shearer achieving the ideal creative partnership, i.e., "based not upon love, but upon suspicion and fear"; versions of William Sansom and Victoria Sackville-West; a promising project collapsing when Pressburger shocks Michael Frayn and Powell verbally slaps Peter Sellers.

The accounts of artistic collaboration, often done as dramatic scripts, are not deep analyses, but something as precious and much rarer – a sense of how ideas knock on, ricochet, dance tangent tangoes through all spirits present. There's careful practical analysis, too, and an inside view of industry history: of how and why The Archers broke up, how very nearly Powell and John Davis buried their legendary hatchet; of Powell, aged sixty, learning on the job how to peddle *They're A Weird Mob* to Australian cinema managers.

His gifts as a gossip rival John Aubrey's in *Brief Lives*, but with more fulsome detail. We get front-row seats for Jennifer Jones in hysterical, helpless and drunken rebellion against Selznick's *amour fou* for her (what an obsession story theirs would, will, make). We read letters from Siobhán McKenna, lamenting Powell's having the mind of, not a Roman Catholic, but "a Canterbury Protestant".

Film theorists will find cues and clues galore for new mutations. Between auteurism, with the great director as great dictator, and structuralism, in which the director is but an intersection point on a socio-ideological grid, maybe there is room for 'collaboration theory' – a fine can of worms – and where better to start than with Powell's box of surprises? Who could have guessed that Pressburger, the writer, not Powell, the pictorialist, conceived in *The Tales of Hoffmann* the breathtaking cross-fade from clockworks springing out of Moira Shearer's head to languorous ripples in a Venetian lagoon? That Powell knew not much about the battle of the River Plate until a German navy man told Pressburger, who told him? That for Powell the arch-colourist, only black and white properly displays the structures of landscape?

The brisker our deconstruction drill becomes, the more we need to relearn an appreciation of beauties à la Sainte-Beuve. To *appreciate*, in this heightened sense, the thinking behind *The Elusive Pimpernel* transforms it from a lame duck with a dodo brain into – a lame swan. Powell himself, although in some ways prone to self-indulgence, was also impossibly exigent, for instance, when he writes of Kathleen Byron in *The Small Back Room*, "only in her brief scenes with Michael Gough did I capture the flutter of an angel's

'The flutter of an angel's wings': Kathleen Byron

wings". His strange mixtures of the clinical and the sensitive give rise to many such unpredictable judgements.

All in all, Powell is honestly self-critical about his career errors and his far from exemplary behaviour (he even calls himself his wife's executioner) – all of which he reviews with a commendable lack of guilt. He understands other people of both sexes, rather well, when he wants to, in that brisk Edwardian way that's more to do with animal psychology than with Freud. But his ruthless innocence about people's vulnerability can amaze, as he flits like a butterfly and stings like a hornet. His tartness was military, without malice, but its patrician quality, its sudden emergence from mellow team spirit, made it more memorable than perhaps he realised.

Million Dollar Movie's mixture of the intimate and the remote, the terse and the elliptical, raises in a useful way most of the problems of the autobiographical genre. Like history generally, it qualifies as 'realism', but can never become 'the whole truth' or even truth 'in the round', except by dint of speculation, hypotheses, invention and the testimony of other people, which makes it tantamount to 'imaginative literature', sometimes, indeed, to fiction, on the understanding that true confessions would embarrass one's loved ones, one's lawyers and oneself. 'The way it was' gets reshaped further by recollection in tranquillity, hindsight and wisdom. And autobiography is always *discourse*, i.e. performance, reshaped to what one's target audiences now ought to know.

There's no ideal solution, only several acceptable ones, and Powell's is of a fresh and vivid kind. Overall, *Million Dollar Movie* is a reliable witness in which many casual details dovetail with other testimony. My various cavils include the non-mention of his novel *A Waiting Game* (1975) and *The Sorcerer's Apprentice*, a fascinating experiment. But that's less serious than the strange omission of anything about that deeply unfashionable masterpiece, *An Airman's Letter to His Mother*.

SOURCE: *SIGHT AND SOUND*, OCTOBER 1992, 22

ANNOTATIONS

ABOUT JOHN FORD

[p. 194] Lindsay **Anderson's own involvement with Joris Ivens**, a Communist documentarist, was his voiceover for the British version of *The Threatening Sky* (1965/7), which Durgnat reviewed on its release in the September 1967 *Films and Filming* and described as simplistic propaganda for the North Vietnamese regime, 'a '30s documentary out of its time' (p. 26). | [p. 197] **John Berger and Alain Tanner** collaborated on, among other films, *Jonah Who Will be 25 in the Year 2000* (1976), which Durgnat showed in his final programme at the PFA. This 'elegy for 60s commune-ism (not just "Paris 68", but the whole swathe of "alternative cultures")', Durgnat wrote later ('The Success and Failure of John Berger', *Art Monthly*, June 1991, pp. 24–5), 'moved me deeply, it had me awash. My sentimentality goaded Jean-Pierre Gorin, my drastically radical sparring partner, to declare that the movie made him want to throw up; it brimmed with unctuous, vague goodwill, denied everything egotistical, irreverent, abrasive, necessary to human activity.' | Lindsay Anderson had shown future **Man of Marble** (1977) director Andrzej Wajda's films under the Free Cinema banner in 1958. | **Lacemaker** (1977) director Claude Goretta had collaborated with Tanner on the Free Cinema short *Nice Time* (1957).

A SKELETON KEY TO STEPHEN DWOSKIN

[p. 197] Peter **Wollen** introduced his idea of the **two avant-gardes**, American ('Co-op') and European ('political'), in his essay 'The Two Avant-Gardes', published in the November–December 1975 *Studio International*. As Durgnat says, it largely ignored the original LFMC. | [p. 199] **'Birth, copulation and death'** – T. S. Eliot. | **INTERLOQUES**, as in Alfred Jarry's *Siloques, Superloques, Soliloques et Interloques de Pataphysique*, written 1905–6. | Dwoskin's *Dyn Amo* was adapted from a play by Christopher **Wilkinson**, author of **I Was Hitler's Maid**. | Dwoskin's **Central Bazaar** seems to have originated in talks with Durgnat in the late 1960s. | [p. 201] Having met Dwoskin through Ron Geesin in the Better Books era, **Gavin Bryars's music** was first used for *Naissant*, filmed in New York but given a soundtrack in London and included in the first LFMC catalogue in 1967.

COOPED IN A CO-OP?

[p. 202] **Hugh Gaitskell As A Famous Monster** of *Filmland* is a 1964 painting by Richard Hamilton, though Durgnat seems to have had not Hamilton but the radical left in mind here. Durgnat had celebrated *Famous Monsters of Filmland*, together with *Mad Monsters*, as 'the mags which Better Books daren't stock' in the *Motion* 'Companion' (p. 17). | Matusow's **The Enchanted Pot** was shown during the Spontaneous Festival of Underground Movies in 1966; Durgnat was constrained to call it merely a 'goading, infuriating collage of outtakes and cutups, a cocked snoot at the consensus' (*IT*, 31 October–13 November 1966, p. 9). | Durgnat wrote the LFMC catalogue entries on **Paul Bartel**'s *Secret Cinema* (1966), **Hilary Harris**'s *Nine Variations on a Dance Theme* (1966), and numerous films by **Hy Hirsh**. Durgnat described Bartel's film as 'the most hilarious twist to cinema-verite since Apollinaire's story of a director who commits the crimes and assassinations which he also films'. | **Ian Hugo**'s *Bells of Atlantis* (1952), made in collaboration with Anaïs Nin and Len Lye, was among the films Bob Cobbing showed at Better Books. | **Michael Nyman**'s contribution to the LFMC catalogue was *Love Love Love* (1967), which married footage of a 'Legalise Cannabis' rally with the Beatles' 'All You Need is Love'. | Apart from his contacts with Peter Whitehead, **Antonioni** attended *IT*'s launch party at the Roundhouse in Camden, which included a film show. | **Castle One** (1966), aka 'The

Light Bulb Film', was the work of Malcolm Le Grice, credited in the first LFMC catalogue as Mihima Haas. | [p. 203] 'Emotionally', **as Dwoskin said** in *Film Is* … (London: Peter Owen, 1975, p. 65), 'the Co-operative never formed a whole, though its members had the same intellectual approach.' | Le Grice's book **Abstract Film and Beyond** was published in 1977. | Peter Gidal's 'Theory and Definition of **Structural/Materialist Film**' appeared in his 1976 *Structuralist Film Anthology*.

JEAN-LUC GODARD: HIS CRUCIFIXION AND RESURRECTION

[p. 208] **Les Blank's** films about the **blues** included *A Well Spent Life* (1971), his portrait of Mance Lipscomb, which Durgnat showed at the PFA. His **garlic** film was *Garlic is as Good as Ten Mothers* (1980). | [p. 209] **Godard's latest film** at the time of writing was *Hail Mary* (1985). | **Carmen x 4**: Brook, Godard, Rosi, Saura.

AIMING AT THE ARCHERS

[p. 215] In his essay 'Made in Ealing' (*Screen*, vol. 16, no. 1, Summer 1975), John Ellis, who went on to write about *A Matter of Life and Death* in Ian Christie's book *Powell Pressburger and Others*, accused **Thorold Dickinson**'s *Secret People* of exhibiting 'an acute suspicion of the left as somehow dehumanised (the product of Stalinism)' (p. 120). Dickinson, who, as Durgnat says, helped found the film workers' union ACT (later **ACTT**) in the mid-1930s, and visited the Soviet Union on its behalf in 1937, did indeed come to take a dim view of Stalinism. | André Maurois invented his affectionately comic Englishman **Colonel Bramble**, popular on both sides of the Channel, having worked as a liaison officer with the British army during the Great War. Another Englishman abroad, Pierre Daninos's **Major Thompson** became the basis for Preston Sturges's last film as director, *The French, They are a Funny Race* (1955). | [p. 216] Durgnat discussed **Asquith**'s *Orders to Kill* (1958), **Val Guest**'s *Yesterday's Enemy* (1959) and **Leslie Norman**'s *The Long and the Short and the Tall* (1961) in *A Mirror for England*. Asquith's film, he wrote, 'suggests a new focus for a standard code of moral decency and oblig-ation' (p. 229), while the latter pair 'deal with atrocities committed by British patrols against Japanese prisoners in Burma' (p. 6). The Jack **Cardiff** film he has in mind is probably *Intent to Kill* (1958). | [p. 217] On 16 October 1978, during the NFT's Powell and Pressburger retro-spective, Durgnat led a seminar after a screening of *A Canterbury Tale* during which **Powell gently but firmly rejected** Durgnat's pet theories. The evening is described in more detail in 'Remembering Michael Powell'. | The **Proppists**, i.e. the cinestructuralists who analysed narratives along the lines laid down by Vladimir Propp, author of *Morphology of the Folk Tale*. | [p. 218] Powell had long wanted to film *The Tempest*, hence **the Caliban of this obses-sion**, etc. | **Renoir** made his version of Andersen's *The Little Match Girl* (1928) in a little stu-dio above the **Vieux-Colombier**, the original Left Bank art cinema. In *Jean Renoir* (Berkeley: University of California Press, 1974), Durgnat wrote that it 'represents the antithesis of the real-ism with which Renoir is usually associated' (p. 49). | In an article on *Peeping Tom* ('The Man(iac) with the Movie Camera', *Framework*, no. 9, Winter 1978–9, p. 8), Durgnat described Powell as the 'third master in this school of "pure cinema" alongside **Gance** and **Hitchcock**'. | Jean Epstein used the phrase **optical phantoms**, 'fantômes optiques' in the original, in the course of a defence of avant-garde optical effects against aesthetic quietism in his 1947 book *Le Cinéma du Diable*. Epstein, as Durgnat noted in 'Brain Drains', straddled avant-garde and documentary forms. Martin Scorsese, in his foreword to Christie's *Arrows of Desire* (London: Faber and Faber, 1994) wrote that Powell's use of superimposition in *The Edge of the World* 'almost looks forward to Stan Brakhage' (p. xix). | **Ian Christie's dossier**, included in *Powell Pressburger and Others*, revealed the depth of Churchill's hostility to *The Life and Death of*

Colonel Blimp. | [p. 219] **Sammy Rice**, as played by David Farrar, is the flawed hero of *The Small Back Room*. | [p. 220] At the start of 1963 Durgnat devoted an entry in the *Motion* 'Companion' to 'Bluebeard', writing that 'the hero of Perrault's fairy-story has, rather surprisingly, never been adapted into the criminal hagiography of the popular cinema (p. 7). | Powell's **Bluebeard's Castle**, adapted from Béla Bartók and Béla Balázs opera, appeared on German television at the year's end. | [p. 221] In his essay on *A Matter of Life and Death*, **John Ellis** scorned Durgnat's search for 'a definite content and message', terms he found 'hopelessly imprecise' (pp. 102–3). | [p. 222] A possible interpretation of **'transferability of effects'** ('transférabilité d'effets' in the original) would begin with Hume's critique of the Cartesian conception of causation in the *Treatise of Human Nature*, in which Hume describes the 'habit or determination to transfer the past to the future' as liable to offer not certain probability but 'a number of disagreeing images in a certain order and proportion'. | [p. 223] Like Wittgenstein and the members of the Vienna Circle, **Pressburger** was born in the Austro-Hungarian Empire. Durgnat may have decided the release of *A Matter of Life and Death* in 1946 coincided with the **triumph** of logical positivism over **metaphysics** on the grounds that A. J. Ayer's *Language, Truth, and Logic*, though first published a decade earlier, began to make waves in non-specialist circles in that year. | Durgnat is likely to have had in mind **Orwell**'s defence of **Kipling**, first published in the February 1942 *Horizon* and many times subsequently. Indeed Orwell, who discusses at more than one point 'the relationship between the highbrow and the blimp' (p. 115), may have provided Durgnat with a model for his defence of Powell. 'Kipling *is* a jingo imperialist,' Orwell wrote, 'he *is* morally insensitive and aesthetically disgusting. It is better to start by admitting that and then to try to find out why it is that he survives while the refined people who have sniggered at him seem to wear so badly.' As Durgnat wrote later, 'What Forster was to *Sequence*, Orwell was to me' (*Movie Scene*, March 1985, p. 29). | [p. 224] **Before going into exile** in New York, **Dickinson made** *The Queen of Spades* and *Secret People*. | [p. 225] Durgnat's friend **Chris Wicking**, horror screenwriter and sometime *Motion*, *Positif* and *Midi-Minuit Fantastique* contributor, eventually wrote about *A Canterbury Tale* in the November 1984 *Monthly Film Bulletin*. | The original stage production of Thornton Wilder's **The Skin of Our Teeth** was directed by Elia Kazan in 1942. | **Michael Walker** took up Durgnat's use of the term melodrama in *Framework*, no. 9, Winter 1978–9.

TRANSLATOR'S ANNOTATIONS: [p. 217] **While Powell realised:** In the original French 'réalisé': this term is resonant with multiple meanings such as directed, produced, achieved, completed. | [p. 218] **He loves to play with special effects:** In the original French 'jouer au trucages', which carries the double meaning 'play tricks' and 'play with special effects'. | **Hence his fate as a cinéaste «maudit»**. A reference to Verlaine's 'cursed poets': *Les Poètes maudits* (1884). | [p. 220] **Renoir dedicated himself to the «little theatre»:** A reference to *Le Petit Théâtre de Jean Renoir* (1970), which comprised three short films (plus musical interlude). | **Renoir's novel:** Like *The Life and Death of Colonel Blimp*, *Les Cahiers du Capitaine Georges*, published in 1966, is told in flashback and partly concerns the titular officer's friendship with a foreigner, in this case British. | [p. 224] **Powell's optimistic, frivolous and crystalline:** Durgnat's use of this term invites productive comparison with Deleuze's concept of *cinéma cristallin*, as outlined in his *Cinéma II: L'Image-Temps* (1985). | [p. 225] **«Oh time, stop your racket …»:** In the original French 'O temps, suspends ta raquette', perhaps a playful reference to a line from de Lamartine's poem 'Le lac' (1820): 'Ô temps! suspends ton vol …' which can be translated as 'Oh time! Arrest your flight!' | **Yvonne Salmon is Preceptor of English Literature, Corpus Christi College, University of Cambridge.**

THE PREWAR BS: REWARDS AND FAIRIES

[p. 228] Durgnat must have known the **servitudes and grandeurs of the shopkeeping trade** in the 1930s through his parents' experience. | [p. 229] Bruce Lacey and the Alberts, part of the 'Edwardian spoof-nostalgia' boom (q.v.), first staged 'An Evening of **British Rubbish'** at the Comedy Theatre in January 1963. The art historian David Mellor has described it in *The Bruce Lacey Experience* (London: Camden Arts Centre, 2012) as a 'hybrid piece of theatre-cum-trad-jazz-cum-comic-sketch-cum-Happening' (p. 42). The show ended with the line 'It may be rubbish, but at least it's British rubbish.'

Notes

1. RCA Archive: Letter from Christopher Frayling to Raymond Durgnat, 14 July 1980.
2. Durgnat, 'Structures and Ruptures', *Literary Review*, June 1981, pp. 34–5; 'Structuralism On Screen', *Times Educational Supplement*, 26 June 1981, p. 41.
3. Peter Wollen, 'The Avant-Gardes: Europe and America', *Framework*, no. 14, Spring 1981, p. 10.
4. Paul Willemen, 'Pesaro', *Framework*, nos 15–17, Summer 1981, p. 96.
5. Email to editor, 4 December 2013.
6. Durgnat, 'Directing the Avant Garde', *Films on Screen and Video*, May 1984, p. 8.
7. Ibid., p. 11.
8. Durgnat, rev. *8½*, in *Monthly Film Bulletin*, January 1990, p. 27.
9. Charles Barr, 'Introduction: Amnesia and Schizophrenia', in Barr (ed.), *All Our Yesterdays: 90 Years of British Cinema* (London: British Film Institute, 1986), pp. 25–6.
10. Durgnat, 'On *The Small Back Room*', in Ian Christie (ed.), *Powell Pressburger And Others* (London: British Film Institute, 1978), p. 77.
11. Leila Wimmer, *Cross-Channel Perspectives: The French Reception of British Cinema* (Oxford: Peter Lang, 2009), p. 187.
12. Durgnat, 'Famous Monsters', *Motion*, no. 4, February 1963, p. 18.
13. Michel Caen, 'Les revues …', *Midi-Minuit Fantastique*, no. 6, June 1963, p. 86.
14. Durgnat, 'How Others See Us', *American Film*, November 1981, p. 64.

APPENDIX I: PACIFIC FILM ARCHIVE PROGRAMMES

MONTAGE RIDES AGAIN!

19 April 1977
Montage A Go-Go: The French
(Dis)Connection
La Conquête du Pôle (George Méliès, 1912,
one-minute extract); *Entr'acte* (René Clair,
1924); *Ballet Mécanique* (Fernand Léger and
Dudley Murphy, 1924); *Ménilmontant* (Dimitri
Kirsanoff, 1926); *Napoléon* (Abel Gance,
1927, twenty minutes of extracts)

21 April 1977
Montage Lets Rip: The Russians are
Cutting! The Russians are Cutting!
October (Sergei Eisenstein, 1928); *Man With
a Movie Camera* (Dziga-Vertov, 1929)

26 April 1977
Montage Marches On: Montage Cuts In
The Murder of Dmitri Karamazov (Fedor
Ozep, 1931); *Song of Ceylon* (Basil Wright,
1934)

28 April 1977
The Montage Story: Alfred Hitchcock,
Master of Montage
Blackmail (Alfred Hitchcock, 1929)

1 May 1977
Montage in the Cinema
Citizen Kane (Orson Welles, 1941);
The Great McGinty (Preston Sturges, 1940)

3 May 1977
Son of Montage – It's Quicker by Montage
La Jetée (Chris Marker, 1962); *Toute la
Mémoire du Monde* (Alain Resnais, 1956);
Letter from Siberia (Chris Marker, 1958)

10 May 1977
The Geography of Montage – Montage
Rising
The Geography of the Body (Willard Maas,
1943); *Cosmic Ray* (Bruce Conner, 1962);
A Movie (Bruce Conner, 1958); *Renaissance*
(Walerian Borowcyzk, 1963)
*A Rough Sketch for a Proposed Film
Dealing With the Powers of Ten and the
Relative Size of Things in the Universe*
(Charles and Ray Eames, 1968); *Scorpio
Rising* (Kenneth Anger, 1963)

17 May 1977
Montage Cut Montage – Scissors and
Splice
Wail (Jeff Keen, 1960); *Like the Time is
Now* (Jeff Keen, 1961); *Frank Film* (Frank
Mourns, 1973); *Toccata for Toy Trains*
(Charles and Ray Eames, 1957); *Les Jeux
des Anges* (Walerian Borowczyk, 1964);
The Koumiko Mystery (Chris Marker, 1965)

19 May 1977
The Editor Regrets – Time Must Have a
Splice
Night and Fog (Alain Resnais, 1955);
Je t'aime, je t'aime (Alain Resnais, 1968)

THE DOCUMENTARY CINEMA

27 September 1977
'A Selection of Films by the Lumière
Brothers' (1895–6, 7 mins); *Daybreak
Express* (D. A. Pennebaker, 1953); *3rd Ave.
El* (Carson Davidson, 1955); *Highway* (Hilary
Harris, 1958); *Overture* (Thorold Dickinson,
1958); *A Well Spent Life* (Les Blank, 1971)

29 September 1977
Nanook of the North (Robert Flaherty, 1922);
Industrial Britain (Robert Flaherty *et al.*, 1933)

4 October 1977
À Propos de Nice (Jean Vigo, 1930); *Berlin: Symphony of a Great City* (Walter Ruttmann, 1927)

6 October 1977
Man With a Movie Camera (Dziga-Vertov, 1929)

11 October 1977
Land Without Bread (Luis Buñuel, 1933);
The River (Pare Lorentz, 1937); *Trade Tattoo* (Len Lye, 1937); *L'Hippocampe* (Jean Painlevé, 1934)

13 October 1977
Triumph of the Will (Leni Riefenstahl, 1935);
Housing Problems (Edgar Anstey and Arthur Elton, 1935)

18 October 1977
Mor'Vran (Jean Epstein, 1931); *Song of Ceylon* (Basil Wright, 1934); *Night Mail* (Harry Watt, 1936)

20 October 1977
New Earth (Joris Ivens, 1934); *Hell-Bent for Election* (Chuck Jones, 1944); *Native Land* (Leo Hurwitz and Paul Strand, 1942)

25 October 1977
The Boy Who Wanted to Know What Fear Was (Paul Diehl, 1935); *The Battle of Midway* (John Ford, 1942); 'Plus, a RARE WARTIME PROPAGANDA FILM'

27 October 1977
Fires Were Started (Humphrey Jennings, 1943)

1 November 1977
Listen to Britain (Humphrey Jennings and Stewart McAllister, 1942); *David* (Paul

Dickson, 1951); *All My Babies* (George C. Stoney, 1952); *O Dreamland* (Lindsay Anderson, 1956)

3 November 1977
Eugène Atget (Harold Becker, 1963); *The Days of Whiskey Gap* (Colin Low, 1961);
Time Is (Don Levy, 1964); *Powers of Ten* (Charles and Ray Eames, 1968); *The Sensory World* (Tom Lazarus, 1971)

8 November 1977
Histoire du Soldat Inconnu (Henri Storck, 1932); *Le Sang des Bêtes* (Georges Franju, 1949); *Hôtel des Invalides* (Georges Franju, 1952); *L'Opéra-Mouffe* (Agnès Varda, 1958);
Du Côté de la Côte (Agnès Varda, 1958)

10 November 1977
Guernica (Alain Resnais, 1950); *Night and Fog* (Alain Resnais, 1955); *Toute la Mémoire du Monde* (Alain Resnais, 1956); *Yunbogi's Diary* (Nagisa Oshima, 1965)

15 November 1977
Les Maîtres Fous (Jean Rouch, 1955); *Cortile Cascino* (Michael Roemer and Robert M. Young, 1962); *Lonely Boy* (Wolf Koenig and Roman Kroitor, 1962); *The Feast* (Timothy Asch and Napoleon Chagnon, 1970)

17 November 1977
Titicut Follies (Frederick Wiseman, 1967);
Chiefs (Richard Leacock, 1968)

22 November 1977
Letter from Siberia (Chris Marker, 1958);
Unidentified Marker film

29 November 1977
Culloden (Peter Watkins, 1964); *The Battle of Algiers* (Gillo Pontecorvo, 1966)

1 December 1977
Loin du Vietnam (Chris Marker *et al.*, 1967);
Pravda (Dziga-Vertov Group, 1970)

The Essential Raymond Durgnat

FILMS SINCE 1962: A PERSONAL SELECTION BY RAYMOND DURGNAT

1 October 1977
The Prisoner, Episode 16: 'Once Upon a Time' (Patrick McGoohan, 1968); *Leo the Last* (John Boorman, 1970) and *The Do-It-Yourself Cartoon Kit* (Bob Godfrey, 1961); *Alone* (Stephen Dwoskin, 1963/6); *Scorpio Rising* (Kenneth Anger, 1963); *The Act of Seeing With One's Own Eyes* (Stan Brakhage, 1971)

8 October 1977
How I Won the War (Richard Lester, 1967); *Martyrs of Love* (Jan Němec, 1967)

15 October 1977
Gertrud (Carl Theodor Dreyer, 1964); *Salvatore Giuliano* (Francesco Rosi, 1961)

22 October 1977
Goto, Island of Love (Walerian Borowczyk, 1968); *Dom* (Borowczyk and Jan Lenica, 1958); *Renaissance* (Borowczyk, 1963); *Les Jeux des Anges* (Borowczyk, 1964); *Point Blank* (John Boorman, 1967)

29 October 1977
Weekend (Jean-Luc Godard, 1967)

5 November 1977
Red Psalm (Miklós Jancsó, 1972); *Shadows of Our Forgotten Ancestors* (Sergei Parajanov, 1965)

12 November 1977
The Firemen's Ball (Milos Forman, 1967); *The Singing Lesson* (Lindsay Anderson, 1967/9); *The Servant* (Joseph Losey, 1963)

19 November 1977
Belle de Jour (Luis Buñuel, 1967); *Performance* (Donald Cammell and Nicolas Roeg, 1970)

26 November 1977
Yellow Submarine (George Dunning, 1968); *Labyrinth* (Jan Lenica, 1962); *Sweet Movie* (Dušan Makavejev, 1974)

3 December 1977
Lisztomania (Ken Russell, 1975); *Jonah Who Will be 25 in the Year 2000* (Alain Tanner, 1976)

APPENDIX II: TOP TENS

1969

DIRECTORS
1. Len Lye
2. Norman McLaren
3. Tex Avery
4. F. W. Murnau
5. G. W. Pabst
6. Carl Dreyer
7. Josef von Sternberg
8. Jean Renoir
9. King Vidor
10. Tony Conrad

FILMS
Le Quai Des Brumes: Jacques Prévert
La Ronde: Max Ophuls
Vampyr: Carl Dreyer
Miracle in Milan: Vittorio De Sica
Duel in the Sun: King Vidor
Saga of Anatahan: Josef von Sternberg
Allegretto: Oskar Fischinger
Duck Soup: Marx Brothers
The Thief of Bagdad: Michael Powell
French Cancan: Jean Renoir

SOURCE: *Cinema*, no. 4, October 1969, 2–3

1982

FILMS
The Big Night (*Losey*)
Blonde Venus
Chinese Checkers (*Stephen Dwoskin*)
Dom (*Borowczyk/Lenica*)
Fellini-Satyricon
The 5,000 Fingers of Dr T (*Roy Rowland*)
Le Mystère Koumiko (*Chris Marker*)
Ruby Gentry
Vampyr
Yellow Submarine

How painful to pass over true friends like Renoir and Franju, Groucho and Kong, who saw me through from infancy to early middle age. Whatever this list suggests, my soul remains a 30s baby's, born of poetic realism and the magic realms around it – of, let's say, **Next of Kin** *and* **Les Enfants du Paradis**, *of* **Hellzapoppin'** *and* **Senza Pietà** ...

SOURCE: *Sight and Sound*, Autumn 1982, 244

1988

FILMS
Yellow Submarine
Ruby Gentry
Look Back in Anger
Tirez sur le Pianiste/Shoot the Pianist
Miracolo a Milano/Miracle in Milan
Leo the Last
Saps at Sea
L'Atalante
French Cancan
Hellzapoppin'

FIRST MOVIE: *The Thief of Bagdad* (Powell/Whelan/Berger).

LEAST FAVOURITE MOVIE: Any radical-dogmatic-Marxist-Formalist British movie!

COMMENT: As I've been teaching film largely through close analysis for nearly thirty years, I really have seen some of these films thirty of forty times, image by image, while discussing every move in them with classroomfuls (from 5 to 300) of students – some touchingly keen, some highly rude – and these films, however many times you analyse them to death, miraculously spring alive again …

SOURCE: *John Kobal Presents The Top 100 Movies* (London: Pavilion Books, 1988), 130

1992

FILMS
Un chien andalou
Dom (Borowczyk/Lenica)
How I Won the War (Richard Lester)
Lettre de Sibérie (Chris Marker)
Miracle in Milan
The Murder of Dmitri Karamazov (Ozep)
Pather Panchali
Powers of Ten (Charles and Ray Eames)
Ruby Gentry
Vampyr

Faced with this impossible assignment, I've chosen films conveying human(ist) content through a diversity of aesthetics. A list of *films*, alas, must eliminate the greatest cinema, which comes in sequences (*The Red Shoes* ballet, *the* peak of cinema, Darrieux and Boyer in Ophüls's *Madame de …*, some musical numbers, etc.).

SOURCE: *Sight and Sound*, December 1992, 20

INDEX

Page numbers in *italics* denote illustrations; subentries ordered chronologically; n = endnote.

Agel, Henri 26, 53
Aldrich, Robert 23, 29–30, 166
  Kiss Me Deadly (1955) 8, 18,
    26, 57
Alloway, Lawrence 3, 7, 10, 70
Althusser, Louis 147–8, 163,
    189*n*26, 202, 204, 208, 211,
    215
Altman, Robert 150–2, 172–87
  M*A*S*H (1969) 135, 186
Anderson, Lindsay
  Writings 11, 15–16, 41–2,
    118–21, 191
  'Stand Up! Stand Up!' (1956)
    2, 7, 15, 120
  About John Ford (1983)
    193–7
  Films 15, 41–2, 118–21, 196–7,
    238–9
  O Dreamland (1956) 2, 15,
    118
  March to Aldermaston (1959)
    15, 119, 143
  If.... (1968) 66, 119–20, 130
  O Lucky Man! (1973) 136
Anderson, Perry 146–7, 189*n*26
Anger, Kenneth 46–8, 142, 188,
    201, 212, 223, 226
  Scorpio Rising (1963) 46, 48,
    155, *158*, 163, 237–9;
    see montageology
Anstey, Edgar 119, 143
  Housing Problems (1935)
    118, 238
Antonioni, Michelangelo 19, 25,
    29, 57, 99, 129, 183–4, 202,
    233
  Le Amiche (1955) 76
  L'Avventura (1960) 19, 53, 96
  Blow Up (1966) 63, 71
Arnheim, Rudolf 4, 74, 164,
    168–70, 188
Arnold, Matthew 3, 10, 13
Artaud, Antonin 9, 49
Arts Lab 48–9, 201–2
Asquith, Anthony 32–3, 117, 129,
    143, 216, 218
Auriol, Jean George 25, 43
Autant-Lara, Claude 8, 88, 116
  En Cas de Malheur (1958) 18
auteurism 7–12, 19–20, 23–4,
    25–31, 32, 165–8, 215, 230–1

Avery, Tex 214, 240
Ayer, A. J. 21, 235

Balázs, Béla 75, 171, 235
Ballard, J. G. 55, 132
Bardot, Brigitte 13, 150
Barr, Charles 11, 115, 140, 192
Bartel, Paul 202, 233
Barthes, Roland 142, 147–9, 154,
    163, 170–1, 175–6, 207, 212,
    222
Bass, Saul 100, 105, 152
Bataille, Georges 142, 199, 214
Baudelaire, Charles 1, 13, 159,
    162
Bauhaus 112, 163, 165
Bava, Mario 9, 105, 113
Bazin, André 11–12, 31, 43, 74–6,
    103, 110, 122, 134, 149, 154,
    156, 163–6, 169–71, 175–80,
    211, 226
Beatles, The 9, 48, 63, 143, 181,
    233; *see Wonderwall*;
    Yellow Submarine
  A Hard Day's Night (1964) 124,
    132, 135
  Help! (1965) 124–5
Becker, Jacques 28–9, 152
  Casque d'Or (1952) 22
Berger, John 138, 197, 201
  *Jonah Who Will be 25 in
    the Year 2000* (1976)
    233, 239
Bergman, Ingmar 14, 23, 25, 37,
    53, 159, 226
  The Virgin Spring (1960) 24
Bergson, Henri 159, 166–7, 185,
    225
Berkeley, Busby 75, 100, 103,
    160, 176, 178, 220
Berlin: Symphony of a Great City
    (1927) 99, 238
Better Books 46–8, *58*, 69, 202,
    233
Biró, Yvette 145, 150
Blank, Les 145, 208, 234, 237
Boetticher, Budd 28–30, 111,
    166
Bolognini, Mauro 14
  La Notte Brava (1959) 18
Bond, James 9, 12, 41, 126, 135,
    216

Boorman, John 9, 116, 125, 129,
    130
  The Newcomers (1964) *9*
  Catch Us If You Can (1965)
    125, 129
  Point Blank (1967) 125, 130, 239
  Leo the Last (1970) 130, 143,
    239, 241
  Zardoz (1974) 130–*3*, 157
Borges, Jorge Luis 132, 159
Borowczyk, Walerian 158–9, 181,
    187–8, 198, 208, 237–9,
    240–1
  Renaissance (1963) 158–9, 181,
    208, 237–9
  Les Jeux des Anges (1964) 89,
    237
Borzage, Frank 28–9, 125, 180
Boulting, John and Roy 121, 129
  The Guinea Pig (1948) 1
Bradley, F. H. 166, 223
Brakhage, Stan 47, 234, 239
Brecht, Bertolt 128, 134–8, 156,
    162–7, 180, 207, 220–1
Bresson, Robert 53–4, 109, 206,
    211, 223–4, 226
British documentary movement
    11, 25, 76, 99–100, 108, 116,
    117–19, 134, 154–5, 165–6,
    170, 176–7, 218, 225, 228
British Film Institute 4–5, 7, 10, 25,
    41, 67, 146–8, 191–2, 201–3
Brooks, Richard 23, 28–30, 166
  Elmer Gantry (1960) 30, 126–8
Bryars, Gavin 201, 233
Buñuel, Luis 29, 49, 125, 163,
    184, 204, 207–9, 238–9
  Un Chien Andalou (1929) 181,
    205, 241
  L'Age d'Or (1930) 138, 207
Burroughs, William 47, 66, 199
Byron, Kathleen 38, 231–*2*

Cabinet of Dr Caligari, The
    (1920) 73, 86, 89, 176–9
Cahiers du Cinéma 7–8, 20–4,
    25, 31, 56, 120, 142, 147–8,
    163–6, 193, 202, 208,
    210, 215, 230
Cameron, Ian 7, 41, 47
Campaign for Nuclear
    Disarmament 41, 143, 146

Capra, Frank 25, 130, 143, 187, 215
  It's A Wonderful Life (1946) 130, 225
Carné, Marcel 27, 37, 117, 212
  Le Quai des Brumes (1938) 22, 125, 129, 240
  Les Enfants du Paradis (1945) 27, 240
Carrà, Carlo 84
Cassavetes, John 30, 132, 166, 173
Cavalcanti, Alberto 163, 170, 218
Cayatte, André 8, 116
  Les Amants de Vérone (1949) vi, 1, 75
Chabrol, Claude 7, 14, 25, 33, 164, 204, 208
Chaplin, Charlie 101, 160
  The Kid (1921) 182
Christie, Ian 192, 203, 218, 234
cinéma vérité 35, 50, 62, 91, 118, 122, 128, 134, 154, 157, 176, 214
Cinémathèque Française 145, 188, 193
Clair, René 117, 135, 163, 184, 237
Clayton, Jack 133
  Room at the Top (1958) 114, 120, 123
  The Pumpkin Eater (1964) 142
Clément, René 8, 10, 28, 57, 116
Clouzot, Henri-Georges 8, 55, 116
Cobbing, Bob 46–8, 72*n*7, 202, 233
Cocteau, Jean 25, 49, 103–4, 119, 226
Coldstream, Sir William 4, 74
Combs, Richard 191–2, 197
Conner, Bruce 145, 157–8, 202, 237
Coppola, Francis Ford 160, 209, 229
  The Godfather Part II (1974) 153
Corman, Roger 27–9, 41, 105, 215
Cottafavi, Vittorio 20, 40–1
Crowley, Aleister 158, 230
Cubism 80, 87, 100, 200–1
Cukor, George 28–9, 93, 187, 202

Dalí, Salvador 82
Dassin, Jules 25
  La Loi (1959) 18
Daves, Delmer 29–30
  Broken Arrow (1950) 14
De Sica, Vittorio 138, 142, 143, 177, 184, 240–1
Definition 15–17, 24, 41–2
Deleuze, Gilles 142, 165, 199, 206, 235
Delluc, Louis 37, 55, 163
DeMille, Cecil B. 30, 59, 95, 102

Demme, Jonathan 132, 150
Demy, Jacques 41
  Lola (1961) 21
Diaghilev, Sergei 227
DIAS 52, 69–70, 144
Dickinson, Thorold 4–5, 9–10, 32–3, 73–6, 111, 113, 115–16, 117, 143, 145–6, 215, 224, 234–5
  The Next of Kin (1942) 240
  The Queen of Spades (1949) 35, 235
  Overture (1958) 76, 108, 145, 237; *see* the essay-film
Disney, Walt 89, 119, 160, 173–6, 182–3
Donen, Stanley 14, 28–30, 37, 105, 119
Doniol-Valcroze, Jacques 43, 122
Dosse, Philip 7–8, 151
Dovzhenko, Alexander 108
  Earth (1930) 16
Dreyer, Carl Theodor 52–3, 73, 206, 230, 240
  La Passion de Jeanne d'Arc (1928) 100
  Vampyr (1932) 107, 240–1
  Gertrud (1964) 239
Duchamp, Marcel 83
Dulac, Germaine 163
Duras, Marguerite 133, 208, 211
Durgnat, Raymond
  Life
    at school 1–2, 15, 41, 161, 195
    at Cambridge 1–4, 11, 42, 116, 144
    at Associated British Picture Corporation 4, 115
    at the Slade 4–5, 7–10, 73–6
    underground activities 46–9, 58, 68, 69–71, 142, 145, 192, 201–4, 233–4
    as art school teacher 1, 46, 74–5, 118
    time in the US 117, 145–6, 150–2
    return to the UK 151, 191–3
  Writings
    'A Look at Old and New Waves' (1960) 8, 116
    'Erotism in Cinema' (1961–2) 9–10
    Nouvelle Vague (1963) 8–9, 42, 116, 117
    Motion 'Companion to Violence and Sadism in the Cinema' (1963) 8–12, 193, 233–5
    'Standing Up for Jesus' (1963) 10, 13–24, 41–2, 192–3, 197
    'Vote for Britain!' (1964) 10–12, 43, 115, 192
    Slade thesis (1964–5) 10–12, 73–6, 112, 117, 188

Writings *(cont.)*
    Eros in the Cinema (1966) 139
    Films and Feelings (1967) 5, 72–6, 112, 142, 151, 188, 191
    'Images of the Mind' (1968–9) 75–6, 91–112, 112–13, 116, 142, 145, 149
    The Crazy Mirror (1969) 73–4, 150
    A Mirror for England (1970) 5, 43, 70, 115–16, 129, 141, 192, 217, 234
    Sexual Alienation in the Cinema (1974) 117, 139–42, 144, 159, 188
    The Strange Case of Alfred Hitchcock (1974) 10, 117, 142
    Jean Renoir (1974) 5, 117, 234
    'The Death of Cinesemiology' (1980) 148–9, 189*n*26, 191
    W.R. – Mysteries of the Organism (1999) 145
    A Long Hard Look at 'Psycho' (2002) 10
Duvivier, Julien 32, 136
Dwan, Allan 25–31, 101, 113
Dwoskin, Stephen 47–9, 59–60, 70, 192, 197–201, 202–3, 233–4
  Alone (1963) 59–60, 108, 198, 239
  Chinese Checkers (1963) 59, 198, 203, 240
  Central Bazaar (1976) 199–200, 233
Dziga-Vertov *see* Vertov, Dziga
Dziga-Vertov Group 146, 204, 207–8, 215, 238

Ealing Studios 118, 134–5, 140, 219–20
Eames, Charles and Ray 158, 174, 237–38, 241
Eco, Umberto 171, 222
Ehrenzweig, Anton 149, 164, 168, 172, 188
Eisenstein, Sergei
  Writings 74–6, 92, 109, 147, 152–5, 166–70, 211; *see* montageology
  Films 25, 49, 73–6, 97–100, 105, 112, 166–70
    Strike (1925) 102, 163
    Battleship Potemkin (1925) 97–8, 110, 168–9
    October (1928) 76, 99, 106, 108, 125, 137, 149, 154, 157, 168–9, 188, 237; *see* the essay-film
    The General Line (1929) 89–90

Films *(cont.)*
    Que Viva Mexico! (1933) 22, 167, 188
    Alexander Nevski (1938) 98, 126, 168–9
    Ivan the Terrible (1944) 156, 168–9, 224
Eliot, T. S. 3, 13, 143
Elster, Michael 77–9, 86–7
Elton, Arthur
    Aero Engine (1933) 134
    Housing Problems (1935) 118, 238
Empson, William 141
Epstein, Jean 117, 163, 218, 234, 238
essay-film, the 55, 76, 106–8, 116, 118, 145, 156–7, 204–5, 237–8

Fainlight, Harry 3, 46–8, 50–*1*, 52, 71
Farber, Manny 145–6, 150, 180
Feiffer, Jules 172–87
Fellini, Federico 75, 117, 126, 140
    La Dolce Vita (1960) 22–4
    8½ (1963) 41, 73, *107*, 122, 132, 192
    Giulietta of the Spirits (1965) 106
    Fellini-Satyricon (1969) 131, 141, 159, 175, 240
    Fellini's Casanova (1976) 173, 175, 188, 226
Fields, W. C. 19, 124, 143, 181, 186–7
Film Comment 117, 146, 151
Films and Filming 7–8, 46, 58, 151, 192, 202
Films on Screen and Video 151, *172*, 192
Fischinger, Oskar 61, 70, 240
Fisher, Terence 115, 193
    Dracula (1958) 89
5,000 Fingers of Dr T, The (1953) 27, 40, 89, 178, 240
Flaherty, Robert 17, 25, 218, 238
    Industrial Britain (1933) 118
Ford, John 7, 14–15, 18–19, 25, 28–30, 119–20, 153, 166–9, 193–7, 224
    The Village Blacksmith (1922) 145
    The Informer (1935) 28, 129, 195
    Stagecoach (1939) 28, 109–11, 134, 152
    Young Mr. Lincoln (1939) 142, 169, 195–6
    The Grapes of Wrath (1940) 15, 116, 196
    The Long Voyage Home (1940) 28, 103, 195

Ford, John *(cont.)*
    The Battle of Midway (1942) 238
    The Man Who Shot Liberty Valance (1962) *195*
Franju, Georges 57, 118, 126, 171, 210–12, 238, 240
Frankfurt School 140, 163, 177
Free Cinema 2, 10, 15–16, 41–2, 118–21, 196–7, 233
French avant-garde 55, 117–18, 132, 152, 163–5, 171, 205
French New Wave 7–8, 12, 37, 64, 76, 116, 120, 123, 164–5, 202, 210
Freud, Sigmund
    see psychoanalysis
Fuller, Samuel 7, 19, 23, 25, 28–30, 138, 166–7, 215
    Run of the Arrow (1957) 18, 25, 28, 196
Futurism 84, 100

Gance, Abel 34, 88, 149, 163, 218, 230, 234, 237
    La Roue (1922/3) 163
    Napoléon (1927) 88, 237
Geesin, Ron 59–60, 198, 202, 233
German Expressionism 28, 34, 41, 73, 96–7, 105, 110, 132, 156, 179–80, 196, 226
gestalt psychology 74–6, 87–8, 90–1, 107, 164, 168, 176–80, 222
Gidal, Peter 198, 201–3, 234
Gillespie, Dizzy 21, 51
Ginsberg, Allen 46–8, 50–*1*, 52, 69, 200
Glover, Edward 167
Godard, Jean-Luc 25, 41, 47, 52–7, 63, 106–8, 116, 121–2, 125, 133–9, 146, 163–8, 188, 204–10; *see* Dziga-Vertov Group
    A Bout de Souffle (1960) 22, 53–7, 73, 106, 136, 204–6
    Weekend (1967) 138, 204, 207, 239
    One Plus One (1968) 49, 63–7, 71, 138, 143, 207
Godden, Rumer 38, 223, 226
Godfrey, Bob 70, 239
Goldmann, Lucien 163, 210
Gombrich, E. H. 149, 188
Gone With the Wind (1939) 27, 101
Goretta, Claude 233
    Nice Time (1957) 15, 24, 118, 121
    The Lacemaker (1977) 197
Gorin, Jean-Pierre 146, 160, 192, 233; *see* Dziga-Vertov Group
    Tout va Bien (1972) 137–8, 207–8
    Poto and Cabengo (1979) 206–8

Gozlan, Gerard 170, 188
Greenaway, Peter 203
Grierson, John 11–12, 16, 25, 97, 118–19, 122, 134, 170, 218
    Drifters (1929) 99
Griffith, D. W. 94–7, 106
    Intolerance (1916) 96, 100

Hall, Stuart 2, 17, 42, 146–7
Hamilton, Richard 3, 233
Harcourt, Peter 140–2
Hardy, Laurel and 19, 27, 36, 186, 241
Harris, Hilary 47, 202, 233, 237
Hauser, Arnold 140, 149, 162, 164
Hawks, Howard 8–10, 23, 25–31, 33, 121–2, 138, 165–7, 215
    Rio Bravo (1959) 123
    'bat it and run' 59, 67, 105, 206
Heath, Stephen 146–7
Heckroth, Hein 37, 217
Heliczer, Piero 49, 69
Hellzapoppin' (1941) 230, 239–40
Hirsh, Hy 202, 233
Hitchcock, Alfred 2, 10, 25–30, 31–4, 121, 153, 166–7, 218, 227, 234
    Blackmail (1929) 34, 75, 237
    Vertigo (1958) 32–3, 54
    Psycho (1960) 7, 9–10, 32–3, 57, 100, 217
Hochberg, Julian 164, 168
Hockney, David 61–2
Hoggart, Richard 2–3, 10, 13, 24, 42
Hollywood, New 34, 121, 132–3, 150–2, 166, 183–7, 215, 223
Hollywood, Old 25–31, 100–5, 150–2, 167, 184, 202, 215, 219
Horovitz, Michael 51, 52, 69
Houston, Penelope 2, 7–10, 19, 75, 146–7
Hugnet, Georges 84
Huillet, Danièle 134, 197, 210
Hume, David 21, 134, 222–3, 235
Huston, John 25, 29–30, 196
    Freud (1962) 133
    Reflections in a Golden Eye (1967) 142

impossible, the 55, 75–6, 82, 105–8, 116–17, 124–5, 132, 166, 171, 179, 203
Ingrams, Michael 119
Institute of Contemporary Arts 3, 9, 46, 48
IT 47–8, 52, 201, 233
Italian Neo-realism 28, 76, 104, 118, 166, 175–80
It Happened Here (1964) 128

The Essential Raymond Durgnat

Itten, Johannes 78, 112
Ivens, Joris 99, 194, 214, 233, 238

Jagger, Mick 62–3, 64–7, 159
Jakobson, Roman 147–9, 162–4, 188
James, Henry 151, 180, 184
Jancsó, Miklós 65, 139, 145, 197, 239
Jarman, Derek 203
Jubilee (1978) 199
Jennings, Humphrey 118, 126, 224–5, 238
Johnson, Ian 8–9, 39, 193
Jones, Jennifer 231
Love Letters (1945) 25
Duel in the Sun (1946) 1, 17, 26, 27, 38–9, 240
Portrait of Jennie (1948) 27, 30
Gone to Earth (1950) 35, 38–9, 219, 230
Carrie (1952) 30, 102
Ruby Gentry (1952) 27, 29, 240–1
Jordine, Merdelle 201

Kafka, Franz 132–3, 183
Kazan, Elia 16, 25, 29–30, 120–1, 173, 235
On the Waterfront (1954) 16–18, 25, 29, 42, 121
A Face in the Crowd (1957) 128, 138
Wild River (1960) 16, 29, 42, 52
Keeler, Christine 55, 70
Keen, Jeff 46–9, 49–50, 63, 67–8, 69–71, 91, 202, 237
Marvo Movie (1967) 48, 60–1
Kipling, Rudyard 35, 196, 216, 221–7, 231, 235
Kirsanoff, Dimitri 49, 54, 237
Klein, William 118, 210, 214–15
Kluge, Alexander 106
Korda, Alexander 35, 38, 129, 216, 219, 230
Kracauer, Siegfried 11–12, 45n42, 73–4, 112, 150–1, 162–4, 175–80, 226
Kren, Kurt 144, 202
Kubrick, Stanley 28
Spartacus (1960) 24
Dr Strangelove (1963) 128
2001: A Space Odyssey (1968) 130
A Clockwork Orange (1971) 130–1
Barry Lyndon (1975) 175
Kuleshov, Lev 76, 84–6, 109, 152–3; *see* montageology

Lacan, Jacques 141, 147, 164, 198–200, 209

Lacey, Bruce 70, 126, 143, 236
Lacombe, Georges 117–18
Lady in the Lake (1947) 101
Laing, R. D. 3–4, 69–70, 144
Lambert, Gavin 1, 14, 193
Lang, Fritz 19–20, 25, 28–30, 96–7, 105, 205
Langlois, Henri 145, 188
Latham, John 47–9, 52, 61, 69–70, 202
Lattuada, Alberto 28
Senza Pietà (1948) 240
Lautréamont, Comte de 86
Lawrence, D. H. 2, 13
Women in Love (1920) 146
Lady Chatterley's Lover (1928/60) 7
Le Corbusier 88, 104, 112, 163
Le Grice, Malcolm 198–201, 202–3, 233–4
L'Herbier, Marcel 37, 55, 163
Lean, David 35, 224–6, 230–1
Brief Encounter (1945) 18, 36, 43, 121, 218
Leavis, F. R. 1–3, 10, 13, 140–1, 151, 163, 195
Lebrun, Rico 82–3
Left Bank Group 55, 132, 145, 156–7, 158–9, 171, 187–8, 192, 210–15
Léger, Fernand 100, 163, 237
Lelouch, Claude 121, 214
Lenica, Jan
Dom (1958) 208, 239, 240–1
Labyrinth (1962) 239
Lessing, Doris 35
Lester, Richard 56, 70, 116–17, 122, 124–5, 135–8, 143, 166
The Knack … and How to Get It (1965) 106, 117, *124*–5, 130, 135
How I Won the War (1967) 125, 129, 135, 215, 239, 241
Petulia (1968) 135, 142
The Three Musketeers (1973) 132, 135
Lévi-Strauss, Claude 142, 147, 163, 166–9, 183, 223
Levy, Don 5, 47–9, 52, 69, 118, 122, 238
Lewis, Jerry 13, 27, 42, 176, 220
Li'l Abner 18, 27, 42, 80, *158*, 178–3, 188
Lindgren, Ernest 33, 43, 75, 154; *see* montageology
Littlewood, Joan 121, 135
London Film-Makers' Co-operative 47–9, 58, 60–1, 68, 70–1, 144, 192, 201–4, 233–4
Lonely Boy (1962) 128, 238
Look Back in Anger (play, 1956) 2, 12, 43, 46, 48, 50, 116, 120–1, 124

Look Back in Anger (film, 1959) *17*–18, 24, 43, 115, 120–1, 241
Losey, Joseph 20, 23, 29, 53–5, 75, 99, 112, 115–16, 122–3, 129, 136–9, 156, 187
The Big Night (1951) 240
The Sleeping Tiger (1954) 120
Time Without Pity (1957) 24, 122
The Criminal (1960) 11, 18
The Damned (1963) 53, 116, 139, 159
The Servant (1963) 159, 239
Modesty Blaise (1966) 125–6, 135, 143
The Romantic Englishwoman (1975) 130
Low, David 207, 215
Lubitsch, Ernst 101
Heaven Can Wait (1943) 130, 225
Lucas, George 151, 160, 174, 182
Luddy, Tom 145–6, 152, 192
Lukács, Georg 163, 180
Lumière, Auguste and Louis 12, 93–4, 104, 145, 237
Luna, Donyale 62
Lye, Len 61, 69, 71, 117, 233, 240
A Colour Box (1935) 50, 69
Trade Tattoo (1937) 238
Lyttelton, Humphrey 13, 41, 201

Maas, Willard 47
The Geography of the Body (1943) 83, 157, 199, 237
MacCabe, Colin 146, 191
McCarey, Leo 29, 216
McLaren, Norman 50, 63, 69, 240
McLuhan, Marshall 105–6, 113
MacMahonism 42, 166
Magritte, René 82, 132
Makavejev, Dušan 138, 145, 160, 201, 212, 239
Malle, Louis 53, 125
Malraux, André 118, 132, 160, 204, 206
Mamoulian, Rouben 37
Queen Christina (1933) 100
Man Ray 80, 163
Manvell, Roger 75, 143, 154, 187; *see* montageology
Marcuse, Herbert 64–6, 163
Marker, Chris 55, 75, 106–8, 117, 118, 134, 164, 171, 188, 210, 214–15, 237–8, 240–1
Letter from Siberia (1958) 108, 132, *155*, 156–7, 171, 206, 214, 237–8, 241; *see* the essay-film
La Jetée (1962) 47, 100, 157–9, 187–8, 214, 237
Marks, Leo 39, 45n49, 217

Marvin, Lee 62, 125, 130
Marxism 109, 134, 140–2, 146–9,
    162–8, 205–6, 225
Mass-Observation 119, 165
Massine, Leonid 162, 231
Matisse, Henri 198, 231
Matusow, Harvey 47, 202, 233
May 1968 64, 117, 140, 146,
    163–4, 202, 233
Mayer, Carl 27–8, 179
Mazzetti, Lorenza
    Together (1956) 2, 119
Mekas, Jonas 47, 108
Méliès, Georges 11–12, 41, 45,
    94, 110, 176, 220, 237
Menzies, William Cameron 27, 101
Metz, Christian 147–9, 154,
    168–71, 175–6, 188
Midi-Minuit Fantastique 193
Millar, Gavin 11, 76
Miller, Lee 82
Milton, John 13, 92, 98, 141, 152
Minnelli, Vincente 23, 25, 28–31,
    119
    Bells Are Ringing (1960) 24, 31
Miss Julie (1951) 88
Mitchell, Adrian 51, 52
Mitry, Jean 147, 162–6, 171–2,
    178
Mocky, Jean-Pierre 204
Moholy-Nagy, László 80, 112
montageology 33, 75–6, 84–5,
    97–100, 106–12, 137, 142,
    145, 152–5, 156–9, 163–71,
    177, 211
Monthly Film Bulletin 1, 21–3,
    145, 191–2
Morin, Edgar 74–5, 162, 222
Motion 8–12, 116, 193
Movie 7–11, 23–4, 25, 47, 113,
    141, 166–7, 201
Muehl, Otto 139, 144
Murder of Dmitri Karamazov, The
    (1931) 237, 241
Murnau, F. W. 28, 33, 73, 97,
    179–80, 240
Museum of Modern Art 8, 180

National Film Theatre 2, 8, 34, 41,
    43, 192, 202, 229–30, 234
Nelson, Zelda 59, 70, 198
Němec, Jan 160
    Martyrs of Love (1967) 139, 142,
    145, 239
New Left 2–3, 10, 15–18, 115,
    140, 146–7, 196–7,
New New Left 121, 140, 146–9,
    161–3, 166–7, 197, 202
New York Film Bulletin 7–8
New York Film-Makers'
    Co-operative 46–7
No Trees in the Street (1958)
    115–16

nouvelle vague see French New
    Wave
Nuttall, Jeff 47, 52, 69
Nyman, Michael 202, 233

O'Brien, Edna 62
    Girl With Green Eyes (1964) 73
Ogden, C. K. 163, 188
Oh! What a Lovely War (1969)
    135, 139, 215
Olivier, Laurence 35, 220
    Henry V (1944) 89, 134–6
Ophüls, Max 25, 28, 33, 73, 89,
    103, 136, 158, 240–1
Orrom, Michael 108, 113, 114n13
Orwell, George 140, 223, 235
    1984 (1949) 56, 128, 216
Osborne, John 7, 18, 42, 120, 124
    Look Back in Anger (play, 1956)
    2, 12, 43, 46, 48, 50, 116,
    120–1, 124
    Look Back in Anger (film, 1959)
    17–18, 24, 43, 115, 120–1,
    241
Oshima, Nagisa 138, 238
Outlaw, The (1943) 30, 177
Oxford Opinion 7–8, 11, 19, 42,
    146
Oz 48, 201

Pabst, G. W. 12, 33, 59, 73, 240
Pacific Film Archive 145–6, 148,
    152–60, *153*, 233–4, 237–9
Pasolini, Pier Paolo 131, 159, 208,
    216, 230
Peirce, C. S. 149, 163–4
Pennebaker, D. A. 69, 237
Perkins, V. F. 11, 44n35
Piaget, Jean 164, 188, 210
Picabia, Francis 163
Picasso, Pablo 56, 78, 80–3, 212,
    219
Pink Floyd 63, 70
Pinter, Harold 139, 159
Poe, Edgar Allen 37, 41, 117, 183
Poetic Realism 117, 192, 195–6,
    212, 240
Polanski, Roman 29, 122
    Repulsion (1965) 32, 40, 131–3
Pontecorvo, Gillo 135, 138, 238
Pop Art 3, 46, 49, 68, 70, 74–5,
    124, 126, 162, 202
Porter, Edwin S. 95, 110
Positif 20, 23–4, 166, 188, 193
Powell, Dilys 23, 202
Powell, Enoch 34, 43, 138, 144
Powell, Michael 11–12, 34–41,
    115–17, 129, 192–3, 215–26,
    227–9, 230–2
    Pre-Pressburger Powell 218,
    227–9
    The Thief of Bagdad (1940) 12,
    40–1, 89, 240

Powell, Michael *(cont.)*
    *The Life and Death of Colonel
    Blimp* (1943) 11–12, 34, 135,
    156, 215–16, 224
    A Canterbury Tale (1944) 35,
    224–5
    I Know Where I'm Going (1945)
    36
    A Matter of Life and Death
    (1946) 11–12, 34, 129, 216,
    221, 225
    Black Narcissus (1947) 38, 225–6
    The Red Shoes (1948) 11–12,
    37, *217*, 241
    The Small Back Room (1949) *232*
    The Tales of Hoffmann (1951)
    12, 37, 45n42, 113, 226
    Peeping Tom (1960) 9, 11, 24,
    35, 39–41, *40*, 193, 217
    The Queen's Guards (1961) 12,
    34–5, 48, 216
Praz, Mario 35, 43
Preminger, Otto 8, 20, 25–31
Presley, Elvis 3, 6n17, *158*
Pressburger, Emeric 36, 217–18,
    223, 231, 235
Prévert, Jacques 1, 27, 37, 125, 240
Propp, Vladimir 217, 234
psychoanalysis 3–4, 8, 41, 56, 82,
    131, 141–2, 166–7
Pudovkin, V. I. 25, 76, 84–5, 136;
    see montageology
Pull My Daisy (1959) 49, 69
Python, Monty 135, 206
    Life of Brian (1979) 209

Quai de Grenelle (1950) 27, 125
Queneau, Raymond 211–12
Quine, Richard 28, 41, 43
    Strangers When We Meet (1960)
    24

Ray, Nicholas 18–19, 25, 29–30
Ray, Satyajit 19, 241
Reed, Carol 89, 129, 133, 224
    The True Glory (1945) 15
Regnier, Carola 199–200
Reich, Wilhelm 199
Reinhardt, Max 96–7
Reisz, Karel
    Writings 75–6, 106, 113, 154;
    see montageology
    Films 2, 15–18, 118–21, 197
    *Morgan: A Suitable Case for
    Treatment* (1966) 119–21,
    130
Renoir, Jean 27–28, 33, 76, 100,
    103–4, 110, 117–18, 120–3,
    153, 180, 219–20, 230, 240
    The Little Match Girl (1928) 178,
    217–18, 234
    Boudu Saved From Drowning
    (1932) 103–4, 110, 152

Renoir, Jean *(cont.)*
  Toni (1935) 118, 180
  La Marseillaise (1938) 122
  La Règle du Jeu (1939) 110,
    220
  The River (1951) 226
  French Cancan (1954) 240–1
  Le Déjeuner sur l'Herbe (1959)
    22, 27
Resnais, Alain 75, 118, 132–3,
    158–9, 171, 210–14, 237–8
  Nuit et Brouillard (1955) 39, 212
  Toute la Mémoire du Monde
    (1956) 157, 212, *213*
  Hiroshima Mon Amour (1959)
    20, 91, 122, 127, 132, 211–13
  Last Year at Marienbad (1961)
    55, 73, 125, 213, 222
  Je t'aime, je t'aime (1968)
    158–9, 213
Rice, Ron 70, 142, 199
Richards, I. A. 140, 163–4, 188
Richardson, Tony 2, 15–16,
    119–21
  Look Back in Anger (play, 1956)
    2, 12, 43, 46, 48, 50, 116,
    120–1, 124
  Look Back in Anger (film, 1959)
    17–18, 24, 43, 115, 120–1,
    241
Rivette, Jacques 122, 159
Roach, Hal 180–1, 186–7
Robbe-Grillet, Alain 60, 133, 163,
    210–11
Roeg, Nicolas 130, 136–7, 166
  Performance (1970) 159–60,
    199, 239
Rohmer, Eric 33, 43, 159
Rolling Stones, The 52, 63–7
Rosenbaum, Jonathan 145–6,
    150
Rosi, Francesco 234, 239
Rossellini, Roberto 166, 170, 177
Rotha, Paul 25, 75, 113
Roud, Richard 7, 19–21
Royal College of Art 74–5, 191–2
Royal Court Theatre 2, 42, 194
Russell, Bertrand 21, 142
Russell, Ken 60, 116, 124, 126,
    130–1, 137, 143
  Billion Dollar Brain (1967) 126,
    129
  Mahler (1974) *130*
  Lisztomania (1975) 130, 137,
    160, 239
Rycroft, Charles 142, 144

Sabu 36, 129, 216, 226
Sadoul, Georges 95, 112
St Martin's School of Art 46–7, 74,
    112, 203
Sarris, Andrew 7–8, 25, 43, 117,
    148, 166, 193

Sartre, Jean-Paul 163, 204, 220,
    222–3
  Les Jeux Sont Faits (1947) 159,
    225
Saussure, Ferdinand de 147–9,
    164, 222
Scharf, Aaron 84, 112
Schlesinger, John 18, 119–21,
    130–3
Schoonmaker, Thelma 230
Schrader, Paul 183
Scorsese, Martin 132, 150, 182–3,
    192, 223, 234
Screen 140, 146–8, 163, 167, 191,
    202
Sebastian (1967), 45*n*49, 216
Sellers, Peter 143, 231
Selznick, David O. 27, 30, 32,
    38–9, 219, 231
Sequence 1–2, 10, 11, 25, 119,
    193, 235
Shearer, Moira 38–39, *217*, 231
Siegel, Don 28, 138
  Invasion of the Body Snatchers
    (1956) *3*
Sight and Sound 1–2, 7–10,
    14–24, 25, 41–2, 56–7
Simenon, Georges 32–3, 228, 231
Sirk, Douglas 28–30, 166–7, 215,
    223
Slade School of Fine Art 4–5,
    10–11, 47, 69, 75–6, 145
Smith, Jack 142, 202
  Flaming Creatures (1963) 46,
    48, 69
Solzhenitsyn, Aleksandr 138–9
Spillane, Mickey 49, 56–7
Steele, Barbara *9*, 193
Steinbeck, John 182, 196
Straub, Jean-Marie 134, 197, 210
Sturges, Preston 28, 166, 181, 187,
    234, 237
  Sullivan's Travels (1941) 136
Suez 2–3, 12, 133, 216
Surrealism 37, 52, 118, 176, 193
Swinging London 61–3, 121, 159,
    197
Syberberg, Hans-Jürgen 209
  Hitler: A Film From Germany
    (1977) 150
Symbolism 55, 85, 130–2, 162–4,
    222–3

Tanner, Alain 138, 197
  Nice Time (1957) 15, 24, 118,
    121
  *Jonah Who Will be 25 in the
    Year 2000* (1976) 233, 239
Tarkovsky, Andrei 139, 159, 213
Tashlin, Frank 23, 30
  The Girl Can't Help It (1956) 24
Tati, Jacques 126, 204
  Mon Oncle (1958) 55

Temperance Seven/Biographic/
    Mukkinese Battle Horn vein
    of Edwardian spoof-nostalgia,
    the 60, 70, 124, 126, 143,
    236
This Island Earth (1955) 27, 89,
    142, 151
Thompson, E. P. 2, 146–8,
    189*n*26
Toland, Gregg 28, 102–3, 110
Triumph of the Will (1935) 18–20,
    238
Truffaut, François 7–8, 14, 25,
    116–17, 164, 220
  Writings
    'A Certain Tendency in French
      Cinema' (1954) 8, 10
    Hitchcock (1968) 31–4
  Films
    Les 400 Coups (1959) 73,
      90, *158*
    Shoot the Pianist (1960) 7–8,
      117, 241
    Jules et Jim (1962) 89
    Tire au Flanc (1961) 135
    Fahrenheit 451 (1966) 130,
      138
Turksib (Victor Turin, 1929) 98

underground, the 6*n*7, 46–52,
    58–72, 108, 157–8, 164,
    197–204, 233–4
University College London
  see Slade School of Fine Art
University of Cambridge 1–2, 4,
    109, 113, 140, 144, 191

Varda, Agnès 41, 55, 118, 213–14,
    239
Vas, Robert 16, 119
Vernon, M. D. 78
Vertov, Dziga 163–8, 207–8, 212,
    220, 237–8
Vidor, King 25–9, 41, 216, 240–1
  The Champ (1931) 182
  Our Daily Bread (1934) 75, 100
  Duel in the Sun (1946) 1, 17,
    26–7, 38–9, 240
Vigo, Jean 37, 117, 120, 212, 238,
    241
Visconti, Luchino 14, 22–3, 33,
    76, 104–5
  Rocco and His Brothers (1960)
    24, 29
Von Sternberg, Josef 38, 54, 73,
    182–3, 206, 226, 240
  The Blue Angel (1930) 75
Von Stroheim, Erich 59, 76, 110
Vorkapich, Slavko 100, 152, 156;
  see montageology

Wajda, Andrzej 25, 233
  Man of Marble (1977) 197, 208

Walsh, Raoul 20, 28–9, 125
Warhol, Andy 46, 59, 65–7, 67–8,
 71, 142, 198
Watkins, Peter 116, 126–9,
 134–8,
 Culloden (1964) 126, 134–5,
 166, 238
 The War Game (1965/6) 122,
 126–8, *127*
 Privilege (1967) 121, 126,
 128–9, 130
Watt, Harry
 Night Mail (1936) 108, 238
 Target for Tonight (1941) 118
Weiss, Peter
 Enligt Lag (1957) 59, 70
 Marat-Sade (1964) 93, 112
Welles, Orson 76, 110, 166
 Citizen Kane (1941) 20, 28,
 102–3, 110, *111*, 156–7,
 170–1, 224, 237
 The Magnificent Ambersons
 (1942) 88, 110
 The Lady from Shanghai (1947)
 30, 75, *85*–6
 Macbeth (1948) 96
 The Trial (1962) 53, 56, 73

Whannel, Paddy 41, 147
Whitehead, Peter 47–9, 52, 69,
 72*n*7, 118, 122–3
 Wholly Communion (1965)
 50–*1*, 52, 62, 69
 *Tonite Let's All Make Love in
 London* (1967) 61–3, 71, 122
Wilden, Anthony 164
Wilder, Billy 28–30, 166
Wilder, Thornton
 Our Town (1938) 173, 181, 184
 The Skin of Our Teeth (1942)
 225, 235
Wilenski, R. H. 77–8, 80–1, 112
Willemen, Paul 147–8, 189*n*26,
 191
Williams, Raymond 6*n*13, 108,
 113, 140, 144
Willis, Baron (Ted) 115
Wilson, Colin 21, 42, 56
Winnington, Richard 1, 11, 35
Wise, Robert 29–30, 88
 Odds Against Tomorrow (1959)
 24
Wiseman, Frederick 187, 238

Wollen, Peter
 Writings 146–9, 154, 160–72,
 188, 191, 193–4, 197
 Films
 Penthesilea (1974) 165
 Riddles of the Sphinx (1977)
 150, 165
Wonderwall (1968) 121, 130
Wood, Robin 7, 11, 25, 32, 44*n*35,
 117, 140–1, 161
Wright, Basil
 Song of Ceylon (1934) 108,
 238; *see* the essay-film
 Night Mail (1936) 118
Wyler, William 27–30, 76, 102–4,
 110–1, 154, 177
 The Best Years of Our Lives
 (1946) 103–*4*

Yellow Submarine (1968) 130,
 136, 239, 240–1
Young, Terence 35
 Dr. No (1962) 9, 12

Zavattini, Cesar 28, 118, 138,
 177–80

List of Illustrations

While considerable effort has been made to correctly identify the copyright holders, this has not been possible in all cases. We apologise for any apparent negligence and any omissions or corrections brought to our attention will be remedied in any future editions.

The Newcomers, BBC; *Look Back in Anger*, © Woodfall Film Productions; *Kiss Me Deadly*, Parklane Pictures; *Peeping Tom*, © Michael Powell (Theatre) Ltd; *Wholly Communion*, Lorrimer Films; *The Lady from Shanghai*, Columbia Pictures Corporation; *Citizen Kane*, © RKO Radio Pictures; *The Best Years of Our Lives*, Samuel Goldwyn Inc.; *8½*, Cineriz di Angelo Rizzoli; *The Knack*, © Woodfall Film Presentations Ltd; *The War Game*, BBC; *Mahler*, © Goodtimes Enterprises Ltd; *Zardoz*, © Twentieth Century-Fox Film Corporation; *Letter from Siberia*, Argos-Films/Procinex; *Scorpio Rising*, © Kenneth Anger; *October*, Sovkino; *The Man Who Shot Liberty Valance*, © Paramount Pictures Corporation/ John Ford Productions; *Toute la Mémoire du Monde*, La Pléiade; *The Red Shoes*, © Independent Producers; *The Small Back Room*, Archers Film Productions/London Film Productions.

The Essential Raymond Durgnat